Israel's Materialist Militarism

Innovations in the Study of World Politics

Series Editor
Zeev Maoz, University of California, Davis

Advisory Board
Michael Barnett, University of Minnesota
Deborah Larson, UCLA
Brett Ashley Leeds, Rice University
Jack Levy, Rutgers University

This series provides a forum for the publication of original theoretical, empirical, and conceptual studies that seek to chart new frontiers in the field of international relations. The key emphasis is on innovation and change. Books in the series will offer insights on and approaches to a broad range of issues facing the modern world, in an effort to revolutionize how contemporary world politics are studied, taught, and practiced.

Forgetting Ourselves: Secession and the (Im)possibility of Territorial Identity,
    by Linda S. Bishai
Multiple Paths to Knowledge in International Relations: Methodology in the Study of Conflict Management and Conflict Resolution,
    edited by Zeev Maoz, Alex Mintz, T. Clifton Morgan, Glenn Palmer, and Richard J. Stoll
New Directions for International Relations: Confronting the Method-of-Analysis Problem,
    edited by Alex Mintz and Bruce Russett
Cycles of Violence: The Evolution of the Israeli Decision Regime Governing the Use of Limited Military Force,
    by Ranan D. Kuperman
Economic Interdependence and Conflict in World Politics,
    by Mark J. C. Crescenzi
Redrawing the Map to Promote Peace: Territorial Dispute Management Via Territorial Changes,
    by Jaroslav Tir

Israel's Materialist Militarism

Yagil Levy

LEXINGTON BOOKS

A division of
ROWMAN & LITTLEFIELD PUBLISHERS, INC.
Lanham • Boulder • New York • Toronto • Plymouth, UK

LEXINGTON BOOKS

A division of Rowman & Littlefield Publishers, Inc.
A wholly owned subsidiary of The Rowman & Littlefield Publishing Group, Inc.
4501 Forbes Boulevard, Suite 200
Lanham, MD 20706

Estover Road
Plymouth PL6 7PY
United Kingdom

Copyright © 2007 by Lexington Books

All rights reserved. No part of this publication may be reproduced, stored in a retrieval system, or transmitted in any form or by any means, electronic, mechanical, photocopying, recording, or otherwise, without the prior permission of the publisher.

British Library Cataloguing in Publication Information Available

Library of Congress Cataloging-in-Publication Data

Levy, Yagil, 1958-
 Israel's materialist militarism / Yagil Levy.
   p. cm. — (Innovations in the study of world politics)
 Includes bibliographical references and index.
 ISBN-13: 978-0-7391-1908-2 (cloth : alk. paper)
 ISBN-10: 0-7391-1908-7 (cloth : alk. paper)
 ISBN-13: 978-0-7391-1909-9 (pbk. : alk. paper)
 ISBN-10: 0-7391-1909-5 (pbk. : alk. paper)
 1. Israel—Military policy. I. Title.
 UA853.I8L445 2007
 355'.03105694—dc22   2007016696

Printed in the United States of America

∞™ The paper used in this publication meets the minimum requirements of American National Standard for Information Sciences—Permanence of Paper for Printed Library Materials, ANSI/NISO Z39.48–1992.

Contents

List of Figures and Tables		vii
Acknowledgments		ix
1	Theoretical Introduction—The Essence and Dynamics of Materialist Militarism	1
2	The Republican Equation and Its Violation	29
3	The Continuation of Oslo by the Al-Aqsa Intifada	77
4	The War of the Peripheries	117
5	From "People's Army" to "Market Army"	147
6	The "Embedded Military" and the Implementation of the Disengagement Plan	181
7	The Second Lebanon War: The "Gap of Legitimacies" Syndrome	213
8	Conclusions: Why Materialist Militarism Matters	247
Bibliography		259
Index		279
About the Author		285

List of Figures and Tables

FIGURES

Figure 1.1.	Reward and Control Matrix	22
Figure 7.1.	The Spiral of Rewards	239
Figure 8.1.	The Republican Equation: Reward versus Military Participation	248

TABLES

Table 4.1.	Comparison between IDF Casualties in the First Week of the Lebanon War and the Al-Aqsa Intifada	119
Table 4.2.	Percentage of Casualties in Proportion to the Population	120
Table 4.3.	Casualties Differentiated by Corps, the First Lebanon War and the Al-Aqsa Intifada.	121
Table 4.4.	Casualties Differentiated by Corps and Ethno-Class Origin	122
Table 7.1.	Comparison between IDF Casualties in the Al-Aqsa Intifada and the Second Lebanon War	230
Table 7.2.	Casualties Differentiated by Corps, the Al-Aqsa Intifada and the Second Lebanon War	231

Acknowledgments

This book would not have come into existence without the support of my colleagues, who provided me with many opportunities to present my work. I am particularly grateful to Guy Ben-Porat, Shlomo Mizrahi, Arie Reichel, and Hanna Yablonka from Ben-Gurion University, to Oren Barak, Amiram Oren, and Gabi Sheffer from the Van Leer Jerusalem Institute, and to Hadas Ben-Eliau, Zeev Lehrer, and Yehudit Sher from the IDF Behavioral Sciences Unit.

I especially thank my colleagues who commented on various parts of the book: Aluf Benn, Chava Brownfield-Stein, Stuart Cohen, Yinon Cohen, Ariel Heiman, Tamar Herman, Yoav Peled, Uri Ram, Orna Sasson-Levy, Yehouda Shenhav, and Yuval Yonai. Chapter 5 partly originated from a collaborative study with Edna Lomsky-Feder, to whom I am indebted.

The theoretical framework was developed in dialogue with Gad Barzilai, Eyal Ben-Ari, Lev Grinberg, Sarit Helman, Ronald Krebs, Kobi Michael, Yoram Peri, Michael Shalev, and Erez Tzfadia, all of whom have my thanks.

I owe a huge debt to Asher Arian for his enduring encouragement, to Charles Tilly for his invaluable guidance and intellectual inspiration, and to Zeev Maoz for his extraordinary support. I would like to thank to Nicholas John, who translated and edited the manuscript. Finally, my special gratitude is extended to my editors at Lexington Books: Joseph Parry, the associate editor, for spearheading this effort and to his assistant Marissa Marro, and to Lynda Phung, the production editor, who took over the project in its final stages.

Chapter One

Theoretical Introduction— The Essence and Dynamics of Materialist Militarism

During the Oslo peace process of the 1990s, *The New York Times* journalist Thomas Friedman (1995) published a pictorial article portraying Israel as a rich, materialist country, driven by its economy to make peace. He cited an Israeli intellectual as claiming that "the cell phone has replaced the gun as the symbol of macho and importance in Israeli society." As Israel has become wealthier, its inclination to fight the Arabs has diminished, asserted Friedman. As evidence, he reported that nine Israelis had just been killed by *Hezbollah*, but that the Israeli government had chosen not to retaliate so as not to disrupt the flourishing tourist season in northern Israel. Five years later, with the eruption of the Al-Aqsa Intifada, Israel once again found itself embroiled in battle against the Palestinians. And yet another five years down the line, Israel launched a round of war in Lebanon, despite a significantly more lucrative tourism industry in the north of the country. The fluctuations of this decade form the subject matter of this book.

THE PUZZLE

Since the First Lebanon War (1982), the Israeli state's internal autonomy in directing and implementing military policies has been eroded, much due to the appearance of protest movements formed by groups of discharged soldiers and their families. This phenomenon reached its climax in the late 1990s with the *Four Mothers* movement, comprised mostly of mothers of soldiers who had served in Lebanon protesting against what they viewed as the pointless sacrifice of lives in the ongoing Lebanon War. The *Four Mothers'* protest was one of the factors that prompted the Israeli government's decision to unilaterally pull the IDF (Israel Defense Forces) out of Lebanon in 2000, after eighteen years of war.

In contrast to the First Lebanon War and the First Intifada (1987–1993), however, the peace movement during the Al-Aqsa Intifada (from 2000) has been almost completely silent, and no public organization of soldiers or their parents has had any significant influence on the political arena. Indeed, support for the army during the Al-Aqsa Intifada was largely enlisted from the Israeli left wing—the traditional supporter of the Oslo Accords—which offered its backing despite heavy losses on both sides and the military's use of excessive and deadly force in dealing with Palestinian riots. First signs of dissent appeared in early 2002, when there was an increase in cases of refusal to serve in the Occupied Territories among reserve soldiers and officers, though this trend receded with the increasing frequency of terror attacks on Israel. It is noteworthy that the decision to implement the *Disengagement Plan* for the unilateral withdrawal from the Gaza Strip and the northern West Bank was not influenced by pressure from Israeli protest movements, unlike the withdrawals from Lebanon, for example (in 1985 and 2000). The Second Lebanon War (2006), which shortly followed the disengagement, at least temporarily reversed what had seemed to be a return to the deescalation of the regional conflict. This time, the government was able to launch a war after hurried discussions in the cabinet, and succeeded in gaining public support that remained in place even when it became apparent that the war had failed to achieve its objectives.

How are we to explain the state's relative autonomy in waging a prolonged military undertaking without significant internal opposition, even though the war signified a shift in Israel's path as characterized by Friedman? How did the state regain the autonomy that had been eroded during the First Lebanon War and the First Intifada? And does the wave of political protests produced by the Second Lebanon War testify to high levels of performance by the state and the IDF during the period that preceded it?

The puzzle becomes even more striking if we recall that from 1985 the military played a pivotal role in helping, and sometimes even driving the political leadership to opt for relatively moderate policies that somewhat deescalated the Arab-Israeli conflict. During the mid-1990s the IDF even drew criticism from the right wing for its part in architecturing the Oslo Accords and blocking Prime Minister Benjamin Netanyahu from undermining them. Conversely, in September 2000, when the Al-Aqsa Intifada broke out, by responding to Palestinian disturbances with excessive and deadly force, the military obstructed the government's pursuit of a more flexible solution, thus bringing about the collapse of the very accords that it had previously helped to design. At the time, the IDF enjoyed wide support, including among members of the moderate left wing, formerly the main advocates of the peace process. However, three years later the IDF was among the first to acknowledge that the fighting had reached a dead end, and in 2005 it efficiently carried out the Disengagement Plan. However, one year later it leveraged an isolated border clash to wage the Second Lebanon War. How are these shifts to be explained?

ALTERNATIVE EXPLANATIONS

So far, very few attempts have been made to tackle this puzzle, and even they have been unsatisfactory. By and large, scholars of Israel's military, politics, and society were highly influenced by the winds of peace that blew across the Middle East during the 1990s, with the Oslo Accords at their center. Israel was portrayed as a state moving toward peace, largely driven by the impacts of globalization on society. This tendency notwithstanding, scholars also indicated the inherent potential that Israeli society might take the road back to war, referring to the remilitarization of the IDF, and the empowerment of the anti-globalization, ethno-national camp (see mainly Ben-Eliezer, 2005; Grinberg, 2000; Kimmerling, 2001; Levy, 1997a; Ram, 2005; Shafir and Peled, 2000; Shafir and Peled, 2002).

I will briefly test two clusters of explanations, the first focused on the external arena, and the second on the internal arena. The tension between them is part of a larger debate among students of Israeli politics and society as to the origins of the Arab-Israeli conflict.

The First Explanation: The International Arena

Israel has long been viewed as a state that responds passively to events in a threatening external arena, with these events seen as fashioning its military policies. Specifically, it is posited that the most enduring threat lies in the systematic reluctance of the Arab states to recognize Israel's right to exist. The empowerment of the military command, albeit within the boundaries of a politically controlled organization, was inevitable. However, given certain shifts in the region —following the First Gulf War (1991), and, concomitantly, the collapse of the Soviet Union, which ceased to support radical elements in the Arab world—the military displayed openness to change and offered its backing to a peace process. Nonetheless, the IDF looked upon the peace process through the lens of security. It is for this reason that it became skeptical of the process, and, fearing that hostilities would resume, prepared itself for a massive response should a second wave of violence break out (Peri 2006, 91–108).[1]

And indeed, the IDF responded to the eruption of the Al-Aqsa Intifada with excessive force and in a manner that gradually led to the escalation of the conflict (Bar-Siman-Tov et al., 2005). Inasmuch as the Al-Aqsa Intifada involved engaging in combat with militias and terror cells that were using firearms of various types, not only against soldiers, but also against civilians in the country's central cities, the use of military violence gained greater legitimacy within the Israeli public relative to the First Lebanon War and the First Intifada. This was because military operations in the First Intifada were aimed at suppressing an unarmed civilian uprising, while the Lebanon War was waged in the north, far from the homes of the Israeli elites. Accordingly, even the advocates of the Oslo Accords were swept up by the new belligerency (Herman, 2002). Furthermore, the IDF itself directed the fighting according to its own interpretation of politicians' intentions, manipulating its professional authority vis-à-vis the latter (Michael, 2007).

Nevertheless, the fighting reached a stalemate in 2003, when the Palestinian Authority portrayed itself as incapable of controlling the armed militias in its territories and bringing about a cessation of hostilities, and the Israelis understood that they could not sustain such exhausting combat. Therefore, with the IDF's support, the government initiated a change in the combat model, namely, the withdrawal from areas populated by Palestinians in the northern West Bank and the Gaza Strip that came to be known as the Disengagement Plan (Caspit, 2002; Druker and Shelah, 2005; Harel and Yissacharoff, 2004).

This, then, is the first explanation, based on changes in the international arena. However, it is far from fully satisfactory. Inherent in it are two binding premises: first, that Israel is a passive actor responding to external events, and second, that it does so in a rational manner. Theoretically speaking, a threatening or friendly external environment is not an objective entity, but rather a discursive construction (Wendt, 1992). Any external event is a real entity only by virtue of the manner in which political agents respond to signals transmitted from the external arena, filter that information, and construct their internal discursive representation of it. Moreover, official state agencies (mainly the army, government ministries, and intelligence agencies) may come into conflict with opposing political groups over the construction of this representation (Levy, 1997a, 16–17). In the absence of significant collective action, such as widespread political protest, state agencies have the power to implant their vision of the external arena within the political discourse. In turn, this power leads to an increase in the state's relative autonomy in implementing policies that might otherwise have been politically disputed.

Approaches that focus on the external arena are anchored on the realist and neorealist schools. Deeply internalized by Israeli academic discourse, these theories see the structure of the global arena as explaining the behavior of the individual state—in this instance, the internal Israeli arena. Given that the state of Israel (and its pre-state configuration) was faced with an external threat, which, at least until the 1970s, was perceived as impinging on its continued existence, the state had no trouble enlisting the societal resources required for the military effort. For such theorists, it is equally clear that when the threat was reduced from the 1970s onward, mostly due to increased U.S. dominance in the region, manifested later on by the breakup of the former Soviet Union and the defeat of Iraq in the two Gulf wars, social motivation to invest in the military was reduced. However, this explanation does not stand the test of empirical examination.

During the 1990s, the exposure of historical documents and/or their reinterpretation enabled the "new historians," together with critical sociologists, to show that at various historical junctions Israel was faced with nonmilitary, or at least only moderately military options, in relation to the path that was actually chosen. This scholarship began to undermine the dominant academic-public discourse in Israel, which saw the Arab side as leaving Israel no choice but to accept the reality of violent conflict with its Arab environment (for the change in the academic discourse in Israel see Ben-Ari et al., 2001; Lustick, 1996).

In particular, the Israeli approach started to change after the Yom Kippur War, when Israeli diplomacy, at least at several crucial junctures, had exhausted political opportunities offered by the regional and international arenas, including initiatives that had previously been rejected, while the Arab environment remained at the same level of threat (or even greater). Indeed, the regional arena offered Israel a vast repertoire of options, each of them with costs and benefits. For instance, Israel could have opted for hawkish policies during the 1990s, as the right wing urged, for the very same reasons that are claimed to have led the country in the opposite direction, primarily Israel's relative power advantage in an unstable region. Similarly, in the 2000s, Israel could have used political means to neutralize Palestinian hostility.

It follows that the external arena does not provide a satisfactory explanation. Indeed, carefully examining critical decisions shows that each juncture also bore the possibility for resisting the military way, even among the ranks of the dominant leadership. Each time, however, this resistance was neutralized. In other words, there were alternative interpretations of the external threat. Therefore, decisions were not based on the external threat alone, but were rather the outcome of political-social choices, which reasonably raises the question as to who gained from them. That is, the focus must be shifted to the very social legitimacy for the centrality of military values. Once it has been shown that such legitimacy is none other than one alternative chosen from a range of others, it cannot be treated as a point of departure, but rather its sources and the process of its establishment should be questioned.

It should be noted that the Israeli case is by no means unique, and is characteristic of the shift from armies prepared for the Cold War to postmodern militaries (see Moskos and Burk, 1994), with reduced social legitimacy for investing in them. This eroded legitimacy is manifested in the allocation of social resources to the army—material and human alike—most strongly felt in Western countries in the gradual abolishment of the draft and the transition to volunteer armies. Here too the popular interpretation holds that the diminished threat to the west from the Soviet bloc played a significant part. However, closer observation reveals that Western armies began to undergo far-reaching transformations even before the supposed threat had been lifted. For instance, the draft was cancelled in the United States because of the controversial war in Vietnam, while criticisms of the budget led Britain to abolish the draft in 1957; at the same time, Sweden, a country not subjected to any external threats, maintains a system of compulsory recruitment to the present day. Hence, the thawing of the Cold War cannot be seen as a crucial factor. This returns us to observations of social processes, and their influence on the internal status of the army (see Leander, 2004a).

Furthermore, the external account fails to explain why, during the Al-Aqsa Intifada, the IDF opted to escalate the conflict, even though the political goals of the fighting were not clearly defined. Following the collapse of the Palestinian Authority, this ultimately created a political vacuum in the Palestinian territories (see Bar-Siman-Tov et al., 2005; Druker and Shelah, 2005; Harel and Yissacharoff, 2004). One should ask, therefore, why the criticism retrospectively directed at the IDF for its part in this (lack of) policy was not sounded during the fighting itself, or did not attract significant political attention. The IDF's mode of reading and interpreting the external arena is viewed simplistically, without analyzing the army's interests, organizational culture, or its relations with the groups that supply its manpower and legitimize its activities in a manner that affects military policies.

The collapse of the Oslo Accords cannot be satisfactorily explained without also taking into account the internal contradictions resulting from the military's crucial role in their very formulation. And even the Disengagement Plan is not adequately engaged with, as the sense of stalemate expressed by its architects was not reflected in public opinion in a manner that suggested it might lead to protest (Caspit, 2005; Shavit, 2004). The political-military bureaucracy worked within a relatively autonomous environment, the essence of which ought to be explained, and not merely treated as a point of departure.

In sum, this externally oriented rationality cannot by itself explain the routes chosen, a weakness that typifies neorealist perspectives in international relations. In consequence, the internal arena must be brought in.

The Second Explanation: The Social-Political Structure

Hazier areas of the first explanation are clarified by explanations that draw on the internal arena. While the Oslo Accords and the economic growth driven by globalization were most advantageous to the interests of the *Ashkenazi*-based upper middle class (the European-descended dominant group in Israeli society), and were backed by the military elites, who had come to acknowledge their inability to sustain military rule over the Palestinians (Grinberg, 2000), the *Mizrachi*-based Jewish working class (the 1950s immigrants from Muslim countries) opposed both Oslo and globalization. Hit hard by the social inequalities emerging from those processes, this class had economic and cultural reasons for opposing them (Peled, 2004). Indeed, Mizrachim have clung ever more strongly to their ethno-national hawkish identity, and perceive the "peace camp" as their societal adversaries. "Civil society" versus "military society" is one possible embodiment of this political-social split (Ben-Eliezer, 2005).

The contradictions within this structure laid the foundations for the resumption of hostilities. Given the political deadlock that followed the assassination of Prime Minister Yitzhak Rabin (in November 1996), and recognizing that Prime Minister Benjamin Netanyahu was stalling the peace process, the military concluded that it should prepare itself for another round of fighting, if only to avoid future accusations of military incompetence. Furthermore, because the Oslo Accords were shaped as a new format of occupation—in keeping with military outlooks—they were prone to collapse (Grinberg, 2002). Naturally, under these circumstances, when the Intifada broke out, the military took the initiative, as stated above. And because the Israeli political and cultural system is unable either to negotiate a costly compromise, or to decide the Israeli-Palestinian conflict by force by carrying out large-scale ethnic cleansing of the area, military escalation leading to an interim path, i.e., the dismantling of the Palestinian Authority, was inevitable (Kimmerling, 2003).

The fighting was also instrumental in mitigating clashes between social groups. It was the Al-Aqsa Intifada that enabled Ariel Sharon's government to legitimize its neoliberal policies—with the retrenchment of the welfare state at their center—by using the new belligerent agenda to politically mobilize the Mizrachi-based, hawkish working class. At the same time, the reduced the tax burden for the shrinking welfare state ensured that the government could mobilize the middle class, the former backbone of the dovish camp, to accept the resumed state of war.

However, coalition requirements meant that one of the political parties representing the Ashkenazi-based middle class—either Labor or *Shinui*—had to be brought in to the coalition. To accommodate this, Sharon had to pursue a more moderate foreign policy, which produced the unilateral withdrawal from the Gaza Strip (Peled, 2004).

While this explanation does indeed bring in aspects from the internal arena lacking from the previous explanation, it does not provide an adequate account of the role of the IDF. According to one view (Peled), the military is a passive actor serving the interests of the upper middle class and the forces of capital without any interests of its own. Alternatively, others see the military as serving its own institutional needs (Grinberg). Yet, both arguments analytically locate the IDF as detached from struggles over societal resources, even though such struggles may well be reflected within its ranks, if only because, as a conscript army, it is highly permeable to social dynamics. The conferral of political legitimacy upon the military's aggressiveness is understandable in the light of the above-mentioned explanations, but its internal legitimacy within the military itself remains unaccounted for. After all, collective action that had previously restricted the military's freedom of operation, such as the *Four Mothers* movement, had sprung from within the ranks of the military, in the form of servicepersons or their families. In other words, the political dormancy of these social cycles during the first years of the Al-Aqsa Intifada still requires explanation. Their awakening during the Second Lebanon War only makes the puzzle more complex.

This missing link between the army's societal setting and its role in generating the dynamics of military policies stands at the heart of this book. The puzzle is broader, however, and extends to the theoretical field. What is at issue here is the dynamics of militarism and the way its expansions and contractions shape military policies.

THE THEORETICAL GAP

According to Mann's famous definition, militarism is a set of attitudes and social practices which regard war and the preparation for war as a normal and desirable social activity (1987, 4). Unlike other definitions, which highlight the role of the military in transcending civilian institutions,[2] Mann moves beyond the narrow focus on military institutions to address militarized political culture. An even broader and complementary perspective has been offered by Enloe (2000, 3), who refers to widely routinized cultural practices, according to which militarization is

> a step-by-step process by which a person or a thing gradually comes to be controlled by the military or comes to depend for its well-being on militaristic ideas. The more militarization transforms an individual or a society, the more that

individual or society comes to imagine military needs and militaristic presumptions to be not only valuable but also normal.

However, this begs the question as to what makes militarism a legitimately routinized pattern. In other words, Mann's and Enloe's conceptualization overlooks the mechanisms that nurture militarism and counterbalance opposing tendencies to civilianization (i.e., the diversion of resources from the military to civilian hands or needs) or demilitarization (i.e., the curtailment of militarization in favor of nonaggressive means for solving interstate disputes).

Let us take two examples of recent writings. In his description of the new American militarism since the Vietnam War, Bacevich (2005) has analyzed this development primarily in relation to the evolution of ideas: from the recovery of the military after Vietnam to the role played by soldiering in embodying America's new national ideals, and, most importantly, the role of the neoconservative movement in redefining America's mission in the world vis-à-vis the perceived forces of evil. What is lacking, however, is an analysis that theoretically links ideas to interests in order to explain what motivates a warprone society, despite the sacrifices entailed by war. Even the Marxist school—which links militarism with the economic benefits that it produces—has failed to expose the mechanisms that motivate the citizenry, and especially soldiers, to sacrifice themselves in the interests of capital (for illustrations of this school, see Baran and Sweezy, 1966; Thompson, 1982).

Another illustration is Goldstein's *War and Gender* (2001), which sets the cross-cultural consistency of gendered war roles—the virtually universal exclusion of women from combat—against the backdrop of the vast diversity of cultural forms of both extra-military gender roles and war. Goldstein argues that to help overcome soldiers' natural reluctance to fight, cultures develop gender roles that equate "manhood" with toughness under fire. In other words, the gendered exclusivity of war roles motivates men to fight. In this way, Goldstein tackles the issue of the motivation to fight, largely unresolved by other scholars. Be that as it may, his explanation cannot fully account for historical fluctuations in the *levels* of motivation to fight, i.e., the dynamics of militarization versus demilitarization. Goldstein may be able to help us understand what motivates desire or readiness to fight among those who potentially or actually do so, but not the changing levels of this desire/readiness.

The school of state formation offers a partial answer to these matters. Central to theories focusing on state formation is the mutually generating mechanism between war and state formation, as mainly reflected in Tilly's war-makes-state argument (Tilly, 1992). Historically, the combination of needs originating from the external arena, and the manipulation of domestic power centers by state rulers, brought about the centralization of the modern state.

The extensive introduction of artillery and gunpowder in sixteenth- and seventeenth-century warfare led state agencies to recruit resources for military buildup whenever necessitated, and permitted, by geopolitical conditions. In particular, conscription was imposed on the domestic population when growing needs for disciplined, loyal, and relatively cheap manpower could no longer be met by mercenaries (Thomson, 1990).

The state then became the only entity able to underwrite and maintain a military, a key component of its monopoly over the use of societal resources of violence (Finer, 1975; Giddens, 1985; Tilly, 1992). At the same time, state activities aimed at preparing for and legitimizing war also became a lever for internal state expansion. Civilian bureaucracies dealing with mass conscription, tax collection, military production, and territorial centralization, were among the outcomes of this process (Barnett, 1992; Tilly, 1992). Administrative concentration led to patterns of bargaining with the groups that controlled the human and material resources needed for waging war, by which military contribution was exchanged for political control over the military via the establishment of representative institutions (Tilly, ibid.).

In sum, the school of state formation has partially filled the gap created by theorists of militarism by addressing the statist mechanism that nurtured and legitimized militarism by means of the *republican contract*. This is a contract that establishes a reciprocal relationship between the state and its citizens, whereby citizens agree to sacrifice their bodies and wealth in bearing the burden of war in return for civil, social, and political rights granted to them by the state. This exchange laid the foundation for the creation of the Western democracies and the development of the welfare state (see Skocpol, 1992). Modern military service, therefore, fulfilled a historical role in defining the boundaries of citizenship by equating the latter with bearing arms. It is against this background that the army became a historical mechanism of mobility for social groups, especially as growing rates of conscription required expanding the social strata from which the conscripts were recruited, primarily by drawing on the middle class (Burk, 1995; Tilly, 1997a). At the same time, the citizen-soldier embodied the republican model of the transfer of sovereignty from the ruler to the community of citizens that staffed and politically controlled the military. The interweaving of democratization with mass conscription generated networks of interpersonal commitment, in which compliance with the draft rested on the citizens' faith in the trustworthiness and legitimacy of the democratic government (Levi, 1997).

Moreover, it is clear from both schools—militarism and state formation—that discursive militarization, i.e., its political and cultural aspects, enabled the state to legitimize the military's needs and prioritize them over other, civilian needs. As military buildup fostered an increasing ratio of soldiers to civilians, political discourse was inevitably militarized.

Nonetheless, while the school of state formation has convincingly addressed the historical mechanisms that generated militarism, it has failed to tackle the dynamics of the fluctuation of societal levels of militarism. Given that militarism rests on the *republican equation*, that is, the equilibrium between the values that constitute the republican contract of sacrifice-for-rights, one should specify the conditions by which the terms of this equation are altered, and how this in turn impacts on the level of militarism in society. Here the usefulness of the notion of *materialist militarism* is revealed.

CONCEPTUALIZING MATERIALIST MILITARISM

The Essence of Materialist Militarism

Protection is the main public good that the state monopolistically provides its citizens. However, it is not supplied for free, but rather in return for military participation, either in the shape of military service or taxation for funding the army. The state is inclined to demand an exaggerated price for its services as a means of retaining "surplus value" in the form of increased internal control, while its citizens prefer to purchase protection at the lowest possible price (Lake, 1992). The state and organized social groups thus bargain over the cost of state-provided protection.

Two main strategies are at the state's disposal in managing this bargaining. First, the state can artificially increase the demand for its protection services by exaggerating the extent of the foreign threats from which it claims it will protect society (Lake, ibid.). As a second and complementary strategy, mostly deployed when the first strategy has proven ineffective on its own, the state offers to reward its citizens for their military sacrifice as taxpayers and, especially, soldiers (see Tilly, 1985, 183–85). This is the background to the historical formation of the republican equation, an outcome of the modes of bargaining that typified the formation of the modern Western military.

Soldiers figure simultaneously in two reward systems: (1) *material rewards*, which are essentially monetary, mostly immediate rewards, such as payments, pensions, job training, housing, financial aid for higher education, and other social goods; and (2) *symbolic rewards*, which stem from the prestige and honor accruing to military service. Whereas material rewards with monetary value are easily deployable outside the military, the value of symbolic rewards in civilian society depends on the social context into which they are introduced. In general, the honor and prestige enjoyed by soldiers are significant to the extent that they are socially recognized in the civil sphere in a manner that facilitates their conversion into social assets. These two modes of reward are mutually related to and partially dependent on one another.

Symbolic rewards are determined by their *convertibility*—that is, the ability of groups to convert the power they acquire within, and owing to, military service into valuable social resources—symbolic and material alike—in the civilian sphere (Levy, 1998). Conversion is the transformation of a symbolic asset from one form to another. While purely monetary rewards are not converted, as their value remains fixed, some material rewards depend on the level of cooperation between the government and civilian organizations, such as educational benefits. Hence, the symbolic status of ex-servicepersons is relevant to the prospective exhaustion of these rewards. At the same time, symbolic rewards are transferable into material rewards, such as civil rights accruing to ex-soldiers, thus modifying their form.

There are different sorts of convertible symbolic resources. First, as mentioned, military service historically shaped the criteria for, and hence was a hallmark of, citizenship and other rights, from political to social rights in the shape of the welfare state. Seeing military sacrifice as the supreme civic obligation fits neatly with the republican tradition, which ascribes great value to active participation in democratic politics in order to promote the common good (Oldfield, 1990; Turner, 2001). Members of groups that had not been recognized as full citizens could improve their social standing by performing military service (Burk, 1995; Janowitz, 1976). Working-class groups, ethnic minorities, and, gradually, women and homosexuals, have all effectively utilized military service as a mechanism for social mobility. Symbolic rewards may be tied to the level of external threats—that is, the state's capacity to artificially increase the demand for its protection services by exaggerating external threats (Lake, 1992)—as the greater the (perceived) threat to the nation's existence, the more worthy military sacrifice is seen to be.

By differentially classifying social groups, military service not only determines uniform eligibility for citizenship, but also its status. The degree of legitimacy that the agents involved confer on the access of groups to power in the military determines whether the conversion of military status into social status will proceed in a stable fashion, or whether it will trigger intergroup tensions. When seemingly universalist criteria for recruitment and promotion are coupled with the conferral of existential meaning on the application and consequences of those criteria, privileged groups are able to invoke their military status to legitimate their social status—the rights, positions, wealth, and power they possess relative to, or at the expense of, their subordinated counterparts (Levy, 1998). At the same time, especially for peripheral groups, their very status within the ranks may serve as a strong signal of the extent to which the state trusts them, and thus signifies the potential ability of such groups to convert military status into social status (Krebs, 2006, 3–4).

Complementing the impact of the military hierarchy, the other form of convertibility is the transferability of skills learned in the military to the civilian labor market. Beyond purely professional skills, military service provides social capital by providing lessons on the value of discipline and responsibility, and how to operate in a bureaucratic environment. Civilian employers may therefore use service in the military to distinguish between more productive and less productive workers, with status attained in the army serving as a screening device (De Tray, 1982; Teachman, 2004). Furthermore, soldiers assigned to labor-intensive jobs are in practice being prepared to hold blue-collar jobs in civilian life—low-status work in advanced capitalist societies. However, officers and soldiers given technology-intensive posts are better prepared to hold white-collar jobs after they are discharged (Weede, 1992).

Military service is also effective as a setting in which different groups can mold their unique identities through dense interactions under the cohesive force of the military unit. Groups can then utilize their emergent identity as leverage for collective action outside the military (Enloe, 1980). Convertibility is also applicable to social networks that connect servicepersons to civilians and work to socially promote their military members (see Mills' classic study [1956]). Consequently, the military hierarchy may influence different groups' social status. At its peak, this influence would imply the replication of the military hierarchy in the social sphere.

To some extent, the profile of militarism in society—itself both a product of and a stimulus to the image of external threat—determines the level of convertibility. Convertibility is higher to the extent that: (1) the prestige, and hence power, that servicepersons can hold relative to militarily excluded groups is discursively constructed such that it relies on the level of social recognition ascribed to military contribution, especially when the republican discourse is deeply established (see Soysal, 1994, 4–32); (2) as stated below, the conversion of military skills into civilian skills rests on the symbolic capital that may confer exceptional worth on soldiering as an occupation; (3) social structures are crystallized in a manner that emulates military values (such as discipline), thus giving preference to the entrance of servicepersons to valuable civilian positions (Dandeker, 1990). To some extent, there is a degree of convergence between the military and civilian hierarchies (Janowitz, 1960; Moskos, 1971); (4) social groups struggle to improve their access to military strongholds, especially when the military plays a key role in constructing national identity in a way that makes it a site for intercultural contentions (Krebs, 2006). In turn, groups import to the civilian sphere some of the values by which they were socialized as soldiers, whether the military is considered an effective "school for the nation" or has only limited influence on its post-recruits (for a critical, comprehensive discussion, see Krebs, 2004); (5) as mentioned, internal social networks in the military attract bonds with social networks, especially when militarization increases the military's resources, and hence also its appeal in the civilian sphere.

In turn, a high level of convertibility nurtures militarization by motivating servicepersons and the social networks in which they are embedded to adhere to and support the military way by allocating resources—material and human alike—to it. This mutual nurturing characterizes materialist militarism, which is the exchange between the ability of social groups to acquire power within, and owing to, military service—that can be converted into valuable social positions in the civilian sphere—and their willingness to legitimize preparations for war and war itself by sacrificing human and material resources and by reinforcing the military effort (as soldiers and their families, and as taxpayers) (see Levy, 2003a). Thus, the equation of *sacrifice for convertible rewards* can be seen as the engine of militarism. In short, the notion of material militarism extends and recontextualizes the essence of the republican equation.

Inverse relations are observed between material and symbolic rewards. Increasing symbolic rewards decreases the expectation for material rewards, as long as the former are highly convertible into valuable assets, such as social rights and professional mobility. Accordingly, attenuated symbolic rewards increase expectations for greater material rewards, as a sort of bridging or substitute compensation. In turn, increased reliance on material rewards frequently devalues symbolic rewards, as it subverts the soldiers' image as bearing the weight of national missions and portrays them as holders of a rewarding occupation instead.

However, although this mode of relationship may typify the overall trend, in other conjunctions direct relations are temporarily observed, that is, a simultaneous increase or decrease in both material and symbolic rewards. At the end of this transitory stage inverse relations undergo a revival (for a theoretical perspective see Levy, 2007a).

Historically, within the process of state-building, material rewards decreased with the end of mercenarism, whereas symbolic rewards increased as the state monopolized the military profession. At this point military service acquired a meaning of service to the nation and civic duty, with the French model of the "citizen-soldier" at the center (see Thomson, 1990). In exchange for these ascending symbolic rates, the recruits, whose social groups had struggled for access to the state's armed forces, accepted a decline in their material rewards (Burk, 2001). Having peaked during World War II, the two forms of reward then simultaneously moved in opposite directions, as the post–Cold War militaries lost prestige concomitant with becoming professional-vocational forces (Moskos, 1977).

The republican equation extends to the mode of political control over the armed forces. As mentioned, the citizen-soldier embodied the republican model of transferring sovereignty from the ruler to the community of citizens that staffed and politically controlled the military, i.e., political rights in exchange for military sacrifice (Tilly, 1997a). As the modern state linked military participation with political participation, the decision to go to war was conditional on the support of the local community, namely, those directly shouldering the burden of war and the groups of citizens that provided them for that mission. In other words, the army is indirectly monitored by the social networks of the very youngsters who staff its ranks. This is why the social composition of the military plays a key role in determining the nature of its political control. The better the composition of the army reflects the diversity of the surrounding society, the more politically balanced it will be. Drafted militaries are therefore not only a mechanism for politically mobilizing the populace, but also for politically restraining the military. Military service thus embodies the duality of sacrifice and control.

As long as the republican equation is balanced, and a symmetrical level of rewards versus sacrifice is sustained, the state enjoys autonomy in administering its military policies. Symbolically, the political community controls the military by constituting formal arrangements of control and by distancing the military from domestic policing missions (see Giddens, 1985; Mann, 1993; Tilly, 1997a). In practice, however, state institutions manage the armed forces pretty autonomously. Only when the republican equation is violated are the foundations laid for increasing the ability of social groups to intervene in military affairs and, by implication, to rein in state autonomy.

The Violation of the Republican Equation

This pattern of exchange is modified when convertibility declines, or, in other words, when the gains made in the military are socially devalued relative to the level of sacrifice. Several sets of conditions may bring this about.

First, leading groups may come to believe that the security provided by the state is too materially or morally expensive, and as such is disproportional to the purported threats. For example, as the Cold War drew to a close, the value of defense was pushed to the bottom of the scale of social priorities in European countries (Inglehart, 1977, 49). Sentiments of this kind reflect the state's failure to artificially increase the demand for its protection services by amplifying external threats (in Lake's terms, 1992). Second, and similarly, the state's failure to provide protection, following a military defeat or blunder, say, exemplifies another form of asymmetric burden that might provoke collective action (see, for example, the case of Argentina, Zagorski, 1994).

Third, leading groups may (implicitly or explicitly) claim breach of contract, especially following the erosion of the republican criterion for the distribution of social goods and the justification for social dominance—with military sacrifice at the center. Erosion of this sort was experienced by upper-middle-class groups in the United States and Western Europe from the 1950s. Whereas the equation of soldiering with citizenship traditionally generated social mobility, as soon as groups attained a status of their own that was no longer conditional on military sacrifice, they lost much of their interest in serving in the army (Burk, 1995; Feld, 1977), especially when social benefits remained stable, or even declined asymmetrically relative to the constant and heavy military burden. Moreover, military sacrifice became increasingly incongruent with ever more widespread post-materialist values and trends toward globalization in Western societies, and the concomitant ascendancy of the market society, highlighting market-based individualist values over nationalist ones. Hence, the legitimation system was reconstituted. More than others, upper-middle-class groups internalized the cultural change that amplified the meaning of the diminished military threat brought about by the waning of the Cold War, as reflected in growing alienation from military service.

Fourth, the decline in convertibility drives and is driven by a deterioration of the military's prestige in a circular fashion. In this regard, one of the impacts of globalization on cultural transformation is the growing divergence between military and civilian organizations, with the latter shifting toward knowledge-based rather than resource- and skill-based organizations. Indeed, military organizations are expected to borrow from civilian values rather than lending military values to civilian management practices (see Fukuyama and Shulsky, 1997). As a result, skills learned in the military might become less transferable to the civilian labor market. The capacity of servicepersons to convert their military contribution into valuable benefits and professional assets after their release is thus eroded.[3]

In short, when the state demands a higher payment for reduced returns, the contract is violated. It is worth emphasizing that the decline in convertibility does not necessarily reflect objective events. Rather, it is the perception of the balance between sacrifice and social gains as perceived by social agents that is more significant. Convertibility declines in relation to the extent that this imbalance is discursively constructed, and is recursively reflected in the declining social merit of military sacrifice. Moreover, the more that leading social groups distance themselves from military service, the more they feel at liberty to disparage the military's image from the outside. Attenuated convertibility brings about demilitarization by reducing the status of those who benefit from war in favor of the expanded coalition of its opponents, or at least those with no interest in promoting militaristic values. Most notable in this regard is the resulting decrease in the social acceptance of casualties (Ben-Ari, 2005), together with pressures to cut military expenditures. In turn, demilitarization further undermines the gains made by social groups owing to their military service, thus accelerating the decline of convertibility.

This state of affairs enables social agents to accumulate autonomous power, particularly when there is a gap between the cost of maintaining militarism and its utility. Attenuated convertibility motivates different combinations of various strategies among servicepersons and their social networks.

The first strategy is a passive approach that typifies the silent majority, namely, "loyalty" (in Hirschman's classic terms, 1970). The second strategy is "exit," that is, beyond the option of emigration, avoiding military service through bargaining power, particularly by middle-class groups even within the terms of compulsory service. Such a strategy was employed by middle-class groups in the United States after World War II. The third strategy is "voice," taking the form of protest groups organized by former soldiers and others, which draw their support from those who have asymmetrically shouldered the military burden. This collective action is aimed at acquiring information about the real cost of protection and examining alternative, sometimes less belligerent, strategies vis-à-vis the external threat (Lake, 1992, 25–26). Its main purpose is to reconstitute the republican equation by decreasing the burden of war or increasing the returns for military service. Collective action of this kind is chiefly patterned by the resources the groups seize, the political and cultural traditions that set the limits of legitimate action, the structure of power in society that affects the degree to which collective action will face support or suppression by adversary groups, and the form of the collective bargaining system (see mainly Tilly, 1978).

A combined exit/voice strategy is one in which groups place conditions on their military participation and bargain over those conditions with the state or the military. Most common are forms of monetary bargaining over the terms of military service. With the military's diminished prestige, and the attendant decline in convertibility, pressure mounts to increase material rewards, or, alternatively, to reduce the length of military service and the social investments in security. What Moskos termed the transition "from institution to occupation" (Moskos, 1977) is in fact an alteration of the mode of reward: from symbolic rewards—based on the soldiers' image as following a calling which is socially rewarded as such—to material ones.

Several factors—partially or entirely manifested in different countries—may be seen as accounting for this process: (1) the military's attenuated appeal and prestige drives it to offer higher material rewards in order to reattract skilled manpower, thus making salary bargaining legitimate (albeit indirectly). Taken to its extreme, the delegitimation of military service may also result in antagonism toward state-coerced military service in favor of market-based mechanisms (for the post-Vietnam era, see Burk, 2001); (2) growing selectivity, such as that generated by the downsizing of Western militaries since the 1950s, amplifies enlistees' bargaining power, forcing governments to increase pay rates so as to make military service more competitive (for the U.S. experience, see Kirby, 1996, 3–6); (3) as the decline in the military's prestige also engenders a decline in convertibility, servicepersons lose part of their capacity to convert their military contribution into valuable benefits and professional assets after their release. Attenuated convertibility motivates servicepersons to demand higher compensation, as they come to see the military as a sort of shelter from the competitive labor market (as illustrated by the case of the United States since the 1980s; see Gilroy et al., 1990); (4) in a cyclical fashion, the more the military rewards its personnel, the more soldiers gradually come to be portrayed as holding a rewarding occupation rather than bearing the burden of a national mission. This alteration in the perception of soldiers is part of the transition from institution to occupation. Hence, eroded prestige once again leads to increased pressure to increase wages.

In short, as patterns of collective action become more widespread, the state loses some of its autonomy in the administration of military policy. Its actions are subjected to bargaining that may restrict its freedom and constrain its policies. From the state's point of view, the reconstitution of the republican equation is crucial to regaining its capacity for autonomous action in the military arena. Under these conditions, a multiphased strategy may be executed, with stages somewhat similar to those of state-building outlined above.

The first phase is to artificially increase the demand for security, or to improve the way security is actually provided by improving the functioning of the armed forces and other security agencies. The creation of an emergency regime—by formal and informal means—in order to overcome perceived external threats forms part of this repertoire. Furthermore, by manipulating the external threat so that military sacrifice is regarded as worthy of greater social recognition, the symbolic rewards reaped from the military sphere are intensified.

In the second phase, the state might increase compensation for military sacrifice in line with the traditional republican ethos, especially if the first phase proved ineffective. As an optional step, the state might grant political rights, some of which would offer increased access to the mechanisms controlling the state's security agencies, as well as social rights.

In the third phase, if the level of rights allocation is threatening to undermine state autonomy, is insufficient to compensate groups that are already privileged, or is too costly, the state looks favorably upon reducing the military burden. In historical terms, this phase typifies Western states from the 1970s to the 2000s.

At first, states will be disposed to adopt what Barnett termed *international strategy*, referring to attempts to deflect the costs of war onto foreign allies (Barnett, 1992, 31–40). Alternatively, if the international strategy fails or is insufficient to overcome domestic constraints, the state might reduce the military burden by deescalating the military conflicts in which it is actually or potentially involved, as seen in the mutual steps taken by all parties that led to the cooling down of the Cold War.

While deescalation is naturally a temporary step, as long as it contradicts the fundamentally violent raison d'être of the state, alternative mechanisms will be sought, central to which is shrinking the circles of military participation and redistributing the burden by diverting it from middle- to lower-class groups. These mechanisms include:

(1) Phasing out the draft in favor of a volunteer-professional army, largely because of new patterns of groups-state bargaining that target conscription and impinge on military professionalism (Ajangiz, 2002).

(2) Employing technology in place of human combatants as a means of reducing the intensity of combat (Ferguson, 2001, 48–50) and the level of military participation. This enables a civilian-managed technological army that largely keeps military policies out of politics (see Edgerton, 2005, on the case of Britain).

(3) Supplementing the use of technology with what Shaw (2002) has termed "risk-transfer war," by which Western states achieve their aim of relatively low casualties by transferring risks away from their own militaries. This goal is achieved primarily by activating local allies to assume the risks of war, as evident in the conflicts in Afghanistan and Kosovo.

(4) Privatizing military missions (Avant, 2005; Mandel, 2001), resulting in the social proliferation, or even banalization, of militarism in a manner that impedes its monitoring (Cock, 2005).

(5) Realigning the army's social composition. While military service lost much of its significance in the eyes of middle-class groups, it gradually attracted relatively low-status groups: women, the lower middle class, ethnic minorities, and, later on, homosexuals.[4] Historically, the transition to a volunteer force was accompanied by a decrease in labor costs by hiring low-income soldiers (for indications see Angrist, 1993, 638–39), that is, by intensively drawing the bulk of the military's personnel from the more skillful of these groups' members (Enloe, 2003, 237–38). For such groups, military

service was uniquely advantageous as a mechanism for eliminating symbolic barriers by offering access to arms and sharing in national responsibilities. In turn, this process laid the foundations for attaining substantive social rights. Because these groups were expecting symbolic rewards, the immediate monetary price for their service was reduced. From the army's perspective, realigning the military's social composition helped to achieve a double goal: first, the military drew upon relatively motivated, and hence loyal, personnel; second, the military reduced its labor costs, or at least avoided the increased costs that hiring soldiers from the middle class—who had lost their interest in the symbolic rewards at the level now being offered to lower-status groups— would have otherwise required.

Insofar as the republican concept of politics is based on the exchange of military obligations for civil rights, the declining level of military participation, resulting from falling rates of conscription and diminished participation in warfare, implies a reduction of the motivation, if not the legitimation, for political participation (Silver, 2004). Reduction of military participation eroded war as a route to active citizenship (Turner, 2001) aimed at controlling the state's apparatuses of violence. Indeed, drawing on processes in the United States, as peripheral social groups filled the vacuum created by the exit of middle-class groups, elite groups distanced themselves from the military and became apathetic toward the consequences of belligerency, including its victims (Vasquez, 2005; Moskos, 2001).

Vocational armies, moreover, brought military service back into the labor market. Advocates of the republican conception of citizenship have criticized this trend on the grounds that "to turn such service into a commodity—a job for pay—is to corrupt or degrade the sense of civic virtue that properly attends it" (Sandel, 1998). That is, soldiers' support for military missions is "purchased" rather than politically mobilized.

Consequently, though, the state's autonomy to administer military policies is enhanced (Shaw, 1988, 45–46), as attested by the wars in Iraq and Afghanistan. Given its greater autonomy, the state can resort to the first phase of the strategy aimed at reconstituting the republican equation, i.e., manipulating the external threat. In short, demilitarization may in turn produce remilitarization. And with changes in the social makeup of the armies, remilitarization can become a weapon wielded by the groups that continue to espouse military service in their efforts to legitimize their demand to recognize it as justifying social rewards.

In our terms, this is a transition from materialist militarism to *postmaterialist militarism*. Several features distinguish post-materialist militarism from the republican-based materialist form:

(1) When the translation of the so-called military calling into valuable social resources proves ineffective, servicepersons demand immediate, liquid rewards. Only the manpower drawn from relatively low-status groups sustains the traditional, republican pattern of materialist militarism, and even then only partially.

(2) Recruits are motivated by self-interest rather than by the army's interests in carrying out national missions, and so material compensation becomes paramount. In short, rather than a calling, being a soldier becomes merely a job, while the military is gradually perceived as just one public institution among others.

(3) The distinction between the market and the military profession is blurred, as soldiering returns to the labor market from which it had departed in the 1800s. In the past it was this very separation that heightened convertibility, as servicepersons were portrayed as sacrificing themselves for the nation and fulfilling an obligation of citizenship, thereby deserving generous compensation in the social sphere. In the era of post-materialist militarism, however, and in contrast to the draft system, military service is allocated by the labor market. Moreover, the symbolic status of servicepersons is further eroded as the professional soldier competes intensely in several jurisdictions with private companies, foreign and allied militaries, and international and nongovernmental organizations (Snider, 2003, 23). In addition, militaries adopt business methods that undermine their professional identity (Snider and Watkins, 2000).

(4) The pattern of exchange that had been internalized as an unquestionable civilian pattern is converted into a form of open—and even direct—bargaining. This is a shift from obligation to contractualism in citizens' and soldiers' relations with the state.

The theoretical-historical argument is schematically presented in the following matrix (figure 1.1), which captures the relations between the modes of reward and the level of political control over the armed forces. High levels of symbolic rewards embodied in mass-drafted armies entail high levels of political control, or at least the foundations for them, as when the republican equation is imbalanced. Conversely, the decline of symbolic rewards simultaneously improves material rewards, but erodes the political community's control over the armed forces, as the transition to vocational armies, and even the discrete return of mercenaries, implies.

In conclusion, the organizing principle of military-society relations as such is the manner by which the army rewards its enlistees and, through them, the social networks within which they are nested. The military's functioning is highly sensitive to the balance between different modes of reward.

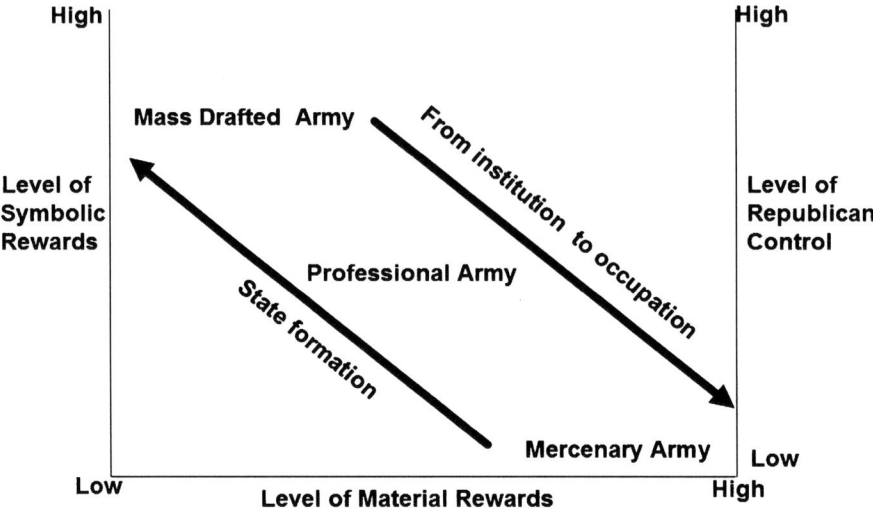

Figure 1.1. Reward and Control Matrix

Historically, the Western nation state was founded on the *republican equation*, which established a reciprocal relationship between the state and its citizens, whereby the former rewarded sacrifices made by the latter. When this equation is violated, such as when the burden exceeds the rewards and the state fails to discursively exaggerate the external threat, the state will tend either to reduce the burden by lowering the profile of its belligerent activity, increase the rewards for sacrifice, or redistribute the internal burden from middle-class to lower-class groups. This dynamic balancing of the republican equation explains the dynamics of war versus deescalation. The case of Israel reflects a similar pattern.

Materialist militarism, therefore, is an advantageous concept for understanding the sources and dynamics of modern militarism at several levels. For the moment, suffice to say that by relying on the notion of convertibility, materialist militarism offers what has been missed by the proponents of state formation and other schools interested in militarism, namely, that levels of militarism vary according to fluctuations in levels of convertibility. High rates of convertibility breed high-profile militarism, and vice versa. Furthermore, the transition from materialist militarism to post-materialist militarism demonstrates the former's contingency upon convertible rewards that may alter their form in accordance with their beneficiaries' motivations. Gender, ethnic, religious, community, and other sources of motivation are rendered obsolete when the gains acquired by groups in the military are poorly translated into civilian benefits. By enabling us to trace the dynamics of these processes, the concept of materialist militarism equips us with the conceptual tools for understanding the dynamics of war and deescalation that characterize Israel during the period in question.

OUTLINE OF THE BOOK

Materialist militarism is Israel's distinctive form of militarism. It is rooted in the exchange pattern developed between the state and the leading secular Ashkenazi social groups. For the Ashkenazi, military service provided symbolic rewards—by converting their military sacrifice into legitimate social dominance—in return for their willingness to invest human and material resources in the upkeep and legitimization of the military effort. This pattern of "reward-for-sacrifice" was constitutive of the republican equation. Therefore, as long as the external arena allowed the state a substantial degree of freedom of choice, and the internal arena endorsed the chosen route by providing resources and legitimation, materialist militarism became the driving force behind Israel's preference for bellicosity.

However, the combination of a decline in the army's status following perceived military failures since the 1973 War, and Israel's becoming a globalized market society, diminished the army's role in determining the social hierarchy. As a result, rewards for military service were devalued while the military burden grew, thus violating the republican equation. Ashkenazi groups began to distance themselves from military service, while making demands at the symbolic-political and material levels that placed restrictions on the state's ability to run its military policies autonomously. This was manifested in the partial demilitarization of Israeli society between 1985 and 2000.

Given this background, the state launched an attempt to reconstitute the republican equation via a twofold balancing strategy: the first phase was a deescalation of military conflict to bring the military burden in line with the rewards offered to those bearing it, with the Oslo Accords playing a crucial part; the second phase was aimed at restoring the state's autonomy in the military arena. This involved a rearchitecturing of the army's social composition, predominantly by turning to religious and peripheral soldiers for whom military service still bore significant symbolic rewards. These took the form of fulfilling their ideological values by protecting the borders of the "Greater Land of Israel," social mobility, and cultural influence within the IDF. These new groups thus displayed loyalty to the military way and internalized the tenets of military culture without mobilizing their civilian networks to protest against the army, as the Ashkenazi groups had done. In short, by relying on peripheral and religious groups, rather than the powerful middle class, the state reconstituted the republican equation, and at a relatively low cost. In exchange for greater symbolic worth, the recruits were satisfied with lower material rewards.

The strategy for reconstituting the republican equation returned a degree of autonomy to the internal management of military policies, and it bore fruit in the Al-Aqsa Intifada. When the army's new social architecture met with the infrastructure for renewed violence, itself brought about by the military nature of the Oslo Accords, a new dynamic was created that escalated the fighting with the Palestinians and temporarily brought the Oslo Accords to their knees. A peace coalition that might have attempted to politically curb the IDF—as had appeared in previous wars—did not emerge (this historical analysis discussed in chapters 2–3).

In earlier wars, the instigators of political protest were mainly ex-soldiers, especially reservists, and their families. Thus, two key mechanisms worked to mitigate the potential for protest flourishing within the IDF's ranks. First, the social composition of the military's casualties in combat in the Occupied Territories changed significantly. A drop was observed in the proportion of Ashkenazi casualties from about 48 percent in the first week of the First Lebanon War (1982) to about 28 percent in the Al-Aqsa Intifada, a considerably larger decline than the relative decrease in this stratum's demographic weight. This social change was reflected in the reshaping of the bereavement ethos from one of protest (typical of the Lebanon War), to one of accepting the sacrifice. The second mechanism was the field units' excessive motivation for combat in which they exhibited much greater enthusiasm than in the past for aggressive missions. Through these missions the religious and peripheral groups expected to prove themselves worthy of status both inside and outside the army, as they struggled both for military status and the ability to increase its convertibility vis-à-vis the Ashkenazi groups (to be detailed in chapter 4).

Nevertheless, despite the broad freedom of operation afforded to the IDF by its new social architecture, the prolonged fighting with the Palestinians and its escalating costs caused the scope of its autonomy to narrow once more. There was renewed tension between the army and the Ashkenazi middle class, the bearers of the market economy, who strove to diminish the IDF's material and human resources. The army's freedom of action became asymmetrical in relation to its contracting resources and attenuated legitimacy to fight. This forms the background to the Disengagement Plan, formulated in 2003 as a withdrawal from the Gaza Strip and the northern West Bank, including the evacuation of about 6,000 Jewish settlers from those areas. The withdrawal was aimed at bringing the fighting in line with the army's narrowing resources by instigating a new model of warfare, one that would decrease the costly military friction with the Palestinian civilian population. This would make it possible for the army to carry on fighting as a way of maintaining its status, though at a lesser cost, especially in the internal arena (the crisis of the IDF vs. the market is discussed in chapter 5).

However, the Disengagement Plan embodied a breakdown in the IDF's new quasi-contractual relationship with religious groups. For these groups, the main symbolic return for their military participation was carrying out the mission of renewing Jewish control over what they perceive as the Holy Land, now partly evacuated by the army. With these groups' massive entrance into the army since the 1980s (and the policies implemented by the IDF in encouraging this trend, by accepting the dual loyalty of the national religious soldiers—to both their commanders and their rabbis), the army became embedded within their social networks. It was in this context that leading rabbis decreed that soldiers were forbidden by religious law to expel Jews from their homes, and urged them to refuse to take any part in uprooting settlements in the Land of Israel.

Despite resistance to the evacuation, however, the IDF carried out the Disengagement Plan most effectively. The army's effective performance was due to its ability to leverage the religious groups' interest in preserving the IDF's capacity to proffer mobility to their members and to improve their own standing within the ranks. This interest committed them to preserving the IDF's status as a "people's army," and ensured that they held themselves back from clashing violently with the evacuating forces. Rather than the military's embeddedness within the religious groups proving to be an obstacle, therefore, it actually enabled the smooth implementation of the withdrawal. Owing to this embeddedness, the military could effectively sharpen the dilemma with which those groups were faced, that is, whether to remain faithful to their ideological and religious principles, but place their accomplishments in the military at risk, or to consent to the pullout (the Disengagement Plan is discussed in chapter 6).

With the disengagement, the social status of the army was further eroded as the empowerment of the market discourse together with the civilian agenda that came to the fore once more threatened the IDF's resources and identity. This laid the foundation for Israel to initiate the Second Lebanon War. This move reflected the syndrome which I term the "gap of legitimacies," that is, the widening gap between high levels of political legitimacy for using force, and low levels of social legitimacy for making the attendant sacrifices, a limitation that is anchored in the market discourse. Paradoxically, this gap strengthens the tendency to speedily deploy excessive military force at a time of crisis, particularly when it appears to exact a reasonable price and offers a good chance of success vis-à-vis a relatively inferior adversary, thus empowering the military's status. However, this gap also imposes limits on the use of military force and may determine its failure, particularly in relation to the ambitious war aims that are leveraged for political mobilization. This was the case in the Second Lebanon War. As a result, the failure of the Second Lebanon War has laid the foundations for accelerating the conversion of the IDF from a drafted to a professional army: the military's arsenal of symbolic rewards has been further depleted following the disengagement and the Second Lebanon War and therefore can only be balanced out by monetary rewards (the war and its consequences are detailed in chapter 7).

The next chapter deals with the construction and subsequent violation of the republican equation that describes the history of materialist militarism in Israel.

NOTES

1. Particularly after clashes in 1996 when the Palestinians responded with a wave of violence to the opening of the "Western Wall Tunnel" in the Muslim sector of the Old City of Jerusalem.

2. See for example: "Militarism refers to excessive levels of military spending by the state and excessive influence of armed forces over civilian life" (Kaldor, 2002, 160).

3. To illustrate, for about ten years after entering the labor market, white veterans of the Vietnam War earned around 5 percent less than their nonveteran counterparts. A possible explanation is that a primary consequence of their military service was a loss of civilian work experience (see for example Angrist, 1990). This loss of experience was aggravated under conditions of increased selectivity, which accompanied the decline in the military's status, as veterans competed with growing numbers of highly qualified nonveterans who were taking advantage of their exemption. Also, it is possible that the diminished prestige of the military as a result of fighting an unpopular war was reflected in the image of ex-servicepersons in the civilian labor market. Incompetence in Vietnam may have been mirrored in the labor market. Even the social networks within which military persons were integrated might have perceived their presence as less attractive and thus been less active in promoting ex-servicepersons.

4. A clear manifestation of this process is provided by the military service of women and the African American group. African American and other working-class groups' participation in the military was boosted during the Vietnam War, particularly with the establishment of the All-Volunteer Force (AVF). It is estimated that working-class and poor youth made up the majority of the enlisted ranks (see Appy, 1993, 35–43; Fallows, 1993, 38–42; for another approach, see Barnett et al., 1992). Later,

during the 1990s, gays and lesbians demanded to be allowed to openly participate in military service and called for the lifting of official bans. For those groups, eradicating discrimination in the military was a crucial step in ending discrimination in the public sphere at large, which is differentiated from private discrimination against homosexuals, and was thus seen as a symbolic reward convertible into other social assets (see Berube, 1990; Sullivan, 1995).

Chapter Two

The Republican Equation and Its Violation

INTRODUCTION

The relationship between Jewish-Israeli society and its army has been a tumultuous one. From its lofty status as a powerful "people's army" in the mid-1950s, the army has met with a succession of crises since the 1973 War which intensified following its display of weakness in the First Lebanon War (1982–1985) and the First Intifada (1987–1993). These crises have led to a dilution of the army's resources, a reduction in its political support, a decline in its symbols, and even its gradual abandonment by social elites. At the peak of this process—the signing and implementation of the Oslo Accords, to a large extent a result of this course of events—the IDF gradually became an "army of peace," thereby losing its central status. However, the Al-Aqsa Intifada filled the army's sails with fresh wind, though even that died down given the ongoing and hopeless fighting in the Occupied Territories, a process signified by the Disengagement Plan of the summer of 2005. The Second Lebanon War worsened the army's status even more, contrary to its expectations at the outbreak of the war. The demobilization of the "people's army" and its replacement with a voluntary-professional military is no longer a distant prospect, as we can see from the public discourse in Israel in the mid-2000s and the recruitment reforms being implemented by the government (see Levy, 2004a).

As mentioned in chapter 1, these are vicissitudes that are inadequately explained by gazing outward at the changing levels of the purported Arab threat on the State of Israel. It is by tracing the very success of Israeli society in preserving the legitimacy of military values over time that we shall be able to decipher the fluctuations in the extent of that legitimacy. Then we shall be able to unravel the more specific problematic that stands at the center of this book, namely, explaining the army's "vacillations" during the decade beginning in 1995: from its leading role in the Oslo process, to fronting the battle against the Palestinian Authority, back to political moderation, and so forth (a problematic to which the following chapters are devoted).

To put it succinctly, in this chapter I shall argue that military service provided symbolic rewards to the dominant groups in Jewish-Israeli society, mainly the secular Ashkenazi middle class, by converting their military sacrifice into legitimate social dominance. These rewards were constitutive of the republican equation, which enabled the state to sustain a situation of conflict for a long time and with a relatively large degree of autonomy. However, as soon as the combination of a decline in the army's status and structural sociopolitical change in Israeli society began to erode the value of the rewards, the equation was violated. Dominant groups began to distance themselves from military service while making demands that placed restrictions on the state's ability to run its military policies autonomously. Demilitarization was at work during the years 1985–2000.

Given this background, the state reconstituted the republican equation via a *twofold balancing strategy*: the first phase was a deescalation of military conflict, meaning that the military burden could be reduced in order to correspond with the rewards offered to those bearing it; the second phase involved a new military "social architecture" which saw the ranks swelled by peripheral and religious groups for whom military service still bore significant symbolic rewards (as described in the following chapter). This reconstruction of the formula returned to the state part of its autonomy, as seen in the performance of the army during the Al-Aqsa Intifada. This chapter deals with developments from the early years of the state up to the period of Oslo. The following chapters focus on the post-Oslo era and address the fluxes of the decade since the Accords were signed.

ETHNO-CLASS REPRODUCTION AS A SYMBOLIC REWARD

The republican principle of the "citizen-soldier," discussed at length in chapter 1, was well assimilated in Israeli society. The IDF was founded along with the establishment of the state in 1948. The army was organized on the basis of compulsory enlistment for every Jewish man and woman, the length of which settled in the 1970s at two years for women and three years for men. In addition, (mostly) men were required to serve in the reserves for a period of a few days up to a number of weeks per year until the age of forty-five or thereabouts. Under the wings of statism (*Mamlachtiyut*)—the state ideology which inculcated the idea that the state is a supreme entity, supplanting any particularist conception incompatible with state-directed goals—mass compulsory recruitment tied a Gordian knot between soldiering and citizenship in its most fundamental sense (Shafir and Peled 2002). Under the halo of the "people's army," this arrangement gave the army a favored symbolic status.

Indeed, the IDF is more than just a conscripted military. Israelis have long viewed it as the "people's army," a crucial institution both for the defense of the state and the self-image of the nation. Furthermore, the IDF cultivated its image as a universal and depoliticized military that stands above society's sectarian divisions. Military service in Israel is not only a legal obligation imbued with symbolic meaning; it is also constructed in terms of a community, which is experienced by its members as overlapping with society (Helman, 1997).

The IDF was consolidated and spearheaded by the dominant social group of middle-class, secular Ashkenazi men—the very group that founded the army, populated its senior ranks, and that was identified with its achievements. High rates of convertibility helped the male members of this Western, secular stratum to reap symbolic rewards from their military participation—rewards that were disproportional to their actual sacrifice—and to attain dominance over two other primary groups—Mizrachi immigrants and Palestinian citizens, who were below them in the emerging class structure. The primary symbolic reward was the legitimacy afforded to Ashkenazi social dominance, which became a central foundation of its own reproduction.

The Ethno-Class Structure

The coalescence and solidification of Israel's ethno-class structure in the early years of the state's existence represented a critical stage in the development of materialist militarism. Three main ethnically differentiated groups stood at the core of this new ethno-class structure, each almost homogenously occupying distinct rungs of the social ladder. The dominant class was largely comprised of the Ashkenazi group, European immigrants who had established the organizational infrastructure of the Zionist project and who represented the vast majority of the waves of immigration in the pre-state years. Members of this group constituted the lion's share of the small business elite, as well as both the upper and middle ranks of the middle class. The middle class was notable for its high representation in the extensive public bureaucracy, which had been set up by the Jewish community during British rule over Palestine (1920–1948), and which grew considerably with the establishment of the state in 1948. Ashkenazi presence in the lower reaches of the social hierarchy was relatively low and, owing to the superior social mobility of Ashkenazim, it tended to be temporary. The control that this stratum enjoyed over the means of economic production and state institutions—especially through the workers' parties, which had almost unbounded power until 1977—enabled it to translate its political power into the imposition of a cultural and normative hegemony, within which socially peripheral groups were incorporated.

The peripheral and semi-peripheral rungs of the ladder were occupied by two groups that had been absorbed by the Ashkenazi collective following the establishment of the state—the Mizrachim, and, beneath them, the Palestinians.

With an initial infrastructure of about 700,000 (mostly Ashkenazi) Jews, between the years 1948 and 1960 Israel absorbed around 500,000 Mizrachi immigrants from Arab countries and a similar number of immigrants from European countries. By the 1970s, the Mizrachi stratum constituted approximately one-half of the entire Jewish population of Israel. State institutions considered and rejected a number of alternative strategies for managing this immigration—from immigrant absorption on a fully equal basis, to treating the immigrants for all intents and purposes as labor migrants—but finally chose a middle path, one which delegated immigrant absorption to the state in a way that combined the construction of inequality with the creation of mechanisms that legitimized it.

The state established an unequal social structure that rigidified the Mizrachi immigrants' peripheral social status. A large proportion of this stratum was settled by the state in the country's hinterlands, along its new borders (especially immigrants from North Africa), and in the outskirts of the large cities (particularly immigrants from Asia), where they lived in overcrowded conditions and substandard housing. Immigrants in these areas were employed as cheap labor in agriculture, industry, construction, and services, with scarce reference to the skills they imported from their home countries (in comparison to the opportunities given to immigrants from Europe). Nor were those skills upgraded so as to adapt them to a modern economy. Mizrachi communities received a ramshackle infrastructure of social services. This was especially true of the education system, which was Ashkenazi-oriented and thus posed a barrier to integration, particularly for the first generation of Mizrachim. However, relations of dependency, which were translated into political power relations, were forged between the immigrants and the old-timers, who provided services to the former in the name of the state.

In contrast to Mizrachi immigrants, most of the immigrants arriving in roughly equal numbers from European countries managed to integrate themselves relatively quickly in the existing middle class. This Ashkenazi group was able to exploit its professional skills, its ethno-social networks, and its dominant Ashkenazi social identity in order to move from the periphery to the center.

Owing to their sheer size as a labor force, the way in which Mizrachi immigrants were absorbed provided an impetus to the economic growth of the absorbing Ashkenazi group. To demonstrate the gaps: in 1972, about 20 years after their absorption, around 30 percent of European immigrants were "white-collar" workers as compared to only 10 percent among the Mizrachim, while 50 percent of Mizrachim were employed in "blue-collar" jobs as compared to roughly 30 percent of Ashkenazim (Swirski, 1981, 59). In the same year, 48 percent of Ashkenazim but only 10 percent of Mizrachim had at least thirteen years' education. These gaps were reflected in the gross difference of income between individuals of European-American extraction and those from Asia-Africa: in 1969, the income of Ashkenazi Israeli-born males was 62 percent higher than that of Mizrachi Israeli-born males; in 1976 the figure was 77 percent (Fishelson et al., 1980, 265). The unavoidable conclusion is that the gaps had been handed down from generation to generation, a process that helps make them permanent.[1]

While the Mizrachim occupied the higher levels of the social periphery, its lower reaches were populated by Palestinian citizens of Israel, those who had not been expelled or fled during the 1948 War and its aftermath. They included about 150,000 residents of territories annexed to Israel as part of the 1949 Armistice Agreements, out of the 800,000 who had been living in them before the war. Their absorption did not pose any particular dilemmas for the state in the beginning of the 1950s. The centerpiece of the new policy was a balance between preserving formal civil rights on the one hand, and preventing the emergence of a potential security risk from a population whose loyalty to the political order was permanently suspected on the other. Accordingly, Palestinian towns and villages were kept under Military Administration between 1948 and 1966, and the rights of Palestinians in acquiring land and in the labor market were restricted. The state expropriated a sizable part of the land owned by Palestinians before the war for the sake of absorbing Jewish immigration. Similarly to the Mizrachim, the Palestinians were also exploited as cheap labor (to the extent that military rule permitted movement from the Palestinian labor market to the Jewish one). Israeli Palestinians received inferior services from the state, which prevented the establishment of an economic infrastructure in their localities. These conditions drove the Palestinian-Israeli population to economic distress, impeded its economic development, and obviously prevented it from attaining equal rights with Jewish groups.[2]

Any inegalitarian ethno-class order is destined for turmoil if unaccompanied by reproductive mechanisms that, over time, maintain social structures that embody arrangements legitimized and internalized by the social actors who are subject to them. As mentioned, while creating this social distortion with one hand, the state simultaneously softened and disguised it as a way of reproducing inequality with the other. The reproduction of the ethno-class structure was critically dependent on the products of militarism, and thus became the central anchor for materialist militarism until the 1980s. Reproducing its social dominance through leveraging its military contribution was the primary symbolic reward extracted from the army by the secular Ashkenazi middle class.

The Reproduction of Ashkenazi Dominance

The reproduction of Ashkenazi dominance rested on the conversion of symbolic resources from the military arena to the social sphere such that the social hierarchy duplicated the military hierarchy, thus legitimizing and solidifying it. The reproductive functions of the army were constructed on a multilevel basis:

(1) *The first level—shaping the intramilitary social hierarchy*, such that dominance was afforded to men from the secular Ashkenazi group, reflecting their dominant status in society. Because the IDF was based on mass compulsory enlistment, and given its form as a modern Western army, the Ashkenazi stratum was marked out as the group intended to give the army its qualitative attributes. Due to its modern nature, the ostensibly rational and general criteria for determining each soldier's status were, in fact, geared more toward the education, values, and primary skills of Ashkenazim, and were less compatible with the background of Mizrachi recruits. During the early 1950s, Mizrachi recruits probably made up 200 of the approximately 4,000 officers in the conscript and career armies (Ben-Gurion, 1981). In the 1970s about 67 percent of the conscripts and squad commanders were Mizrachi, but they accounted for only about 30 percent of the junior officers and 10 to 17 percent of the senior officers (Smooha, 1984, 19).

Other social groups were located in peripheral positions, particularly auxiliary and administrative roles. As Mizrachi youngsters were gradually integrated into combat units, they were represented as contributing to the army's quantitave needs but not to its quality, as "Orientals" who were "joining" Israeli society. While Mizrachim were notably present in combat units during the first years of the state, their proportion declined from the end of the 1950s as the army once more attracted educated Ashkenazim (see below). However, their numbers began to climb again during the 1960s with the emergence of a relatively educated stratum among the younger generation of Mizrachim (for various aspects of this see Erez et al., 1993; Yinon and Friedman, 1977; Smooha, 1984).

Women, who were primarily deployed in auxiliary roles, as well as standing as mothers at the forefront of the demographic (Jewish) struggle, were forced to the margins as well (Yuval-Davis, 1985). Religious recruits were also excluded on account of their fear of the secularizing influence of the army, an anxiety that led many of them into auxiliary roles and away from the possibility of a military career. The exclusion of other groups—Palestinian citizens and Ultra-Orthodox youngsters—from any kind of service distanced them from the construction site of the new Jewish Israeliness, and added to the value of those who did serve, especially Mizrachim. The growth of the army after the Six Day War further entrenched Ashkenazi dominance by opening up new possibilities for promotion in the enlarged command and logistics sections, possibilities that gave preference to people with a high level of schooling, namely, Ashkenazi high school graduates.

(2) *The second level—legitimizing intra-army inequality* by wrapping it up in an ethos of egalitarianism flagrantly at odds with prevailing patterns of civilian inequality. The ethos of egalitarianism was supported by a number of mechanisms: (1) inclusive compulsory recruitment; (2) a purportedly achievement-oriented, non-ascriptive system of criteria for job allocation and promotion (at least in relation to Jews); (3) the army's image as a "melting pot" for Jewish youngsters of the mass immigration in which, purportedly, all young Jews densely interacted with one another; (4) the informal nature of military discipline, which blurs hierarchy; (5) the uniform induction process for both soldiers and officers, in contrast to most other armies; (6) the detachment of the army from party politics and its subjection to civilian supervision, thus undermining its identification with any specific center of Ashkenazi-based social power. Thus, the ethos of egalitarianism constitutive of the army had two simultaneous effects: it became a mechanism that intensified inequality, in the name of equality, by making access to military positions ever more inequitable due to the equal entrance of unequal groups; and at the same time it also camouflaged this inequality, thereby helping its subjects to accept it. The army's façade of egalitarianism helped instill in the Mizrachi recruits the recognition that their personal status in the army was determined by objective criteria inherent in the military's needs, and not by ascriptive criteria of ethnic affiliation. Accordingly, inequality in the army was perceived (and represented by the heads of the army and the state) as a temporary phenomenon that contradicted the army's goals.

(3) *The third level—duplicating the military hierarchy in the civilian social sphere*. Ashkenazim could smoothly translate their legitimated dominance within the military into social status in the civilian sphere, with this consolidation of their social dominance over the Mizrachim helping to avert interethnic unrest. This state of affairs lasted for as long as military service encapsulated the new society's code of civic virtue by defining the criteria for

becoming a participating member in it. As such, not only did it distinguish between Jews and Palestinians, but also between different Jewish groups. This idea formed the anchor of the statist republican discourse, which saw contributing to the state as a supreme value. Replacing the *pioneering spirit*—the dominant criterion in the pre-state community (the *Yishuv*), which had been associated with the Ashkenazi settler—the ethos of *Mamlachtiyut* put forward a criterion that favored a collective or individual acting in the service of the state. Citizenship was perceived as an active form, focused on promoting the community's "common good" (Shafir and Peled, 2002). This paved the way for the appearance of new status symbols that were identified with the state, and thus ostensibly available to all, the most important of which was the *warrior*, who came to supplant the *pioneer*—the dominant icon of the pre-state period (for more see Levy, 2003b, 50–81).

The linkage between the statist republican criterion and contribution to the military was constructed through the militarization of the political discourse. Militarization combined a discursive intensification of the existential threat posed to the country by the Arabs, with a delegation of the roles of "nation builder" and "melting pot" to the army. Gradually, the boundaries of Israeli militarism expanded, blurring the dividing lines between army and society, and directly and indirectly making the military a project for (Jewish) society at large. Moreover, the conceptual distinction between the "army" and "national security" collapsed, and the major civilian institutions and concerns—education, science, birth-rates, and more—were defined in terms of the military functions they fulfilled. At this point, the term "security" took on mythic standing in Israeli public discourse (Arian, 1995; Ben-Eliezer, 1998).

The militarization of the discourse amplified the significance attributed to military service and its location in the most critical of positions, namely, guaranteeing personal and communal existence. This rhetoric gave meaning to the figure of the warrior and cemented its dominance over every other vocation that was not involved with protecting the country.

However, a social criterion is not enough to establish social dominance, unless it is identified with the group that is seeking dominance. The warrior was empowered by being identified with the image of the *Sabre*. The Sabre was the prototype of the young, male, secular Ashkenazi, held up in contrast to the diasporic Jew. He was a hale and hearty man, the embodiment of the pioneering spirit, a child of the new Hebrew land, and a product of its educational and social frameworks, or the graduate of a youth movement. He lived in an agricultural settlement and was well-educated. In short, the Sabre was the distilled expression of the pre-1948 secular Ashkenazi middle class, and as such became a model for imitation and a source of jealousy among other groups (Almog, 1997). Its coalescence with the warrior brought about the image of the *warrior-Sabre*. The warrior-Sabre represented the dominant and proper (non-diasporic) masculinity of men who could pass the ultimate test of masculinity, namely, combat. This test included sacrifice, courage, heroism, danger, bodily discipline, emotional control, and more. Military service tested the masculinity of young men through a series of physical and emotional trials, which formed a "rite of passage" from youth to manhood (Ben-Ari and Levy-Schreiber, 2000). Because it fully linked masculinity with nationalism, the image of the combat soldier was bestowed with special powers.

The inequitable power division within the military meant that the crucial status of warrior was achievable mainly by Ashkenazim. In practice, this identification came through the success of the veteran secular Ashkenazi segment in gaining control over both the formal and informal rituals for commemorating fallen soldiers from the 1948 War as a means of reglorifying its national achievements. Secular Ashkenazim's institutional power, their organizational and economic clout, their presence in the relevant social networks, and their human capital, all accounted for this success without any real relation to their actual rate of participation in the war. It is against this background that the fallen were commemorated and the warriors were celebrated, just as the role of those who were not Sabre-Ashkenazim was belittled, such as Mizrachi recruits, the children of new immigrants from European countries, fighters from right-wing underground militias, and others. This resulted in the mythologization of the Sabre, who would from now on also be identified with military heroism (Almog, 1997, 190–97; Sivan, 1991, 55–101; see also Aronoff, 1993, 53). The Suez War (1956) and Six Day War (1967) would further strengthen this symbol (see Almog, 1997, 165, 209–15).

Warrior-based symbols concurrently imbued the Mizrachim with the idea that their social position depended solely on their contribution to the state. Accordingly, they expected that they would only be able to enter society through "contributory" social activity. But until Mizrachim could affirm their contribution they had to accept their inferiority vis-à-vis the Ashkenazim, whose contribution (certainly in historical terms) was portrayed as greater than that of the Mizrachim. The more a group is portrayed as shouldering the glamorous burden of national redemption, the less other groups are able to blame it for having achieved social superiority, especially as the former group's achievements make their way into the public discourse as the criterion for determining the status of individuals or groups in the social hierarchy. At least in the short term, conditions were created in Israeli society for legitimizing this social dominance by ruling out social protest by Mizrachim against the very social arrangements that structured the reproduction of interethnic inequality. Inequality in the military was thus instilled into societal relations, a mutual reinforcement of the structure of inequality.

Furthermore, to the extent that officers were able to successfully convert their military profession into a fitting civilian one upon their release from the army (including political mobility), much owing to their ability to build powerful social networks (Maman and Lissak, 1990), convertibility could be seen as spreading from the group to the personal level. A range of classificatory practices also helped enlistees translate the social capital provided to them by the army into professional mobility. The central practice was the status of the "ex-soldier," which served until the 1990s as a criterion for access to various civilian jobs and state allowances, with the consequence that Palestinian and low-status Jewish citizens were excluded from those benefits by an apparently universal criterion. In other words, in the shift from the military to the social sphere, symbolic rewards were converted into material ones.

Just as military dominance was converted into social dominance, peripheral status in the army was converted into and entrenched social marginality. Gradually abandoned by Ashkenazim, "blue-collar" jobs in the civilian labor market were staffed by Mizrachi immigrants, who had been partially prepared for those positions by the army (Roumani, 1979, 70–86). Thus, in the context of the decline of the pioneering manual laborer and the rise of the middle-class "working intelligentsia," they found themselves in possession of a slowly waning status symbol (see Keren, 1989).

The Mizrachim acquiesced in their inferior status in the army due to the aforementioned mechanisms that legitimized it. Because the Mizrachi immigrants believed the official ideology that military service constituted an entry ticket to society, their very induction, rather than their status in the organization, became a symbolic resource in itself, motivating them to accept what was perceived as temporary preferentiality enjoyed by the Ashkenazim. Evidence for this can be seen in the Mizrachim's mode of protest (such as the events in Wadi Salib in 1959).[3] Although during the 1950s they became increasingly conscious of the built-in inequality of civilian institutions, they placed their confidence in the IDF and its emphasis on the ethos of equality, thus placing the army beyond political conflict (Swirski, 1995, 107). Their acquiescence with their inferior status was also strengthened by the way that the Israeli-Arab conflict was constructed in the consciousness of Mizrachim—they were presented with a reality of enmity between themselves and the Arab world from which they had emigrated, as well as between themselves and Israel's Palestinian citizens (see Levy, 2003b, 66–67, 75–76; Shenhav, 2006; Yiftachel and Tzfadia, 2004). The Mizrachim, therefore, were also symbolically rewarded, but not in a way that challenged the symbolic rewards of their Ashkenazi counterparts. This encouraged them to perceive the army as an important site in which to demonstrate their abilities and strive for advancement, and to treat their achievements as a social criterion.

The legitimacy of this unequal access to symbolic rewards took on additional meaning as the direct fruits of war were gathered. First and foremost, the 1948 War enabled the establishment of a state-led property regime that ensured that the state could take control of Palestinian-owned land, either by confiscating land owned by people who had now become refugees, or by claiming security considerations and thereby expropriating a large amount of the land that remained in the hands of those who had become citizens. The state simultaneously took steps to assume control of houses and property left behind by Palestinian refugees as they were driven out or fled (Yiftachel and Kedar, 2000, 77–85). In the early years of the state, most of the immigrants were settled in new communities set up on this land. This regime ensured the reproduction of Ashkenazi dominance in two ways. First, it enabled the state to absorb huge waves of immigration without having to carry out any kind of redistributive reforms that might have harmed the dominance of the Ashkenazi middle class, or that might at least have reduced its members' standard of living over time. Had Israel chosen to absorb Palestinian refugees or return land, it almost certainly would have had to undertake such reforms (see Carmi and Rosenfeld, 1989). Second, the regime created distributive arrangements for the allocation of land that, by means of various universal legal devices, favored the founding Ashkenazi groups, which in turn served as an engine for growth in agriculture and construction (ibid.).

At the same time, the 1948 War made full employment a possibility, critical mainly for Mizrachi immigrants, thereby preventing their competition with cheap Palestinian workers. Control over the labor market rested on the exclusion of Palestinian labor from the Jewish labor market. This was achieved by imposing Military Administration on Palestinian areas and preventing the entrance of refugees or infiltrators from the Palestinian communities that had been annexed to Egypt or Jordan, both mechanisms that served to perpetuate the state of war (see Shalev, 1992, 203–4). This meant that the unemployment of the state's early years was eliminated, and the 1960s were characterized as a period of full employment. Unemployment among Mizrachi immigrants, or a fatal blow to their earning capabilities due to competition with cheap Palestinian labor, bore the potential for social unrest that could endanger the legitimacy of Ashkenazi dominance (such the quickly quelled Wadi Salib riots).

The dominance of the secular Ashkenazi middle class was entrenched by the 1967 Six Day War. Leading up to the war the economy was deep in recession. A recessive policy had been adopted by the political leadership as a strategy to fight off a severe economic crisis. The crisis had emerged as a result of a steep rise in labor costs and a decline in productivity, which was brought about by the conditions of full employment in the 1960s, because of which the state had lost much of its moderating control, via the *Histadrut*—the powerful trade union umbrella organization—over organized labor. The large number of strikes was symptomatic of that structure. However, the significant reduction in imported capital prevented the state from subsidizing the economy to the extent that it had done in the past in order to ensure full employment and prevent social unrest. Following a drastic reduction in government spending, as a strategy for restraining both workers and employers, the recession brought about widespread unemployment and economic slowdown. At the same time, efforts were made to increase the supply of cheap labor by abolishing the Military Administration over the Palestinian citizens in 1966, thereby enabling their gradual integration within the primary Jewish labor market.

The 1967 War reversed this trend by creating new resources, enjoyed mainly by the secular Ashkenazi middle class, but which also enabled mobility for the more educated stratum of the Mizrachim, and even for a small number of Palestinian citizens, a process that helped divide the social periphery and further reproduce the social hierarchy. The occupation of the Palestinian-populated West Bank and Gaza Strip enabled their exploitation as captured markets for products, as a source of land for new settlement, and mainly as a supply of cheap Palestinian labor. Indeed, this workforce boosted the building industry while also weakening the lesser-skilled Mizrachim and Israeli Palestinians, who had to cope with the influx of cheap labor. As well as gaining control of the oil fields in the Sinai Peninsula, lands were taken in the Jordan Valley and the Golan Heights that offered the potential for agricultural development. In addition, the years following the war saw the Israeli arms industry become a leading sector in the economy, with no small part played by the tightening of the strategic alliance with the United States, which laid down an infrastructure for arming the military and directing generous aid to Israel (see Levy, 1997a, 113–31).

To sum up, converting military status into civilian social status, which in turn was converted into material rewards in the civil sphere, was the main symbolic reward of military service. The symmetry between rewards and sacrifice constituted the republican equation in Israel. Conceptually speaking, it follows that the Israeli version of the republican contract embodies a broader form of exchange. Military sacrifice was not traded for formal rights alone, but also for social dominance, which extended to the fruits of war and consequently shaped the social hierarchy.

Two interrelated consequences then laid the foundations for the state's ability to implement militaristic policies over time: (1) the creation of conditions for low-cost social recruitment for military participation, with the result that (2) the state had greater autonomy in the internal sphere to manage its military policies.

THE STATE'S ABILITY TO WAGE WAR

Low-Cost Military Participation

The secular Ashkenazi group bore the ideology of militarism for as long as it advanced its social status. Other groups—mainly Mizrachim, women, the national religious, and, later on, immigrants from the former Soviet Union and Ethiopia—assimilated the principle of the citizen-soldier and its anticipated social rewards. This could be seen in their efforts to be integrated into the military, to stand out from other soldiers, and to invoke their military contribution in order to demand social recognition and its associated array of rights.

As a result, the high convertibility of resources from the military to the social sphere was translated into a militarization that augmented the legitimacy for greater military participation, primarily by expanding the army's resources. This process involved overcoming the significant obstacle of the "bourgeois" tendencies of the middle class in the early years of the state's existence. These inclinations could be seen in the tendency of high school graduates to serve in the rear and not in combat units, and in the propensity of the veteran cooperative farming communities—the *kibbutzim* and *moshavim*,[4] who were symbolically identified with having made a vital contribution to the establishment of the state—to retain their control over a large part of the draftees and to keep their youngsters away from the combatant core of the military in favor of two alternative forms: the *Nahal* and the *Territorial Defense Organization*.[5] This had the effect of denying the army the resources required to maintain its belligerent agenda.

The military elite attempted to lure Ashkenazi youngsters back into combat units in order to meet the growing needs of the IDF. The transformation of the character of military activity due to the escalation of the reprisal raids against Jordan and Egypt, in response to infiltrations of Palestinian refuges into Israel, lent urgency to the effort. The turning point came in 1953, when General Moshe Dayan (who would be appointed Chief of the General Staff a year later) decided to establish the elite Unit 101 to execute cross-border reprisals. The operations carried out by the unit under the command of (then) Lieutenant Colonel Ariel Sharon, beginning with Qibya Raid (against the Qibya village in Jordan in 1953), vastly enhanced the IDF's prestige, in sharp contrast with the period between 1951–1953, when the first reprisal raids took place, and which revealed the low standard of the combat units. Their inadequate professionalism was attributed by their commanders to the high percentage of unskilled Mizrachi inductees (Rabin, 1979, 88; Dayan, 1976, 111). Following the launch of Unit 101, young people, particularly from the agricultural sector, began to be attracted to it and other combat units, and started to view service in them as a challenge (Benziman, 1985, 61–62).

In a circular fashion, the escalation of the retaliation raids, then, restored the army's status as a magnet for Ashkenazi youngsters as it bestowed renewed meaning and prestige on young people's military contribution (on this historical process, see Levy, 2003b, 56–63).

In other words, the military burden was not only balanced out by the fruits of militarism, but also by the direct translation of the burden into the symbolic utility of the "serving elite," taking the form of the warrior-Sabre. This shift in the first years of the state was reflected by a number of processes: the enlistment of high school pupils and youngsters from the agricultural sector into combat units; shortening the year spent in the *Nahal* doing agricultural work in favor of combat missions; and increasing the length of compulsory service from twenty-four to thirty months (this is dealt with more extensively in Levy, 1997a, 57–100). After 1967, military service was once more extended, this time from thirty to thirty-six months (during the 1968–1970 War of Attrition). In addition, after 1967 the burden began to be shared by reserve soldiers too, who now started to serve in the newly occupied territories instead of just being called up for training, as in the past. At the same time, expenditure on security as a proportion of GDP rose from 7.7 percent in 1952–1955 to around 10 percent from the mid-1950s, before soaring to around 23 percent between 1968 and 1973. Only a third of this was covered by American military aid, which had grown significantly after the Six Day War (Lifshitz, 2000, 170). Owing to these increased resources the army could modernize, mostly through acquisitions from France and later from the United States.

Not only did the convertibility of resources enable the maintenance of a high level of military participation, it did so at a low economic cost: regular soldiers received a miniscule salary in return for their service. Their parents were thus faced with a kind of indirect tax, as they had to top up their children's earnings from the army. Reserve soldiers were not even given that, instead receiving compensation for lost earnings. Indeed, it was only in 1967, following the Six Day War, that a uniform rate of 100 percent of their salary was guaranteed to reservists, and not a lesser proportion of it as in the past. Even then, some of the costs of reserve duty were not met by the army or the National Insurance Institution, but rather by the soldier or his/her employer (Shai, 2003). Sizable symbolic rewards, convertible into material rewards in the social sphere, thus compensated for the poor material rewards that were directly given to soldiers.

The State's Internal Military Autonomy

The strengthening of the army fed into the increasingly bellicose profile of Israeli policy. During its early years, Israel was exposed to a limited existential threat insofar as it had to face up to rundown, underequipped, and unmotivated Arab armies. Not for nothing did the political sphere offer opportunities for a settlement of the Arab-Israeli conflict, reflected in various talks and initiatives, which Israel did not try to fully exhaust. The most notable cases from the period include Israel's contribution to the failure of the Arab-Israeli peace conference at Lausanne (1949), and the way Israel ignored gestures toward peace made by Egypt, Jordan, and Syria in the early 1950s: they were demanding the readmission of refugees (even if only partially) and the return of certain territories (such as adjusting the border around the Sea of Galilee and in the Negev, including giving Jordan an outlet to the Mediterranean Sea). Perhaps it was not in Israel's capacity to change the belligerent reality, but for anyone placing Israel at the center of their analysis, it is particularly significant that Israel refrained from exhausting the potential of diplomatic maneuvers and opted instead to preserve the fruits of war on which the social order had been anchored.

At that time, the political leadership of two schools of thought, represented by Prime Minister Ben-Gurion on the one hand, and Foreign Minister Moshe Sharett on the other, found themselves in disagreement. The "security," hawkish school, whose views were expressed by Ben-Gurion and his younger associates—most notably Chief of the General Staff General Moshe Dayan, who would be nominated as the Minister of Defense in 1967, and Shimon Peres, who served as Deputy Minister of Defense—espoused a proactive approach toward Arab countries, driven by their fear of the anticipated "second round," and based on their assumption that "the Arabs only understand the language of force." Political and military preparations for what was perceived as the inevitable second round of fighting became the cornerstone of their politics, assuming that the military answer to that threat was the exclusive one. On the other hand, the diplomatic, dovish school, represented by Foreign Minister Sharett (who served as Prime Minister between 1953–1955), received support from much of the *Mapai* (the ruling party) leadership, and tended to advocate political agreements, with guarantees from the international community. Accordingly, as Ben-Gurion's activist stance came to be embodied by the escalation of the retaliatory operations, sympathizers of the diplomatic school tried to hold him back, but to no avail (see, for instance, Maoz, 2006a, 386–404; Morris, 2001, 259–69; Pappe, 1992; Rabinovich, 1991; Shlaim, 2001).

By missing these diplomatic opportunities, a vacuum was created, which meant that priority had to be given to the use of military force to solidify the territorial and demographic status quo, and, given the lack of political will for a negotiated settlement, to prepare for a second round of fighting with Arab countries. It was against this background that Israel escalated its reactions to attempts made by Palestinian refugees to cross the border into the country. Following these violent responses, incursions that had primarily been economically motivated became organized and violent. Thus began a succession of violent actions and counteractions in the shape of the reprisal raids. With this process at its peak, and with Anglo-French backing, in 1956 Israel initiated the Suez War. The aim of that operation was to eliminate the perceived existential threat to Israel as a result of Egypt's decision in 1955 to arm itself with modern Soviet weaponry, a decision brought about by the threat posed to Nasser's young revolutionary regime by Israel's retaliatory operations. This escalation subjected statesmanship to military modes of thought, and saw the ejection of Moshe Sharett from the political arena.

To a large extent, the congruence between the bellicose approach and the interests of those who had benefited from the social and material fruits of the 1948 War made the attitude of Ben-Gurion and his supporters more relevant than Sharett's, the adoption of which may have endangered those fruits of war. An inequitable social structure constrained the dominance of the military way and the military establishment. In other words, the moment the political leadership opted to create a "mobilized," disciplined, and inequitable society by turning the army into a "nation builder" and making war a constant, politicians became dependent on the army. This was not just dependence on the army as an organization, but rather on military thinking itself.

The subjection of statesmanship to military logic paved the way to the 1967 War. Border disputes between Israel and Syria, including those initiated by Israel in an attempt to take control of the buffer zones under its sovereignty, could not be settled by the Armistice Agreement. Instead, they were gradually escalated, mostly by the Israeli side through the use of tanks, artillery, and the Air Force (for greater detail see Levy, 1997a, 106–10).

At the same time, the construction of the nuclear reactor with French assistance, and the concealment of the motivations behind it (as part of the opaque doctrine of nuclear deterrent) were a further source of anxiety for the Arabs, especially Egypt, which in turn stoked Israeli counter-anxieties that Egypt might try to attack the reactor (Aronson, 1992, 109; Cohen, 2000, 329–56). Accordingly, when Egypt moved troops into Sinai in May 1967, and subsequently closed the Straits of Tiran to Israeli shipping—in reaction, if only indirectly, to Israel's nuclear project, and as a direct response to Syria's call for help in curbing Israel—Israel's almost automatic response was a public and widespread mobilization of the reserves. This narrowed the scope of Israel's diplomatic actions and channeled the country into a preemptive strike, which ended with the occupation of large territories, in contrast to the war's original defensive targets.

In the light of the IDF's achievements, Israel's new political aims were subjected to military thinking. This trend could be seen in the devotion to the metaphysical idea of total security ("security borders") by preserving the territorial status quo as an alternative to converting military achievements into political assets, even at the price of a calculated military risk (Wald, 1987, 202–6). Boundaries between "left" and "right" were redrawn according to the depth of one's willingness to withdraw from the Occupied Territories, rather than differentiating between socioeconomic attitudes. Political discourse became a military discourse in every way. As Israel's hold on the Territories strengthened, the military discourse came to take on religious tones, as seen in the development of the idea of returning the people of Israel to lands of religious importance, and the gradual erasure of the "Green Line" (the line that separated Israel and its new territories) from both physical and cognitive maps (Lustick, 1993, 275–76).

Another aspect of the symbolization of militarism as a public asset was the seemingly natural yet dramatic increase of military figures taking up eminent positions in politics. Because army officers brought with them a military outlook to politics, one which defined national security in narrow military terms, and because they functioned as representatives of the army in the government, and not vice versa, this process intensified the militarization of the political discourse (Wald, 1987, 224–26).

Beyond the militaristic rhetoric, Israel's foreign policy utterly resisted the exchange of a full withdrawal from the territories conquered in 1967 for peace. This policy was realized in the government's disinclination to follow through on various diplomatic initiatives, such as King Hussain's proposal for autonomy for the West Bank, and American initiatives for a peace agreement with Egypt (Maoz, 2006a, 409–28). Thus Israel marched toward the Yom Kippur War with the clear knowledge that continued diplomatic stalemate would lead to more bloodshed (Bar-Joseph, 2001, 140–45; Golani, 2002, 215–18).

As long as the utility borne by the status quo strengthened the elements of the (informal) coalition that benefited from the occupation, primarily the secular Ashkenazi elites, the government could lead a line that stabilized it. Those elites showed low receptiveness to various options of a political settlement to the conflict. In particular, the economic growth made it very clear to the political leadership and the social elites that a fast withdrawal from the Occupied Territories would push Israel back into recession and unemployment, with all its problematic consequences for the reproduction of the ethno-class hierarchy. Clearly, the war rescued the middle-class groups from having to reallocate societal resources in order to ensure social stability in the face of deep unemployment and subsequent unrest among the

Mizrachim. Furthermore, the United States put no pressure on Israel to change its policy. Indeed, together with economic growth, American subsidies enabled Israel to increase its defense spending without lowering the standard of living or damaging the interests of capital, which would have been the price had Israel needed to fund its arms by itself (see Sussman 1984, 21–25). This, in turn, would have provided the incentive for renewed political thinking. Add to this the tendency of neighboring Arab states to communicate belligerent messages, and not only moderate ones, and we have an explanation for the absence of counter-pressures for a less warmongering policy that would have balanced out the interests of the war-prone coalition. Au contraire, the dominant policy was to become more permanent (in relation to expressions of relative moderation subsequent to the war), and spread from the practical field to the cultural, discursive one. In such circumstances, groups that were determined to establish the occupation—be they settlement organizations and nationalist circles, or sections of the military establishment and their political allies—found no effective obstacles in their path. On the other hand, groups who had initially voiced relatively moderate views, including a number of ministers and "new left" circles that had formed during the prewar period (which saw the strengthening of liberal trends), were neutralized.

In sum, the militarization behind the construction of the ethno-class structure reinforces the argument that the military's legitimacy should not be taken for granted, in contradiction to the assumption that the state of war was forced on Israel by the hostile Arab world. Instead, the endurance of the military way and its domination over diplomatic thought should be explained (for a comprehensive analysis see Maoz, 2006a). High rates of convertibility created conditions in which the more bellicose approach could overcome internal resistance to it by relying on a coalition of forces that were benefiting from the fruits of war, such that a tight affinity was forged between militarism and social interests.

The Ashkenazi groups accepted this line, despite early uneasiness concerning the choice of a belligerent path and the price to be paid for it. Nonetheless, it is reasonable to assume that had the result been unsatisfactory from the point of view of the Ashkenazi groups, and especially if the management of this bellicosity had come at a price that outweighed the fruits of war, that is, negative convertibility, then they would have adhered to their original skeptical attitudes. These groups then would have resisted belligerent moves at an earlier stage, including paying more attention to the relatively moderate messages emanating from the Arab world, and acting to turn the progress of history on its head. For example, in the early 1950s the middle class thwarted the policy of austerity—the attempt, which was damaging to its interests, to implement a budgetary policy that allocated essential products equally to all citizens regardless of their economic means—thus demonstrating its ability to overturn state-led processes (Levy, 1997a, 29).

As a consequence of this affinity between the state of war and social interests, political participation in military matters was the exception, and could mainly be found in times of crisis. Even then, such participation was only focused on the first stage of state-citizen bargaining, as outlined theoretically in chapter 1, that is, on the demand that the state improve the quality of the security product, though not necessarily through the transparency of the means of its attainment (supervision over the army), or by offering alternatives to it (diplomatic alternatives to the military way). This mode of participation characterized the quiet protest among Mizrachim in border settlements in the early 1950s, which, following the damage caused by infiltrators to their settlements, took the form of attempts at abandonment (see Morris, 1993, 108–15). It was also characteristic of moves before and during the 1967 War to appoint General Moshe Dayan to the position of Security Minister in place of Prime Minister Levi Eshkol, and later on to occupy the Golan Heights under pressure from settlers in the north of Israel.

The state thus acquired its freedom of action thanks to the formation of the republican equation: it exchanged the allocation of symbolic rewards, later to be converted into material ones, to the dominant group, in return for the latter's support in providing the army with a relatively broad autonomy. The army was supervised by the political elites, and even then only partially, far from the reach of the social groups that staffed it.

This saw the consolidation of an interwoven and circular process over time: the results of practical bellicosity (the fruits of war and military prestige) strengthened the foundations that legitimized its upkeep, even as it became more costly; this was translated into the flow of resources to the army, which in turn intensified and further established bellicosity, and so on and so forth. Social interests entrenched security ones for the sake of preserving the territorial and demographic status quo (for more see Levy, 1997a).

This affinity is the essence of the Israeli variant of materialist militarism: an exchange pattern developed between the state and the leading social groups in such a way as to construct the republican equation, according to which the groups acquired the ability to extract rewards from their activities in the military sphere in return for their willingness to invest human and material resources (as soldiers and their families, and as taxpayers) in the upkeep of the military effort and its legitimization.

Materialist militarism is Israel's distinctive form of militarism. It was cultivated by the dominant social stratum as leverage for the accumulation of social rewards. This form of militarism, contrary to alternative models that are familiar from other countries, was not cultivated by a peripheral group, by a dominant group in decline, by the military establishment alone, or by business corporations. Materialist militarism became the driving force behind Israel's preference for bellicosity for as long as the regional and international arenas allowed the state a substantial degree of freedom of choice, and the internal arena backed up the chosen route with resources. The violation of this equation would instigate a turning point and the erosion of this freedom of action.

THE VIOLATION OF THE REPUBLICAN EQUATION

The Israeli form of the republican equation has been gradually violated since the 1973 Yom Kippur War, in which the army was surprised by an Arab attack and Israel suffered about 3,000 fatalities, about 0.1 percent of the total population. Up until then, the state had effectively balanced the price of security with satisfactory rewards to its citizens, mainly symbolic rewards for servicepersons and their convertibility into material ones. Significant increases in the cost of security had been met until then by external sources, namely, the economic gains of occupation (since 1948) and foreign aid. Used to spur growth in the Israeli economy, these sources even left a sizable profit in the hands of the middle class. Beginning in the 1970s, however, tension developed between *militarism* and *materialism* as they became competitive rather than mutually complementary values.

Herein lies the contradiction: militarism rested on a state-led discourse that heightened the security threat, making Israeli military readiness, with its demands for social, bodily, and material sacrifice, seem an appropriate response. However, following 1967, people felt more secure, and the idea that Israel was in danger of being wiped out was replaced by the motif of "security borders." This was a concept that dismissed existential danger and aggrandized Israel's military might, if only it would be allowed to preserve its new borders. Even recurrent military failures—such as the 1973 War and the subsequent First Lebanon War (1982–1985) and the First Intifada (1987–1993)—did not shake the assumption that the state provided a high enough level of security to its citizens. And if this were not enough, the war in Lebanon and the First Intifada were portrayed as serving the security interests of the state's geographical and social peripheries (northern settlements and settlements in the Occupied Territories respectively), and not its "center." Accordingly, those years saw a decline in the price that citizens, the "consumers of security," were prepared to pay for security goods that had been partially damaged—because of military failures—and devalued—because of the removal of the existential threat.

At the same time, citizens were required to pay a heavier price for this lesser return as the security burden increased. The need to rehabilitate the army after the 1973 War increased the fiscal burden by enlarging external and internal government debts (despite American aid), and elevated the investment in security to a peak of about 30 percent of GDP in 1974–1976. Similarly, the burden of military service became weightier as the human resources of both regular and reserve soldiers were more deeply utilized (Barnett, 1992, 185–209). In short, this asymmetry laid the foundations for the state's failure in deploying its strategy of discursively increasing the demand for its protection services by exaggerating foreign threats. As suggested in chapter 1, this is the first bargaining strategy that the state will undertake when the republican equation is violated.

An attempt to revalidate this strategy by initiating the First Lebanon War quite simply failed. The First Lebanon War was initiated by Israel in 1982 in order to eradicate the PLO-controlled quasi-state that had been formed in South Lebanon, and that was perceived as a threat to the Israeli population living near the border. The government expanded the original goals of the war—which had been partially agreed upon by the main political parties—to include the reshaping of the political order in Lebanon, a move that entailed an unsuccessful military clash with the Syrian army stationed in Lebanon. Consequently, the IDF was forced to remain as a conquering army in South Lebanon for almost three more years, suffering heavy losses. Eventually, Lebanese Shiite groups were successful in their resistance to the Israeli occupation, and in 1985 the government ordered the IDF to partially withdraw, though without having come to a formal agreement with the Lebanese government.

This is not to imply that the army initiated combative moves in order to establish its legitimacy, but that rather, like every institutionalized mechanism of "protection" (Tilly, 1985), it leveraged external threats so as to strengthen the recognition of its monopolistic function in providing the response to them. *Military thought* is the main repertoire available for the army, hence its endeavors to inculcate it as much as the geopolitical conditions permit. Bureaucratic inertia (in the terms of Maoz, 2006a, 293–96) imbued within the strategic culture was also at work, as repetitive patterns of operation and familiar tactics were borrowed in dealing with Arab hostility in a manner that escalated warfare.

Structurally speaking, for the state this is an attempt to attribute excess meaning to an external threat in order to: (1) show its citizens that it is charging a reasonable price for its services; (2) increase demand for security, thereby reducing pressures to provide any service other than security; (3) increase rewards for the bearers of the security burden, or resist pressures to lessen the overall burden. We recall that manipulating the external threat increases the symbolic rewards to the bearers of security burden and thereby decreases pressures for material rewards.

In this case, had it ended with a glorious and swift victory, a battle against a "demonic" yet inferior enemy (the PLO), could have annulled the effects of the 1973 War on the IDF's position as much as it could have defeated the Palestinian national spirit. Increased bellicosity, however, only helped to further dilute the army's standing in a changing social environment, especially given the heavy losses and the economic price of the war.

Along with the erosion of the sacrifice/reward symmetry, the very anchor of the republican equation, the second strategy—raising the rewards for sacrifice—also showed signs of crisis. First and foremost, because of the decline in security consumers' motivation for sacrifice, the relative price of expected rewards went up. A heavier security burden became more and more incongruent with the consumerist values with which Israeli society was infused from the late 1970s, owing to the rise in the standard of living stimulated by the 1967 War (see Gottlieb and Yuchtman-Yaar, 1985; Ram, 2005; Talmud, 1985). The newly expanded, consumerist, Western-style middle class that had evolved in the post-1967 economic boom now displayed a distinct lack of enthusiasm for making sacrifices to retain the Occupied Territories, the very source of its profits. This was part of the paradox characteristic of symbolic rewards: the ongoing conversion of the military burden into symbolic rewards, which change their shape to material rewards in the shift from the military arena to the civil one, strengthened materialistic behavioral patterns. Militarism raised materialism to a new pinnacle, at which over-materialism sat uneasily with military sacrifice. In these circumstances, and beyond the change in objective values, the military burden became relatively greater and the rewards relatively smaller, while expectations for compensatory rewards increased.

In many ways, the post-1967 period saw the rates of military participation and the rewards for it reach their maximal values. After all, the increased security burden after 1967 could not have come about without the utility that the fruits of war provided to those who bore it. This state of affairs, which laid the basis for future crises, meant that one of two paths should have been followed after the 1973 War—reaping new fruits of war, or, alternatively, reducing the rates of military participation. In practice, the opposite took place in both cases.

Indeed, the value of the symbolic rewards started to erode with the diminishment of the external threat. With a diminished threat, military sacrifice lost part of its meaning as a struggle over the national existence. Concurrently, as a result of the failures attached to army, in acute contrast to its previous image as omnipotent, the erosion of symbolic rewards intensified. Meanwhile, sociocultural change, in the form of the new materialism, recontextualized those failures and increased their significance. Because the symbolic rewards given by the army to the secular Ashkenazi group made the army its "social property," the IDF's failures were of particular significance: after all, the army's prestige gave meaning to the military contribution of that class, which in turn legitimized its favored social status. Moreover, the decline of the secular Ashkenazi warrior-Sabre created a new space in which groups that had been expelled to the social periphery by that very figure could now challenge it (Mizrachim, women, the national religious, and so on; see below). Accordingly, damage inflicted on the army's prestige by its failures motivated some Ashkenazi sections to abandon their "ownership" and pursue alternative sources of legitimacy for the group's dominance. Lastly, the erosion of the worth of symbolic rewards also stemmed from the army's becoming a site for political clashes, especially after 1973, when the argument over the state's borders sharpened (see Barzilai, 1996). Disagreements over the army's conduct heightened, and its universal status and prestige, that is, its symbolic rewards for servicepersons, were gradually devalued.

The erosion of symbolic rewards intensified from the mid-1980s along with the penetration of cultural and economic globalization into Israeli society. Globalization was accompanied by structural changes in the economy in the spirit of the neoliberal doctrine. The state-led "economic stabilization plan" of 1985, which eradicated the hyperinflation that the Israeli economy had been dealing with, was an important milestone in this regard. These changes made the economy more open to investment, the bidirectional migration of capital, and international business relationships.

Globalization strengthened the ethos of the market economy with its characteristic liberal discourse, and was accompanied by a new political discourse that it simultaneously fed into. *Mamlachtiyut*, collectivism and the pioneering spirit—the central symbols of the republican discourse (according to Shafir and Peled, 2002), which had been dominant ever since the consolidation of the Jewish-Israeli political community—faded away, to be replaced by a liberal agenda, at least among the secular Ashkenazi middle and upper classes. Prominent in this agenda were new values such as individualism, privatization, competition, achievement, efficiency, consumerism, democratization, sensitivity to civil rights, and so on. The foundations of this new discourse heralded the expansion of the boundaries of the economy at the expense of society and politics. This new agenda, with its leanings toward globalization, neoliberal policies, and demilitarization, was adopted by the upper reaches of the middle class and market forces, and was given political expression by left-centrist parties. These were the social groups for whom bursting into the international economic scene required that they free themselves of the intrusiveness of the statist and collectivist welfare state. They also wished to remove the limitations placed on the accumulation of capital in the local market, and on the movement of capital, labor power, and goods between the Israeli market and global ones.

A cosmopolitan and liberal outlook that weakened nationalist orientations thus helped construct the cultural and ideological basis for demilitarization. In this framework, the violent conflict was portrayed as an obstacle to Israel's participation in the global economy insofar as investment in security was no longer seen as profitable, but rather as interfering with the reaping of new fruits that required the end to, or at least the toning down of, the Arab-Israeli conflict.

The market economy discourse also laid down the basis for an increasingly strident critique of the army's resources, as its budget was the largest single proportion of government spending. Indeed, the neoliberal ethos of "small government" did not leave the army untouched. This illustrated an equation that positioned the growth of the economy against cutbacks in security spending as a way of redirecting resources from inherently wasteful usage (strictly military spending) to ways that would advance economic targets (Tov, 1998, 127–38). In the past, the army had been placed above the market. At the same time, exacting military service contradicted the materialist ethos that had taken hold of parts of society (see more in chapter 5).[6]

The ethos of the market economy thus eroded the army's role in defining the social hierarchy. The value of one's contribution to the state through military service was no longer the criterion that would necessarily determine the distribution of social goods and justify social domination, as individual achievement replaced the test of statism. Diminished symbolic rewards among the traditionally elite groups, with a special impact on the members of the kibbutzim and moshavim, was the outcome (see Ram, 2005). Equally, groups that did not serve in the army, or who made a lesser contribution—such as the Ultra-Orthodox Jews, Palestinian citizens of Israel, and women—recorded certain achievements that were no longer dependent on the test of military service, but rather were based on their own political power, wrapped in the liberal discourse of citizenship. Nothing was more symbolic of this than decisions made by Yitzhak Rabin's government (in the early 1990s) to drop the requirement for military service as a basic condition for employment in the public sector, and to cancel the payment of child benefits to ex-servicepersons alone (see Aronoff, 1999, 44).

At the same time, the republican ethos was also challenged by the ethnonational discourse, which gives center stage to the individual's Jewish ethnic belonging, and not his/her civic contribution. Religious and peripheral groups became the main bearers of this discourse, to a large extent as a counter-reaction to the empowerment of the market economy (see more below). The erosion of the social value of military service, with consequences for groups' motivation to serve, originated from the opposite direction as well.

Not only did the symbolic rewards of the traditional middle class decline, but the more peripheral Mizrachi groups simultaneously improved their status, thus heralding a reduction in the convertibility of Ashkenazi military contribution into symbolic rewards such as social and political dominance. Three major aspects are relevant here. First, the Mizrachi groups gained from their deeper assimilation in the political system (through the *Likud* Party) and their involvement in an ethno-national political discourse that, unlike previous attempts to belittle it, highlighted their historical contribution (see more below). From this perspective, the governmental reversal that in 1977 brought the *Likud* to power (a party supported by large a proportion of Mizrachim, thus ending decades of Ashkenazi-supported Labor Party rule), was both a consequence and a cause of the violation of the republican equation. It was a consequence of its violation in that the decline of the army's prestige, the source of symbolic capital for the secular Ashkenazi middle class, opened up a new space for challenges and criticisms that spread into the political sphere. At the same time, the upheaval furthered the violation of the equation by creating the sense among members of the middle class that the state had been "taken away" from them. In other words, they felt that they were receiving less for their contribution, especially regarding the conversion of their military contribution into political dominance. Second, in the 1970s the welfare state had expanded, especially in terms of child benefits, unemployment payments, and income security, benefits which were mainly to the advantage of ex-servicepersons (Rosenhek, in print). This was part of the Israeli republican order, which strove to preserve a high level of legitimacy for almost universal conscription. However, in this instance, more peripheral groups, and especially Mizrachim, slowly became the main beneficiaries, instead of the secular Ashkenazi middle class. Third, peripheral groups also began to expand their military service, which, despite the army's declining prestige, became more meaningful for them (see more in chapter 3).

Military service lost even more of its value as the army became a less relevant source for acquiring professional skills for a contracting technology-based and capital-intensive labor market. The army's vertical hierarchy failed to offer professional socialization for an economy characterized by hi-tech organizations with horizontal structures, the rise in the value of business entrepreneurship, and a shift in management focus from the product to the customer. Indeed, lengthy military service gradually became an obstacle for middle-class youngsters trying to exploit their head start in the labor market (see, for example, Avrahami and Lerner, 2003), and the ability of enlistees to reap social capital from their military service deteriorated; in other words, its convertibility declined. Reserve duty also became a heavier burden in both absolute and relative terms, and it began to hamper reserve soldiers both from effectively contending in an increasingly competitive labor market, and fulfilling their roles as fathers within a more equal division of labor in the family (Nevo and Shor, 2002a, 18). In short, competition evolved between "military time" and "civilian time."

The ethos of the market economy even laid down the infrastructure for a number of market-economy–based mechanisms that replaced statist ones in reproducing the ethno-class hierarchy, a situation that could not have come about in the years after the state's establishment. These mechanisms were no longer based on transforming military contribution into social dominance, the central anchor of the Ashkenazim's convertibility. Three alternative mechanisms are worthy of note (Levy, 1998): (1) *Mobility*—motivating some of the members of peripheral groups to adhere to the path of social mobility out of a belief in its validity. Some of this mobility was through the military, which was by and large isolated from ethno-class tensions; (2) *Split*—positioning certain peripheral groups—mainly Russian immigrants, Israeli Palestinians, and nonmobile Mizrachim—opposite one another in peripheral segments of the labor market; and as a consequence, (3) *Identity construction*—the construction of ethno-religious identity as an extreme instance of sectorial identity. This would bring parts of the Palestinian-Israeli and Mizrachi communities to establish breakaway institutional networks based on that separate identity, which they would reinforce among their members as an alternative to class struggle with the state.

These new reproductive mechanisms made it largely unnecessary to rely on military statism, and allowed a partial withdrawal from bellicosity without significantly endangering the social hierarchy that military statism had legitimized. Furthermore, these mechanisms channeled collective action among the Mizrachim to the political and cultural arenas, thus sidelining the option of ethnic-class action in order to effect a drastic change in ethno-class power relations, i.e., a demand to remove structural barriers to social mobility. With this relegitimization of the social order, Israeli governments from the center-left and center-right alike could uninterruptedly administer policies that worked to widen ethno-class social gaps from the mid-1980s onward.

In short, the symbolic rewards for military sacrifice were diminished. As a result of the combination of social, cultural, and political change, the rate of convertibility between military and social resources dropped. The status of the warrior, the dominant figure in Jewish-Israeli society since the 1940s, was on the ebb, to be replaced by alternative status symbols. From the 1980s onward, warriors were no longer included among Israeli cultural icons.

Historically speaking, this was the stage at which the status of groups that had attained mobility through army-based symbolic rewards was no longer dependent on their military sacrifice. Its usefulness had disappeared, leaving only the burden. As mentioned in chapter 1, this stage is characteristic of the relationship between the middle class and the army in many Western countries, and is not unique to the Israeli context.

However, not only did the symbolic rewards drop in value, their translation into material rewards in the shape of the fruits of war also suffered. The Yom Kippur War was the first total war that ended without yielding new economic gains. Instead, it produced a significant slowdown of the growth that had characterized the Israeli economy until then. At the same time, given that it paid most of the taxes, the secular Ashkenazi middle class funded both the growing burden of maintaining and strengthening the army, and the cost of the welfare state, which gradually came to serve other social groups. This funding was both direct and indirect, insofar as the budget was overburdened, thus setting the scene for a severe and lengthy fiscal crisis. At its peak, this crisis resulted in hyperinflation (around 400 percent per annum) and undermined the stability of the middle class, the bearer of the military effort (see Bichler and Nitzan, 2001, 277–98; Shalev, 1992, 236–306). The First Lebanon War only intensified the trend that saw the middle class taking on a greater burden just as the army's prestige was in decline, and without itself gaining any utility, certainly not financial, from this new situation. On the contrary, further taxation was needed to fund the war. Later on, the First Intifada contributed to the devaluation of some of the original fruits of war: the ability to economically exploit the Occupied Territories was almost lost (including cheap manpower, as Palestinian day laborers were replaced by foreign labor migrants), and the arms industry was plunged into crisis as the Cold War abated and harsh competition with American and European industries emerged.

To summarize, the state demanded of its upper middle class an exaggerated price for a devalued security product, while the increased burden of military service was no longer balanced by symbolic rewards, which had been diminished, and material rewards remained unchanged. *This was a violated equation.*

This analysis thus suggests that, taken on their own, the consequences of the 1973 War cannot explain the army's declining standing. The image of failure was accompanied by a burden imposed in order to strengthen the military and reduce economic growth. However, these processes were taking place on the back of the infrastructure of a society adopting the tenets of the market economy. Without this infrastructure, the motivation for military sacrifice would have remained higher, expectations for rewards would have been lower, and the role of military service in defining the social hierarchy—the central symbolic reward of military service—would have remained in place. As we shall now see, the violation of the republican equation triggered collective action.

THE REACTION TO THE VIOLATION OF THE EQUATION

As mentioned in chapter 1, when the republican equation is violated, civil groups that wish to reconstitute it on their terms may turn to collective action. Alongside passive acceptance (loyalty/neglect) and a migratory pattern (exit), which characterized a relatively high proportion of the secular Ashkenazi stratum after 1973 (Cohen 1988; Shavit et al., 1999), the most remarkable and unprecedented reaction among middle-class groups was the attempt to wield influence over the production of the security product (voice). This reaction drove, and was driven by, challenges posited by more peripheral groups and was reflected in the Ashkenazi "motivation crisis" regarding militarily sacrifice.

The Ashkenazim's Protest

Mass participation in a military that rewards its members created the potential for broad resistance to develop among the ranks. Social groups could exploit their own or their children's military participation in order to demand civil, social, and economic rights from the state in return, and as compensation for the decline of other symbolic rewards. The wars of 1973 and 1982 thus created a political opportunity structure (in Tarrow's terms, 1994), of which mass protest movements took advantage.

The first wave of protest movements focused on supervising "production," that is, activities aimed at subjecting the army to more effective political-civilian scrutiny, primarily by making information more transparent to the consumer-civilian public.

The first protests came right after the war and were spearheaded by ex-reservists demanding the resignation of the government and an inquiry into the events that had led to the blunder. Until then, the Israeli citizenry had not played any active role in monitoring military activities, but rather had passively tolerated military policies. Following this protest, the government established a judicial commission of inquiry (the Agranat Commission) to investigate the military's performance in the war. The commission's findings led to the dismissal of several generals. This was followed by the resignation of Prime Minister Golda Meir and Defense Minister Moshe Dayan (in 1974), signifying unprecedented impact of political protest on oversight of the military.

This collective activity simultaneously helped and was assisted by the development of a press that became relatively autonomous vis-à-vis the political elites, and not as uncritical of it as in the past. After the watershed of the 1973 War, the press gradually shifted its commitment from the ruling establishment to its reading/consuming public, to whom it felt primarily obliged (Peri, 2001, 240–41).

While the first wave of protest followed the 1973 War, the second wave appeared at the end of the 1970s (following the political upheaval of 1977) and the beginning of the 1980s (after the First Lebanon War). *Peace Now* was the most notable organization in this regard. A mass movement of young, mainly Ashkenazi, ex-servicepersons, led by officers in the reserves, it called on Menachem Begin's government (the first to be led by the *Likud* Party) to exhaust all political opportunities for peace against the background of what had been viewed as Israel's reluctance to accommodate the Egyptian President Sadat's moves toward peace. This was the first time a mass movement had been organized outside a political party, and it was natural that it should be led by the social stratum that experienced an asymmetry between its military contribution and its sociopolitical status, which had been on the wane ever since the Mizrachi-based *Likud* Party had come to power.

During the war in Lebanon, several new protest movements emerged and left their imprint on society-military relations. *Yesh Gvul* ("There is a limit/border") represented for the first time reserve soldiers who organized to selectively refuse to carry out military missions in Lebanon and the Occupied Territories because of the IDF's allegedly aggressive behavior. Nothing can testify more eloquently to the violated equation than the emergence of conscientious objection, which overcame the republican rhetoric that set cultural barriers to collective action by challenging the very underpinnings of the totality of conscription. Yet, to overcome those barriers, *Yesh Gvul* was inclined to use a communitarian discourse and employ national symbols without questioning the state's authority to conscript its youth (Vos, 2006, 286–87).

In tandem, other organizations, most prominently *Soldiers against Silence* and *Parents against Silence*, sprang up to protest against the transformation of the war in Lebanon from a quick operation into the attempt to shape a "new order," culminating in a siege of Beirut. By demanding an alternative to the accepted military way, these movements broadened their critical scope to include not only the army's modus operandum, but also its very purpose (see Helman, 1999). In other words, not only were the security product and its price put to the test, but alternatives to its production were examined as well. Central to this discourse was the definition of the First Lebanon War as a "war of choice," distinguished from what had been described as earlier "wars of no choice," thus instilling the notion of an alternative to bellicosity. Much owing to these protests, the IDF partly and unilaterally withdrew from Lebanon in 1985. Later on, *Peace Now*, *Yesh Gvul*, and other new groups that emerged during the First Intifada (1987–1993), endeavored to restrict the IDF's freedom of operation in quelling the Palestinian uprising. Additional protest groups followed in the footsteps of *Peace Now*, the most notable of which was *Four Mothers*, composed of parents of soldiers who had served in Lebanon, who demanded an immediate and full withdrawal from this front in the mid-1990s (see chapter 4).

Not only was the IDF's subordination to the political level consolidated, but the professional autonomy enjoyed by the military was also sharply reduced. Assisted by the press, groups such as soldiers' parents and reservists amplified their scrutiny of traditionally professional issues, thus undermining the IDF's autonomy at several levels: journalists' and parents' scrutiny of accidents in military operations and training; reservists' critique of the distribution of the military burden, generating legislative attempts at limiting the IDF's powers to call up reservists; homosexuals' and women's successful struggles to lift limitations on their military promotion; press scrutiny of budgets, nominations, and military performance; the lifting of civilian restrictions on those who had not done military service; moderating military discipline—all these and more were among the manifestations of this trend (see Levy, 2003b, 193–235). While up until this point political monitoring of the army had mainly increased in its formal, institutional aspects, from now on it also took the form of wider public supervision carried out by social groups.

Observation of political-military relations in Israel reveals an apparent paradox: within a period of about seventy years, the more the militarization of Israeli society and politics gradually increased, the more politicians were successful in institutionalizing effective control over the IDF. Militarization passed through three main stages: (1) accepting the use of force as a legitimate political instrument during the pre-state period (1920–1948); (2) giving this instrument priority over political-diplomatic means in the state's first years up to the point in which (3) military discourse gradually predominated over political discourse after the 1967 War. Each stage was accompanied by the gradual intensification of resources devoted to war preparation and the amplification of force-oriented preferences as reflected in foreign policy.

At the same time, political control over the IDF was tightened. The principle of subordination of the armed forces to the political leadership during the pre-state period gave way to the construction of formal and informal restraints on autonomous military action. During the 1980s, the principle of the responsibility of the political echelon for the army was institutionalized when a state commission of inquiry held the political echelon liable for the massacre perpetrated by the Christian Phalange in the Palestinian refugee camps of Sabra and Shatilla in Beirut, and forced Defense Minister Ariel Sharon to resign. Later, other areas were gradually monitored (such as the defense budget), with greater involvement of the Knesset and civilian agencies

By increasing the state's capacity to extract resources and mobilize legitimacy for military buildup during the 1950s–1970s, militarization had shaped *relations of exchange* between military and civilian state institutions. Within this framework, the military exchanged the cumulatively acquired multiple rewards of militarization—material resources, social prestige, political power, and the political mobilization of retired officers—for its acceptance of political control. And paradoxically, the very increase of military figures taking up eminent positions in politics, as a result of their attractiveness in a militarized culture, contributed to the tightening of operative control over the IDF. Thus fewer and fewer spheres of military action remained autonomous. Had the IDF not accepted political control, it might have lost those gains. The gains of militarization thus functioned as engines of political control: they imposed limitations on the military's leverage for behaving in defiance of state civilian agencies. Paradoxically, therefore, to the extent that Israeli politics has been militarized, political control over the military has been enhanced (Ben-Eliezer, 1997; Levy, 1997b).

From the mid-1980s, institutional monitoring by civilian agencies has become much more powerful, and has been backed up by public monitoring, as social movements have stepped into the arena. Growing political participation then went beyond the level of political control and prompted demilitarization. The very activities of these groups undermined the status of militarism in Israel, be it through their demands for an alternative to the traditional military way, or via calls for restrictions on the army's professional autonomy for the sake of more penetrative civilian supervision. At the same time, demilitarization found its expression in the opening of a new cultural space for voices challenging the centrality of the military and the state of war in Israel (Levy, 2003b, 193–222).

The partial success of these two waves of protest was embodied in the increased allocation of political rights to the middle class in the form of its ability to influence military policy, a capability it had previously been denied. Political rights replaced and compensated for the attenuation of the old, symbolic rewards, namely, the military-based legitimation of social dominance. As a dominant group that had exhausted its ability to reap more significant benefits from military service, Ashkenazim focused on the other side of the equation, namely, reducing the military burden by seeking to limit the autonomy of the army. Clearly, this process nicely demonstrates that external events are not real entities but rather are discursively constructed in a manner that may change when leading groups come to believe that military sacrifice harms their interests, and therefore bringing them to respond with more openness to signals transmitted from the external arena.

The violation of the republican equation was both affected by and influenced the response of other social groups.

The Ethno-National Challenge

With the downturn in the image of the omnipotent Ashkenazi warrior-Sabre, other groups, who had been asymmetrically rewarded for their military contribution, were able to enter the political scene and challenge, directly and indirectly, the hegemonic military symbols. Furthermore, as the army came to need new reserves of manpower, because of its massive post-1973 buildup that encountered a reduced motivation among the secular Ashkenazi middle class, the bargaining power of other groups increased.

The *ethno-national ethos* was at the center of the challenges issued by the more peripheral groups. Ethno-nationalism had strengthened in response to the Six Day War's aftermath in which the encounter between the Israeli-Jewish community and historically venerated sites, such as the Old City of Jerusalem and Hebron, was renewed. For religious and rightist groups, the occupation was a stimulus to reassert their identification with Jewish tradition. Symptomatic was the revival of the religious concept of *Eretz Israel* (Land of Israel) rather than *Medinat Israel* (State of Israel), the term prevalent in the statist rhetoric of *Mamlachtiyut* until the 1970s (Kimmerling, 1985). Traditional Judaism, which invoked the primordial in the building of the Israeli-Jewish community, became for many a crucial factor in redemarcating the boundaries of Israeli society.

Thus, as opposed to the republican ethos, the ethno-national ethos saw the state as an extension and the embodiment of the Jewish community, not as an instrumental entity separate from it. Therefore, citizenship was not viewed as based on individual rights or duties deriving from the individual's formally belonging to the state. Instead, status was expected to be attained merely by belonging to the Jewish collective, and was no longer seen as dependent on historical or contemporary contributions—military or otherwise—as associated with Ashkenazi dominance and legitimized by the statist, republican discourse. This new discourse thus laid the foundations for the systematic erosion of the value of the symbols of the Ashkenzai elites, especially the kibbutz. At the same time, the ethno-national discourse sharpened the distinction between Jews and Arabs, seeing them as primordial identities. This distinction created a hierarchy defined by ascriptive belonging. Two sets of attitudes followed: the first was an aggressive stance toward the Arab surroundings, rooted in a theocratic or nationalist rationale; while the second set of attitudes aimed at restricting the liberal civil rights enjoyed by the Palestinian-Israeli minority, especially since the revocation of Military Administration in 1966.

Originally borne by the *Likud* and *Gush Emunim* (see below), the ethno-national discourse was a magnet for less-mobile Mizrachi and religious groups—who had been marginalized and thereby alienated by the ethos of *Mamlachtiyut*—and offered them meaningful partnership in shaping the "common good" of the Jewish-Israeli community. The Mizrachim in particular were attracted by a discourse that, unlike secular Israeliness, gave them a sense of belonging to society as equal partners without blurring their ethnic distinctiveness and without making their membership conditional on their contribution to the state—primarily through military service—as entailed by the *Mamlachtiyut* (see Shafir and Peled, 2002, 87–94).

In the spirit of this change, three types of challenge to the Ashkenazi hegemony in the army can be identified (see also Levy, 2003b, 121–33): *Challenge A—the struggle for accessibility*—Acceptance of the principle that the army defines the social hierarchy, but challenging the criteria for role allocation within the IDF.

This challenge characterized the (Israeli) *Black Panthers*—a movement of young men of North African extraction, inspired by their counterparts in the United States—who, in the early 1970s, demanded that the army draft groups of socially distressed Mizrachim that it hitherto had screened out because of their lack of education. Women and homosexuals made similar demands in the 1990s. By and large the army met these demands, as the universalist image of the "people's army" constrained it to recruit even those people whose perceived abilities did not match the IDF's needs.

Challenge B—the struggle for rights—Acceptance of the principle that the army defines the social hierarchy and acceptance of the criteria for role allocation in the military, but challenging the allocation of the rewards that derive from military service.

This challenge sprung from the increasing consciousness among Mizrachim that the republican equation did not work for them. In other words, they were not rewarded for their military sacrifice as well as their Ashkenazi peers had been. This consciousness about the linkage between army service and the allocation of resources was heightened by the 1973 War and the subsequent wars in which many soldiers from Mizrachi communities participated and died in significant numbers, as the ranks were gradually opened for them. While the Black Panthers' demand to be recruited reflected their internalization of the republican equation, this later wave of Mizrachi protest demanded recognition for their military contribution in defiance of Ashkenazi failure to do so, and as a springboard for more substantial political involvement. To some degree, these expectations for increased rewards gave rise to the construction of a hawkish identity and stimulated the massive flocking of Mizrachim from the Labor to the *Likud* Party, the right-wing party that in the elections of 1977 ousted the Labor Party from power after almost fifty years of dominance.

Speeches made in town squares by Menachem Begin, the *Likud* leader, in the 1981 election campaign, in which he played up the historical contribution of Mizrachim to the establishment of the state as a riposte to comments made by Labor Party spokesmen that hinted at a devaluation of their contribution, were an indication of this discourse. Thus, the *Likud*'s hawkish political identity defended the Mizrachim's battlefield gains and counteracted what had been portrayed as the Ashkenazi left's attempt to devalue these gains by criticizing the IDF and advocating the end of the Arab-Israeli conflict. Bluntly put, the same "melting-pot" symbols previously invoked to obstruct ethnic organization were now utilized to justify the demand for social rights.

Challenge C—the struggle for an alternative equation—Challenging the principle that the army defines the social hierarchy, but internalizing the criteria for role allocation in the army and the social rewards that derive from such participation.

Groups who had been disappointed by their inability to gain the recognition embodied in the previous challenge, especially their inability to attain positions associated with some degree of status in the army, adopted other forms of protest. Two major organizations associated with this form of protest were the *Shas* Party and *Gush Emunim*.

Shas, a Mizrachi Ultra-Orthodox movement set up in the 1980s by youngsters, attracted the less upwardly mobile Mizrachi segments that were disappointed with the neoliberal social policies of the *Likud*-led governments. Given that social mobility in civilian tracks was blocked and these youngsters had limited opportunities in the army, especially as the military itself lost much of its status following the Lebanon War, these Mizrachi elements sought social status divorced from the military. For such disadvantaged Mizrachi youngsters, military service would have meant either dropping out or a marginal position in the "blue-collar" segments of the military.

Shas did impressively well in the elections of 1984, becoming a part of most of the governing coalitions. Armed with the power of this success, *Shas* successfully demanded that yeshiva students' exemption from military service be increased, but not at the expense of the privileges awarded to ex-servicepersons. This demand was an alternative to the centrality of the army and the Gordian knot that had been tied between soldiering and citizenship. A few hundred youngsters were exempted in the early years of the state, as part of a gesture made by Ben-Gurion to the Ultra-Orthodox rabbinate during the early 1950s to assist in rebuilding the Orthodox yeshivas after the devastation of the Holocaust. In the 1990s this number climbed to around 10 percent of potential recruits. It was mostly *Shas* that contributed to the institutionalization of the military exemption given to yeshiva students under the slogan of *Torato Omanuto* ("the study of Torah is his livelihood"). Furthermore, unlike the Ashkenazi Ultra-Orthodox parties, *Shas* refused to bow down to hegemonic secular militarism, instead unhesitatingly presenting the route of studying Torah as no less worthy, if not more so, than the military one.

Shas thus constructed an alternative pattern of rewards for an increasingly Ultra-Orthodox population in the form of huge funding for state-subsidized Mizrachi yeshivas. This route offered greater material and symbolic rewards than military participation did (on *Shas* see Peled, 2001).

However, the increase in the number of exemptions given to yeshiva students was also due to a social shift, and not only because of political arrangements. First, as the Israeli labor market was hit with relatively high structural unemployment from the mid-1980s as part of the neoliberal agenda, Mizrachi youngsters showed greater motivation to enter religious frameworks, mainly yeshivas, which promised a basic income. At the same time, as the welfare state atrophied, more non-Orthodox parents began to send their children to Torah-based educational frameworks, mostly those run by *Shas* and *Chabad*, because they offered better services than the state education system. In other words, the withdrawal of the state in favor of a market economy not only weakened the army but also indirectly undermined the welfare infrastructure that had enabled mass conscription. Second, *Shas* flowered precisely because of the erosion of secular militarism's symbolic status and its implications for the rates of convertibility. This made military service even less attractive for people who would potentially have received training in the army for "blue-collar" positions in the civilian labor market.

What these three forms of protest by Mizrachim—the *Black Panthers*, *Likud* and *Shas*—had in common was the absence from the discursive repertoire of any explicit criticism of the army for its part in creating social inequality, an approach that had its roots in the deep-seated legitimacy of the IDF's ethos of egalitarianism. Thus, Mizrachi social protest was channeled into indirect strategies, even after many of the Mizrachim had become aware of the illusory nature of the ethos.

A parallel challenge with similar characteristics was also made by the religious Zionist movement in the form of *Gush Emunim* ("Bloc of the

Faithful"). Ideologically, the organization of *Gush Emunim* was related to the renewal of the discourse concerning the state's borders following the 1967 War. This debate was fueled by the 1973 War that, as noted above, highlighted ethno-national patterns in politics. However, the social aspects of this organization were no less significant: *Gush Emunim* was a group of young religious people, largely from the Ashkenazi middle class, identifiable by their "knitted skullcaps." They were graduates of religious high schools and yeshivas, and had served in the army, many as officers.

The appearance of the *Gush* reflected a rebellion on the part of the younger generation of the national religious sector against their parents' generation, whom they accused of a timid approach to politics, of being dragged along by the Labor Party, and of making pragmatic comprises in the "rearguard battle" over the religious character of Israeli society.

This was an uprising of the religious Ashkenazi middle class protesting against their marginal cultural and political status and their exclusion from equal participation with the secular Ashkenazi stratum in shaping the "common good" of the Zionist project. Their activities demonstrated their disappointment not only with the weakness of their parents' generation, but also with their semi-peripheral status in the army, where they played only a secondary role, partly because of their rabbis' concerns about the army's secularizing influence and the secular nature of the organization. With the refutation of the myth of the Ashkenazi warrior's military omnipotence following the failure of the Yom Kippur War, the recognition of the combat capabilities of religious youngsters served as a catalyst for their organization. Hence, as an alternative to the symbols of army service, the *Gush* put forward the idea of settlement in the territories (see Levy and Peled, 1994, 221–23).

The *Gush* believed in the idea of the "Greater Land of Israel," that is, an Israeli state spreading from the Jordan River to the Mediterranean. *Gush Emunim* acted on this belief by initiating protest activities against political concessions, but its main agenda was the establishment of Jewish settlement in populated areas of the West Bank. This program contradicted the government's policies and sometimes led to violent clashes with the army, which tried to block the *Gush*. The hegemony of materialist militarism was thus eroded, for this was a challenge that came from a group that belonged to the middle class, and was thereby fed by the fruits of materialist militarism. Nonetheless, by imposing a historical, metaphysical mission on the state, one that absolved itself of rationally calculated diplomatic action, this group stood against the statist rationale, which represented the lap of militarism. It also undermined the army's universality by immersing it in internal political wranglings, and even posited an antimaterialist logic when demanding unconditional sacrifice. Moreover, the *Gush* even disputed the secular militarist approach by putting forward religious criteria (such as the sanctity of the land) for deploying military force over and above the standard, secular criteria that were based on considerations such as the balance of forces (see Kimmlerling, 1993). Thus, *Gush Emunim* was quite willing to confront head-on one of the state's most lofty symbols and the embodiment of secular militarism, namely, the IDF itself.

Over time, those religious youngsters, many of whom who had not got involved in settlement activity, strengthened their hold on the combat units from which they had been culturally excluded in the past. In other words, they returned to the first mode of challenge, that is, they internalized the principle that the army defines the social hierarchy, and insisted on improving their status within that organization; some of them even challenged the authority of the secular military command (see more in chapter 6).

In a circular fashion, therefore, as the groups that laid down challenges to the army deepened their hold on it, among them the Mizrachim and the "knitted skullcaps," as part of the necessity to expand the manpower of a heavily burdened army, the "sense of ownership" among secular Ashkenazi middle class youngsters declined, and their motivation to abandon the army heightened; as a result, they took more liberty and legitimacy in criticizing the army, which accelerated the decline in its status, thus further distancing the Ashkenazim, and so on and so forth.

From the reactions of *Gush Emunim* and *Shas*, it would appear that the ethno-national ethos itself developed as an expression of the erosion of the army's symbolic rewards. Groups legitimized an alternative ethos, in the shape of an alternative route, that represented a counter-reaction to the decline in the convertibility of military service. The decline in the army's status spurred them on, either because the barriers preventing activities that would undermine the foundations of traditional militarism had fallen, or because of the reduced attractiveness of an organization on the wane that drove the construction of alternative routes.

The "Motivation Crisis"

After exhausting their ability to broaden their political right to supervise the army and military policy, secular Ashkenazim made relatively fewer demands for more rights from the state than other groups. As the dominant stratum, its strategy was to reduce the security burden while increasing its resources through the market in a way that would lessen state involvement. Accordingly, along with protest activities, secular Ashkenazis tried to exert pressure to reduce military sacrifice or increase the rewards for it by turning to more individual tactics. This was part of an attempt to oversee the "production" of the security product, in this instance by reducing its price.

Accordingly, one mode of action was reflected in the cultivation of internal pressures of various kinds to divert resources from military reinforcement to private consumption (including reducing tax burdens). This reduced investment in security (as a proportion of GDP) from a peak of 31 percent in 1974–1976 to around 17 percent between 1986–1990 (Lifshitz, 2000, 170).

A second mode of action could be seen in the gradual forsaking of the army, and especially a reduction in motivation for combat duty—the "motivation crisis" syndrome, as some aspects of this were termed in public discourse during the mid-1990s. This trend had a number of aspects: a slow and continual decline in the general willingness to enlist, particularly to combat units; fewer volunteers for officer training; a rise in the number of potential recruits purposely trying to alter their medical profile—which determines the soldier's qualification to perform his/her duties—as a means to avoid combat duty; a rise in the number of enlistees requesting to serve at a base close to their home; and a significant increase in the number of youngsters dropping out before and during their service on the grounds of apparent mental ill-health (for various aspects see Mayseless, 1993; Nevo and Shor, 2002b, 9–35). The reduced symbolic rewards of military service thus led the secular Ashkenazi groups to untie the republican Gordian knot between soldiering and citizenship by distancing themselves from combat service—in the past the ethos that had constructed their preferential status—and by either partially or totally abstaining from military service.

By its own doing, the state exacerbated the violation of the republican equation. Not only did it contribute to the erosion of symbolic rewards by directing the IDF to politically disputed missions in Lebanon and the Occupied Territories, it also began to reform the conscription system from being inclusionist to selective. Two processes are particularly worth mentioning.

First, in 1985 the reserve army was reformed and the burden was reduced. The main thrust of the reform was to gradually transfer the cost of reserve duty from the National Insurance Institute to the army. Previously, the daily cost of a reserve soldier (primarily compensating him/her for loss of earnings) was not borne by the security budget, and so the reserve army was largely managed in isolation from economic considerations. The reform provided an incentive for the army to rein in its usage of reservists and divert resources to other purposes. This process was part of a broad cutback in the security budget in the framework of the "Economic Stability Plan," which, in 1985, eliminated the hyperinflation and heralded the gradual shift to a market society. Indeed, beyond its budgetary implications, the reform meant that the reserves began to be managed according to the prerequisites of the market economy, and a price tag was attached to the service of reserve soldiers. This resulted in a dramatic reduction in the number of overall reserve duty days, and an easing of the burden of reserve duties. To illustrate: in 2001, reserve duty was funded on the basis of 3.8 million days per year instead of 10 million in 1985, before the reform.[7] At the same time, the number of days served by reservists dropped from an average of twenty-six days per year in 1990, to sixteen in 2000 (Nevo and Shor, 2002a, 57). In short, the reform of the reserves brought about for the first time a semi-selective recruitment model, one which deviated from the universalist principles of an inclusive "people's army." The high cost of reserve duty (following the First Lebanon War) led to a policy of selectiveness based on giving the reservist a price tag.

However, this is a case of trying to right one wrong with another: the army's inefficiency, characterized by the wasteful recruitment of reservists, was resolved by increasing inequality in the reserves. The cutback in reserve duty days weighed most heavily on combat units, where the middle class was bearing most of the burden, in terms of both the reservists and their employers. The burden placed on noncombat forces, with their larger representation of other social strata, was lightened as reserve duty days were reduced and cheaper, civilian alternatives to reservists were found. A new contradiction thus emerged from the directives of the market economy: economic savings for the army at the cost of an increased financial burden on the middle class, itself already faced with a high tax burden and the contradictory pressures of the market economy (such as competitiveness and pressure from employers).

Second, selectivity encompassed the compulsory army as well. Numerically speaking, the defection of secular Ashkenazim, together with the expansion of the nonmilitary Torah-study route, and the disqualification of low-educated draftees, largely owing to the growing human reservoir following the mass immigration from the former Soviet Union in the 1990s, led to a reduction in recruitment rates: in the 1990s less than 60 percent of Jewish men were serving full military service, and this number continues to drop. As mentioned above with regard to *Shas*, the exemptions given to yeshiva students, which, as noted, account for around 10 percent of all exemptions, are the result of the broad social processes that produced the "motivation crisis," and so they too can be seen as part of this general "crisis."

As in other societies, upsetting the republican equation with the growing selectivity that accompanied this process amplified the enlisted persons' bargaining power vis-à-vis the IDF. Especially so as selectivity also further cracked the military's image as an inclusionist "people's army," the boundaries of which overlap with those of the Israeli-Jewish community, thus further devaluing the symbolic rewards. The model of reserve duty is highly sensitive to social changes, as it is based on "civilianized soldiers" who simultaneously live in two worlds (see Ben-Ari et al., 2004), unlike the model of compulsory service, which suspends citizenship, and the career army, populated by professionals in uniform.

Indeed, examples of this bargaining included: (1) pressure to increase the material rewards for reservists and their employers, which was partially answered by improved compensation for reservists (especially those serving for longer periods of time); (2) pressure to redistribute the burden, especially the demand in the 1990s to recruit yeshiva students. This was the rearguard battle to piece together the republican equation out of its remnants, if not by increasing the rights of those who bear the burden or negating the rights of those who do not, then by making greater demands of the latter. Amendments to legislation only partially met this demand, however. This struggle showed how the burden of military service—formerly part of the symbolic capital of the middle class, and the basis for the exclusion of other groups from the army—had become a burden that justified demands for its alleviation, or even for it to be shared with previously excluded groups. Theoretically, the extent to which citizens acquiesce with their mass recruitment, itself a kind of taxation, rests on the depth of their trust that the state will treat them fairly, including the just distribution of the burden of service among other citizens (Levi, 1997). By exempting more and more yeshiva students without limiting their social rights while constricting the rewards given to enlistees, the state upset this principle. Groups demanding to recruit other groups in order to justify rights that have already been granted to them is not a unique phenomenon (see Brubaker, 1992, 92–94); (3) pressures for political selectivity regarding military missions, reflected in various forms of explicit and "grey" refusal to participate in politically controversial missions, from the First Lebanon War to the First Intifada (Helman 1999).

The combination of the "motivation crisis" with growing selectiveness also necessitated an increase in the material compensation of compulsory servicepersons. In 1994, a law was passed that defined a package of financial assistance to be given to conscript soldiers upon their release. In 2000, this law was amended to allow for differential payouts to be given to combat as compared with noncombat soldiers, as well as the higher salary regular combat soldiers were paid. In the compulsory army as well, then, material rewards were given in compensation for the reduction in symbolic rewards.

The "motivation crisis" spread out to include the behavior of bereaved families. From the late 1990s, these families began a struggle to improve their compensation, and some war widows even took their cases to court, where they demanded that they receive the same preferential package as that given to the widows of reserve pilots. Here too the demand for material rewards intensified as the symbolic compensation for bereavement declined. An indication of these processes can be seen in the privatization and individualization of bereavement during the 1990s. An illustration was the struggle of bereaved parents to write the wording on their sons' gravestones themselves, instead of the uniform text imposed by the state (see Rosental, 2001).

Arguably, the 1990s saw the gradual dismantling of materialist militarism and the appearance of a new hybrid form of post-materialist militarism, signaling a shift from symbolically based rewards to materially based ones. As mentioned, the traditional form of materialist militarism represented a militarism nurtured by the dominant social strata as a symbolic impetus for attaining social rewards, primarily using its military contribution to legitimize its social dominance. Post-materialist militarism differs from its traditional shape in that it emphasizes the expectation for liquid material rewards instead of symbolic rewards that may later be converted into liquid material ones, while blurring the separation between the military and the market. The army variously incorporated itself in the market economy, and the driving force behind actors' motivations shifted from openly declared ideology, whose representatives were depicted as the "service elite," which was also rewarded for its service, to utilitarian motivations. Equally, the relationship between the individual and the army also shifted from *obligatory militarism*, which sees compulsory service in terms of unconditional contribution to the state, to *contractual militarism*, which makes military service conditional on the aspirations or interests of the group or individual (Levy et al., 2007, see more in chapter 5). The transition from obligatory to contractual militarism is one of the expressions of the violation of the republican equation. Only among Mizrachi and religious groups is the motivation to serve based on the traditional republican patterns of materialist militarism.

To sum up, the violation of the equation led to pressure from secular Ashkenazi groups to rebalance it by raising material rewards to compensate for the devaluation of symbolic ones, and by reducing the burden of military service through direct and the indirect action, namely, the political restraint of the military by amplifying its monitoring. These modes of action, together with attenuated convertibility, spurred on national religious and Mizrachi groups to integrate themselves in the traditional equation, or to formulate an alternative one (the *Gush Emunim* and the Orthodox route). As a result, the army's political freedom of action and its control over human, material, and legitimizing resources were limited. The state exhausted its initial strategic mechanisms, namely, discursively reintensifying the sense of threat (especially during the First Lebanon War), and granting political rights in a way that ultimately narrowed the army's autonomy. Improving the material rewards given to those who bore the burden only partially helped to balance the equation. After all, it did not deflect pressure from middle-class groups in the mid-1990s to end the IDF's presence on Lebanon soil, as groups for whom such minor material rewards lacked significance.

However, the state could have provided much greater material rewards. In many instances, the various occasions of a "motivation crisis" could have been solved through improved financial rewards, but this was restrained by two contradictory factors: on the one hand, the volunteer ethos of the "people's army," as opposed to the principle of remunerating either regular or reserve soldiers; and on the other, the ethos of the market economy, which restricted the army's resources, thereby impeding its ability to reward its enlistees. From now on, the army's conduct would face an inherent contradiction in its legitimacy system: the Ashkenazi bearers of the ethos of the market economy raised their expectations for greater material rewards for their military service in light of their declining symbolic rewards. At the same time, however, that same group also curbed the price that the state could pay in order to meet those expectations because of its market-oriented interest in "small government," which entailed a reduction in military expenditure. Therefore, the state had to find alternative modes of action that would rebalance the equation. Thus, in consequence, if not on purpose, a two-phased balancing strategy was adopted that embodied the third strategic mechanism at the state's disposal, namely, reducing the rates of military participation.

BALANCING THE EQUATION

The first phase of the balancing strategy was to significantly reduce the security burden by deescalating military friction, while the second and parallel one was a new "social architecture" for the army (to be dealt with in the next chapter).

The first phase—reducing the burden—enabled the discrepancy between the burden and the rewards given to those bearing it to be narrowed. Both the restrictions placed by the internal arena on its professional autonomy, and the expectation that it would reduce its holdings of social resources, were well internalized by the army.

Protective of its internal integration, social status, and its decreasing human and material resources, the IDF found itself being increasingly driven to adjust to a civilian set of considerations under pressure from civilian groups. It was precisely because it was a "people's army," with the resources, prestige, and the professional mobility of the officer corps in the civilian labor market that this status entails, that the IDF was sensitive to shifts in the profile of the social legitimacy it enjoyed.

Clearly, moreover, the more that political disputes over the use of military force intensified, the more Israel's capacity to use force declined, because the state bureaucracy and the military establishment had to carefully calculate the expected political outcomes. Manifestly, the expansion of the boundaries of political debate over the use of force illustrates the linkage between social interests and deterrence. The greater the hesitation to use force, the less deterrence enjoys credibility (Inbar and Sandler, 1995). Grasping these lessons, the self-restrained use of military force, along with considerations of international politics, was reflected in the relatively moderate policy adopted by the *Likud*-led governments in the First Intifada (the reluctance to use massive firepower to quell the uprising) and the First Gulf War (refraining from retaliating against Iraq's scud missile attacks). Later on, the Labor-led government displayed a similar pattern by refraining from embarking on massive ground operations against the Shiite militia in South Lebanon. Central to self-restraint was Israel's gradual internalization of the limitation of using force, in sharp contrast to the sense of total omnipotence inherent within Israeli political thought until the 1973 War.

Consequently, the army's conduct has been characterized by cycles of escalation and deescalation, and not only by the escalations common before 1973 when the IDF had attracted a high degree of legitimacy. Furthermore, the political leadership itself internalized the limited capacity of the IDF, especially vis-à-vis the challenge presented by Shiite and Palestinian militias. Israeli statesmanship, in which the army had played such a central role, was therefore channeled into exhausting nonmilitary options.

First was the full withdrawal from the Sinai Peninsula in return for peace with Egypt (1979), and this after the army had been one of the architects of the approach calling for uncompromisingly holding on to territories, at least up until the Yom Kippur War. In return, the army's human and material costs were decreased by eliminating the Egyptian threat and gaining American aid that helped to rebuild the army. Yet, more than attempting to cool down the conflict, the government and the army were geared to divert resources (including legitimation) from the Egyptian arena to the Palestinian one, through which the main battle over the "Land of Israel" would be determined. Indirectly, this move helped to launch the First Lebanon War.

Indeed, the next phase was an attempt to return to the army some of the centrality and prestige it had lost following the withdrawal from Sinai and the failures of the Yom Kippur War. This effort took the shape of a rapid operation to conquer South Lebanon in 1982. However, a lightning raid became a lengthy war, the extended target of which had been to impose a new order on Lebanon. In fact, the war actually strengthened Hezbollah as a force that Israel failed to deal with, at least party because of the complex restrictions placed on its combat capabilities. The imbroglio in Lebanon shifted the direction of the trend—a partial and unilateral withdrawal in 1985—with the IDF making efforts to persuade the politicians to speed up the withdrawal (Inbar, 2004, 152). As part of the withdrawal, the mercenary South Lebanese Army (SLA) was left behind to separate Israeli towns in the Galilee from Shiite militias deployed in South Lebanon. In the mid-1990s it turned out that the IDF was continuing to pay a price for its presence in Lebanon because of difficulties with the functioning of the SLA that required direct IDF involvement. And so, in 2000, owing to political pressure, including from the *Four Mothers* movement, Israel fully and unilaterally withdrew from Lebanon.

At the same time, the effective occupation of the West Bank and the Gaza Strip expanded into the settlement project that peaked to about 60,000 settlers and more than 100 settlements in the mid-1980s. This was among the factors leading to the national Palestinian uprising known as the First Intifada (1987–1993). When the IDF acknowledged its failure to quell the uprising, it was brought to an end with the Oslo agreements with the Palestinians in 1993–1995.

These cycles of escalation and moderation as a counter-reaction to the over-exploitation of military power embody a failure typical of the "security dilemma." In other words, actions by the state intended to increase its security undermine the security of the other side, which intensifies threats to the state's security. Redefining the state's security interests and the threat evaluations they imply could vanquish this shortcoming (see Collins, 2004). Indeed, this is what happened in between cycles, as the security interest was gradually reformulated in terms which shifted the responsibility for Israel's security from being exclusively reliant on Israel's military power to regional and even global "security regimes." These regimes have brought about cooperation between Israel and pragmatic Arab states, and have deepened the involvement of the United States (Bar-Siman-Tov, 1995). However, the security dilemma has been solidified by Israel's insistence on secretly developing a nuclear project which has gradually placed Israel under a regional nuclear threat, or may lead to pressures for nuclear disarmament (Maoz, 2003).

At the same time, in an attempt to prevent the burden from becoming even heavier, as early as the 1970s the state changed its financial strategy from self-reliantly funding security to resting on American aid, in the shape of either credit or increased foreign military financing (Barnett, 1992, 194–96, 232–33). This strategy was reflected in foreign policy too: the withdrawal from the Sinai Peninsula was traded for American aid that financed the post-1973 military buildup. Similarly, the eradication of hyperinflation in 1985 was combined with a partial withdrawal from Lebanon in return for generous American aid, along with a cutback in the defense budget and a downsizing of military industries. Likewise, fears of a reduction in American assistance in absorbing the mass immigration from the former Soviet Union played a part in immigrants' support for the relatively dovish Rabin-led Labor Party in 1992; this accelerated political processes, at the center of which stood Oslo.

However, from the point of view of the state and its army, these developments wore down its internal autonomy in the military sphere and eroded the IDF's status. It was only an interim strategy helping to reduce political pressures, but it could not last long, especially when demilitarization and the peace process, which involved territorial concessions, gave rise to a counter-reaction among peripheral and religious groups. Therefore, the second and parallel phase was the army's new "social architecture," which yielded the political rehabilitation of military capabilities by refilling its ranks with religious and peripheral groups who would display more loyalty to the military way. This new architecture and its military-political expressions are the subject of the next chapter.

CONCLUSIONS

This chapter's point of departure was the need to get to the root of the success of Jewish-Israeli society in maintaining firm legitimacy for its militaristic orientation over time. It was assumed that unraveling this success would help us understand the subsequent erosion of that legitimacy, which, in the 1990s, plunged the army's relationship with civil society into a state of crisis. This need was sharpened given the alternatives to a militaristic orientation posited by the external arena, as the revisionist historical writing cited above has clearly shown. Recognition of these alternatives undermined the widespread assumption that the reality of conflict was imposed on Israel, at least until the 1970s, an assumption that would seem to make any discussion of the origins of Israeli militarism superfluous.

Accordingly, this discussion has focused on social, political, and cultural processes. Instead of focusing on the external arena, this chapter has looked at the Israeli form of the republican equation, which constituted materialist militarism. This equation involved an exchange between the military sacrifice made by leading social groups and symbolic rewards in the military sphere, which are converted into material rewards in the social sphere, central to which are the fruits of war and legitimacy for social dominance. The conversion of resources from the military to the social sphere rested on a high rate of convertibility, which simultaneously fed into and was fed by the level of militarism in society. This created the energy that enlisted groups from the dominant social class to a demanding yet low-cost military effort, and which gave the state a relatively high degree of autonomy in running its military policies, at least until the 1970s.

The Israeli version of the republican equation was gradually violated from 1973 as the symbolic rewards lost part of their value without the burden of military sacrifice decreasing, but rather growing. The violation of the equation gave rise to a "progressive motivation crisis," led by groups from the secular Ashkenazi middle class: at first the military way lost some of its legitimacy (in the 1970s), as seen through the appearance of protest groups; later on, support for the allocation of material resources to the army declined (1980s); and finally, abandonment of the army was expressed in the various ways in which people distanced themselves from military service (1990s).

Demilitarization was at work. Yet because of its dependence on rewards, the "motivation crisis" in its broader context shows the extent to which materialist militarism was built on shaky foundations, like every social structure that rests on pragmatic interests and lacks deep ideological, religious or historical roots. It is no wonder, therefore, that as soon as it ceased to harvest utility from militarism, the dominant class in Israel relatively quickly shed its responsibility for its upkeep and turned to alternative ways of accumulating utility. This is not to ignore the cultural, communal, and ideological aspects of Israeli militarism (emphasized by some researchers; see for instance Helman 1997), but they were not as crucial as the material, utilitarian aspects, which, when they contracted, shrunk the entire militarist project. It follows that the Israeli version of demilitarization had not originated from a deep-rooted cultural change, but rather from the encounter of waning of militaristic utility and the internalization of the limitations to use force.

At first, a process of deescalation of the Arab-Israeli conflict with the army's cooperation revealed itself. This was the last strategic option adopted by the state, that is, to rebalance the republican equation by reducing the military burden, after it had exhausted the initial strategies at its disposal for dealing with a violated equation, namely, manipulating the external threat, allocating rights and monetary rewards, and reducing the burden by modifying financial strategy. While in the short term this strategy led to the withdrawal of militarism in the form of the Oslo process, in the long term it brought about the state's renewed ability to manage autonomous militaristic policies in the internal arena, largely because of the new architecture of the army's social composition that made it reliant on ethno-nationalist groups.

However, deescalation and rearchitecturing were not separate, but rather combined phases. Owing to this amalgamation, the IDF and its political supervisors were provided with the ability to politically recruit passive support among ethno-nationalist groups for the peace process as much as to prepare for the future clash with the Palestinians when the political arrangements collapsed. Oslo and Intifada Al-Aqsa were mutually tied, as the next chapter shows.

NOTES

1. On the Ashkenazi-Mizrachi gap, see also Ben-Porath, 1986; Nahon, 1987; Shalev, 1992; Swirski, 1990; Yiftachel, 1998.

2. As an indication of this, in 1961, 10 percent of the Jewish population had at least thirteen years' education, compared to a mere 2 percent among the Palestinian-Druze population (Ben-Porath, 1986, 165–66).

3. A series of street demonstrations in the Wadi Salib neighborhood of Haifa as a social protest against ethnic discrimination organized by young immigrants from Morocco.

4. The veteran Ashkenazi-dominated moshavim are to be distinguished from the immigrants' moshavim (*moshav olim*), which were the form of absorbing the Mizrachim.

5. *Nahal*, a Hebrew acronym for "Fighting Pioneer Youth," is a special military framework that combines agricultural work in border settlements with military service. The *Territorial Defense Organization* relied—as a heritage of the pre-state defense conception—on veteran-Ashkenazi agricultural border settlements (differentiated from the new settlements mainly populated by Mizrachim) as forward outposts.

6. On this structural and discursive change see Grinberg and Shafir, 2000; Ram, 2005; Shafir and Peled, 2002, 238–45; Shalev, 2000.

7. According to a report made to the Knesset by MK Raanan Cohen, *Proceedings of the Knesset*, 16 April, 2001.

Chapter Three

The Continuation of Oslo by the Al-Aqsa Intifada

The strategy for reconstituting the republican equation returned a degree of autonomy to the internal management of military policies, and it bore fruit in the Al-Aqsa Intifada. When the army's new social architecture met with the infrastructure for renewed violence, brought about by the military nature of the Oslo Accords, a new dynamic was created that escalated the fighting with the Palestinians and temporarily brought the Oslo Accords to its knees.

REBALANCING THE EQUATION—THE ARMY'S NEW SOCIAL ARCHITECTURE

In the medium term, the army internalized the external limitations placed on it and cooperated with the political leadership in deescalating the conflict. However, it simultaneously implemented a social rearchitecture as a way of constructing the army out of social groups that were loyal to the military way—the second phase of the balancing strategy of the republican equation (for more see Levy, 2003b, 285–307). Inasmuch as the IDF found itself coping with the contradictory prerequisites of the market economy, namely, greater material rewards for military service concurrent with cutbacks in the military's resources, the IDF turned to increase its reliance on religious and ethno-nationalist groups offering their services for degraded monetary rewards but high symbolic rewards.

The social rearchitecturing of the military implies a structural change in the social composition of those performing the military's missions or in the nature of the armaments that they operate. It is an outcome of the implicit or explicit linkage between the political orientation or potential for collective action of the social group (that is executing the mission or operating the arms) and its mission. In this case, the rearchitecturing may result in the downsizing of missions assigned to middle-class groups, either by reallocating them to other groups or by reducing the intensity of the mission by increasing the use of technology.

The army's new social architecture had a number of components:

Satellite armies—from the 1980s Israel started trying out a new model of delegating problematic missions to satellite armies. The first such army was formed in the early 1980s and comprised armed Jewish militias in the Occupied Territories. They operated within the framework of the Territorial Defense Organization with the backing of the IDF. In practice, they were reserve units staffed by settlers who participated in the day-to-day defense of their settlements. Accordingly, the settlers were armed by the army as befitting reservists. The function of these militias was to contribute to the maintenance of the military occupation.

The South Lebanese Army (SLA) was built on a similar model. In 1985, Israel unilaterally withdrew from Lebanon, leaving the multiethnic and mercenary SLA to keep Shiite forces away from Israel's northern border. The SLA was funded, trained, politically backed, and monitored by the IDF. But because the SLA was not alone in paying the price for increasingly efficient Shiite actions—they were also costly in terms of IDF soldiers—the army was forced to readapt and withdrew from Lebanon entirely in 2000.

In both of these instances, Israel armed local inhabitants as a human defensive shield against majority Arab populations, and used salaried soldiers in place of official IDF manpower. Soldiers in the SLA were mercenaries who kept Hezbollah away from the northern border with their bodies. Recruits to the Territorial Defense Organization in the Territories were also more akin to mercenaries than regular conscripts or reservists in the formal IDF. This could be most clearly seen in the principle of using a Jewish civilian population for military purposes in return for generous state subsidies of the settlements and their armed inhabitants. In both cases the state led its missionaries to believe that they were carrying out a righteous task, while not hesitating to abandon them (as in the withdrawals from Lebanon and the Gaza Strip in the early 2000s) as soon as its interests changed.

In certain respects the Oslo process also involved a kind of "subcontracting" to the Palestinians in the shape of the security forces that were deployed under Israeli auspices. However, this model collapsed with the outbreak of the Al-Aqsa Intifada in 2000.

This kind of utilization of satellite armies, termed risk-transfer militarism by Martin Shaw (2002), is not very different from that characteristic of Western countries in similar circumstances.

The partial transformation of the army from a labor-intensive to a technology-intensive organization—the IDF began increasing its use of technology-intensive armaments that distance the warrior from his victim, thus dulling his political consciousness and placing him under less risk, which may in itself reduce the political cost of his deployment. The two large operations embarked upon in South Lebanon in the 1990s against an emerging Hezbollah-run mini-state—*Operation Accountability* and *Operation Grapes of Wrath*—illustrated the new model. Here, the conception called for "counter fire," that is, heavy reliance on aerial assaults with no use of ground troops. The new approach involved the use of accurate and long-range munitions that aimed at pressuring the local population into restraining Hezbollah's activities (Levy, 1995). The use of the Air Force in various missions in the second Intifada represented a similar model, as did the Second Lebanon War of 2006.

Removing reservists from friction zones—the First Lebanon War laid bare the political collapse of the model of a middle-class–based reserve army. This stratum levered its military participation into political involvement—mainly in the shape of protest organizations—which contributed to the fracturing of the army's professional autonomy. The lesson that had been learned was implemented in Lebanon from 1985–2000, as the fighting was increasingly carried out by the conscript army. One of the senior field officers in Lebanon testified that relying on enlistees meant that warfare could be managed far from the public's consciousness and free from public criticism (Tamir, 2005, 10–11, 274).

The final process—*Change in the composition of the field forces*—is significant enough to deserve its own section.

THE NEW SOLDIERS

Five groups (hereinafter the *new groups*) that had previously been relegated into a peripheral status in the army's ranks came to fill the vacuum created by the secular Ashkenazi middle class' partial abandonment of combat units. They were: Mizrachim—at first the relatively mobile Mizrachim, and later the less-mobile ones; the national religious youngsters together with a small number of Ultra-Orthodox; new immigrants, mainly those from the former Soviet Union and Ethiopia; Druze and Bedouin citizens of Israel; and, more slowly, women. This change in the army's composition began in the 1980s, though along with the Oslo process and the withdrawal from Lebanon, it sped up during the 1990s (Levy, 2003b, 236–63).

These new groups strove to construct their unique warrior identity so as to bring them closer to the main site in which the communal "common good" is constructed. The status emanating from participating in the advancement of the common good was seen as valuable in and of itself. The desire to succeed in the army blurred prior political and even ethical orientations. As many of their members bear ethno-national values, these groups viewed military duties as a means to fulfill their ideological values by protecting the borders of the "Greater Land of Israel" vis-à-vis the seemingly hostile Arab world. The new groups thus forged for themselves a new symbolic resource, and the army started to become a locale for the construction of differentiated identities for servicemen and women from groups located outside its secular Ashkenazi historical core (see for instance Cohen, 2004; Hakak, 2005; Kaplan, 2002; Lomsky-Feder and Ben-Ari, 1999; Lomsky-Feder and Rapoport, 2003; Sasson-Levy, 2006; Shabtay, 1999).

The new groups also saw military service as a pathway for legitimately attaining social and political rights and privileges. However, they were not seeking legitimacy for deep-rooted social dominance, as the secular Ashkenazi groups had done. Instead, they primarily sought to legitimize demands for improving their status, and maybe, among some of the groups, expectations of future dominance. The buds of this orientation had already started appearing in the shape of attitudes among Mizrachim and, more notably, the "knitted skullcaps," who were attributed with the intention of capturing senior positions at the top of the military hierarchy, thus making their mark on the entire society.

The new groups were also motivated by the need to delineate new paths of mobility. This was certainly the case when, among other strategies, the army tried to deal with the "motivation crisis" by offering enlistees improved material rewards, while at the same time, youngsters from the new groups were increasingly integrating themselves in the officer corps, in the light of its abandonment by traditionally elite groups. The new groups thus created an alternative to the civilian paths of mobility that were blocked off to them, or were at least less accessible in a professionalizing, competitive, and unstable labor market. In short, for the new groups, the traditional foundations of materialist militarism, and not its "post" form, still bore significance. Remilitarization, then, became the weapon wielded by these groups, which espoused military service in order to legitimate their expectations that military service be recognized as a source of social rewards.

While the increased presence of Mizrachim was the continuation of a process that had begun back in the 1960s, the army's treatment of other groups was more singular, as detailed below.

The Ashkenazi and Mizrachi middle class—while religious groups, women, and the social periphery gradually began to populate "blue-collar" combat positions in greater numbers, the secular Ashkenazi middle class, joined by mobile Mizrachim located in the upper middle class, reformulated their military contribution. Under the mantle of the concept of a "small and intelligent army"—a phrase coined by Dan Shomron, Chief of the General Staff in the second half of the 1980s as part of his planned structural reforms—the army gradually shifted from being labor-intensive to being technology- and knowledge-intensive.

New status symbols thus appeared in the army that were identified with the *warrior-technologist*. This warrior carries sophisticated weapons, is equipped with control and information systems, and operates these technological systems without coming into direct contact with the enemy. Technological auxiliary units also appeared (such as the 8200 Intelligence Unit) with a distinctly hi-tech image. Along with the high convertibility of skills acquired in these units in the civilian hi-tech labor market, they were also seen as prestigious on account of the way that they conflated one of the more notable symbols of the market economy discourse—technological supremacy—with national security (see Sasson-Levy, 2006, 218–22).

Women—the lack of high quality manpower, as defined by IDF officers, was functional for the advancement of women in the army. Demands from women's organizations, the "motivation crisis," and calls from servicemen for greater financial rewards, all spurred on the army to expand the recruitment of women, whom, until the 1980s, had been restricted to auxiliary roles. For women, the symbolic incentive, that is, the very accessibility to combat or combat support positions, with all that meant for gender power relations, reduced the need for financial rewards. Field positions had been slowly opened up to women since the First Lebanon War, and they were gradually given greater access to combat roles. The watershed was Alice Miller's petition to the High Court of Justice in 1995. The court accepted Miller's complaint regarding the rejection of her application to the pilot training course, and these courses were consequently opened up to women.[1] More combat professions were subsequently made available to women too. In 2000, the *Security Service Law* was amended to allow the Defense Minister to define a list of voluntary positions for women for which existing legal distinctions between men and women would be cancelled. These distinctions mostly related to women's shorter duration of service in both the conscript and reserve forces. In 2003 it was decided that women serving in such positions would have to serve for thirty-six months, like their male counterparts, instead of twenty-four months.

Schematically speaking, women developed two separate systems of motivation. The first pertained to high school graduates, mostly from the secular Ashkenazi middle class. For these young women, the struggle for equality in the army was part of a gender test to challenge or imitate masculinity (Dahan

Kalev, 2001; Sasson-Levy, 2003). The second related to secular or traditional Mizrachi women, for whom military service was a pathway for mobility as it was an experience that weakened their dependency on their families and strengthened their self-confidence in a masculine environment (see findings in Dar and Kimhi, 2004).

The Mizrachim—the army was relatively opened up to Mizrachim from the 1980s onward, though their mode of integration reflected changes in their internal stratification. The most mobile Mizrachi groups had internalized the republican principle from the outset, understanding that military service was a tool for social mobility, and deepened their hold on the army accordingly. However, at the end of the 1980s, the republican conception of citizenship came under attack, both from the liberal discourse (one of the ideological anchors of the Oslo process) and the ethno-national discourse, both of which weakened the Gordian knot linking soldiering to citizenship (Shafir and Peled, 2002). Many Mizrachim gradually attained mobility into the middle class without any relation to their military achievements, thus devaluing the significance of military service. Mizrachi youngsters from the upper echelons of the middle class, who lived in the large cities in the center of the country and graduated from prestigious high schools, and whose parents were on the verge of the upper middle class, began to adopt modes of behavior in relation to the army that were similar to those of their Ashkenazi friends: in other words, their motivation declined. On the other hand, for Mizrachi youngsters from the lower strata of the middle class—mostly graduates of high schools from peripheral cities, or peripheral high schools in the big cities—military service remained an important test of citizenship. In fact, these youngsters renewed the traditional military ethos of the sacrificial service elite. This could be seen as an act of defiance in the face of the secular Ashkenazi service elite, and can be operationalized in terms of this group's increased presence in combat units and among officers (see more in chapter 4).

The same is true for the Mizrachi settlers, who can be grouped in the same class stratum as peripheral Mizrachim. Their peripheral class status led them to migrate from towns inside the Green Line to settlements in the Occupied Territories in return for subsidies from the government, which then maintained the welfare system that was collapsing within the Green Line (Gutwein, 2004).

Four groups can be identified within the nonmobile Mizrachi sector, located beneath the middle class: (1) a group excluded by the army and not recruited on the grounds of unsuitability, mostly because of low educational achievements; (2) a group for whom military service was superfluous in the light of the minimal rewards given to those fulfilling marginal roles in the army when compared with studying in a yeshiva, which provided both an income and symbolic capital. Because the ethno-national ethos did not make civilian status conditional on military service, instead giving prominence to ethno-national belonging, forgoing military service was perceived as legitimate; (3) a group for whom military service, and especially fighting the Palestinians, remained meaningful. Members of this group saw the combination of globalization and peace as posing a threat to their symbols, status, and level of earning; (4) a group fulfilling administrative roles whose self-image, and hence motivation, were low (see Sasson-Levy, 2002).

As mentioned, the image of the army as an egalitarian "melting pot" serving as a significant path for Mizrachi mobility was one of the main sources of legitimacy for inequality in the military. Israeli sociologists also inflated this idea over the years (see mainly Lissak, 1984). However, the mobility theory does not stand the test of empirical enquiry. Looking at the empirical data, the rate of mobility among Mizrachim in the civilian hierarchy is similar to that in the military hierarchy. In the 1990s Mizrachim comprised about 25 percent of the middle- to high-ranking officers (from majors to generals), while constituting about 50 percent of NCOs. At the same time they manned about 18 percent of the four leading professional civilian sectors which are approximately equivalent to those military ranks (data compiled from Kashti, 1997; Yaish, 2001).

In consequence, Mizrachim failed to significantly achieve mobility within the military (including the second generation of immigrants). More significantly, the close similarity between the hierarchies attests to the fact that military promotion does not necessarily lead to advancement within the civilian hierarchy in such as way as to reconstruct the social hierarchy. Indeed, the opposite may even be the case: the most qualified among the Mizrachim may advance within the labor market even without the military's assistance; in fact, military service may even disrupt the mobility of talented youngsters as it removes them from the labor market and reduces their experience relative to those who serve for a shorter period, thus returning them to the civilian labor market in a disadvantageous position. (For the conceptual framework of this approach see MacLean, 2005; Teachman, 2004.)

Moreover, it is possible that before the advent of accelerated mobility among Mizrachim within the military following the "motivation crisis" among secular Ashkenazis, there was even greater similarity between the hierarchies.

This would seem to be an instance of the "climbing down the escalator" syndrome: in other words, although Mizrachim increased their grasp on senior positions, these steps forward were paralleled by a devaluation of the convertibility of such positions in the civilian labor market.

Immigrants from the former Soviet Union—similar to the Mizrachim, immigrants from the former Soviet Union also saw military service as a symbolic "entrance pass" into Israeli society, and even as a test for gaining formal citizenship. This also applied to Christian immigrants (who came to Israel as part of mixed-religion families), who found the army to be a fast and convenient route for converting to Judaism. Immigrants from the first wave of migration in the 1970s (comprising around 200,000 people) were mostly recruited into service and administration units with low prestige, meaning that the army did not contribute to their social mobility (Azarya and Kimmerling, 1998). In contrast, not only did the immigrants from the 1990s (the main wave, comprising around 700,000 people) leverage the "motivation crisis" to gain promotion through the ranks, but from the mid-1990s their ethno-nationalist orientation strengthened: just as they were crystallizing their identity as part of the majority Jewish group in their new country, they began to perceive the Palestinian minority as threatening the Jewish majority. According to their emerging group mythology, these immigrants saw themselves as a kind of vanguard unit that would put the brakes on the Al-Aqsa Intifada (Shumsky, 2001). For some of them, this ethno-nationalist orientation even had the character of Islamophobic ideology imported from the former Soviet Union (Shumsky, 2005).

Therefore, it is possible that greater meaning was attributed to military service as contributing to the community, and that the immigrants thereby appropriated for themselves a stake in the construction of society. Their encounter with the warrior-Sabre also enabled many immigrants to consolidate their "Russian" masculinity, presented as a challenge to the hegemonic military masculinity of their fellow servicemen, which they perceived as childish and spoiled (Lomsky-Feder and Rapoport, 2003). At the same time, a utilitarian orientation also developed among certain of the immigrants, largely expressed through seeing acquiring a profession as preferable to actually going to battle (Carmeli and Fadlon, 1997).

Immigrants from Ethiopia—for young immigrants from Ethiopia (this immigration comprised around 120,000 people) military service not only provided access to an Israeli identity, but was also a way of improving their self-confidence and even finding a certain feeling of superiority over their old-timer counterparts. This was based on their self-image as more ascetic soldiers who were prepared to serve far from their family homes, and to internalize the military hierarchy (Shabtay, 1999).

The Druze, Bedouins, and Palestinian Citizens—from the 1980s the IDF began to make a greater effort to persuade Bedouins—who are part of but separate from the Palestinian minority, and who are not subject to the draft—to volunteer for combat duty and not only to serve as trackers, which had been their traditional role in the military. These efforts resulted in the establishment (in the early 1990s) of a patrol battalion (Desert Patrol Battalion) that served during the Intifada on Israel's border with the Palestinian Authority in the area of Rafah in the Gaza Strip. The battalion was comprised mainly of Bedouins, along with Christians and Muslims from the north of the country. Their motivation was manifold: an ambition to attain equal rights through signing up for the army; an attraction to military activities, channeled into serving in the IDF; and seeing service in the army as a profession at a time of unemployment and economic instability. For the army, recruiting the Bedouins was not only a way of dealing with a lack of manpower, but also an attempt at damming increased Islamization among that group.

Men from the Druze community are subject to compulsory recruitment, and from the 1990s some of the restrictions regarding their service were lifted and they began to be integrated into combat units alongside Jewish soldiers. At the same time, they continued to be recruited to the Border Police—a military police force that mainly carries out policing missions in the Occupied Territories. Unlike the Bedouins, for the Druze, fighting the Palestinians is a tool in shaping an Israeli, and not Arab, identity. In return, the state provides preferential rewards in comparison to Palestinian citizens of Israel (see Frisch, 1993; Kanaaneh, 2003). Adopting the framework of the traditional militaristic-materialistic discourse, both groups, Bedouin and Druze, try to leverage their military contribution into improved material status for their communities.

The religious—a major part of the army's changing social architecture could be seen in the increasing number of "knitted skullcaps" in the army from the 1980s onward. Two interacting factors stood behind the entrance of this group into the army, following years of alienation and marginalization: the first was the gradual cognizance among religious Zionist youth that the time had come to challenge the secular Ashkenazi nation-founding stratum, identified with the Labor and leftist parties. The establishment of *Gush Emunim*, and the ensuing massive influx of national religious conscripts into the army as a counterbalance to youngsters from the kibbutzim, were two of the more notable aspects of this challenge. This factor overlapped with the secular Ashkenazi "motivation crisis," of which the "knitted skullcaps" took advantage, whether consciously or not, in order to stand out in the army and endeavor to replace the social stratum historically identified with the IDF.

This was a process with several stages. It started with the foundation of the *yeshivot hesder* ("arrangement academies")—a special program that enabled Torah study in a yeshiva alongside combat service in homogeneously religious companies—beginning in 1965 and expanding following the 1973 War.

It is important to recall that when the army was established the rabbis demanded that Prime Minister Ben-Gurion set up separate units for religious soldiers. Ben-Gurion refused, however, citing the ethos of the "people's army." It was only after his retirement that his successor, Levi Eshkol, saw fit to institute a separate framework in the shape of the *yeshivot hesder*. They were an apparatus that enabled the army to make a breakthrough in recruiting for combat duty a social group which it had previously not recruited, or which had preferred to staff rear positions, not infrequently owing to pressure from its rabbis, and which was therefore underrepresented in combat units. The rabbis' earlier reticence centered on their concern that religious youngsters would be exposed to the secularizing influences of the army, and that they would quite literally remove their skullcaps following their service or during it, a concern that had some basis in reality. The *yeshivot hesder* helped to overcome this resistance.

This process expanded after the First Lebanon War and coincided with the "motivation crisis" among secular Ashkenazi youth. Following the First Intifada this process progressed at an even faster pace: many religious youngsters, including religious Mizrachim, were recruited to regular army units, and not only to those associated with *yeshivot hesder*, and gained promotion through the ranks. One of the consequences of this was the removal of obstacles to a lengthy period of service in the standing army, a necessary condition for promotion through the ranks. These obstacles were faced by soldiers following the special *hesder* program, as it limited their possibilities for promotion.

Later, the army also allowed many of the religious conscripts to defer their induction so that they could study for a year at pre-military Torah colleges (*Mechinot*), the first of which was set up at the end of the 1980s, for "spiritual fortification" prior to their enlistment as a means of balancing out the army's secular influences. The establishment of these preparatory programs increased the religious legitimacy for enlistment to field units. According to published data, around 85 percent of their graduates sign up for combat duty, and 30 percent become officers, three times above the national average (Harel, 2003).

By the end of the 1990s, national religious soldiers started to appear among the ranks of senior officers, as well as strengthening their presence in field units, where they had filled about 30 percent of the junior command positions since the mid-1990s, more than their relative weight in the population, which stood at around 20 percent. These young men came both from Israel within the Green Line and from settlements in the West Bank and the Gaza Strip.

In parallel with these developments, and following years of being exempted from the army in order to study at yeshiva, the end of the 1990s also saw the establishment of the Ultra-Orthodox *Nahal* battalion. At first the battalion comprised people who had been emitted from Ultra-Orthodox yeshivas and who subsequently volunteered for military service. Later on they were joined by "knitted skullcaps." Their primary motivations in signing up were to learn a profession, to extract themselves from the margins of Ultra-Orthodox society, and to reap the financial rewards of military service (Drori, 2005, 79–82).

The recruitment of religious youngsters served the army at two levels. On the surface, it was required to overcome the lack of manpower caused by the expansion of the conscript army from the 1973 War and the First Lebanon War. On a deeper level, however, the army drew into its ranks what it perceived to be a pool of high-quality soldiers who remained loyal to the military way throughout the "motivation crisis," and who were motivated by their ethno-national ethos and the desire to attain parity with their secular peers. Yeshiva students thus came to fill a vacuum, though without making the political and material demands of their secular counterparts. It is unsurprising, therefore, that the proportion of religious youngsters in the army grew during the Al-Aqsa Intifada.

In other words, the army made political use of the yeshiva students at a time when it was embroiled in politically controversial fighting in Lebanon, which had driven away a considerable proportion of the secular Ashkenazim. In these circumstances, encouraging the enlistment of yeshiva students should not merely be seen as a manpower policy, but rather as the establishment of a contract. The terms of this contract revealed a willingness among religious youngsters to serve and make sacrifices, but not free of charge. What they received in return was the freedom to demarcate a pathway by which the rabbis and their students would leave their ideological mark on the army by molding its culture in a less secular direction, and make their military service a springboard for an ideological/religious mission, namely, protecting the borders of the "Greater Land of Israel." Military sacrifice was traded for new symbolic rewards. This calling, with its belligerent tone in the Lebanese arena, and later in the Palestinian one, was encouraged by the military, whose needs it suited very well.

Over the years the *hesder* and *mechina* rabbis were used by the army to "market" it to potential enlistees who otherwise would not have reached prestigious units. It was the army that operated rabbinical "mediators" in order to provide it with manpower whose commonly known political orientation was actually welcomed by the military, which was managing a politically controversial battle. As a result, it was the army itself that created what was sometimes called "the dual hierarchy"—the simultaneous subordination among part of the religious enlistees to both their officers and their rabbis. The army entered into a dialogue with the heads of the yeshivas over the terms and character of their students' service, which is not something it does with the leadership of most other social groups. This dialogue led the army to instigate cultural arrangements that made it easier to integrate religious youngsters into military service (also bearing in mind the parallel incorporation of women), and to recognize special enlistment programs as mentioned above. This had the effect of creating frameworks that were either homogenously or markedly religious. The IDF even came to terms with the fact that its religious officers did not make do with their professional service, but strove to stamp their values on the army too, as borne out by the public appearances of senior religious officers, some of whom aroused public controversy.

As the numbers of religious combat soldiers grew, their rabbis had a stronger position of power from which to negotiate with the army on various issues. In the 1990s this bargaining involved the call to refusal, that is, making military obedience conditional on the political character of the mission at hand, especially when the evacuation of territories perceived as holy is involved (see chapter 6) (the analysis drawn from Cohen, 1993; Cohen, 2004).

This survey of changes in the army suggests that the sociocultural meaning of military service deviated from materialistic and employment concerns. Military service directed a range of symbolic rewards to the new groups discussed above, or at least the expectation of them. These rewards lowered the expectations among members of those groups for immediate returns: material compensation, such as that anticipated by secular Ashkenazi groups, in return for symbolic compensation of a kind that matched their preferences. This no longer suited the secular Ashkenazi groups, and so they gradually left the military path. In other words, the new groups consolidated a new exchange system built on the provision of military sacrifice in return for high symbolic but low material rewards.

Accordingly, from the state's point of view, the Ashkenazi abandonment of the army was a problem, but also provided its solution. The army's new social architecture was the answer to its lack of soldiers who would be loyal to the army's mode of conduct. Military service gradually came to be based on social groups who had internalized the fundamentals of military culture and were supportive of the army's role in the Occupied Territories and elsewhere without stimulating their civilian social networks to act outside, or even against, the army, as long as it carried out belligerent missions. In contrast, the criticism of the IDF and the restrictions placed on its functioning from the 1980s were largely the result of secular Ashkenazi organizational activities. These organizations strove to subject the army's behavior to a logic that was at least partially nonmilitary, and even when it was military, it contradicted the army's organizational rationale. This formed the common ground of movements such as *Peace Now*, *Yesh Gvul*, *Soldiers against Silence*, and *Four Mothers*.

The IDF was not a passive actor, simply accepting its enlistees' changing orientations. Instead, it played an active role in creating arrangements that would actually make the army a multicultural site and thus encourage members of the new groups to join the forces, in other words, the army administered policies of diversity management (Lomsky-Feder and Ben-Ari, 1999). As special recruitment programs were established for women, Druze, Bedouins, Ultra-Orthodox, and more, special attention was paid to the recruitment of national religious youngsters to replace their departing secular counterparts. This kind of proactive approach also characterized the army's actions in other fields, such as specifically incentivizing peripheral groups, by developing the pre-army technology ROTC program designated for youngsters from underprivileged communities, for example, or establishing a fast-track conversion process for non-Jewish immigrants from the former Soviet Union, and offering financial support for soldiers from underprivileged families.

Therefore, with the attenuation of symbolic rewards, the cultural changes in the IDF became one of the ways to symbolically reward its recruits. At the same time, with the reduction of the symbolic rewards that were based on the conversion of resources from the military arena to the social one, enlistees and their social networks tended to focus on the terms of their service, that is, looking inward at the army and not outward from it. In other words, multiculturalism became an alternative symbolic reward.

This is not to imply, however, that the army initiated these processes in order to intentionally fill its ranks with loyal soldiers. However, the proactive incorporation of new groups, together with the army's satisfaction with the results, mean that it can be represented as a strategic architectural move, even if not an intentional one.

The state thus reformulated the republican equation, though from its perspective, at a lower cost: instead of allocating material and other rewards on the basis of military contribution, thus making military service more expensive, and instead of undercutting the army's autonomy by tempering its activities in order to slow down the departure of the secular Ashkenazi stratum, the state rewarded the new groups merely by making the army accessible to them in cultural and ideological terms. The embodiment of the traditional patterns of materialist militarism was set in motion with regard to the new groups.

The army does not publish data on its soldiers' ethnicity and class. Nonetheless, based on a variety of reports we can schematically posit that in the years following the new millennium, around 20 percent of the army's regular combat corps were Ashkenazi "knitted skullcaps," at least 20 percent were immigrants from the former Soviet Union, about 35 percent were

Mizrachim (including Mizrachi "knitted skullcaps"), about another 20 percent were secular Ashkenazim, with the remaining few percent made up of women, Bedouins, Druze, and Ethiopian and other immigrants (Levy, 2003b, 305–66). Mapping the casualties of the Al-Aqsa Intifada and the First Lebanon War can provide another indication of the army's realignment (see chapters 4 and 7).

As mentioned, the new architecture started taking shape in the 1980s at the same time as the first phase of conflict deescalation, and received a further boost in the mid-1990s following Oslo. As well as laying down an infrastructure for the recruitment of soldiers with higher motivation for combat duty, the architectural change also increased the army's ability to politically recruit passive support among ethno-nationalist groups for the peace process, or, at the very least, to weaken their opposition to it. An infrastructure was thus prepared for shaping the Oslo Accords as military agreements, and later on for escalating the violence against the Palestinians when the Accords would be beset by crisis.

THE OSLO ACCORDS AS MILITARY AGREEMENTS

Until the outbreak of the First Intifada (1987–1993), between the years 1967–1987 Israel gave relative civilian autonomy to Palestinian institutions in the Gaza Strip and West Bank as a means of controlling the population at a relatively low cost. Those institutions, however, failed to restrain the First Intifada. The Intifada broke out in 1987 as a popular uprising inspired by Palestinian political achievements in the First Lebanon War; it was also a response to increasing unemployment in the Palestinian labor market as a result of Israeli cutbacks, and a counterresponse to the Jewish settlement project in the West Bank that was dramatically expanded during the 1980s and comprised of about 60,000 settlers and more than 100 settlements.

Under instructions from the government, the army acted forcefully to suppress the Palestinian revolt. It failed to do so, however, succeeding only in curbing the uprising somewhat. Even this success was questioned when the first signs that the fighting was spilling over the Green Line appeared in the form of knifing attacks in 1992.

The Intifada brought the army into political warfare, not only in the sense that the fighting involved political aims, as is always the case, but in the sense that the theater of war was a political struggle for control over a population. Therefore, both aims and methods were involved in politics. This was a situation that threatened to fracture the ranks of the army, populated by soldiers from Israel's left and right wings. It also threatened to drive a wedge between military commanders and political forces that were in conflict over the appropriate strategy for the army to adopt—the left demanded that the army restrain its repressive activities, while the right called for wiping out the civilian uprising via military means. This heightened the effects of the 1973 and First Lebanon Wars, both of which had harmed the army's symbolic status. Cracks in the army's unity were added to by additional factors, such as policing missions, bereft of the glory of combat and without existential meaning. These missions also involved problematic behavior on the part of the army (the abuse of a civilian population, sometimes the subject of public and legal approbation), all the more so given that it was portrayed as ineffective, and the soldiers carrying it out were increasingly seen as failing in a struggle against a militarily inferior population. Moreover, much of the work was delegated to reserve units, by now worn out following the First Lebanon War, which only served to strengthen the feeling of crisis surrounding the Intifada. As mentioned in chapter 2, moreover, the Intifada even further devalued the fruits of occupation with the waning ability to economically exploit the Occupied Territories. As a result, political protests were renewed with fresh vigor, led by *Peace Now* and *Yesh Gvul* (see mainly Ben-Eliezer, 2001, 70–71; Helman, 1999; Peri, 1990).

Concerned about the possibility of an internal split in the army, the Chief of the General Staff at the time, Dan Shomron, declared that the Intifada could only be resolved by political means. In doing so he contributed to the restraint of military force and laid the ground for finding such a solution. By making Israel's rule over the Occupied Territories more costly, with the entailed violation of the republican equation, the path to Oslo was laid. However, this could not happen until the hawkish *Likud* government, led by Yitzhak Shamir (Prime Minister Begin's heir), had been replaced by a Labor government under Yitzhak Rabin in 1992.

Rabin had been the celebrated Chief of the General Staff during the Six Day War, and was a former Prime Minister and Defense Minister. He made a commitment to bring an end to the Intifada, which by then had gradually spread from the West Bank into Israeli towns.

The Oslo model was born out of secret talks held during 1993 between Israel and the PLO under Norwegian patronage, concluded in the Declaration of Principles that was signed in November 1993 on the lawn of the White House, and sealed with the historic handshake between Yitzhak Rabin and Yasser Arafat under the auspices of President Clinton. By this declaration, both parties agreed to establish a Palestinian autonomy in the West Bank and the Gaza Strip. The model was founded on the belief held by Rabin and his military advisors that a new functional division of labor needed to be implemented in the Occupied Territories: Israel would maintain its external military control (demilitarization along with responsibility for the borders, airspace, access to the sea and water resources, and more), while the Palestinian leadership would be entrusted with authority over internal security. Its job would be to put down terrorist organizations in place of Israel, which had failed to do so. Rabin believed that the Palestinians would do it better than Israel; or as he famously said, "without the Supreme Court of Justice and without B'Tselem [a human rights group]." Moreover, should the Palestinian Authority fall short of proving its military capabilities, the Oslo Accords were seen as reversible, and the Territories could be reconquered (Inbar, 2004, 201–6).

To a large extent, as delineated by the Israeli team (led by Foreign Minister and ex-Prime Minister Shimon Peres and his deputy, Yossi Beilin), the original Oslo agreement rested on foundations of civilian thought. This mode of thought placed the economy, and not the army, at the center of foreign politics, and preferred to establish Palestinian interests on military quiet rather than permanent Israeli military control. This thinking was influenced by Peres' vision of the "New Middle East"—a new regional order founded on economic cooperation. However, after a short civilian intermezzo, the army resumed its lead of the diplomatic process. A new form of indirect Israeli military rule of the Occupied Territories was stabilized, one that was combined with economic control (see Grinberg, 2002). The army, whose status had been tarnished during the First Intifada, thus returned to its leading position. How is this to be explained?

The explanation for the temporary rehabilitation of the army's status does not necessarily lie in Rabin's affinity with the army and his desire to use the Oslo process to improve its standing and halt the neutralization of its impact on Israeli statesmanship. After all, had Rabin wanted to, he could have involved the army in talks with the PLO from the outset, instead of fully delegating the process to "civilian" politicians. Rather, the explanation lies in the army's new role in counteracting the ethno-nationalist coalition, the emergence of which was dealt with in the previous chapter.

The ethno-nationalist discourse, which had originated following the Six Day War, strengthened from the second half of 1980s as a reaction to globalization, the withdrawal of the welfare state as expressed in the Economic Stabilization Plan of 1985 with the institutionalization of unemployment, the partial withdrawal from Lebanon (in 1985), and the eruption of the First Intifada. The Oslo Accords provided a more significant impetus, and bolstered the attempt to reinforce ethno-Jewish identity. This in turn embodied the attempt at halting efforts toward peace and liberalization-globalization, which accompanied, and maybe even spearheaded, the peace process. Peace-with-globalization, with its inherent social and economic structural reforms, was portrayed as a typical "Ashkenazi" creation, which barred broad social segments from shaping it, and certainly from enjoying its benefits (Raz-Krakotzkin, 2000). The process even carried a threat—real or imagined—to sections of those excluded groups for a number of reasons: it was perceived to threaten their array of Jewish symbols, which were historically nourished by the cultivation of animosity with the Arab world; their affinity to the idea of the "Land of Israel" which the government actually abandoned in Oslo; their civil status as compared to that of the Palestinian citizens, whose standing improved as a result of the Accords; and their ability to make a living now that processes of globalization were bringing about the relocation of labor-intensive industries to Arab countries, the West Bank, and the Gaza Strip.

Those years also saw the unprecedented sharpening of the contradictory meanings of the concept of a "Jewish-democratic state." This could be seen, for example, in the way that the idea of equal civil rights impinged on sensitive issues, such as limiting the ability of Palestinian citizens to purchase land and houses in Jewish communities. The contradiction between "Jewish" and "democratic" was built in to Israel's political order from the outset (when the state absorbed the Palestinian minority in 1949), but was now being sharpened in the political discourse.

The political union of the ethno-national groups created an (informal) ethno-national coalition. This coalition included peripheral Mizrachim (mainly organized through *Shas*); semi-peripheral Mizrachim (part of the *Likud*); the "knitted skullcaps" (the National Religious Party, the right-wing *Moledet* party, and other satellite parties); most of the immigrants from the former Soviet Union (the "Russian" parties, which were ethno-national in the national, but not in the religious sense); and the Ultra-Orthodox (*Shas*, *Agudat Yisrael*, and its offshoots). In short, this coalition comprised about one-half of the electorate, among which were the more organized political groups, such as the settlers and the Ultra-Orthodox. Largely by means of electoral politics (ousting Shimon Peres and Ehud Bark from the Prime Minister's office in the elections of 1996 and 2001 respectively), this coalition succeeded in slowing down the Oslo process.

From the 1990s onward, the two discursive schemas—ethno-nationalism versus the market economy—were simultaneously and conflictually enacted by different wings of Israeli society, to the extent that it became very difficult to explicitly decide politically disputed issues. Consequently, the remilitarization of one part of the society was taking place just as another part was becoming demilitarized (for different aspects of the conflict between the ethoses see Calderon, 2000; Grinberg, 2000; Kimmerling, 2001; Liebman, 1989; Ram, 2005; Raz-Krakotzkin, 2000; Shafir and Peled, 2002).

With the intensification of the ethno-national discourse from the 1980s, the political role of the military shifted. From the very beginnings of the state's existence to the first withdrawal from Lebanon, the army initiated escalatory moves: from the retaliatory raids that led to the Sinai Campaign in 1956, through the escalation that led to the Six Day War and the stabilization of the occupation that led to the 1973 War, to the instigation of the First Lebanon War. As mentioned above, the army's privileged status, part of the supremacy of military thinking in politics, was explained in terms of the emergent congruence between the military agenda and a broad range of social interests. Predominant in this was the army's role in helping to dampen ethno-class tensions, thus reproducing the inegalitarian social structure. This task was made conditional on giving the army a central status, alongside its role in nurturing the fruits of the occupations of 1948 and 1967, enjoyed by many social groups. This was the essence of materialist militarism.

In the 1980s the fruits of war declined and the market economy created alternative mechanisms for maintaining ethno-class calm and reshaping the social criterion. On the one hand, the army adapted itself to this change in its status and began restraining the political echelon, or at least cooperating with it in heading moderating political processes. On the other hand, the army still maintained central components of its privileged status by becoming a mediator between social groups belonging to the ethno-national coalition and the state. In practice, the army was expected to provide military legitimacy to the state's controversial and relatively dovish policies.

The ethno-national discourse challenged rational military thinking by positing an alternative approach that subjected security concerns, including shaping the state's borders, to considerations to do with the "Greater Land of Israel," control over what were seen as holy sites, and ensuring Jewish demographic hegemony in the State of Israel. Moreover, even at the beginning of the Oslo process calls could be heard from a small number of rabbis for soldiers to refuse to evacuate territories in the West Bank; in other words, an attempt was made to subjugate the army's operational conduct, including military discipline, to theological considerations (Kimmerling, 1993).

Nonetheless, even though the ethno-national coalition confronted and criticized rational military thinking, it did not negate it entirely, and military thought was still located somewhere between ethno-national challenges and civilian-political thought. The latter aimed at making concessions in order to end the Arab-Israeli conflict, offering justifications such as ending the occupation, seeing the economy as the primary means for managing international politics, acknowledging the role of the international community in preserving the world order, placing humanitarian restrictions on military force, and so on. Not only did these patterns alienate the ethno-national coalition, the coalition even invoked them as part of rhetoric aimed at undermining the legitimacy of political concessions. As mentioned, the original Oslo agreement was based on some of the foundations of that mode of thinking, but only for a short time. Moreover, for most segments in the ethno-national coalition, the army remained an important symbol deserving of continued respect, particularly as a site that enabled mobility for the coalition's constituent groups, as illustrated by the army's new social architecture.

The army's part in recruiting the ethno-national coalition increased for as long as both right- and left-wing governments abstained from constructing a social agenda that incorporated a strategy for ending the conflict. Rabin had been one of the first architects of the amalgamation of peace and globalization. Indeed, he tied in the first withdrawal from Lebanon (in return for generous American subsidies) with the "Stabilization Plan" of 1985, which accelerated the gradual transformation of the Israeli economy into a market economy. Ever since then, military retreats have been combined with the retreat of the welfare state and the consolidation of the foundations of the market economy.

It was in these circumstances that the army became the institution that bridged the gap between the state's neoliberal social and economic policies and the interests of the social periphery, from which the ethno-national coalition drew much of its strength. During those years, the other institution that had traditionally mediated between the periphery and the state, namely, the *Histadrut*—the federal umbrella organization for Israel's workers' unions—had been atrophying as a result of financial distress and structural reform, thus intensifying the army's significance in this respect. The army attained this mediating role because it was a site for mobility, and thus for self-expression for groups that lacked alternative apparatuses, including political means.

Therefore, respecting the army's status, including accepting its professionally cloaked involvement in political moves, became, to a point, a structural interest among ethno-national groups. Were they not to respect the army's status, they would be strengthening its political image, which would lay bare its symbolic status, thus turning it into an exclusively professional sector. Weakening the army's symbolic status would also undermine the significance of those groups' achievements, or their potential for achievements, in the organization. In a political army, achievements in the battlefield would lose part of their value, as the test of military service would lose what was left of its ability to provide access to civil rights. This conclusion is not based on explicit statements made by spokespersons for those groups, but rather on interpretations of their behavior, central to which was the respectful attitude these groups maintained toward the IDF and their utmost endeavors to leave it out of political debate. Interestingly, even *Shas*, which practically confronted military symbols, refrained from clashing with the institution itself, through which many of its supporters established a path of mobility.

In summary, the exchange arrangements latent in the army's new social architecture—military sacrifice in return for symbolic rewards for religious and peripheral groups—laid the foundations for strengthening the state's internal autonomy in implementing political, and not just military, processes. Thus, the state's ability to realize a dovish policy that contradicted the subjective interests of the groups that made up the ethno-national coalition was made conditional on the ability of the political leadership to recruit the army's support. Put negatively, the army's indirect or especially explicit resistance to moderate political initiatives could have goaded the ethno-national coalition into political activity, as a move that had been given legitimacy owing to the IDF's stand.

If the political leadership wished to reduce its dependency on the army, the only alternative was to change the direction of social policy. It is not for nothing that political leaderships tend to strengthen the welfare state after war in order to balance out the surplus power accumulated by the army (Andreski, 1968). It would appear that the Israeli political leadership did not internalize this affinity, instead making a historical decision to position the army center stage at the same time as speeding up the weakening of the welfare state. This made the two processes dependent on one another: the army served as a mechanism for recruiting those groups most affected by the retreat of the welfare state. This was the juncture that was reached in the 1990s.

On a practical level, Rabin internalized the link between recruiting support from the army and the ability to recruit the ethno-national groups. His government did not in any way deal with the political mobilization of the social periphery, instead making do with investing in physical infrastructures. He paid no regard to cultural aspects, and did not enter into dialogue with the groups that represented the periphery. During those years the welfare state was strengthened in only two ways—the education budget was expanded, and child benefits were raised and no longer made dependent on military service. However, privatization was accelerated, the minimum wage remained low, and capital gains remained untaxed, while company taxes and employers' payments to the National Insurance Institute were reduced. As a result, the Oslo years heralded increased social inequality (Swirski et al., 1998).[2]

At the same time, the peace process became a kind of ongoing and extroverted celebration for the business community and government ministers (Ben-Porat, 2005). The unequal distribution of the fruits of Oslo nourished the ethno-national coalition, and would later bring about the election of Benjamin Netanyahu as Prime Minister (in 1996). In other words, as the welfare state was weakened, the political dependency of the "peace camp" on political mobilization via the army increased. It is not surprising, therefore, that we can see a clear correlation between increased opposition to the Oslo process and the expansion of the army's freedom of operation, as shall now be described.

THE ARMY'S ROLE IN OSLO

At first the army was entirely excluded from the process that brought about the Oslo Accords and had no influence over its outcome. It had been possible to neutralize the army by conducting secret diplomatic negotiations that aroused no public antagonism, and quickly ratifying them in a surprised Knesset. The Oslo Accords were the result of secret diplomacy managed by Foreign Minster Shimon Peres and his deputy, Yossi Beilin, under the direction of Prime Minister Rabin. The army was informed via intelligence it picked up from Palestinian sources, and had no influence at decisive junctures of the process (Sagie, 1998, 184–87). Accordingly, figures from the military criticized the Oslo Accords for being overly guided by diplomatic thought; the map it drew was like "Swiss cheese, full of holes," they said. The then Chief of the General Staff, Ehud Barak, also fundamentally refuted the possibility of intermediate agreements. Nonetheless, in a spirit of pragmatism and utilitarianism, the general attitude among the heads of the army was positive, and a number of generals even expressed public support for the principles embodied by the Accords and their basic logic, and set about implementing them.

The second stage began when the program was made public and opposition began to appear. Simultaneously, *Shas*—the only representative of peripheral groups in the government—left the coalition. At the same time, it became incumbent on the army to conduct talks with representatives of the PLO regarding the implementation of the Declaration of Principles. Involving the army in negotiations was the Prime Minister's direct response to public criticism (Caspit, 2001). Rabin could have set up a special civilian department within his office for planning and carrying out the talks (as previous Defense Ministers had done), but instead he chose to rely on the military. Given the army's organizational capabilities, and Rabin's personal experience from taking part in the Rhodes armistice talks in 1949 when still a soldier, this could appear to have been a natural move for him (Peri, 2002, 25–29). However, because Rabin was reshaping the profile of future arrangements, this decision requires deeper understanding from the perspective proposed in this chapter. The army, which was then running the West Bank and Gaza Strip by means of military administration, was given responsibility for diplomacy, the desired outcome of which was purportedly the end of military occupation. However, this actually strengthened the infrastructure for shaping mechanisms of indirect or "refined" occupation, rather than realizing an alternative, political paradigm, conditional on civilian, not military, management of the negotiations. We should note that later on, when Benjamin Netanyahu was Prime Minister, negotiations over similar issues (such as evacuating Hebron in 1997) were taken out of the army's hands and delegated to the Ministry of Foreign Affairs and the Prime Minister's emissaries.

During 1994, opposition to Oslo among members of the ethno-national coalition increased. By this point the army had become the major implementing body of the Accords while interpreting the Declaration of Principles from its military point of view. Disagreements between the army and the Ministry of Foreign Affairs were usually settled in favor of the military approach. The military interpretation of the Accords had a number of aspects: (1) the army controlled the pace of the establishment of the Palestinian Authority; (2) the army decided on the date of Yasser Arafat's arrival in the Occupied Territories, an event that symbolized the formation of the Authority; (3) the army controlled the timing of elections, which were conditioned on its withdrawal from the Palestinian cities; (4) the army translated Israel's commitment to withdrawal as a redeployment of IDF forces in the Occupied Territories. Furthermore, while it had been agreed that army and police bases located outside Palestinian population concentrations would remain under Israeli control, the army interpreted this as applying to much larger territories; (5) the army insisted on retaining control over border crossings between the Palestinian Authority's territories and Jordan and Egypt, thus subjecting them to a form of indirect occupation; (6) arrangements were made that allowed the IDF to enter areas controlled by the Palestinian Authority in order to pursue suspects, and the army enforced joint Israeli-Palestinian patrols in areas under Palestinian security control.

In contrast to the army's interpretation, the Declaration of Principles had originally intended that the IDF withdraw in a way that would create Palestinian territorial contiguity. This was not only meant to assist in the Palestinian Authority's economic development and prevent humiliating encounters with the army, but mainly to forge a dialogue between equals, and not between occupier and occupied. The Cairo Agreement of May 1994, however, which saw the implementation of the Oslo Accords in the Gaza Strip and Jericho, was entirely formulated as a military arrangement (see Caspit, 2001; Pundak, 2001; Savir, 1998, 115–44).

Following the Cairo Agreement and the start of negotiations on the implementation of the Accords in West Bank cities (Oslo B), opposition to the agreements in Israel further increased. In the summer of 1994 the first mass rally was held in Jerusalem's Zion Square in which the decision makers' legitimacy was undermined. Against this background, negotiations over the signing of the Oslo B Accords were also led by the army, together with the General Security Services (the *Shabak*). This agreement (the "Taba Agreement" of September 1995), raised military dominance a notch by creating a new form of occupation. Crucially, the Jewish settlement project was made permanent, around which indirect Israeli military rule would continue. In practice, the agreement divided the West Bank into three separate administrative areas, with only one category ("Area A") designated for (partial) Palestinian rule. The IDF's thinking was short term and focused on ongoing security concerns. This led it to create the category of Area B, defined as territory under Israeli security control and Palestinian civilian rule, as part of an attempt to reach a compromise with settlers residing near to Palestinian cities. However, this merely created sites of violent friction.[3] The Taba Agreement also established the composition of the Palestinian Legislative Council and the principle of "safe passage" between the West Bank and the Gaza Strip.

The arrangements that the army shaped were an attempt at dealing with the contradiction between setting up the Palestinian Authority as a statelike entity on the one hand, and leaving the Jewish settlements in place on the other. In leaving the settlement project in place, the military foundations of the agreements were fortified, because it denied the Palestinian Authority territorial contiguity, and the presence of IDF forces in the Occupied Territories was made permanent as a means to protect the settlers. Moreover, the Palestinian security forces were perceived as "operational contractors" for the IDF and the *Shabak*. Their relationship with the Israeli security forces was grounded in understandings between the two sides, the transfer of funds from Israel to the Palestinian Authority, the granting of permission to Palestinian security personnel to bear arms, and the provision of intelligence and professional support. Meanwhile, the army developed a system of encirclements and roadblocks around Palestinian towns, which were tightened whenever the Palestinian Authority displayed operational deficiencies.

In sum, the military approach illustrated Israel's lack of a strategy for building a Palestinian state (see Zureik, 2001), which could have given the Palestinian Authority, a state in the making, more sophisticated tools for preventing threats on Israel. Shimon Peres' civilian-economic vision of the privatization of peace and of the "New Middle East" was demeaned. Especially so, as the business community's primary concern was to see the restrictions of the Arab boycott lifted, and not necessarily regional development. Hence it was not particularly interested in the militaristic implementation of the agreements (Selby, 2005).

The decision to leave the settlement project untouched, including the refusal to evacuate isolated settlements or even extremist elements in Hebron (following Baruch Goldstein's massacre of Muslim worshippers in the Cave of the Patriarchs in February 1994), had a similar origin to the army's empowerment, namely, fear of confronting the organizational capabilities of the settlers. This apprehension was a feature of Rabin's first government (which failed to cope with the establishment of illegal settlements) and continued into his second. In both instances the government acted as if acknowledging that it could not legitimately deal with the settlement project. Accordingly, the years 1993–1996 saw the number of settlers in the West Bank increase by about 40 percent (Lein, 2002), under the auspices of an agreement between Rabin and the Bush administration that froze the establishment of new settlements but did not prevent existing ones from expanding. This project, including laying down a system of bypass roads that allowed settlers freedom of movement through the heart of the Palestinian population, was managed by the army, and not by civilian government offices as in the past.

Mass resistance increased during the talks over Oslo B, which were later brought to a temporary halt with the assassination of Prime Minister Rabin in November 1995. Following the assassination, attempts were made at reconciliation between the leaderships of the secular center-left and the ethno-national coalition, and the role of the military was therefore strengthened. The army started to carry out invasive operations in Palestinian Authority territories in response to the terror attacks of March 1996, and in an attempt to push President Arafat into restraining the military wing of *Hamas*. These incursions were followed by *Operation Grapes of Wrath* in Lebanon, aimed at forcing the population of South Lebanon to put pressure on Hezbollah by subjecting the region to aerial bombardments. Israel's internal "reconciliation" after the assassination also had the character of an aggressive militaristic policy.

The complementary foundation of the political leadership's dependency on the military was its abstention from any efforts at instigating structural reforms in the army, or at significantly cutting back its budget. The vision of a "small and intelligent army" that some generals voiced at that time—downsizing the army, including changing its model of recruitment, alongside professionalization and increased usage of technology—was not realized. Rabin's main cutback in military spending was at the time of the partial withdrawal from Lebanon in 1985. That withdrawal was overseen by a Labor-*Likud* unity government and enjoyed relatively wide support, which reduced the dependency of the political echelon on the army.

This is not to argue that Rabin consciously linked the social power structure to the utilization of the IDF in controversial sites. Indeed, this is a pattern that is well rooted in the "institutional heritage" that perceives the "people's army" as the preferred way of legitimizing politically contentious policies, precisely because it is a "people's army." This institutional heritage had developed along with the establishment of the state, and like any such heritage it had emerged from a series of events that shaped a certain path while rejecting alternatives by means of "trial and error." To the extent that the chosen path produces satisfactory results for the relevant actors, it reshapes or solidifies the institutional heritage and restricts policy making in the future. The institutional heritage shapes a repertoire of desirable actions that can be called upon at a time of political crisis. In this instance, the repertoire included deploying the army to stifle the ethno-national coalition during the Oslo years, to dealing with the Al-Aqsa Intifada. It is this institutional heritage that, a decade after Rabin's assassination, would turn the army into the effective executioner of the withdrawal from the Gaza Strip and the northern West Bank, including the evacuation of Jewish settlements in those areas (for different theoretical aspects see: Johnston, 1995; Krasner, 1984; Levy, 1997a; Tilly, 1997b).

The unequal distribution of the fruits of Oslo nourished the ethno-national coalition and brought about the election of Benjamin Netanyahu as Prime Minister in 1996, and the defeat of Shimon Peres, who had succeeded Rabin following his assassination. This was portrayed as "the rebellion of the new elites," that is, as an ethnic-Jewish attack on the old-new Israeliness historically identified with Ashkenazi statism, the ideology of the "melting pot," and now with globalization (Ben-Ami, 1998, 334–39; Ben Simon, 1997; Filc, 1996). Netanyahu managed to recruit the ethno-national coalition and win the election by systematically attacking the Oslo agreements. Even though he proposed a neoliberal economic policy even more stringent than that of his predecessors, Netanyahu succeeded in reconstituting the identity of members of the coalition as part of a united social force defending itself against external threats, such as the terror attacks of 1996 and the threats of globalization (Filc, 1996).

For its part, the army was not only acting to mobilize the ethno-national coalition as in the days of Rabin and Peres, but became the main supporter of the Oslo process as against Netanyahu. To a large extent, the army had been trapped by its support for Oslo, and this grasp tightened for as long as it was criticized by Netanyahu's coalition. The army did not necessarily support Oslo because of its support for the process in and of itself, but rather, and perhaps mainly, as an oppositional counterreaction to Netanyahu, whose attack on the Oslo process was interpreted as an attack on the army that had been identified with its implementation. The Oslo process reinvigorated the coalition between the army and the center-left representative of the Ashkenazi middle class, against the ethno-national coalition that had put Netanyahu in power.

Therefore, while his predecessors had mobilized the army in order to neutralize the ethno-national coalition, Netanyahu needed the IDF to retain a high level of legitimacy for his administration in relation to the forces identified with the secular Ashkenazi elites and the interests of the market economy that they represented, forces that opposed Netanyahu. This came at the cost of military restraint, and forged a complex balance of power: on the one hand, Netanyahu, as a hawkish politician, displayed reluctance to make concessions to the Palestinians when it came to implementing the Oslo agreements. On the other hand, the army kept him in check lest he should translate his diplomatic steadfastness into military aggression, especially after the troubling clashes following the "Western Wall Tunnel" incident in the autumn of 1996.[4]

This shows the army's dual character: while the highest military ranks at that time mostly came from the secular Ashkenazi middle class and mobile Mizrachim, the combatants were being recruited to an ever increasing extent from the social periphery and ethno-nationalist groups. The army's new social architecture enabled the mobilization of these groups as a way of legitimizing a moderate military-diplomatic policy, which, paradoxically, alienated the civilian social networks from which the soldiers were recruited. At the same time, the composition of the senior command prevented the political leadership from initiating and implementing belligerent policies that contradicted the interests of the market, that is, of the class from which the high ranking officers had been drawn.

As a result of this balance of power, not only did Netanyahu's government formally acknowledge the Oslo Accords and carry out a controversial withdrawal from Hebron, it actually internalized the military logic upon which they were founded. This was a logic that entrusted the reining in of Palestinian terror organizations to the Palestinian Authority, which Israel was arming, while Israel withdrew most of its military control from civilian population centers. By insisting that the Palestinian Authority respect its own commitments and hold back the terrorist organizations ("If they give, they'll get," as Netanyahu famously said) without Israel invasively harming its sovereignty (unlike the Rabin-Peres government previously, and the Barak government subsequently), Netanyahu's government helped strengthen the Palestinian Authority's internal rule and tighten security cooperation between the sides. The consequence was a tiny number of terror attacks between the years 1996–2000. The seal of legitimacy that Netanyahu's government stamped on the Oslo process, alongside its contribution to strengthening the logic upon which it was based, were more important than the government not fully implementing Oslo B (particularly completing a withdrawal from the West Bank) and its ongoing support for the settler project, albeit at a significantly lower level than that of Rabin and Peres' government (the number of settlers rose by only 25 percent as compared to 40 percent under Rabin-Peres [Lein, 2002]).

By confusing facts with nostalgia, those who remember the period prior to Rabin's assassination with fondness paint a rosy picture of a systematic process of statesmanship that, were it not for the assassination, would have gained momentum. This description ignores the signs of its slowdown toward the end of Rabin's term. The Oslo Accords were designed as a quick process that was ratified and implemented before the right wing, which had been taken by surprise, could organize its opposition, and without Rabin's government concerning itself with recruiting widespread support. Right-wing resistance increased after the signing of Oslo B, which relinquished control over cities in the West Bank, thus signifying the end of the vision of the "Greater Land of Israel." Mass protest increased, which intensified and hardened around the ratification of the agreements in the Knesset. This protest would undoubtedly have increased as the withdrawal from the West Bank cities drew nearer, and would have trickled down to the army. Even then rabbis were appealing to conscript soldiers to refuse to take part in the evacuation of military bases in the West Bank. It is quite likely that this pressure would have intensified, making it harder for the government to implement the Oslo Accords. It would certainly have slowed down any progress toward the next stages. Even if Rabin had planned on seeing through an accelerated political process following Oslo B, it is more likely that he would have had to proceed much more slowly. Of course, this is a tentative interpretation of a historical process, but it is worth positing it against Israel's collective memory, which seems to have erased those aspects that may have threatened the advance of Oslo even if Rabin had not been assassinated.

Paradoxically, Rabin's murder enabled the rapid withdrawal from most of the cities in the West Bank. The right wing, temporarily stunned by the force of the assassination, struggled to pick itself up, thus making it easier for Prime Minister Peres to implement the withdrawal. However, trends to halt the Oslo process gradually gained strength once more, and one can assume that had he been re-elected Prime Minister in 1996, Peres would have been unable to prevent them from neutralizing his government. Nowhere is this seen more clearly than in Peres' hesitancy in following in his predecessor's footsteps. On the one hand, he did not evacuate Hebron, as required by Oslo B; he stopped the peace process with the Palestinians (he rejected the "Beilin Abu-Mazen Document" with its principles for a final status agreement); and he even missed the opportunity to make peace with Syria when he cut off talks that were being held under the auspices of the United States. At the same time, he unnecessarily escalated military reactions to the Palestinian Authority, not to mention *Operation Grapes of Wrath* in Lebanon, in which the bombardment of South Lebanon and the suffering of its citizens were seen as a means of applying pressure on Hezbollah, which itself had been bombing settlements in the Galilee.

Although Netanyahu's government was instrumental in legitimizing the Oslo agreements, it also acted under the influence of the ethno-national coalition that had put him in power. Thus, the government desisted from carrying out the little it could to advance the political process (such as implementing the Wye Plantation Agreement of 1998 regarding Israel's withdrawals from the West Bank), and bringing forward the withdrawal from Lebanon. Thus, the Oslo Accords created the infrastructure for the outbreak of the Al-Aqsa Intifada.

THE AL-AQSA INTIFADA

The Al-Aqsa Intifada broke out during Ehud Barak's term as Prime Minister following the failure to arrive at a final agreement during the Camp David talks in the summer of 2000. The talks were held between Barak and Arafat under the auspices of President Clinton. Ariel Sharon's visit, as the *Likud* leader, to the Temple Mount served as the trigger for the riots.

When the violence erupted, the army systematically acted to escalate its response to the uprising. The opening moves of the Intifada mainly involved Palestinian attacks on symbols of the occupation—IDF positions near Palestinian towns, and isolated settlements. Not all of these attacks involved the use of firearms, and they were mostly carried out by forces that were not part of the Palestinian Authority. Nonetheless, the IDF adopted a policy of heavy gunfire aimed at harming Palestinian Authority institutions and the *Fatah* organization, which were held responsible for the uprising, even though the initial instigators of the violence came from other groups.

The Israeli response exacted a large number of fatalities on the Palestinian side, with only a few casualties to Israel. In return, attacks on Israel were escalated from demonstrations to firing on roads and settlements, and later on to terror attacks against civilians beyond the Green Line. From October 2000 the army began its unprecedented use of combat helicopters against Palestinian city-center headquarters; later on fighter planes would also be deployed. At the same time, aerial assassinations were employed that targeted those suspected of planning to initiate terror attacks. Every now and then a cease-fire would be declared, arrangements would be made to reduce the violence, and an internal dynamic in the Palestinian political system would often be created for restraining violent forces. A number of times the Palestinian Authority enjoyed relative success in reining in its organizations, and even came to certain understandings with them. However, because it never achieved a total cease-fire, the Israeli side was never satisfied. Deviating from the instructions of the political echelon, the IDF itself put paid to a number of cease-fires and agreements. Sometimes, army operations would interfere with internal Palestinian processes to temper the violence. All the while the blockade of West Bank cities was tightened, breaking the territorial contiguity of the Palestinian Authority, and causing heavy human suffering and economic damage to the civilian population (this description is based on: Caspit, 2002; Druker and Shelah, 2005, 28–53; Harel and Yissacharoff, 2004, 35–38; Meital, 2004, 148; Morris, 2001, 664–69; Peri, 2006, 91–108).

An immediate consequence was a reduction in the Palestinian Authority's ability, not to mention its motivation and legitimacy, to assume the role assigned to it by the Oslo framework, namely, to rein in acts of terror on the part of radical Muslim groups. In response, the Israeli military and political leadership held the Palestinian Authority responsible for the collapse of Oslo. Absurdly, the Israeli solution was to intensify the breakdown of the Palestinian Authority rather than working toward its rehabilitation ("politicide," in Kimmerling's terms, 2003).

The most significant escalation was in March 2001, shortly after the establishment of Ariel Sharon's *Likud*-Labor government with the participation of Shimon Peres, one of the architects of Oslo, when political talks with the Palestinian Authority were suspended. The circle of violence gradually expanded, taking the form of the renewal and, later on, the significant intensification of acts of terror in Israeli cities, which had virtually ceased between 1996–2000. These acts caused serious harm to Israel: hundreds of civilians were killed, thousands were wounded, and the economy was gravely damaged. As expected, the Palestinians paid a dramatically higher price, with thousands of fatalities and casualties, and the collapse of governmental and economic systems.

The final attempt made by the Palestinian Authority, under heavy international pressure, to reestablish its power was also impaired with no little "help" from Israel. The period December 2001 to January 2002 was one of relative calm, during which the Palestinian Authority made greater efforts than before to get Palestinian groups to hold their fire (as reflected in a 75 percent reduction in attacks). However, it was disrupted when the IDF killed one of the prominent *Tanzim* leaders, Ra'ad Carmi, thus reigniting the violence. If previously it had cooperated with the cease-fire, this time, the *Tanzim*—a force made up of the younger generation of the *Fatah* organization—headed efforts at attacking Israel, efforts which resulted in the heavy wave of terror attacks during Passover of 2002, most notably the attack on celebrants at the Park Hotel in Netanya (Druker and Shelah, 2005, 170–74; Harel and Yissacharoff, 2004, 184–88, 213–15). During the period of calm, the President of Israel, Moshe Katsav, was even invited to address the Palestinian Legislative Council in Ramallah as part of efforts to promote the cease-fire (the *Hudna*). However, the Israeli government prevented him from doing so.

The Passover attacks and the Palestinian power vacuum pushed the IDF into embarking on *Operation Defensive Shield* (in April 2002), during which the army temporarily reoccupied cities in the West Bank, only withdrawing in response to American pressure. Despite the withdrawal, talks were not resumed with the Palestinian Authority, and no efforts were made at rehabilitating its sovereignty. As a result, terror attacks resumed a number of weeks after the operation. From that point until the time of writing the army has entered cities in the West Bank from time to time, and they have been placed under de facto military rule, while the IDF has avoided entering the cities in the Gaza Strip.

A spiral process thus took shape: the IDF attacks the Palestinian Authority and its institutions, security forces, and sovereignty; the Palestinian Authority's ability to rein in terror is thus weakened, and terror attacks increase; Israel holds the Palestinian Authority responsible and escalates its punitive actions against it and other Palestinian organizations, thus further weakening their ability to rein in terror attacks; and so on and so forth, until the Palestinian Authority collapses. In short, military logic brought about its own self-destruction: the exertion of excessive military force led to the collapse of the mechanisms by which the Palestinian Authority controlled its security forces, mechanisms which had proved their efficiency in serving Israel's security interests between the years 1996–2000.

Despite the army's active role, there is no evidence that it developed an agenda for bringing down the Oslo regime, which it had actually constructed itself. Shaul Mofaz's tenure as Chief of the General Staff, which overlapped with the Intifada, was even characterized by a rhetoric of turning the military into a "peace army." These were also years when the army began to initiate and implement internal organizational reforms. On the other hand, the militaristic thought behind Oslo served as a catalyst for instigating and escalating the Al-Aqsa Intifada. The key to this does not lie in Barak's maneuverings at Camp David. It may be that he erred in trying to accelerate negotiations so as to reach a final and permanent agreement before the Palestinians were ripe for it and without them being properly prepared (see Barak, 2005); however, this alone was not enough to stimulate such a violent response from the Palestinians to the extent that the Palestinian Authority lost control over its armed elements while still conducting diplomatic negotiations. Equally, the failure of the negotiations does not explain the IDF's excessively forceful response to the renewed Palestinian uprising.

Rather, the key lies in the conditions created by the military shaping of the Oslo Accords across a number of dimensions. First, the Al-Aqsa Intifada was in part a popular revolt against the model by which the Palestinian Authority was run under Israeli supervision. Inasmuch as this model generated a mini-state that lacked territorial contiguity and that was indirectly controlled by the occupying mechanisms of the IDF, its leadership lacked full legitimacy, especially given the extremely difficult conditions of the Palestinians' day-to-day lives (Morris, 2001, 662–64). Legitimacy problems gave rise to internal challenges. In many ways, the riots that sparked the Al-Aqsa Intifada were the result of competition between *Fatah-Tanzim*, which challenged what was known as the Palestinian Authority's "Tunisian leadership," and *Hamas*, which had developed an alternative institutional network to the Palestinian Authority's formal system (Druker and Shelah, 2005, 52–53).

Furthermore, protest extended to accusations that the leadership, headed by Arafat, was corrupt (see for instance Beilin, 2001, 112–13). The propensity to corruption largely resulted from the Oslo model of relationships between the Palestinian Authority and Israel. The new arrangements made the Palestinian citizenry increasingly dependent on reshaped Israeli devices of occupation, mediated by the Palestinian leadership. This made the Palestinian security forces stronger and enabled them to run local "protection rackets." Equally, the agreements gave Israel responsibility for charging duties in lieu of the Palestinian Authority and depositing the monies unchecked in the Authority's bank accounts (part of the "Paris Agreements" of 1994 for regulating economic relations between the two sides), thus discouraging the Palestinian Authority's internal control mechanisms (for a different conceptualization of those arrangements, see Bergman, 2002; Lev, 2005; Meital, 2004, 72).

Second, because the Oslo Accords were formulated in military terms that created a "client-contractor" relationship between Israel and the Palestinian Authority, their collapse legitimized a military response, precisely on the part of one of their previous supporters. The task that had been contracted out was returned by the major customer. The spread of the Intifada in the first few weeks to include violent confrontations with large rallies held by Palestinian civilians also added to the feeling among political centrists in Israel that their trust had been betrayed by the very people whom the peace process was meant to benefit. Anxiety among the public made it prefer a military solution (Druker and Shelah, 2005, 28–30).

The supremacy of military thinking encountered the strengthening of the ethno-national coalition. The coalition had the power to prevent political steps or tendencies to compromise, which limited the ability of Barak's government to initiate a political understanding or to respond only moderately, imposing its authority on the army, when the clashes started.

Third, the army's leading role in the Oslo process turned out to be a double-edged sword. On the one hand, the army had an interest in protecting the Oslo Accords from the political coalition that questioned them, especially after Netanyahu was elected Prime Minister. However, out of concern for its image the army necessarily had to try and prepare itself for a renewal of violence in such a way that would ensure that it controlled events. This would enable it to shed criticism for its part in the "Oslo formula," which was liable to be portrayed as a failure. In other words, the army tried to minimize its risks.

And indeed, at the same time as supporting the Oslo arrangements and implementing them according to its own understanding, the army prepared itself for a renewal of armed conflict with the Palestinians in the way that any army readies itself for a range of external threats. In particular, having learned from its failures in the First Intifada, the First Lebanon War, and the "Western Wall Tunnel" events, the IDF prepared a set of scenarios and their attendant operational responses. The army's "reference threat" was the expected unilateral declaration of statehood by the Palestinian Authority in 2000, for which the army prepared to react with force and renew the violence along the border between the two entities. These provisions were accompanied by the development of a military doctrine that enhanced the concept of "low intensity conflict"—not all-out war, but not peace either (Michael, 2007).

These operational plans had two effects. The first was an organizational rigidity and loss of flexibility. As a result, when the first clashes broke out with unarmed protesters in September 2000, the army responded with excessive force almost out of inertia, deploying its full arsenal, including, for the first time, combat helicopters and tanks, thus unnecessarily escalating the violence as described above. Second, as far as is known, the army's plan was the only one available, thereby restricting politicians' ability to pick and choose at a time of crisis, such as the unexpected circumstances of the outbreak of the Al-Aqsa Intifada (ibid.; for a theoretical perspective see Levy, 1986).

The supremacy of military thinking also enabled the army to construct a media discourse that delegitimized the Palestinian Authority (Meital, 2004, 162–65). As soon as the Intifada broke out the IDF took control of the discourse and presented the clashes as bounded within the military sphere. However, while at first the army presented the violence as aimed at bringing the sides back to the negotiating table, thus providing the political echelon with some freedom of action, later on it presented its perception of reality as a war that required a decisive military outcome (Ratner, 2004). The domination of military thinking thus laid the grounds for the management of the crisis in Israeli-Palestinian relations according to military precepts.

Even if those were not its intentions at the outset, the escalation was fed by the utility it brought to the army, who saw in the conflict with the Palestinians a good opportunity to halt the decline of the IDF's lofty social status. Just before the Intifada the IDF had hurriedly and unilaterally retreated from

Lebanon on the government's orders, with Hezbollah's militias snapping at its heels. Moreover, since the mid-1990s the army had been dealing with the above-mentioned "motivation crisis," which saw the secular Ashkenazi stratum gradually abandoning its ranks. And if this were not enough, not only did the army's primary mission come to an end, namely, fighting in Lebanon, but this itself intensified the "threat" that the market economy would eat away at its resources; and indeed, the budget proposal of the year 2001 included a relatively deep cutback in the army's spending (Benn, 2002).

The satisfaction that the army's commanders felt in returning the army to the center of society following its renewed fighting in the Occupied Territories can be seen in comments made by the Chief of the General Staff Moshe Yaalon after *Operation Defensive Shield*:

> I think that since [the Intifada's eruption in] September 2000 something has happened to Israeli society's priorities. We were a society busy with self-realization—are you familiar with that phrase?—it means me, me, me! And it means that my needs come first . . . I think that the security situation since September 2000 was a kind of wake-up call to some people. [Up until] then people had been saying that we don't need an army, for example. (cited in Kaplan, 2003)

The key, therefore, to the renewal of violence lies in the army's centrality and its ability to impose its mode of thinking on Israeli statesmanship. If the Oslo Accords had not had such a military character (whose repressive features intensified under Barak), the failure of the negotiations would not necessarily have ended the chances of reaching an agreement, and so Palestinian resistance might have been weaker with stronger legitimacy at home. Equally, had the army not acquired renewed dominance following its internal political role during the Oslo process, it may have been possible for it to react in a more restrained and proportional manner to the Palestinian uprising, thus dissipating it relatively quickly. The unavoidable conclusion, therefore, is that the power structure that came into being during the 1990s paved the way to the renewal of intercommunal violence after the intermezzo of Oslo.

However, this does not explain why a coalition of forces from the "peace camp" did not organize protest activities with the aim of restraining the army, as had happened during the First Lebanon War and the First Intifada. The explanation lies in the high level of legitimacy enjoyed by the army.

THE LEGITIMACY OF THE ESCALATION

The legitimacy of the military reaction was not necessarily based on the reaction to terror attacks on Israeli cities: those attacks only began in early 2001 in a gradual fashion, while the army's "firm handedness" toward the Palestinian Authority enjoyed high legitimacy from the outset, that is, from the outbreak of the clashes in September 2000.

The legitimacy of the military response was the direct result of the spiral process of escalation: the IDF damaged the Palestinian Authority, following which the latter's ability to control its armed forces was lessened, meaning that terror attacks became more frequent, which legitimized the next escalation in the army's attacks on the Palestinian Authority, and so on and so forth. At the zenith of this process the Palestinian Authority stopped functioning as an effective military force (see Bar-Siman-Tov et al., 2005; Kimmerling, 2003). Therefore, the attack on the Passover celebrants at the Park Hotel in Netanya in 2002, a reflection of the collapse of the Palestinian Authority, legitimized *Operation Defensive Shield*, in which the IDF reoccupied the cities of the West Bank. This vicious circle mainly served in enlisting support for the army's activities among the Israeli left-wing, the traditional supporter of the Oslo Accords (see Ofir, 2001), and helped delegitimize challenging voices, such as those of conscientious objectors (see chapter 4).

The media played an important part in creating this legitimacy. It contributed to the representation of the conduct of the Palestinians as another failure in a long history of wrongheaded behavior and missed opportunities. While Prime Minister Barak was portrayed as having offered the Palestinians "everything" at Camp David, the Palestinians were represented as being unwilling to make peace. This was the basis of the "no partner" theory. Later on, the media helped (along with the army, as mentioned above) to consolidate the consensus around the idea that Sharon's government was being dragged into a war by terrorists. Even if doubts were expressed about the precise aims of the fighting and whether there was an orderly plan for when the Palestinian Authority would collapse, the possibility that there might be nonmilitary alternatives and that the government was initiating the fighting, and not being dragged into it, was nowhere on the media's agenda (Dor, 2004).

The legitimacy of the fighting was also buttressed by its very nature, especially because it was so different from the First Intifada, during which the army was criticized. The First Intifada was an unarmed civilian uprising by a population officially under occupation, with the occupying army as its target. Israel thus responded with a policy of violently repressing that civilian population, though under certain limitations (including legal ones) relevant to fighting an occupied population that is officially subjected to military rule. Deployment of rubber bullets for use against the unarmed Palestinian insurgents was among the symbols of Israel's recognition of its limits to the use of force (Ezrahi, 1997). In contrast, the second Intifada was seen by the army and its political superiors as a clash between two statelike entities, and so the army shaped its response in the context of what it perceived as an act of hostility by another state, which blurred the distinction between the "enemy" and the civilian population. From the army's point of view the occupation had ended, and even if it was reinstated in practice, this was to be seen in the context of fighting an enemy terrorist state, and not as the renewal of policing activities. It was against this background that the army did not hesitate to deploy the kind of armaments it would use against an enemy state, and not a civilian population, particularly aerial bombardments. There was no clearer demonstration of this than in the distinction drawn by the Military Attorney General between the First Intifada, in which the army was carrying out policing missions, and the second, in which the army was involved in a battle.[5]

Political legitimizing mechanisms came together with the army's new social architecture. From one point of view, the increased use of technology, primarily fighter planes, helped alienate the fighter from his victim, which served to reduce the potential among soldiers to be struck by pangs of conscience. This alienation was clearly illustrated in a statement made by the commander of the Air Force, General Dan Halutz: in August 2002, the army assassinated the leader of the *Hamas*' military wing, Salah Shahada, by dropping a bomb from a fighter plane on a residential neighborhood in Gaza, killing Shahada, but also a number of civilians. When asked how he felt about this, Halutz replied that the only thing he felt when a bomb was released was "a slight knock on the wing of the plane." At the same time, the new social architecture of the combat units also assigned most of the fighting to compulsory soldiers, and not to reservists. Unlike compulsory conscripts, reservists bear a greater potential for political protest as "civilianized soldiers."

More significantly, however, was the aspect of the architecture that saw soldiers from the ethno-national coalition tighten their grip on the army, simultaneously with the weakening of the more dovish and critical secular Ashkenazi backbone. As a result, two phenomena stood out during the clashes, which prevented them from being a short and passing episode.

First, most of the casualties in combat with the Palestinians were from peripheral groups. This did not spur the elite groups into protest, as they were hardly affected. When bereaved parents from the elite groups tried to remonstrate, their minority status meant they could not attain the critical mass needed for effective protest. At the same time, for the affected groups, notably immigrants from the former Soviet Union, Mizrachim, settlers, and the "knitted skullcaps," the victims became a part of the new ethos of national contribution. In this way they filled the vacuum left by the traditionally elite groups, as the ethos of bereavement helped legitimize the fighting, and did not contest it.

Second, the field forces were quite willing to carry out controversial missions without enacting their social networks in collective action against the military way, as the secular Ashkenazi groups had done in the past. They were even overly enthusiastic to carry out aggressive missions, as it meant they could prove their worthiness both within the army and outside it, in the context of their competition with other groups. The change in the army's social composition thus reduced the potential that soldiers would provoke public opinion via their civilian social networks. (These two phenomena are detailed in chapter 4.)

Thus the army regained a sufficient level of autonomy to gradually escalate its response to the uprising until it had destroyed the Palestinian Authority. Not only was the army acting within a more supportive political milieu, but the fact that it was relying on combat soldiers from the more conservative segments of Jewish-Israeli society meant that the high command could be less sensitive to the possibility that the army might crumble when carrying out controversial missions. By way of illustration, when the First Intifada broke out in 1987, the Chief of the General Staff, Dan Shomron, appeared before the government and declared that the uprising called for a political, and not military, solution. Accordingly, he requested that the government temper the kind of mission it asked the army to carry out in putting down the uprising. Shomron's rationale was to prevent the disintegration of the army at a time when left-wing and right-wing soldiers were equally represented in its ranks.

Thirteen years later this sensitivity had dwindled, and met with the senior ranks' satisfaction with the escalated fighting. The army even allowed itself to set a political goal for its actions, namely, the need to "burn into the Palestinian consciousness" the recognition that violence will not bring them political gain. This goal also shows how autonomous the army's top command was in comparison with the General Staff during the First Intifada, which asserted that only a political solution could stop the violence. If we add to this the influence of the spiraling escalation on the legitimacy of the use of force, we can see that the shift in the army's social composition, and the partial departure of the left wing from its ranks, gave it renewed autonomy, which paradoxically enabled the left to reinstate its support for the army via that same spiral process. Thus, a moderating counter-coalition failed to emerge.

The non-emergence of a moderating counter-coalition rested on a set of complementary mechanisms related to the remnants of the army's symbolic rewards in the eyes of the secular Ashkenazi middle class. In a dialectical fashion, the strengthening of the ethno-national discourse increased the tendency among parts of the middle class to preserve the army's symbolic status. This served the nostalgia of center-left old-timers—some of whom had been notable figures in the military—in the light of the ethno-national coalition's attempt to forge an alternative narrative of the establishment of the state, one that would diminish the contribution of Ashkenazi groups, or even undermine the legitimacy of their actions. The ethno-national discourse also temporarily revitalized the republican array of symbols: by rhetorically reemphasizing military contribution as the criterion for social rewards (rendered obsolete by the market-oriented discourse), the center-left was trying to deflect ethno-national trends, especially as represented by *Shas*, which, as mentioned, helped disentangle soldiering from citizenship. This goes some way to explaining the success of the *Shinui* ("Change") party, and its meteoric growth at the beginning of the new millennium. On the strength of its call to draft the Ultra-Orthodox, weaken state support for the Ultra-Orthodox that do not sign up, and improve the rewards for ex-servicepersons as compared to religious "parasites," *Shinui* recruited the support of wide sections of the Israel center-left (see Shalev and Levy, 2005). In other words, republican rhetoric was utilized more negatively than positively: not as a meaningful criterion that affected the upper middle class as it gradually retreated from its civic duties, but rather as a means to block the upward mobility of others.

Similarly, the military discourse received significant support from the feminist discourse. Women's representatives, mostly identified with the left wing, adopted a model of *militaristic feminism* that internalized masculine symbols. They demanded increased access for women to combat positions, and saw the army as a site for women to attain equal status with men (see Sasson-Levy, 2003). They even accepted the widespread assumption concerning the centrality of military service and its being a test of civil status, and refrained from challenging arrangements in the army that discriminated against women (see Barak-Erez, 2005; and for a broader perspective on gender relations, see Gross, 2002). Here too, the symbolic rewards seemingly offered to women by the army were perceived as an incentive to maintain the exchange between military sacrifice and the legitimacy for attaining social rights, and this helped preserve a relatively high level of militarism.

Women's organizations did not formulate a radical strategy: they did not incorporate their criticism of militarism into a wide-ranging platform for political change that would deprive masculine organizations of their symbolic power and undermine the military criteria for evaluating personal and group-level activities, thus fragmenting society's gender hierarchy. Women were coerced into acting in a dominantly masculine sphere where they were not struggling for equality, but rather for recognition of their ability to appear masculine in a way that expressed their internalization of men's superiority. Their limited achievements merely ratified once more the dominance of militarism, which as such may be termed "gendered militarization." Only in the mid-2000s have voices been heard at the margins of the discourse calling for the cancellation of compulsory recruitment, including for women (for a theoretical discussion of the feminist dilemma, see Giles and Hyndman, 2004).

Finally, the business community, generally supportive of globalization, cooperated with the fighting, not least because of its ability to transfer its business and capital to overseas markets, thus reducing the damage sustained by the Intifada. At the same time, it expressed a degree of satisfaction (though not explicitly) with the effect of the terror attacks on disciplining the labor market and reducing employment costs. This was also accompanied by the withering away of the welfare state, enacted by a liberal ethno-national coalition (comprised of the right-wing National Unity Party, the liberal *Shinui*, and, for a while, *Shas*). This had the effect of weakening the organizational infrastructure of the business community (see Peled, 2004; Swirski, 2005, 94–98).

In short, the remnants of the symbolic rewards of military service led certain groups, which had in the past been critical of the army for violating the republican equation, to try and balance it by raising the value of the symbolic rewards that stemmed from the army and its combat activities. In such circumstances, this very attempt to restitute the equation gave the army greater autonomy in managing military affairs.

CONCLUSIONS

The army regained its legitimacy for operating forcefully and enjoyed a high level of autonomy in doing so. This resulted from the two-phased political strategy for rebalancing the republican equation. The first phase saw the burden on the middle class reduced as militarism retreated. This could be seen in moves to deescalate the violent Arab-Israeli conflict, with the Oslo process at the center. However, the Oslo Accords were constructed as military agreements with the army at the head of the process, much owing to its role in legitimizing a moderate military policy by militarily, and hence politically, mobilizing ethno-national groups.

In the second phase, largely integrated into the first one, the army's new social architecture helped to balance the equation and reconstitute it in a way that limited the boundaries of this equation. The new equation was based on symbolic rewards given to the new groups and by forsaking the contribution of the traditionally elite groups, which in practice continued to demand relatively high rewards, especially in material and political-symbolic terms. The further the middle-class groups positioned themselves from the military, the less interest they had in exercising control over it, leading to the weakening of the political monitoring of the IDF's conduct. This change in the army's composition had clear consequences in terms of sharpening its combat profile. It was an army that relied on social groups for whom fighting was a critical social test that bore rewards. This structural change merged with a renewed combat infrastructure created by the Oslo Accords, due to their military character.

Therefore, the encounter between the internally contradictory military arrangements of Oslo, the supremacy of military thinking when dealing with crises that resulted from those very arrangements, and the restoration of the army's professional autonomy, all gave the army extensive freedom of action in managing its response to the second Palestinian uprising. In short, demilitarization prompted remilitarization in peripheral sectors of society, beginning in the late 1990s. Central to this process was the declined motivation of the middle-class groups, incited by demilitarization, which brought about the remilitarization of policies in the form of a social new architecture.

The next chapter will analyze in greater detail the part played by the social architecture in reinforcing the army's professional authority in two ways—the changing social map of fatalities, and its impact on the discourse of bereavement, and the shifting motivation of the new combat soldiers.

NOTES

1. The court ruling did not negate the legitimacy of differentially allocating men and women to combat positions. Rather, it merely toned down its implementation and preserved the model whereby women would have to volunteer for combat positions, unlike men, who could be posted to them against their will (Barak-Erez, 2005).

2. To illustrate, wage gaps increased by 32 percent at the end of the 1990s when compared to the early 1980s. Deepening social gaps (among Israeli citizens) were reflected in changes in the Jinny Coefficient for income inequality: it showed a 7.5 percent increase in inequality from 1980 to 1997 (Dahan, 2002).

3. See the criticism made by reserves Colonel Shaul Arieli, who had held senior positions in the army in implementing the agreements, as quoted in Eldar (2004): "At no stage did we offer them more than 88 percent," *Haaretz*, 11 March 2003.

4. In this incident, Palestinian forces opened fire along the border, causing a relatively high number of casualties to Israeli soldiers. This was in response to the opening of an ancient tunnel in Jerusalem, a move perceived as an Israeli attempt to establish facts on the ground in that politically contentious city.

5. This is a theoretical distinction between "ghetto" and "frontier," as proposed by Ron (2003): during the First Intifada, cities and villages in the West Bank and Gaza Strip were part of a ghetto, in that they were under the full control of the Israeli state, which also had legal responsibility for the welfare of their inhabitants. Accordingly, when the uprising broke out, Israel was dealing with forceful policing, but without using firearms. In the Second Intifada, after the Oslo process, the Occupied Territories were part of Israel's frontier region, and the lack of Israeli control meant that the state was not committed to the inhabitants. Restrictions on the use of force were therefore eased.

Chapter Four

The War of the Peripheries

By the time the Al-Aqsa Intifada erupted in September 2000, the army's composition was based mainly on the new groups. As a result, the IDF could deploy force with renewed legitimacy. A peace coalition that might have attempted to politically curb the IDF, as in previous wars, did not emerge. Given that the instigators of political protest were mainly ex-soldiers, especially reservists and their families, two key mechanisms worked to mitigate the potential for protest flourishing from within the military ranks: the composition of casualties, with its effects on the reshaping of the bereavement ethos, and the field units' overmotivation to fight, both of which rested on the realigned composition of the army.

Unlike in other armies, the ethno-class stratification of the IDF is considered a taboo subject. In keeping with the discourse that portrays the "people's army" as being above ethno-class divisions in Israeli society, no official statistics are available regarding the representation of different groups. Although the IDF's claim of being a "people's army" is no longer tenable, with less than 50 percent of the Jewish population completing military service, the army clings on to the rhetoric and doctrine of the "people's army," the source of its preferential status in Israeli society. This being the case, mapping the casualties in the Al-Aqsa Intifada could provide an indication of the change in the social composition of the army.

MAPPING IDF CASUALTIES IN THE AL-AQSA INTIFADA[1]

From the outbreak of the Al-Aqsa Intifada in September 2000 until December 2006, 244 IDF soldiers, including soldiers from the Border Police,[2] were killed in combat as a result of Palestinian fire or in operational accidents. In order to examine the extent of the change in the casualties map over time, I compare the casualties of the Al-Aqsa Intifada with those of the First Lebanon War, specifically the 231 fatalities from the first week of the war (June 6–11, 1982). Information on these casualties was taken from private and public Internet sites (Levy, 2005).

The first week of the Lebanon War was chosen for several reasons: first, most of the military forces, both regular soldiers and reservists, were active that week, a phenomenon that has not been repeated since. Second, this was the first war since 1973, and the social composition of the combat soldiers was similar to that of the 1973 War, when groups of secular Ashkenazim were at the core of the fighting. After the first week, however, the composition of the forces altered, not only due to the changing character of the combat from full-blown military clashes to guerilla warfare, but also because the expansion of the war prompted the first signs of the above-mentioned "motivation crisis," which hastened the entry of other groups into combat. Third, the first week aroused the most significant protest Israel had ever seen, as will be clarified below. It should be noted that, even though these wars featured different types of combat, my interest is in comparing the politics of war: who was sacrificed, and what were the political ramifications of the changing composition of the casualties? Basic ethno-class categories (with consistency over time) were used for the mapping, given the correlation between ethno-class affiliation and military motivation (Enloe, 1980).

A comparison of the casualties of the first week of the Lebanon War and the Al-Aqsa Intifada clearly indicates the change in the social composition of those bearing the burden of the fighting, as detailed in Table 4.1

The data clearly show that the Al-Aqsa Intifada is the war of the social peripheries, with the traditional elite groups being replaced by peripheral ones. A comparison of the first week of the Lebanon War and the Al-Aqsa Intifada reveals a drop in the proportion of casualties from the three Ashkenazi groups from about 48 percent to about 28 percent. This cluster also includes the veteran, secular Ashkenazi kibbutzim and moshavim—in the past the most prominent elite group within the military—though the decline is particularly prominent among the upper middle class. If we add to this cluster the Mizrachi middle class, the entire middle class reduced its share in the casualties from about 68 percent to around 45 percent. Countering this decline in the casualty rolls is the conspicuous entry of Russian and Ethiopian immigrants from the 1990s (about 15 percent), Druze and Bedouins (about 8 percent), and residents of settlements in the Occupied Territories, Mizrachim and Ashkenazim alike (about 7 percent). The Al-Aqsa Intifada also saw casualties among women (about 1 percent) for the first time since the 1948 War. The

Table 4.1. Comparison between IDF Casualties in the First Week of the Lebanon War and the Al-Aqsa Intifada (Percentage, Rounded)

The group	Lebanon War, Week 1	Al-Aqsa Intifada	Change
Secular Ashkenazim—upper middle class	19.5	7.8	−11.7
Veteran kibbutzim & moshavim	12.6	7.0	−5.6
Secular Ashkenazim—middle class and below	15.6	13.1	−2.5
Mizrachim—middle class and higher, secular and religious, resident within the Green Line	20.8	17.6	−3.2
Mizrachim—lower middle class and below, secular and religious, resident within the Green Line	19.0	15.2	−3.8
Mizrachi settlers in the Occupied Territories, secular and religious	0.0	3.3	3.3
Religious Ashkenazim, resident within the Green Line, including immigrants (except from the former Soviet Union)	9.1	5.7	−3.4
Religious Ashkenazi settlers, including immigrants (except from the former Soviet Union)	0.4	3.7	3.3
Russian immigrants (including settlers)	0.9	12.3	11.4
Ethiopian immigrants	0.0	2.5	2.5
Other secular immigrants (except from the former Soviet Union and Ethiopia), resident within the Green Line	1.7	2.9	1.2
Druze, Bedouins, and Israeli Palestinians	0.4	7.8	7.4
Women (all backgrounds)	0.0	1.2	1.2
TOTAL	100	100	
N =	231	244	

presence of the Mizrachi and religious Ashkenazi groups remained fairly steady, since the decline in participation by the groups living inside the Green Line was balanced by a rise in casualties among settlers from the Occupied Territories.

Nevertheless, this comparison is insignificant without comparing the casualties in relation to the proportion of each group in the general population. After all, it is possible that the change is simply the result of demographics, mostly due to the immigration from Russia and Ethiopia in the 1990s, which greatly affected Israeli society. Table 4.2 presents this comparison.

Table 4.2 shows that demographics alone cannot explain the change. The middle and upper middle classes—Ashkenazi and Mizrachi alike—reduced their representation among the casualties by more than the change in their demographic weight, while groups from the middle class and below increased their representation in the army's casualties despite the reduction in their demographic weight. In short, the four leading groups—the three secular Ashkenazi groups

Table 4.2. Percentage of Casualties in Proportion to the Population (Percentage, Rounded)*

The Group	First Lebanon War, Week 1			Al-Aqsa Intifada			Change in the proportional share between the wars
	Percentage of casualties	Proportion in the population	Percentage of casualties in proportion to the population	Percentage of casualties	Proportion in the population	Percentage of casualties in proportion to the population	
Secular Ashkenazim— upper middle class	19.5	6.0	325	7.8	8.0	98	−70
Veteran kibbutzim & moshavim	12.6	4.0	315	7.0	2.5	280	−11
Secular Ashkenazim—middle class and below	15.6	16.0	98	13.1	9.0	146	49
Mizrachim—middle class and higher	20.8	11.0	189	17.6	14.0	126	−33
Mizrachim—lower middle class	19.0	33.0	58	15.2	20.0	76	32
Mizrachi settlers	0.0	0.0	0	3.3	1.5	220	new group
Religious Ashkenazim (Green Line)	9.1	6.5	140	5.7	7.0	81	−42
Religious Ashkenazi settlers	0.4	0.5	80	3.7	1.5	247	208
Russian immigrants	0.9	3.0	30	12.3	13.0	95	215
Ethiopian immigrants	0.0	0.0	0	2.5	2.0	125	new group
Other secular immigrants	1.7	2.5	68	2.9	2.0	145	113
Druze, Bedouins, etc.	0.4	17.0	2	7.8	19.0	41	1950
Women	0.0	0.0	0	1.2	1.0	—	new group
TOTAL	100	100		100	100		

*Data regarding the demographic weight were compiled from several sources, mainly the Israel Central Bureau of Statistics (reports of 1995, 2001, 2003, 2005); Lein, 2002; Smooha, 1993; Swirski, 1981; Yaish, 2001; Yaish 2003. Categorization was built according to the analysis at the group level offered in chapter 3. In order to avoid distortions in calculating the weight of the female casualties in the Intifada, the proportion of the male groups was calculated in keeping with their weight in the general population, including both men and women. That figure was then reduced by the female casualties (1.2%). For example, if a group was 10% of the population, even if the proportion of men was just 5%, its weight was calculated at 9.88%. In other words, women were analyzed as a new group, since during the First Lebanon War they were totally excluded from the battlefield.

and the middle-class Mizrachim—who compose the core of the middle class, reduced their representation by 25 percent more than their demographic weight. Furthermore, demographics alone cannot explain variations in groups' behavior, such as women, Druze and Bedouins, and Russian immigrants, whose contribution shifted dramatically relative to their demographic weight. This leads to the conclusion that the attenuated motivation of the leading groups, which stemmed from the reduced convertibility of their military service, resulted in the new groups taking their place in the ranks.

However, perhaps the change in casualties can be accounted for by the shift in the nature of the fighting between the First Lebanon War and the Al-Aqsa Intifada, which was characterized by a transition from combat between a standing army and militias, to policing activities against a civilian population. Accordingly, Tables 4.3 and 4.4 map the composition of the casualties by their military corps and ethno-class origin.[3]

Tables 4.3 and 4.4 indicate the army's tracking policy: the policing missions rely on the Border Police and the special policing units set up specifically for this purpose. The ranks of these units were filled with a relatively high ratio of peripheral groups, namely, lower-middle-class Mizrachim, Russian and Ethiopian immigrants, and Druze and Bedouins. This policy is based on the categorization and placement of recruits in keeping with their perceived human capital and the army's cultural preferences. Thus, the fighting units, which require low-tech personnel, were manned by groups with relatively low educational achievements. In contrast, the army channels secular Ashkenazim and upwardly mobile Mizrachim to highly technological units, such as the Air Force and artillery corps (see Sasson-Levy, 2002). Because of the nature of the combat with the Palestinians, the participation of these units in the Intifada was relatively low, and even low risk, in contrast to their assignments in the First Lebanon War, and resulted in their suffering zero casualties. Still, there is a strong linkage between the erosion in motivation

Table 4.3. Casualties Differentiated by Corps, the First Lebanon War and the Al-Aqsa Intifada (Percentage, Rounded)

War/corps	Proportion of each corps in total casualties	
	First Lebanon War	Intifada
Infantry and elite units	42	44
Armor and engineering	40	6
Artillery and Air Force	6	0
Special policing units	0	37
Border Police	0	7
Auxiliary units	12	6
TOTAL	100	100
Ratio of officers	25	18

Table 4.4. Casualties Differentiated by Corps and Ethno-Class Origin (Percentage, Rounded)

The corps/group	Infantry & elite units		Armor & Engineer		Artillery & Air Force		Special policing units		Border Police		Auxiliary units		Ratio of officers	
	L	l	L	l	L	l	L	l	L	l	L	l	L	l
Secular Ashkenazim—upper	16	8	20	12	54	0	0	6	0	0	14	7	37	11
kibbutzim & moshavim	19	13	11	0	8	0	0	3	0	6	0	0	23	13
Secular Ashkenazim—lower	21	10	10	16	23	0	0	21	0	0	14	7	14	13
Mizrachim—middle class	19	18	24	23	8	0	0	17	0	6	28	14	11	24
Mizrachim—lower	20	15	15	28	8	0	0	6	0	6	31	29	5	9
Mizrachi settlers	0	4	0	0	0	0	0	2	0	0	0	21	0	7
Religious Ashkenazim Green Line	3	10	17	2	0	0	0	3	0	0	7	0	9	4
Religious Ashkenazi settlers	0	7	1	2	0	0	0	0	0	0	0	0	0	7
Russian immigrants	1	9	0	14	0	0	0	8	0	35	3	21	0	7
Ethiopian immigrants	0	0	0	0	0	0	0	5	0	18	0	0	0	2
Other secular immigrants	1	5	2	0	0	0	0	0	0	12	3	0	2	2
Druze, Bedouin, etc.	1	0	0	2	0	0	0	24	0	18	0	0	0	0
Women	0	0	0	0	0	0	0	5	0	0	0	0	0	0
TOTAL	100	100	100	100	100	0	0	100	0	100	100	100	100	100

and the channeling of specific groups to units that did not participate in the Intifada, and there are several reasons why this channeling cannot be attributed to the change in the nature of the fighting alone.

First, in both wars most of the casualties (in almost identical ratios of 40 percent) were from infantry units, whose initial purpose was not policing but rather participation in offensive operations. Even so, the rate of casualties among the three secular Ashkenazi groups in infantry units declined significantly, from 56 percent to 31 percent. This decline is only partially offset by the relative proportion of secular Ashkenazi casualties in the armored and engineering corps, which fell from 41 percent to 28 percent, while the relative proportion of all casualties in armored and engineering units fell from 40 percent to 18 percent (including casualties in missions for which the corps had not been originally trained). Furthermore, while the rate of officers among the casualties dropped by about 25 percent from the First Lebanon War to the Al-Aqsa Intifada (from 25 percent to 18 percent), the decline among the upper-middle-class Ashkenazim was dramatically higher: from 37 percent to 11 percent, a decline of about 70 percent. Despite the change in the mode of fighting in the two wars, the structure of the combat forces largely remained the same. In short, the presence of the Ashkenazim in high-risk missions was reduced.

For the sake of illustration, based on a simulation, let us assume that a war identical to the First Lebanon War had broken out in the early 2000s, meaning that the army had not had to deploy policing units in the Occupied Territories, and that it had therefore not needed to populate them with peripheral groups that had previously been channeled away from combat positions. Let us then compare the two main corps—the armored and engineering corps, and the infantry—and assume identical casualty rates in the First Lebanon War and the Intifada. To them we shall add the casualties from the artillery corps and the Air Force at identical rates to those of the First Lebanon War (in other words, we are leaving unchanged the almost complete Ashkenazi hegemony)—corps that lost no soldiers during the Intifada—and also auxiliary units.

Analysis of the data shows that the rate of casualties among the three Ashkenazi groups and the Mizrachi middle class would have dropped by 18 percent in relation to their demographic proportion, and not by 25 percent as it did in practice (largely because of the "contribution" of the artillery and the Air Force). At the same time, the nonmobile Mizrachi groups would have been overrepresented in relation to their proportion of the population at large. There would have been no significant changes among religious groups and Russian immigrants, though women and Ethiopian immigrants would not have been represented, while the proportion of Druze and Bedouins would have plummeted. Even had the type of warfare been identical, then, the trend would nonetheless have persisted. Indeed, even when we calculate altogether the 363 soldiers fallen in the Al-Aqsa Intifada and the Second Lebanon War (which displayed a mid-pattern between the two wars) to further scrutinize the social realignment of the IDF, the overall picture remains intact and similar to the simulation, and hence also to the Intifada's map, with a major growth in the presence of recruits from kibbutzim and moshavim, as elaborated in chapter 7. Therefore, the change in the nature of the fighting does not provide a robust explanation.

Second, the Intifada was perceived by the Israeli-Jewish public as an existential war. Had military service in general, and combat experience in the Intifada in particular, been viewed by the dominant groups as equally worthwhile as in the wars that preceded the First Lebanon War, it might have been expected that in the five years of fighting, Ashkenazim and upwardly mobile Mizrachim would have been contending for a place in the battlefront against the Palestinians, despite the army's channeling policy. Given that this was not the case, one can only conclude that the composition of the casualties greatly reflects changes in the level of motivation.

Evidently, the upper-middle-class groups had managed to exploit their bargaining power vis-à-vis the army to attain their preferences (one example is the dropout rate due to mental health before or during service). This bargaining power grew when the army adopted semi-selective conscription in the mid-1990s, largely a result of the new sources of manpower available to it. Youngsters from elite high schools relied on their power to be assigned to units that do not participate in combat against the Palestinians, such as artillery, antiaircraft units, and the navy (Makover-Blikov, 2005). By so doing, they maintained the aura of combat service while avoiding the risk that it naturally entails.

Third, the casualty map of the Al-Aqsa Intifada reflects the relatively lower sacrifice made by reserve forces as compared with the First Lebanon War. Since that war, reserve units have been gradually distanced from politically contentious missions, such as policing the occupied Palestinian population, which reservists could translate into political protest. After all, Ashkenazim and upwardly mobile Mizrachim are particularly prominent in the reserve units, reflecting to a great extent the character of the army before the realignment in its social composition. An examination of the ethno-class structure of the refuseniks shows that it reflects "yesterday's" army, and provides an understanding of how the army increased the potential for loyal soldiering by decreasing the role of reservists. This being the case, the channeling of manpower is also a political construction based on the soldiers' motivation.

In short, ethno-class channeling is highly influenced by the different orientations and motivations of the various groups. For this reason I will now focus on explaining the motivation of the different groups.

THE CHANGE IN THE COMPOSITION OF THE ARMY

As indicated in Table 4.2, the contribution of the secular upper-middle-class Ashkenazi groups, which had traditionally constituted the military's backbone, declined by about 70 percent relative to their increase in demographic weight. In the veteran kibbutzim and moshavim, there was a relative decline of about 10 percent. Although this group's contribution still exceeds its relative demographic weight, it lost its status as the leading group among the combat units. The "motivation crisis" significantly affected this group after the 1977 political upheaval, as the mélange of ethno-national and market-oriented discourse cracked the historic symbolic status of the kibbutz/moshav, which combined a national contribution in republican terms and a collectivist alternative to the market. The alienation of the group's youngsters thus resulted from the same factors that caused the IDF to lose its social status.

At the same time, the proportion of the secular Ashkenazim from the middle class and below—those whose parents are employed in middle- and lower-status jobs—rose by about 50 percent. Although its proportional share was somewhat decreased, its relative demographic weight significantly shrunk as part of the mobility to the upper middle class within the Ashkenazi segment and the overall proportional decrease of the Ashkenazi groups owing to demographic changes. This group, which in the past had benefited less from the profits of war, was therefore less sensitive to their decline. It is also likely that this group's bargaining power vis-à-vis the army's tracking policy was weaker than that of the secular upper-middle-class Ashkenazim. In the final analysis, both secular male Ashkenazi groups decreased their presence among the casualties by about 20 percent relative to their reduced demographic weight.

The Mizrachi groups maintained similar fatality rates in both wars, but their relative weight rose a little due to their demographic decline. While the proportion of the casualties declined slightly among the upwardly mobile Mizrachi group, which had gained mobility to the middle-upper levels of the middle class, the decline in proportional terms was more pronounced—about 35 percent—due to the increase in its demographic weight. It seems that this group adopted a similar pattern of motivation to that of the secular Ashkenazim, with whom they share a similar social status, mainly by not being overly motivated to take part in high-risk missions.

Still, the group maintained its strongholds in the armored, engineering, and infantry corps, and increased its presence among the officers.

Among the peripheral Mizrachi groups, those living in outlying areas and positioned in the lower sector of the middle class and below, the proportional sacrifice declined as well. Due to the reduction in the group's demographic weight, however, its representation in the casualties map rose by about 30 percent relative to its demographic weight, with a salient presence in the armored and engineering corps. The absolute decline in the rate of casualties among the peripheral Mizrachim is offset by the Mizrachim who settled in the Occupied Territories. In the First Lebanon War only a minute proportion of Mizrachim lived in such settlements, and so there were no casualties from this group in the first week of the war. In the Al-Aqsa Intifada, on the other hand, about 3.5 percent of the fatalities were Mizrachi settlers. This is a significantly greater representation relative to the group's demographic weight, which is about 1 percent of the general population.

This picture shows that among Mizrachi youths from the lower middle class, mainly graduates of high schools in the periphery and low-prestige high schools in the big cities, army service remains an important test of civic duty, sometimes in defiance of the elite secular Ashkenazim's "motivation crisis." For many members of this group, fighting the Palestinians is another way of expressing the traditional enmity that was created between Mizrachim and Palestinians during the early stages of the Zionist project (see Shenhav, 2006). As for the settlers, the importance of military service is viewed as the very defense of their own communities. Meanwhile, the poorest, nonmobile sector of the Mizrachi population is partially screened out by the army due to disqualification for service, while many other members of this sector have abandoned the track of military mobility by opting to study in yeshivas, whose students are exempted from military service (Levy, 2003b, 308–70).

The contribution made by religious Ashkenazim is characterized by strong stability alongside an internal shift between residents inside the Green Line and those in the settlements. Since the 1973 War, the national religious groups have strengthened their presence in the army, as the traditional reservoirs of manpower could no longer meet the IDF's growing needs. Gradually, with the aggravation of the "motivation crisis," these groups filled the vacuum left by youngsters from the kibbutzim and moshavim and became the most prominent militarized group. For the national religious sector, serving in the military helped forge an alternative autonomous identity to the dominant secular Zionist ethos. After years of displaying a largely passive posture in the military, the national religious sector began to flaunt its presence. From their point of view, their military mission embodied a kind of psychological contract, enabling them to exchange their sacrifice by realizing their ideology of maintaining Israel's hold on areas of religious symbolism (see Cohen, 2004).

Table 4.4 shows the shift of religious Ashkenazim from armored units in the First Lebanon War to infantry units in the Intifada. In practice, this group thereby adapted itself to the major battlefront, thus maintaining its earlier casualty rates. However, it is interesting to note the decline in the proportion of casualties among residents from within the Green Line relative to their demographic weight. Two explanations are crucial here: first, the slight demographic growth shown by this group is largely felt in the Ultra-Orthodox sector, which is entirely unrepresented in the map of military casualties. Meanwhile, the demographic weight of non-Orthodox (and non-settler) elements even dropped somewhat between the two wars. Therefore, in relative terms, the national religious group's share slightly dropped between the wars. Second, since the 1990s, a new identity—that of the "new national religious"—has been developing, primarily within the Green Line. The behavioral patterns of the new national religious Jew are not considerably different from those of his secular peers, as the former has been undergoing a process of secular Ashkenazi "embourgeoisment." Here too, the drain on the inclination to social elitism, which in the past had led the "knitted skullcaps," has been reducing military motivation (Sheleg, 2000, 101–2).

Immigrants from the former Soviet Union increased their share of the casualties as well. The new immigrants who participated in the Intifada had arrived in the 1990s, while the immigrants who fought in the First Lebanon War had come to Israel in the 1970s. Between the two wars there was a clear transition from underrepresentation to representation that approached the group's demographic weight. The IDF relegated the 1970s immigrants to peripheral positions in the military, mostly because of their shorter terms of service (Azarya and Kimmerling, 1998). In the 1990s, however, part of this group strengthened its ethno-national identity, viewing itself as protecting the Jewish majority in Israel and blocking the strengthening of the Palestinian minority (Shumsky, 2001). It is therefore possible to attribute the increase in the relative weight of the immigrants both to the construction of a newly found motivation and the withdrawal of the veteran secular Ashkenazi group, which vacated military positions in favor of other groups.

Indeed, immigrants from Russia became the backbone of the Border Police, as is reflected in the casualties map (about 35 percent). Others among the Russian immigrants internalized the individual advantage they could gain from military service, and so sought logistical and technologically rich positions.

The participation of other immigrant groups is also conspicuous. For instance, the proportion of fatalities in the Al-Aqsa Intifada among Ethiopian immigrants is greater than their demographic weight. Young men from this group view army service not only as their entry ticket for an Israeli identity, but also as a tool that can help them fortify their self-confidence and even achieve a certain sense of advantage over their veteran compatriots (Shabtay, 1999). This group is also prominent in the proportion of casualties in the Border Police and special policing units.

Another group is secular Ashkenazi immigrants. American immigrants, who came in various waves in the 1970s and 1980s, are particularly prominent in the map of casualties, and the ideological character of this immigration is reflected in the military motivation of its first and second generation descendants.

About 8 percent of all Intifada fatalities were Druze, Bedouin, Circassian, and other Israeli-Palestinian citizens. Their motivation to enlist (conscription applies only to the Druze) stems from considerations of social mobility and obtaining employment in an environment with high rates of joblessness.

Last but not least, for the first time since the 1948 War, the Al-Aqsa Intifada also saw 3 female casualties (about 1 percent). This minor change is indicative of women's increased accessibility to combat positions since the First Lebanon War, and particularly in the special policing forces.

In conclusion, in the first week of the Lebanon War, about 48 percent of the fallen were secular Ashkenazim, who had previously manned core roles in the military. In contrast, in the Al-Aqsa Intifada, only about 28 percent of the casualties came from this group, with soldiers from the more peripheral groups taking their place. If we calculate the fatality rates of the core of the secular middle class, the drop is from about 68 percent to around 45 percent. The change in the casualties map increased the army's room to maneuver in the direction of autonomous action. The bereavement discourse served as a mediating mechanism between the composition of the casualties and political and operational outcomes.

THE BEREAVEMENT DISCOURSE

For some of the new groups, their fallen gradually became part of the new ethos of national sacrifice, filling the vacuum left by the traditional elite groups. Accordingly, casualties from the new groups did not inspire protest. The families tended to accept their sacrifice submissively, with conciliation, forgiveness, and even pride. Bereaved parents sometimes found significance and purpose to their loss. This reaction is compatible with their motivational ethos and their approach to military service, as well as with their hawkish, ethno-nationalist orientation in general. Even parents who voiced criticism usually endeavored to serve as advocates for the army, calling on the political leadership to lift restrictions on military activity in order to reduce the number of injured soldiers, as indicated by an analysis of reactions of families to their loss. Another segment of these families remained passive, though sometimes their passivity stemmed from limited political awareness and a lack of access to the networks and resources that might facilitate collective action, as is typical of lower-middle-class groups.

In contrast, bereaved parents from the secular Ashkenazi middle class have quite often expressed objections, casting doubt on the necessity of the war, directing their anger at senior IDF commanders, and translating their pain into public activity, typically through the media. Nevertheless, due to the relatively low proportion of fallen soldiers from this group, the Al-Aqsa Intifada has not generated a critical mass for effective opposition. Against this background, one can understand why the military casualties did not spawn a protest movement similar to the Lebanon War's *Four Mothers* movement, and this despite the growing public feeling that the victims were being sacrificed for no good purpose. Not only did the fallen fail to arouse massive protest among the elite groups, which were only marginally affected, but the peripheral groups that were highly affected did not protest either, instead accepting their loss.

These reactions reflect the unequivocal relationship between ethno-class status and the bereavement discourse. Not only is the bereavement discourse a response to disaster, it has largely become a symbolic resource by which those who need to can attain a feeling of contribution or communal belonging, especially among the social periphery. For others belonging to the upper middle class, bereavement is a resource that helps challenge the dominant political culture (on the bereavement discourse see Lebel and Ronel, 2005; Levy, 2005).

Theoretically, "the voice of the people is heard loudest when governments require either their gold or their bodies in defense of the state" (Porter, 1994, 10). Nevertheless, here we see a differential pattern of voice: since the 1990s, the middle class has mainly voiced against its "gold sacrifice," i.e., the monetary burden of the fighting, and has adopted a market-oriented criticism of the military. This group, however, remained silent regarding the "body sacrifice" of other groups. It is therefore not the human price, but rather strategic considerations and the internalization of the affinity between economic growth and military calm, that motivated the withdrawal from Gaza initiated by Ariel Sharon's government in 2005 (see more in chapter 5).

Unlike the Al-Aqsa Intifada, the First Lebanon War was a catalyst that spurred parents of fallen soldiers into action in the public arena in order to protest against the army's operations. Later, as bereavement became a lever for political action, parents also acted to increase scrutiny over the army's handling of safety in operational activities and training exercises (Lebel, 2006). Although parents bereaved by the 1973 War had criticized the military's failures, the First Lebanon War triggered unprecedented protests that targeted the war's very political goals rather than just the army's performance.

These activities had a clear ethnic-class character, being driven mainly by the relatively high proportions of the secular Ashkenazi middle class, as its symbolic rewards were drying up and it was estranging itself from the army. The parents took advantage of their resources—organizational skills, money, motivation, and free time—to bargain with the state over the character of the missions their sons undertook. The catalytic event took place in the first week of the First Lebanon War: following the fatalities during that week, the families of soldiers killed in the battle to conquer the Beaufort post in South Lebanon formed a group known as the "Beaufort Family." The parents, who could have interpreted the mission in which their sons had fallen as heroic (as bereaved parents had done in previous wars), instead viewed it as an unnecessary operation, and accused the government of the death of their sons. The protest they sparked was one of the driving forces behind the unprecedented and extremely effective protest movement against the First Lebanon War (Rosental, 2001, 95–98). It is notable that three of the Beaufort casualties were kibbutz members and a fourth was the son of a veteran Jerusalem family with involvement in the media. This change in the bereavement ethos makes the comparison between the composition of the casualties in the two wars relevant, despite the differences in the character of the fighting.

Later on, following the helicopter accident of February 1997, in which seventy-three soldiers were killed en route to Lebanon, the middle-class–based *Four Mothers* movement was founded. In response to that accident, the *Four Mothers* movement attempted to launch a grassroots organization that would spearhead the demand to quit Lebanon unilaterally. The *Four Mothers'* protest was most effectual, and triggered Ehud Barak's vow to withdraw from Lebanon, a promise that helped him win the general elections in 1999 and to be elected as Prime Minister. In May 2000, Israeli troops withdrew from Lebanese soil.

Interestingly, while the war in Lebanon exacted about twenty casualties every year, this sacrifice did not arouse effective political protest, largely due to the social rearchitecturing of the IDF, a process that had started in the mid-1980s, as well as the distancing of reservists from the battlefield (Tamir, 2005, 10–11, 274). However, the social composition of the casualties in the helicopter accident was similar to that of the first week of the Lebanon War: in other words, about 70 percent came from the middle to upper levels of the secular middle class. This was because air transport was used mainly for elite units and the *Nahal*, largely staffed by the veteran kibbutz and moshav communities.[4] The accident stimulated protest that originated in the social networks to which the fallen had belonged. This was another clear indication of the linkage between the social composition of fatalities and the prospects for political protest.

Change in the IDF's social composition was also mirrored in the soldiers' over-motivation to fight.

THE FIELD UNITS' OVER-MOTIVATION

In the summer of 2004, the organization *Breaking the Silence* appeared on the public scene. This was an organization of released conscripts who presented a photography exhibition in Tel Aviv. The exhibition incorporated testimonies concerning the abuse of Palestinians as presented by soldiers who had been released from regular service in Hebron. The exhibition stirred up a public storm, which strengthened the organization and expanded the project of documenting abuses carried out against the Palestinian population. The media then began to flood their outlets with information on violent behavior, while the IDF rushed to declare that all alleged cases of misconduct would be investigated. As a result, a range of incidents were brought to light, including looting and destruction, various methods of punishing civilians, humiliating experiences at checkpoints, improper shooting practices, such as "confirming the kill" (shooting a corpse to "confirm" that the enemy is dead, even when he may only be wounded), and more.

The late arrival of *Breaking the Silence*, four years after violent conflict with the Palestinians had actually commenced, is an indication of the high legitimacy the fighting enjoyed among the ranks of the IDF. This phenomenon complemented and intensified the effect of the change in the bereavement discourse, and together they served to strengthen the army's professional autonomy during the first years of the Al-Aqsa Intifada. Here, then, is another aspect of the changing composition of the combat soldiers in the Occupied Territories and its role in reconstructing the republican equation.

Comparing the Intifadas

A comparison between the soldiers' pattern of behavior during the First Intifada and the Al-Aqsa Intifada—both types of warfare against the occupied Palestinian population—reveals that during the Al-Aqsa Intifada the IDF General Staff refrained from curbing aggressiveness among the units, in sharp contrast to its approach during the First Intifada.

As mentioned in chapter 3, in the First Intifada, the army implemented a policy of relatively restrained use of force. Of especial significance was the Chief Military Attorney's directive to the Military Police to open an investigation into every incident in which a Palestinian was killed as a result of IDF action, unless the Palestinian was involved in hostile terrorist activities at the time (Strashnov, 1994, 177–90). This directive was annulled in the Al-Aqsa Intifada.[5] Furthermore, while in the First Intifada the army distributed written open-fire orders to its soldiers, it did not do so in the Al-Aqsa Intifada, in keeping with a reality defined as warfare.

For the sake of comparison, in the first three years of the First Intifada, around 1,200 such cases were opened, and hundreds of soldiers were court-martialed. This policy was not repeated in the Al-Aqsa Intifada: indeed, from September 2000 to December 2005, Israeli security forces in the Occupied Territories killed 3,289 Palestinians, of whom 1,594 had not been participating in battle, including 669 minors. In contrast, during the six years of the First Intifada, 1,070 Palestinians were killed, of whom 237 were minors. In the equivalent period in the Al-Aqsa Intifada (until June 2005), only 131 military criminal investigations were opened in relation to the killing or wounding of Palestinians by soldiers in the Occupied Territories (and most of those were opened since 2004), of which merely 52 resulted in an indictment. The army justified its policy by claiming that it was involved in battle, and not just policing an occupied population (*B'Tselem* site).

From this perspective, as information flowed from the army into the public sphere, during the First Intifada there was a certain level of internal pressure for restraint, which in turn led the IDF to moderate its use of force. In the Al-Aqsa Intifada, on the other hand, the lack of restraint was particularly notable, at least until its fourth year.

Chapter 3 explained the disparity between the two Intifadas in terms of a disparity in the legitimacy of the fighting due to the nature of the threat (uprising versus terror), the changing status of the Palestinian entity (occupied population versus quasi-state), and the IDF's interest in escalating the fighting without the limitations of politically balanced ground forces, the social composition of which changed as part of the rearchitecturing of the army. These mechanisms flowed not only from the army to the political discourse, but also from the military command into the ranks of the army. This explains the barrier preventing internal resistance within the ranks to the use of force in the form of *Breaking the Silence* and conscientious objection. Even when such groups eventually raised their voice, they faced political obstacles.

For illustration, in 2002 the long-standing *Yesh Gvul* movement was joined by *Courage to Refuse (*in Hebrew, *Ometz Lesarev*), a movement based on selectively refusing to serve in the Occupied Territories in what its members perceived as a battle to expand the Jewish settlements at the cost of oppressing the local Palestinian population. Moreover, they saw this as contradicting Israel's security interests (*Courage to Refuse* website). *Courage to Refuse* distinguished itself from *Yesh Gvul* by positioning itself at the heart of left-wing Zionism (Dloomy, 2005, 713). More than five hundred reservist combat soldiers and officers expressed their willingness to refuse, many more than had done so during the First Lebanon War and the First Intifada, and the movement gained momentum. However, *Operation Defensive Shield* in March 2002, launched in response to the Passover attack at the Park Hotel in the town of Netanya, stopped the momentum. Again, with high rates of public support for the government's military policies, which were portrayed as a battle against Palestinian terror, the moderate left wing was effectively swept away, and the opportunities for institutionalized collective action aimed at curbing military policies were once again limited. In other words, the legitimacy of the fighting negated the legitimacy of any challenge to limit it, and largely blocked off attentiveness in public opinion to the little information concerning improper behavior that was available.

As much as their over-motivation for aggressive conduct, these mechanisms therefore explain why soldiers refrained from arousing public opinion through their social networks, or from curbing aggressiveness through dialogue with their commanders, in contrast to their predecessors in the First Intifada. Nonetheless, the very appearance of *Breaking the Silence* testifies to the potential for such activity. A high profile of aggressiveness may increase the likelihood of protest or resistance. Furthermore, the external legitimacy for the excessive use of force cannot be accepted as a point of departure given that it embodies a discursive interpretation of the external threat, which may itself be politically questioned. Further, soldiers' acceptance or resistance of the use of force is not only shaped by external legitimacy, but also shapes it by mobilizing support through their social networks to challenge military policies or by refraining from so doing. Complementary explanations are thus needed.

With the change in the social composition of the field units, the forces exhibited much greater enthusiasm than in the past for aggressive missions. It became less likely that sensitive soldiers would arouse public opinion via their extra-military social networks, as their Ashkenazi predecessors had done in the past.

To better understand the new groups' orientation, as the new bereavement ethos served as a mediating mechanism between the social composition of the IDF and its rehabilitated military autonomy, I thus offer another mediating mechanism that worked within the ranks and impacted on the way soldiers interpret their missions.

Aggressiveness is very much traceable to the unique situation in which the new groups found themselves. They were functioning in a competitive arena in which they were struggling over their military status and the ability to increase the convertibility of this status, i.e., its translation into valuable assets in the social sphere. Through their military performance, the new groups hoped to prove themselves worthy of status both inside and outside the army.

Competition and Aggressiveness

Theoretically, the military organization plays a major role in curbing inappropriate conduct among soldiers (see Cockerham and Cohen, 1980; Ficarrotta, 1997).[6] Still, as complementing practices of management within the organization, or in cases in which the organization fails to discipline its soldiers, behavioral mechanisms come into play.

Anthropologists and psychologists have focused on the power relations that generate compliance to immoral orders.[7] Others have focused on moral dilemmas in perpetrating violence, and have mapped the mechanisms that help resolve those dilemmas and legitimize violence, such as reconstructing reality, coping with cognitive dissonance, denial, the deployment of distancing mechanisms aimed at dehumanizing enemies, constructing an artificial partition between the ostensibly moral civilian sphere and the immoral military sphere, emotional-cognitive mechanisms of dichotomizing the self and the enemy in order to create a state of moral exclusion, and so on.[8] However, the social context of the soldiers' activity has been overlooked.

Soldiers import values from the civilian sphere, including those related to violence. Of great importance is the social context in which those values were constructed, including inequitable schooling (Mateu-Gelabert and Lune, 2003; Speaker and Petersen, 2000). In this case, it is safe to assume that the level of violence in Israeli society somewhat grew between the Intifadas, although comparative monitoring is not available. Yet, given that the new groups are partly povertized with the linkage between schooling, violence, and poverty (Benbenishty and Avi Astor, 2005), it is reasonable to expect a slight increase in the initial adherence to violent values and norms. This impact, however, is hardly measurable provided the units' heterogeneous composition. Thus, imported values cannot serve as the main explanatory variables.

Nonetheless, soldiers do not only import norms; they also interact with their peers in both the military and civilian environments in a manner that may mitigate or aggravate previous proclivities toward violence. As with any agentic action, soldiers' actions arguably take place within a plurality of environments or structural contexts simultaneously, which intersect and overlap with one another while remaining mutually autonomous. Those environments shape the actors' normative commitments, social ties, and emotional solidarity, by which the agents are guided and channeled (Emirbayer, 1997). Soldiers' expectations before and after military service derive from interethnic or interclass power relations (see Enloe, 1980), and as such should be analyzed at the group, rather than the individual, level, especially given that social inequalities between groups construct categories that are often emulated in the military (Tilly, 1998).

Given these environmental terms of entrance, soldiers compete against one another, mainly in the form of group behavior, over the resources the army can provide and to which the groups may attribute symbolic importance. Military achievements embody the initial symbolic rewards the new groups can reap from the army. Competition intensifies the significance of battlefield achievements as the supreme test of fighting, and might overshadow the warriors' previous ethical standards, even including matters of conscience. In this case, competitiveness is applied mainly to the relations between the new groups and the secular Ashkenazi groups, within the new groups themselves, and within their civilian, social networks, in which the groups compete over the social recognition of military accomplishments.

The lower the social status of the competing group, the more competitive it is within the army: because it has fewer opportunities in the civilian sphere, the army is a more important site in determining one's status, hence the more critical significance of battlefield achievements, which shape the amount of symbolic rewards. Inversely, as Liebes and Blum-Kulka have argued (1994), soldiers who are self-propelled can be expected to adopt a critical attitude toward orders that generate immoral behavior, while in lower-status families one is more likely to grow up with the awareness of being at the mercy of the hegemony, which leads to keeping a low profile and the compliance patterns that this entails. Drawing from theories of collective action (Lyons and Lowery, 1986), the availability of a good alternative outside the organizational framework—that is, if the military were less valuable as a mobility track because of attenuated convertibility—would increase the likelihood that soldiers will react strongly to any dissatisfaction. In the context of military service, dissatisfaction may result from a situation that generates inconsistency with the soldier's imported ethic. Being of lower status implies having reduced alternatives, thus making conservative responses more likely. In sum, behavioral norms may matter more than organizational mechanisms in restraining violence, whereas those norms are elicited from the encounter between imported values and competitive social interaction.

Three overlapping sites of competition can be observed that increase the proclivity of religious and peripheral groups to violence as compared to their

Ashkenazi predecessors. It is worth emphasizing that social status accounts for this tendency, rather than any organic pattern.

(1) *The struggle for recognition within the army*: The new groups strove to prove that they were capable of achievements on the battlefield equal to, or even surpassing, those of the secular Ashkenazi groups. Here, the struggle was also over "historical memory," as the Ashkenazi elites had denigrated the other groups' capacity to fight, or had discredited their actual accomplishments. To some extent, these groups even acted in defiance of their predecessors' perceived "soft" masculinity and their evasion of military service, as summarized in chapter 3. The high motivation that these sentiments elicited was translated into a willingness to undertake combat missions without political or conscientious constraints, even displaying excessive enthusiasm for aggressive missions that involved belligerent behavior toward the occupied Palestinian population.

Part of this aggressiveness stems from a struggle over the recognition of the particular unit's combat heritage, especially in units that had been established to carry out policing missions in the Occupied Territories vis-à-vis the more established and prestigious units (in which the presence of their Ashkenazi predecessors is more pronounced). The formation of "instant units," consisting of several groups with different professions bought together from different organic units, created the competitive conditions that could aggravate aggressiveness (see Ben-Shalom et al., 2005).

A representative illustration of this is the conduct of soldiers and border policepersons enforcing the policy of closures on Palestinian towns, most of who belonged to "instant units" assembled for that mission. As the mission was prolonged, the soldiers' identification with it reached the level of full devotion to, and the drawing of satisfaction from, denying Palestinians their humanitarian rights. Rosenfeld (2004) has called this "a false consciousness of combat," which blinds soldiers to the essence, meaning, and consequences of their mission.

Struggles over recognition are intensified when the opportunity to gain a temporary sense of power within military service is exploited. Unlike their Ashkenazi counterparts, for whom military service is a kind of moratorium from their social mobility or part of their mobility track when high rates of convertibility are available, for soldiers from peripheral groups, military service might signify an apex in their career that is most unlikely to repeat itself in the near future. Hence, the totality of the military experience offers a unique opportunity to exhibit power, in this case in relation to a weaker group, i.e., the Palestinians. As testified by a soldier who served at a checkpoint:

> You start playing with them [the Palestinians], like a computer game. You come here, you go there, like this. You barely move, you make them obey the tip of your finger. It's a mighty feeling. It's something you don't experience elsewhere. You know it's because you have a weapon, you know it's because you are a soldier, you know all this, but it is addictive.[9]

The Palestinians themselves are aware of differences between the soldiers according to the ethnic map of the army, as documented in a discussion with children from the Balata refugee camp.

> Rasmi: "all the soldiers are bad, but we see in the camp that the youngest soldiers [the compulsory soldiers] are worst, they hit us more, they are even more violent one with us. The large ones [the reservists] are also bad, but they hit us less."
> Mu'tazz: "They are Ashkenazim."
> [reporter]: "How do you know that they are Ashkenazim"?
> [Mu'tazz]: "We see that."[10]

(2) *The struggle for recognition within the civilian sphere*: This struggle is over the political construction of the groups' achievements, with efforts made to discursively ascribe national meaning to their respective contributions. These efforts became significant in light of what is perceived as a repetitive historical pattern whereby the Ashkenazi-dominated "peace camp" attempts to downgrade, or even delegitimize military contribution.

Frustration of this kind is voiced by Colonel Harel Knafo, commander of the Samaria Brigade during the Al-Aqsa Intifada. Knafo, born to a Moroccan family, grew up in the peripheral town of Mitzpeh Ramon and had been educated at a yeshiva.

> In the fighting units that have passed through this district there were dozens of Meir Har Zions [referring to the legendary commando who fought alongside Ariel Sharon in the Unit 101 of the 1950s]. Twenty years ago, books would have been written about the amazing operations carried out here by the elite units . . . Today? There's not a word about it in the newspaper. It isn't newsworthy. I don't remember a single instance of messing up or of cowardice under fire. I've been in the army for twenty-one years and I don't remember as glorious a period. The achievements are tremendous. The tragedy is that the feeling among the public is the opposite of what the army itself feels.[11]

(3) *The struggle for social recognition within the soldiers' original civilian social networks*: The new groups' communities are partly imbued with the ethno-national ethos, which highlights the individual's Jewish ethnic belonging, and not his/her civic contribution, thus weakening the motivation to serve

within those communities. Soldiering is not necessarily perceived as the determinant test for meaningful citizenship, especially after the IDF had relegated many members of these groups to peripheral positions. Therefore, members of these new groups who choose to serve (mainly some Ultra-Orthodox and youngsters from the lowest social stratum) struggle for recognition vis-à-vis those who have avoided service, with the latter sometimes gaining more prestige within their home communities than their peers doing military service.

For illustration, in 2004 combatants from the Ultra-Orthodox *Nahal* battalion abused the bodies of dead Palestinians and were photographed with them. One of the soldiers attributed this behavior to the lowly status of the soldiers, who had been estranged by their Ultra-Orthodox communities, in which recruitment is delegitimized. A suicide bombing, he claimed, became an exciting attraction for the soldiers, and bestowed meaning on missions they perceived as "grey" in comparison with the more prestigious operations performed by other units (Gonen, 2004).

In sum, this multisited competition intensively and unidirectionally made soldiers from the new groups overly motivated to fight and prove their ability in relation to other groups (more testimonies documented in Levy, forthcoming). Remilitarization became the peripheral groups' interest as a means of conferring their military service with special worth.

Unlike these groups, their Ashkenazi predecessors (during the 1950s–1980s) came from social networks that were imbued with the republican ethos, which, given the high convertibility rates of military contribution within the structure of materialist militarism, encouraged youngsters to contribute to the army. Because of the lack of environmental alienation, competitiveness was weaker within the social networks themselves. Furthermore, military service was utilized to consolidate a preexisting social dominance rather than to acquire an "entry ticket" to society, as some of the new groups attempted to do, and as such was less determinant. Nonetheless, for as long as these groups struggled for the recognition of their military achievements during the state's first years, mainly vis-à-vis the political establishment, battlefield achievements served as the supreme test of contribution, and as such triggered aggressiveness (see Ben–Eliezer, 1998). Only after the Ashkenazi groups had established their social dominance, with the Six Day War as the main watershed, did soldiers begin to display more sensitivity and criticism toward their missions. Furthermore, when rates of convertibility decreased following the 1973 War, competition over military gains lessened and increased sensitivity was translated into political action that challenged the military mind-set, as attested to by the protest movements set up by ex-soldiers.

The Soldiers' Response to Violence

Although conditions were created that increased the inclination toward violence, the key lies in the military unit's composition and the climate that it produces. Due to the realignment of the IDF's social composition, the socially imbalanced field units of the Al-Aqsa Intifada did not generate the critical mass for launching effective resistance to aggressive conduct, whether perceived as a pattern encouraged by the high command, or as deviant behavior. Because of the IDF's altered social composition, sensitive soldiers, mainly those who had been drawn from the more educated social strata, found themselves in the minority. Accordingly, they could embark on one of four alternative paths: (1) to be swept away by the majority, the path chosen by most of these soldiers; (2) to opt for "exit" by leaving the unit (especially in the reserve system); (3) to restrain the use of force within the unit by interacting with their peers or commanders. This pattern declined in the Al-Aqsa Intifada because of the social imbalance of the units. The effect of this social realignment is illustrated by the testimony of one of the leaders of *Courage to Refuse*, who described what happened in his military unit after he and his friends had left it:

> I was sitting with a group of ten combat platoon commanders . . . They told me that because we refused to serve during the past year [2002], we have no idea what's happening there, that it's an entirely new ballgame now. They described the horrors that were committed in their units—looting, abuse, you name it. Everything but rape. The experiences that caused us to come out with the letter pale in comparison to this. (Lavie, 2002)

And finally, (4) to voice their reluctance to use excessive force by turning to post-service protest or even conscientious objection, patterns familiar from former wars. This final option was late to appear because the imbalanced social composition had not generated a critical mass of assertive, relatively conscientious soldiers, and because public opinion delegitimized alternative voices as the case of *Courage to Refuse* attests.[12]

It was only in 2004, four years after the Intifada had erupted, that the *Breaking the Silence* movement entered the scene. Made up of discharged soldiers, mostly from the secular Ashkenazi middle class, *Breaking the Silence* exposed animalistic behavior toward the Palestinian population in the West Bank and Gaza Strip. This movement drove the IDF's high command to rein in aggressiveness and clamp down on violations of military codes. Still, the very late appearance of this group—much due to the narrowing social base of potential protestors—testifies both to the reduced potential for sensitive soldiers to arouse public opinion, and the considerable autonomy the IDF had enjoyed up until then in dealing with the occupied Palestinian population without facing effective public criticism initiated by its own soldiers.

The partial exit of many male, secular, middle-class Ashkenazim from combat roles—as part of the social rearchitecturing of the IDF prior to the Intifada—created a vacuum that was to some extent filled by the *Machsom Watch* movement (*machsom* being the Hebrew word for "checkpoint" or "barrier"). *Machsom Watch* was a civil rights movement, consisting exclusively of middle-class and conspicuously Ashkenazi women. It was founded in 2001, inspired by reports of human rights abuses of Palestinians at the many checkpoints the IDF had set up throughout the West Bank, allegedly to perform security checks on the Palestinian population. *Machsom Watch* monitored the behavior of soldiers and police at the checkpoints through which Palestinians enter Israel so as to ensure that the human and civil rights of the latter were protected, and reported the results of their observations. Their primary modus operandum was to stand at each of the main checkpoints, observing how Palestinian civilians were treated by the soldiers. Perceived patterns of abuse and humiliation were documented and reported, and very often activists intervened with the soldiers in situ, or even helped Palestinians in their interactions with the IDF (*Machsom Watch* site).

In short, *Machsom Watch* offers a unique model of civilian monitoring of the military. As an alternative to the customary model of monitoring, by which civilian groups raise issues and approach the political echelon via the media, interests groups, politicians, and so on, *Machsom Watch* has taken an active role in the monitoring process itself, directly observing military practices.

Still, had the secular Ashkenazi exit not occurred, the more dovish Ashkenazi group might have increased its presence at the checkpoints, and hence improved its ability to inform the high command from within of any wrongdoings by soldiers, and even to rally public opinion through its social networks, as it had often done in the past and as the testimony cited above (from the *Courage to Refuse* activist) indicates.

In other words, the exit of the male group triggered the entrance of the female group, whose social background was for the most part identical. On the other hand, the organization did not restrict itself only to "voice," as it did not simply protest against military practices in the West Bank. It is safe to assume that it is precisely the same mood of apathy that brings many members of the upper middle class to exit the public sphere that directed *Machsom Watch* away from futile voicing in favor of this unique mode of action.

These phenomena—*Machsom Watch*, *Breaking the Silence* and *Courage to Refuse*—embody the emergence of alternative channels of information and supervision—either supervision by external organizations, or calls for soldiers to protest or refuse, i.e., "supervision from within." In the First Intifada the IDF deployed effective legitimizing mechanisms that preserved unity within the army for a long time owing to the policy of the relatively restrained use of force. Both within the organization and beyond it, the army's command thus broadcast that it took responsibility for what was being done, thereby relieving the soldiers of a feeling of responsibility that would make them act outside the army in order to restrain the use of excessive violence. The Al-Aqsa Intifada, in contrast, was notable for its lack of restraint, at least until its fourth year.

However, not only were intramilitary routes of action blocked, but political ones were too. Middle-class groups, formerly the backbone of the peace coalition, reacted to the Al-Aqsa Intifada with a passivity mixed with the delegitimization of the institutionalized peace organizations (Herman, 2002). In particular, the steps to war were headed by the partnership in government of representatives of the "peace camp," namely, the Labor Party and *Shinui*. This was a process that created a space in which political initiatives by small groups and organizations could appear. It is possible that had there been mass resistance to the fighting then this kind of space would not have opened up, with most political energy channeled into putting forward diplomatic alternatives to warfare. Conversely, the experience of the European pacifist movements in the early 1980s suggests that the movements struggle to improve the profile of conscientious objection, rather than focusing on ending conscription itself, resulted in only a small number of conscientious objectors and practices of disobedience (Ajangiz, 2002).

Such circumstances nurture an *alternative politics* that bypasses the blocked institutional channels of influence, and adopts what can be conceptualized as a *quasi-exit* (Lehman-Wilzig, 1991, following Hirschman's [1970] terminology). Quasi-exit is an alternative type of action that is neither regular protest (voice), nor a mode of leaving the system or rebelling against it (exit), but rather an intermediate path that is either illegal (*Courage to Refuse*), or legal but operates outside institutional channels (*Breaking the Silence* and *Machsom Watch*) (Levy and Mizrahi, n.d.). In the final analysis, alternative politics played a significant role in eroding the IDF's legitimacy for fighting, thus paving the road to the Disengagement Plan, as chapter 5 illustrates.

CONCLUSIONS

This chapter has highlighted the realignment in the social composition of the IDF in an attempt to tackle part of the puzzle posed in chapter 1, namely, the Israeli state's relative autonomy in waging a prolonged military undertaking without significant internal opposition, in contrast to the erosion in autonomy during the First Lebanon War and the First Intifada. While chapter 3 outlined in general terms the mechanisms behind the political generation of new patterns of violence management, this chapter has zoomed in on the role of the social composition of the IDF in affording it the autonomy to keep the violence alive. Two mechanisms were analyzed as mediating variables between the social realignment and the military's conduct: (1) the change of the bereavement ethos due to the alteration of the casualties map in a manner that did not elicit political protest; and, (2) army units becoming competitive sites triggering the new groups to demonstrate aggressiveness. Common to both mechanisms is the state's production of symbolic rewards for the new groups, by which bereaved parents accept their loss and for which these groups compete.

This social change greatly influenced the functioning of the senior command, as illustrated by a comparison between the First and second Intifadas. While the Chief of the General Staff during First Intifada, General Dan Shomron, blocked political pressures to vigorously quell the uprising, with his externally oriented efforts internally mirrored in the Chief Military Attorney's restraining directives, thirteen years later this approach was altered. As the secular Ashkenazim partly exited, the senior command became less sensitive about the disintegration of the army when executing controversial missions. Thus, the military command enjoyed considerable autonomy and was able to gradually escalate its response to the Palestinian uprising and infuse its action with political goals. Only the combined efforts of *Machsom Watch*, *Breaking the Silence*, and *Courage to Refuse* brought about some moderation in the form of the more stringent directives issued by the Chief Military Attorney.

It follows that the command's policies not only determine the soldiers' conduct but, at the same time, are determined by it. Therefore, the legitimacy of violence cannot be simply regarded as a point of departure but is rather the variable to be explained. Soldiers' acceptance of or aversion to the command's directives not only mirror existing levels of legitimacy, but to a large extent also shape them by their very response. Hence, the social composition of the military politically matters.

As the Israeli case shows, the model of the "citizen-soldier" combines symbolic rewards with a pattern of political control over the military. The more the state rewarded its soldiers and their families by enabling the bidirectional replication of the military and civilian social hierarchies, the greater internal autonomy the state enjoyed regarding military affairs, as seen through the 1940s–1970s. Attenuated convertibility, asymmetrical with the increased military burden following the 1973 War, greatly extended the leverage for any collective action that invoked the equation "military burden = political participation" (see Tilly, 1997a at the theoretical level). Thus, eroded state autonomy paved the way for both the deescalation of military policies with the trend toward cultural demilitarization that this entails, and the simultaneous rearchitecturing of the IDF's social composition as a low-cost way of reconstituting the republican equation by symbolically rewarding religious and peripheral groups. Thus, by altering its social composition, the army partially restored the levels of autonomy that it had previously possessed until the 1980s.

In other words, the state opted for the third mechanism at its disposal to reconstitute the violated republican equation, namely, reducing the circle of military participation by redistributing the burden and diverting the weight from middle-class to lower-class groups. That is, after other mechanisms — manipulating the external threat and allocating rights — had failed to improve the state's autonomous capacity, it had been forced to decrease military participation by embarking on deescalation. With this mode of action described in this chapter, the state could resort once more to the first mechanism and leverage the Intifada to manipulate the external threat.

Indeed, the alteration of the military's social makeup reflects a global trend. The realignment of the social composition of Western armies in general since the 1980s indicates a mounting alienation between the upper middle class and the military. Elite groups distance themselves from the army, consequently displaying apathy to the implications of its belligerency, including the victims that that belligerency entails (see Moskos, 2001; Ricks, 1997). Here, as noted in chapter 1, the corruption of the republican conception (as put by Sandel, 1998) takes the shape of diminished motivation, if not also reduced legitimacy, for collective action aimed at substantively controlling the state's military policies (Silver, 2004), the ultimate epitaph for the republican principle of the political community's control over its violent resources.

Consequently, democracies with conscript armies experience fewer combat casualties than democracies with volunteer or professional forces, because the societal actors most closely affected by conscript casualties utilize their political power to constrain policy makers (Vasquez, 2005). Indeed, since the 1980s, the discourse in the United States has debated the question of whether American casualties in the Vietnam War came disproportionately from the working class and the poorer sectors of society (Appy, 1993; Barnett et al., 1992; Fallows, 1993). Likewise, the ethno-class categorization of the casualties of the war in Iraq has triggered public debate as to the possibility of bringing back the draft as a way of dividing the burden more equally.

Small wonder, then, that historian Richard Kohn (2002) expresses the paradox of political control over the armed forces in the postmodern era thus: though the public has more tools to supervise the military, it has less incentive to do so. Part of this orientation is ascribed to the shrinking rates of military participation. In Tilly's terms (2004), this phenomenon is no less than a partial withdrawal of trust networks (whose historical emergence owed much to the imposition of recruitment) from public politics in a manner that undermines democracy. Political control over the armed forces is thus put at risk.

This process deserves special attention, as foundations have simultaneously been laid for the remilitarization of Western militaries, as they become increasingly staffed by peripheral groups. As the ties between citizens and soldiers are loosened, a gap is created that poses questions about how effectively the military will reflect and support the values of contemporary democratic society (Burk, 2002, 19). In this spirit, overaggressive behavior among soldiers (such as the 2004 Abu Ghraib prison scandal in Iraq) has been traced to those soldiers' disadvantageous position in the labor market, which had impelled their recruitment in the first place (Klein, 2004). Peripheral groups, moreover, have displayed hyper-motivation to engage in belligerent activity (Karsten, 2001) as a means of upgrading the military's status, to which their own social and professional status is linked.

It follows that states regain their internal autonomy by reconstituting the republican equation based on the exchange of military obligations for social rewards, in other words, by intensively drawing the bulk of military personnel from the more skillful members of the lower middle class, women, and ethnic minorities, rather than adopting more costly strategies. Increasing the community's substantive control over the armed forces, concomitant with reintroducing conscription or simply demilitarizing foreign policy, is an exemplary alternative strategy. In sum, the Israeli case is representative of a broader trend: Western militaries may be more militarized, but they are less politically monitored.

Nevertheless, despite this increased autonomy, the Israeli state shifted and modified its mode of warfare and initiated the partial withdrawal from the Palestinian-populated territories, starting with the Disengagement Plan from the Gaza Strip. Greater autonomy in managing military policies was paradoxically expanded to the implementation of the Disengagement Plan, even though this was an outcome of the attenuated legitimacy of warfare. Chapter 5 will deal with this shift.

NOTES

1. Part of this chapter was first published as "The War of the Peripheries: A Social Mapping of IDF Casualties in the Al-Aqsa Intifada," *Social Identities* 12 (3), (2006): 309–24 (http://www.tandf.co.uk/journals/titles/13504630.asp).

2. A paramilitary force within the Israel Police Force composed of career officers and conscripts from the IDF.

3. Table 4.3 maps the casualties according to the mode of their military action rather than their corps' assignment, as many armored and engineering units functioned in the Intifada as infantry policing units. Table 4.4 maps the original corps' assignment to analyze the changes in the IDF's social composition.

4. This data was surveyed by the same method as the overall mapping.

5. *The Association for Civil Rights in Israel and B'Tselem v. the Military Attorney General*, High Court of Justice 9594/03.

6. Indeed, the scandal of the Abu Ghraib prison in Iraq was largely related to the failure of command monitoring (see Badger, 2005).

7. See, for example, Browning, 1992; Kelman and Hamilton, 1989; Szegedy-Maszak, 2004.

8. See Bar and Ben-Ari, 2005; Ben-Ari, 1999; Helman, 1997; Liebes and Blum-Kulka, 1994; Linn, 1996; Maoz, 2001.

9. Breaking the Silence website.

10. Cited in Ali Waked, "Children of the Camp of Balata," *Ynet*, 2 April 2004 (Hebrew).

11. Cited in Avihai Becker, "A Job Well Done," *Haaretz*, 26 June, 2005.

12. This analysis is based on testimonies documented in the Soldier Testimony and Breaking the Silence websites.

Chapter Five

From "People's Army" to "Market Army"

In 2003, the army could point to real achievements in reducing the number of terrorist attacks carried out by Palestinian organizations. Paradoxically, it was also the year that saw a rise in public criticism over the IDF's performance in the Occupied Territories. Two years later, the result was the unilateral withdrawal from the Gaza Strip and the northern West Bank in what was termed the Disengagement Plan.

    At the center of the decline in the army's legitimacy stood a contradiction latent in its activities. As mentioned, the bearers of the ethos of the market economy, mostly identified with the secular Ashkenazi middle class, raised their expectations of greater material rewards for their military service, and applied added pressure so as to attain them, especially given the reduction in value of symbolic rewards. At the same time, however, because it thought that military expenditure should be reduced, that same group also curbed the price that the state could pay in order to meet those expectations. Accordingly, the army increasingly relied on religious and peripheral groups, which offered their services to the IDF in return for low material rewards on the one hand, while being able to realize relatively high symbolic rewards on the other. The army's new social architecture thus broadened its freedom of action by creating, at least temporarily, the conditions that enabled it to autonomously escalate the fighting while enjoying wide political support, which also led to a temporary increase in its resources. However, to the extent that military activities contradicted the interests of the bearers of the ethos of the market economy, the prolonged fighting with the Palestinians and its growing cost once more added tension to the relations between the army and the relatively higher reaches of the middle class. The army's freedom of action was unsymmetrical in relation to its contracting resources, an asymmetry that renewed the decline in the legitimacy afforded to military activities. To be sure, the first years of the Al-Aqsa Intifada tempered this decline and put it on hold, but they did not entirely deflect a process that had begun following the 1973 War and heightened during the 1980s. The army's reduced legitimacy would eventually lead to the Disengagement Plan.

THE ARMY VERSUS THE MARKET

The theoretical-historical starting point for this chapter is that Western armies are undergoing processes of adaptation to the market that impinge on military policy. This trend offers a conceptual framework for the Israeli case.

As previously indicated, the state provides its citizens with a security product, but not for free. The price is a combination of taxes and military service, with citizens bargaining with the state as to their exact composition (Lake, 1992). The neoliberal ethos of the market economy takes these negotiations a step further. Not only does it expose alternative modes of resource allocation (war versus other options), and not only does it energize the exposure of information concerning the "manufacture" of the security product (i.e., political supervision of the army), but it also creates the expectation of being able to attach a price tag to such security services as are provided, thus enabling them to be weighed against alternatives. This also raises the possibility of consuming security in a way that sidesteps the state (including bringing mercenaries in through the back door).

As a result, the adaptation of armies to the market stems from a number of interrelated factors: first, the delegitimization of compulsory recruitment (that had been developed in tandem with the neoliberal discourse) meant that the recruitment model based on administrative imposition (the draft) was converted into one regulated by the market, in other words, a voluntary model. This delegitimization largely resulted from the fundamental detachment of citizenship from soldiering, which weakened the middle class' motivation to serve in the military—after all, it was able to attain considerable achievements that were no longer dependent on military service (Burk, 1995). The army thereby became an employer in every way, and rather than following a calling, the serviceperson became the holder of an occupation (Moskos, 1977). Insofar as military service is reconstituted as a service provided by the market, a gradual process of commodification is thus instigated. Not only does soldiering return to the labor market, but complementary military services are increasingly provided by private companies (Avant, 2005; Mandel, 2001).

Second, the traditional territorial basis of warfare is gradually undermined as part of a change in the constitutive principle of the state in the global era:

the state mainly serves as a mediator between internal and external forces, and does not require territorial expansion in order to recruit capital and maintain a bureaucracy for that purpose as in the past. Western countries have thus been gradually shrinking their armies and increasingly relying on privatized services (Leander, 2004b). Third, because of their organizational stagnancy, armies ceased to be inspirational in the formation of modern organizations. Indeed, the opposite is the case. A gap opened up between those two sets of organizations, and, if it wished to maintain organizational innovation, the army had to borrow organizational values from the business sector, and not vice versa (Fukuyama and Shulsky, 1997). Fourth, military failures, changes in warfare, the increasing similarity between military and civilian technologies, and the general crisis of confidence in civilian professions, have led to a weakening of the professional jurisdiction of the military and to the fracture of its monopoly, as competing occupations and, later on, organizations, entered the field (such as private organizations, other state security agencies, and so on), a process that forces the army to adapt itself to operating in conditions of competition (Segal and Schwartz, 1981; Snider and Watkins, 2000). In short, due to the tension between the constitutive rules of the market economy and those of the military organization, the challenge from the former on the latter is of the utmost significance to the army's legitimacy. Values such as hierarchy, discipline, uniformity, and sacrifice on the part of the provider of a public product are held up against the contradictory values of business organizations and others modeling themselves on them, which provide mainly private goods. At the same time, the neoliberal ethos contradicts the state's ability to raise large funds for the military effort, thus eroding the legitimacy of deploying force. Accordingly, as armies find themselves struggling for resources in a competitive environment, they learn how to pursue alternative sources of legitimacy. This leads them to adapt themselves to the hegemonic culture of the market economy. Part of this adaptation process is a conscious mode of action by the army, and another part lies in the military organization's deep-rooted strategic culture.

Indeed, with the appropriate adjustments, this theoretical starting point can assist in studying the Israeli case. Until the 1980s the army was seen as above the market. The widespread legitimacy enjoyed by the state in controlling the economy, along with its status as the main provider of civil services and a high level of militarism, ensured that military expenditure as a proportion of GDP rose systematically. Military expenditure competed with other clauses in the state's budget, but not with the market. The state's supremacy over the market rested on the ethos of statism (*Mamlachtiyut*), while the high rates of convertibility that this afforded strengthened the affinity of the middle class to the state rather than the market in the form of materialist militarism.

During the 1980s, a process of change got underway with the decline of materialist militarism and the evolving tension between materialism and militarism. The equation that positioned financial growth alongside cutbacks to the security budget was presented as a way of routing resources away from inherently wasteful (purely military) usage, to usage that promoted economic growth (Tov, 1998, 127–38). The "Economic Stabilization Plan," implemented by Shimon Peres' government in 1985 in order to eliminate the hyperinflation, incorporated a deep cutback in army spending, a reduction in government military industrial activity, and a toning down of the army's belligerent profile, as manifested by the unilateral, partial withdrawal from Lebanon in 1985. This juncture signifies the period of time during which Israel became a market economy society. State involvement in the economy was largely shaped by the neoliberal agenda, which called for the state's retreat in the face of the market and sanctified the values of the free market in the name of individual freedom, while seeing government interference as an obstacle to economic growth. Israel's political economy from the second half of the 1980s was thus characterized by the transfer of regulatory activities away from the state. The neoliberal doctrine created a broad political-cultural base from which to criticize the army's resources, thereby forcing the military to adapt its internal management to the new cultural rules. In practice, in the years 1980–2003, military spending as a proportion of GDP dropped by more than 50 percent, while GDP rose by about 200 percent (according to the Central Bureau of Statistics), with most of the cutbacks directed at private consumption (on the cultural and political changes in Israel see: Grinberg and Shafir, 2000; Shafir and Peled, 2002; Shalev, 2000).

During the early 1990s, with the winds of peace blowing across the region (with the Oslo process at the center), this trend intensified. The IDF was no longer positioned above the market, nor even as a competitor with it; instead, it was gradually subjugated to the market. With the state perceived as interfering in the market, and with warfare perceived as interfering with Israel's integration into the global economy, the army, as a state-run tool of warfare, came to represent both of those "evils," and was subjected to increasing criticism. The ethos of the market economy was borne by the relatively upper reaches of the middle class, notably by secular Ashkenazi groups and upwardly mobile Mizrachim who had made it to the upper rungs of the middle class.

While the state's supremacy had depended on the social criterion embedded in statism, the strengthening of the market in relation to the state was related to a reverse process. Let us recall the argument made in this context in chapter 2.

A series of factors were responsible for empowering the ethos of the market while weakening statism. These included the intensification of a materialist ethos as a direct result of the strengthening of the middle class, the primary beneficiaries of the fruits of economic growth after the Six Day War; Israel's exposure to globalization in a way that was conditional on deescalating the violent Arab-Israeli conflict; the decline in the economic fruits of war simultaneously with increased security costs following the 1973 and First Lebanon Wars; the state-sponsored growth of business corporations; and other processes. The ethos of the market economy eroded the value of contributing to the state as the criterion determining the distribution of social rewards and as the justification for social dominance. Individualist, achievement-oriented values dominated the traditional tenets of statism.

In other words, convertibility declined. As social inequality expanded, the middle class succeeded in establishing its dominant status, relying on the reproductive mechanisms of the market economy rather than statist or military symbols. Those leading groups that in that past had been the bearers of the statist ethos, to their clear benefit, now turned their back on it, seeing statism as superfluous, or even bothersome.

The clash of militarism with the market had additional causes. First, a gap in organizational culture opened up between civilian and military organizations, which lessened professional convertibility among servicepersons. Second, although the ethos of the market economy is not necessarily a liberal one, its elements of entrepreneurship and competition strengthen individualist values, values that contradict with a military culture based on discipline, sacrifice, and even totalism. Third, in the context of a competitive labor market, "military time" and "civilian time" began to compete with one another. It is not for nothing that reserve army duties, once a status symbol for Israeli men, became an obstacle in finding work, and not an advantage, as had previously been the case, to the level that the state turned to protect via legislation the reservists' rights vis-à-vis their employers.

It is the bearers of the market ethos, mainly from the upper middle class, who have ceased to see militarism as a central symbol. That is, they do not reap significant symbolic rewards in the form of convertible military assets, and so, in the light of the violation of the republican equation, they seek to reduce the costs. This can take the shape of demands for compensatory material rewards, or for a reduction of the military burden, partially by subjugating it to the rules of the market, as we can see from the relationship between the IDF and the middle class since the 1980s. This process undermined the legitimacy of the army and forced it to match its conduct to the directives of the market economy. As mentioned, the Al-Aqsa Intifada slowed this process down; however, contrary to what the army's most senior officers might have expected, it did not reverse its course. Indeed, the erosion of the IDF's legitimacy was renewed even as the army was fighting. While the IDF's new social architecture gave the army more room to maneuver in creating the conditions—albeit temporary ones—for autonomously escalating the fighting, the increasingly expensive and ongoing warfare with the Palestinians once more made the army's relationship with the upper middle class tense, thus renewing the erosion of its legitimacy.

Indeed, just as the army could point to a reduction in the number of terror attacks as a positive outcome of the fighting, mainly in 2002, a gradual decline in the public's confidence in the IDF's personnel was identified (Vigoda-Gadot and Mizrahi, 2005, 17). Nonetheless, public confidence in the army remained high, as expressed in occasional surveys that measure confidence in the IDF as compared with civilian institutions (see Arian et al., 2005). However, the concept of "confidence" should be taken in context: this is not the same unconditional confidence, or even blind faith, of the pre-1973 years, but confidence relative to that given to other civilian institutions. It can be termed "critical confidence," a clear indication of which can be found in measurements of democracy in Israel that show a high level of confidence in the army contemporaneous with increasing recognition of the right to refuse to serve.

Several dimensions of the erosion of legitimacy shall now be presented: financial resources, human resources, the legitimacy of the fighting, and the contradictions inherent in the politics of a market economy. Eroded legitimacy generated the disengagement.

THE EROSION OF THE LEGITIMACY OF THE ARMY'S FINANCIAL RESOURCES

Even as the army was at war against the Palestinians, criticism of its resources resurfaced more intensely. However, this was not only a budgetary issue, but a clash that spread to cultural and symbolic dimensions, and which could be seen in the demand to subject the military's management to the rules of the market economy even while it was involved in battle.

This was notably manifested in the renewal of the assault on the terms of employment enjoyed by career servicepersons. As part of the reduction in the security budget in 2003, career servicepersons saw their salaries cut (civilian public sector employees also suffered similar cutbacks), and their favorable retirement packages were downgraded.[1] At the same time, the army implemented a large redundancy program. For the first time, then, serving in the standing army was, for all intents and purposes, seen as a profession, comparable in status to that of other civil servants. This was not only the case at the discursive level (a process that had begun from the mid-1990s), but also in practical terms, and is a clear illustration of the declining status of an army that, as mentioned, was perceived as a fighting force.

In 2004 the government ratified another cut in the budget, while simultaneously providing tax relief to the benefit of the middle class and above. Here too the military budget was subjected to the neoliberal principles of "small government" and strong public purchasing power, despite the IDF being at battle. Historically, cutbacks in the defense budget in the years 1952 and 2000 largely succeeded in driving the army to construct external threats (intentionally or not) as a way of struggling for resources (the retaliatory operations and the Al-Aqsa Intifada, respectively). In contrast, however, after the cutbacks of 1985 were implemented, having failed to construct a threat (the First Lebanon War), the military underwent a process of moderation. The circumstances of the cutbacks in 2004 were similar to those of 1985. They arose following the collapse of the army's effectiveness in the Palestinian front, along with the consequences of the Second Gulf War, which was the catalyst for a reexamination of the IDF's military rationale to prepare itself for dealing with a number of simultaneous threats. This was the result of the neutralization of what was perceived as the Iraqi threat, which had implications for other perceived threats, primarily the Syrian. At the same time, the budget was debated as the *Shinui* Party led a kind of middle class uprising against increased burdens in taxation (mainly in the shape of payments to the National Insurance Institute), and reserve duties. Demands for reducing the security budget thus became *bon ton* in the political discourse around mid-2000. These circumstances led to the return of the 1985 scenario, namely, military restraint and moderation.

The budgetary problem was sharpened by the expectation that a price tag be put on the security product provided by the state, thus enabling it to be compared with other products and alternative ways of delivering that particular product. This is a mode of action typical of security consumers in the light of an increasingly costly security product or a perceived decline in its quality, and incorporates pressure for greater transparency in the "manufacture" of the security product and its alternatives (at the theoretical level see Lake, 1992). Militarism was subjugated to the rules of the market.

In a way, the argument over the *security fence*, the wall that has been constructed since 2003 along the border between Israel and the Palestinian Authority, illustrates this cultural change. Lowly social groups paid the bulk of the human and economic price for terror attacks on cities during the Al-Aqsa Intifada, attacks that public discourse in Israel attributed to the lack of a separation wall. However, while the victimhood of those groups fitted the ethos of sacrifice without inspiring protest, a debate was conducted over the financial efficiency of the proposed barrier. This resulted from the very affinity between reducing the profile of terror attacks and increasing economic activity at the price of funding the wall from internal resources (for example, see Eckstein and Tsiddon, 2004).

A security-related ecological discourse was also integrated within the market economy discourse: the army, which controls most of the territory in the country (Oren, 2005), was criticized for causing environmental damage. This criticism intensified as the massive building projects of the 1990s (following the huge wave of immigration from the former Soviet Union) made land a scarce resource. In this case, the discourse of the market economy merged with a civic enthusiasm for environmental issues (see Ben-Eliezer, 2003). Civil groups acted in the legal and public spheres to prevent the army and military industries from realizing their environmentally damaging plans. To the extent that the environmental discourse served to bypass frontal attacks on the military establishment and its values, deployment of the issue of the environment increased criticism of the army. This can be seen no more clearly than with regard to the nuclear bomb: the most significant challenge—albeit limited—to have developed since 2000 to the secrecy of Israel's nuclear projects was the environmental one, drawing on ecological damage caused by the nuclear reactor in the town of Dimona, the fear of leakage from the aging reactor, and illness among workers exposed to radiation. Were it not for these harms, the nuclear project would have remained in the shadows. After all, its existence was not perceived as incurring significant costs until the appearance of the environmental aspect.

THE EROSION OF THE LEGITIMACY OF HUMAN INVESTMENT: FROM "OBLIGATORY MILITARISM" TO "CONTRACTUAL MILITARISM"[2]

The "motivation crisis" produced by the market ethos embodied a retreat from "obligatory militarism," which sees compulsory military service as an unconditional contribution to the state, and the adoption of "contractual militarism," that is, making service conditional on its meeting the individual's ambitions and interests. This transformation is one of the expressions of the violation of the republican equation that gave rise to post-materialist militarism.

Based on an exchange of resources in return for military sacrifice, the republican order was a veiled arrangement between the state and leading groups of its citizens. This arrangement did not require ongoing bargaining, in particular because it had a universalistic character, at least at the declarative and formal level, in that it posited a uniform set of criteria for military service based on universal, and not attributive, principles for recruitment and promotion. Accordingly, this arrangement assured a high level of obligatory citizenship, in other words, internalizing the state's authority while also internalizing the reciprocal relations established by the state with its citizens (Giddens, 1985).

The violation of the republican equation gave rise to patterns of bargaining between individuals and groups on the one hand, and the state on the other, negotiations that took place via the army. With a decreased return for military sacrifice, bargaining became necessary, from the dominant groups' point of view, to increase their rewards or to redefine them in material terms. Although the IDF's new social architecture could have countered this trend, it was not sufficient as the social composition of the reserve army naturally mirrors the composition of the compulsory army of about ten to fifteen years previously, with the middle class in the center.

Several patterns of bargaining can thus be observed.

Personal bargaining: Since the 1990s, soldiers have begun to negotiate with the army in person or via their families or other networks. These negotiations can determine the individual's role in the army, the conditions under which he/she serves, restrictions on his/her service and military function, and even the very fact of his/her serving at all. The strengthening of liberal values and their partial infiltration into modes of action among governmental institutions have empowered the individual's standpoint and put him/her in a stronger negotiating position, sometimes with the assistance of the legal system, while the penetration of the media into the army impedes it from efficiently imposing internal discipline. The individual's ability to shorten or cancel his/her service due to apparent "mental health" issues, and the weight the army gives to personal preferences with regard to one's role in the military, are but two of the expressions of this bargaining. Youngsters make their considerations based on the package of incentives that the army offers them and their own expectations for self-fulfillment as compared to alternative, extra-military routes (mainly employment or studying). Only a reasonable match between the individual's expectations, originating from his/her private sphere, and what the army has to offer will be incentive enough for the youngster to agree to serve in a demanding position, or at least to see out the entire period of his/her service (Gon-Gross, 2003; Nevo and Shor, 2002b, 9–35).

As we saw in chapter 4, this bargaining power was sustained even during the Intifada, as manifested by youngsters from elite high schools who relied on their power to be assigned to noncombat units in the battle against the Palestinians (Makover-Blikov, 2005).

Military parenting: This can be seen in the increasing and quite open involvement of parents, mostly from the Ashkenazi secular stratum (who were later followed by other groups as well), in affairs of the army. Parents, among them bereaved parents, even get involved in matters such as training accidents, operational accidents, the political justification of missions, and military service conditions. They do not restrict themselves to expressions of anger or pain, but rather issue penetrative criticism that directly or indirectly strikes at the root of professional practices in the army. The combination of a lack of faith in the military, mostly since the First Lebanon War, along with a culture of consumerist privatization, in which parents can be perceived as customers who paid society with the lives of their sons and are now demanding payment in the form of compensation, an explanation, or a change in patterns of behavior, has ensured that the parents, acting as social-political entrepreneurs, have attracted the attention of the public (Ben-Eliezer, 2005; Doron and Lebel, 2004; Herzog, 2004).

The political selection of missions: This can be seen in the strengthening of the phenomena of both explicit and selective, and "grey" conscientious objection, and the appearance of political movements that ideologically endorse it (Helman, 1999), especially in the first years of the Al-Aqsa Intifada. Because of the particularly strong grip of this phenomenon among reservists, the IDF limits their use in politically contentious missions. It is against this background that pressure has been mounting to recognize national service as an alternative to compulsory military service.

Monetary bargaining: Military duties became conditional on economic remuneration. The most striking illustration is the "revolts" in the late 1990s among reservists (such as pilots) due to a lack of insurance cover, and consumerist-style associations of reserve soldiers demanding easier conditions or a redistribution of the burden, as well as appropriate financial compensation for their service. Such ad hoc organizations bear the threat—overt or latent— that the recruits' motivation is dependent on the army's response to their demands (Levy, 2003b, 253–55; Ben-Ari et al., 2004).

This pattern of collective bargaining, which appeared during the mid-1990s, as shown in chapter 2, saw a revival while the army was fighting in the Al-Aqsa Intifada. As a response, in 2002–2003 the government established two new posts—Chief Reserves Officer and a Ministerial Committee—that would handle the service conditions of reservists. And even though the army was under fire, the defense establishment barely succeeded in its efforts during 2002–2003 to extend the emergency orders allowing the IDF to draft reservists from thirty-three to up to forty-three days a year in order to take part in the fighting. Eventually, the IDF was constrained to shorten the period again (*Ynet*, 10 June 2002; *Ynet*, 18 March 2003).

In sum, at the heart of these patterns of bargaining are demands and expectations at the individual level. With the violation of the republican equation and the erosion of symbolic rewards, new spaces of bargaining were opening up for the secular Ashkenazi middle class. Symbolic rewards in terms of convertibility were gradually displaced by maneuvers to decrease or even avoid the burden, or to make sacrifice conditional on material rewards. Such rewards included improvements in service conditions, and professional rewards, in the shape of the enlistee's self-fulfillment. Besides, expectations of more meaningful service were raised by eliminating "brokerage fees," in the form of accidents or perceived negative political costs emanating from military duties.

Contractual militarism therefore contextualizes the notion of the "motivation crisis." The drop in motivation does not only apply to avoiding military service in its entirety, but also to the motivation of the recruits themselves. Patterns of bargaining over the conditions of military duties signify an aspect of the "crisis" that restricted the IDF's freedom of operation. Even among the upper-middle-class groups with high motivation to serve, the youngsters present their willingness to serve in the military as conditional, its essence lying in the common Israeli expression *sayeret o'nayeret*, literally translated as "[high status] elite unit or [low status] paperwork." Those imbued with motivation to serve represent their motivation as conditional: if they are not admitted to the select combat units they wish to join, they prefer a noncombat position, even if it lacks prestige.

A central mechanism that links agents' behavior with structural outcomes—in this instance the retreat from canonic militarism, or a change in its form—can be found in sites of socialization that are formally managed by the state, mainly school memorial ceremonies and pre-military preparatory frameworks. These arenas are changing their patterns of behavior as a result of being caught in a two-way "pincer movement": given feelings of unease concerning the compensation offered by the state for their military sacrifice, the subjects of socialization are demanding alternative content to it, both directly and via their families. In other words, there is a growing expectation that agencies of socialization should reflect the changes in the structure of interests among their subjects. At the same time, these sites are becoming more autonomous: the retreat of the welfare state is making the state education system more independent, enabling it to develop an affinity with pupils and their parents, whom it increasingly sees as its customers. The subjugation of state mechanisms to the market is advantageous for the upper-middle-class groups, who can convert their purchasing power into the ability to shape the content of these sites of socialization. In turn, these sites of socialization are therefore empowering the young recruit by giving him/her tools with which to bargain with the army over the conditions of his/her service and the values that it embodies. This shift in orientation quite clearly reflects a change in the institution of citizenship in

Israel—at least among the secular Ashkenazi middle class—from republican citizenship to a form that has diluted its republican foundations with liberal ones (Ram, 2005; Shafir and Peled, 2002), or, in other words, one that supports processes that place individual utility and a redefinition of citizen-state relations at the top of the pyramid. A pattern of citizenship is thus developing that wishes to detach civil status from contribution to the army.

With the erosion of the canonical military ethos, it became more legitimate for other groups to see the military ethos as a flexible text with multiple interpretations that can be deployed in the construction of a range of identities, and no longer as a collection of binding state directives.

For the secular Ashkenazi groups, the utility of military service is measured against the utility of civilian spheres (work, studying, leisure, etc.) in the light of available exchangeable resources, and this comparison shapes the level of motivation to serve. In contrast, the ethno-national groups perceive the army as a more significant sphere in which to produce symbolic resources, as shown in chapters 3 and 4.

Similar to their middle-class counterparts, these groups are also developing contractual patterns of exchange with the army, though not necessarily in the same way as their predecessors. The most notable of these groups is the national religious. A striking example was the way some of them, with the mediation of their rabbis, made their military service conditional on the army taking no part in the Disengagement Plan. However, the "knitted skullcap" group differs from secular groups in two ways: first, they were bargaining as a distinct group with unique characteristics and did not enter into individual or sectorial-professional negotiations (as the representatives of reservists did, for instance); second, their bargaining would seem to be driven, or at least legitimized, by ideology, and not utilitarian interests.

Negotiations typify the approach of other groups as well, who utilize bargaining tools according to their power. Thus, for illustration, feminist organizations use the court system and the media, while Druze and Bedouins act through political channels.

The relationship between the phenomena is obvious: the retreat of the secular Ashkenazi stratum from the army strengthens the motivation of peripheral and religious groups to build up their hold on the military. However, the erosion of the canonic military ethos and the strengthening of cultural diversity within the IDF gives these groups an incentive not to settle for participation in the army for its own sake, but rather to make it conditional on the improvement of their status, primarily in the civilian political sphere. These groups have taken on board the old, republican model that tied military participation to social and symbolic remuneration, and have projected it onto their own status, while the erosion of the canonic ethos together with the empowerment of their bargaining power due to the military's need for their service, enables them to discuss these exchange relations increasingly overtly. This is another by-product of contractual militarism, but in a different form from that characteristic of secular Ashkenazi youth.

As a result, the army has gradually been becoming an arena for multicultural distributive struggles, partly because of the penetration of "identity politics" that has taken root in the surrounding society. This identity politics has supplanted the Ashkenazi-dominated symbol of the "melting pot" by giving voice to culturally excluded groups, particularly Mizrachi and religious groups (see Ben-Eliezer, 2003). Internal competition is therefore set in motion, competition that may be shrouded with cultural symbols insofar as the struggling groups believe that this form of identity politics strengthens their bargaining power vis-à-vis the military command and other groups. The most conspicuous manifestation of this trend is the emerging clash between religious groups and women over the mode of their integration in combat units, with the rabbis demanding that men and women be kept separate. In this clash, both sides invoke their symbols—feminism versus religion—to legitimize their demands. In this regard, the IDF is not exceptional as a postmodern military (Moskos and Burk, 1994), with destructive implications for the cohesiveness and the impermeability to politics of a fighting army that endeavors to reflect at least part of the mosaic of Israeli-Jewish society.

With these patterns of bargaining restricting the IDF's freedom of operation, the army and its political supervisors were propelled to reform recruitment policies. Advocates of the reform adamantly claimed that refraining from taking harsh steps might lead to the collapse of the reserve system (Lubin, 2001), or at least warned against the crisis that the system was facing (Heiman et al., 2004). Consequently, in 2005 the government adopted a reform plan that would reduce the load on army reserve soldiers by dropping the exemption age to forty, deploying reserves in emergencies only, thus abolishing such missions and duties as border policing, shortening the period of service, and releasing thousands of soldiers from the army.[3] At the same time, the government also reformed compulsory service by adopting a plan that would gradually shorten it from three years to two, while keeping the original length for those (especially combatants) whose service is highly needed, in return for a special monetary reward.[4]

In short, the IDF downsized its human resources, with clear implications for the military's ability to endure high-cost belligerent policies. Furthermore, by incorporating selectivity within its formal policies of recruitment in an unprecedented fashion, the IDF retreated from the constitutive principle of the "people's army" that had traditionally subjected its effectiveness and economic considerations to the universalist principle of nonselective recruitment.

Here, as in other fields, the market ethos prevailed over previous traditional tenets. Erosion of the available resources dovetailed with the erosion in the legitimacy of warfare.

THE EROSION OF THE LEGITIMACY OF FIGHTING

Exposure to globalization did not only create an affinity between the credit ratings given to Israel by international credit agencies and the performance of Israeli companies in Western stock markets on the one hand, and the state's subsequent budgetary and socioeconomic policies on the other, but also between normative judgments passed by global institutions and the state's military activities. The sensitivity to globalization among the bearers of the market discourse was reflected, even if only indirectly, in increased openness to international norms. Limits on force were more deeply recognized, increased weight was given to international law, and global security regimes were seen as more capable of ensuring Israel's security. The legitimacy for deploying force was clearly impacted by this.

Following the First Lebanon War, Israel internalized the need to adapt itself to international codes of military conduct, a trend that intensified during the Al-Aqsa Intifada. Furthermore, the liberal discourse, which expanded protection for individual rights, even when the individual is an enemy, took shape on the basis of the infrastructure of the market economy, particularly as liberal legislation that intensified during the 1990s was elicited from the doctrine of protecting private property (Hirschel, 1997). This was another point at which the market met with the limitations of military power.

First and foremost, globalization spread out into the security field. Along with other countries, Israel internalized the recognition that it must entrust certain aspects of its security to international institutions. After all, the Iraqi threat was (temporarily) removed by a U.S.-led military coalition in the 2002 Gulf War. Equally, a similar coalition began dealing with the elimination of the Iranian threat, just as other international efforts brought Libya to drop its nuclear projects, and led to the withdrawal of the Syrian army from Lebanon in 2005. The 9/11 attack on the United States also contributed to the consolidation of global cooperation in the face of threats to Western countries, thereby strengthening Israel's dependence on the United States. This also helps explain how the First Gulf War (1991) served as a catalyst in dispelling the Israeli conception that territory is a central part of national security (Barzilai, 1999, 325). In sum, in the 1950s, security was conceptualized in military terms alone, including subjugating civilian missions to this outlook. However, recognizing that the army forms only one aspect of security, it gradually came to be understood in diplomatic terms as well.

In practical terms, tracing the decision-making procedures during the Al-Aqsa Intifada reveals that Sharon's government—on the face of it, one of the most militant governments in Israel's history—actually punctiliously coordinated its moves with the American government, which was quite supportive of Israel's combative steps, especially in the shadow of 9/11. It was against this background that America could force the *Road Map* on Israel in 2003. The Road Map accepted the establishment of a Palestinian state in principle, but without imposing final borders on Israel or forcing it to accept Palestinian refugees from 1948. Israeli diplomacy was thus channeled into accepting steps that would preserve the Road Map, as opposed to other, less comfortable political alternatives, such as the *Geneva Initiative*.[5] To the extent that it could be presented as incorporated within the Road Map, but also as a move that prevented alternative initiatives to it, the Disengagement Plan would serve this purpose.

International norms also accelerated the Disengagement Plan by bringing the debate over the "demographic problem" back into the political discourse. Supporters of the Plan argued that unless Israel separated itself from the Palestinians it would become a binational state, and thus compelled to award civil rights to its Palestinian citizens, over and above the rights already given to those who were annexed to Israel's territory following the 1948 War. More than giving voice to a demographic concern that is deeply rooted in Israeli political culture, Israelis paradoxically expressed global values having to do with ethnic anxiety. Israeli statesmanship internalized the lesson from South Africa, where international pressure led to equal rights and the dismantling of the Apartheid regime, ultimately bringing about the collapse of white rule over the country. The moral that was learned in Israel was that, under the current international regime, continued rule over the Occupied Territories will compel Israel to award civil rights to the Palestinians in such a way as to bring about the future collapse of the rule of the Jewish elites over the State of Israel.

International norms also influenced practical codes of behavior. At the turn of the millennium, the concept of "war crimes" gradually began to be introduced to Israeli public discourse as international norms were internalized, and the International Court of Justice at The Hague was rehabilitated. International pressures were also given voice in Israeli public discourse, which heightened internal criticism of the army on account of its attacks on a civilian population, gradually leading to increased restrictions on the use of force.

For example, comments made by the then-Air Force Commander General Dan Halutz caused a public storm: when asked how he felt following the killing in August 2002 of the head of *Hamas*' military wing, Salah Shahada, by a bomb dropped by a fighter plane on his neighborhood in Gaza, Halutz said that he "slept well," despite the death of fifteen civilians, among them children. In light of this declaration, a group of intellectuals submitted a petition to the Israeli High Court of Justice in order to prevent his promotion to the position of Deputy Chief of the General Staff. In an unprecedented move, the Court requested that General Halutz lay out his moral worldview, and in doing so Halutz in practice retracted his original comments. Halutz's remarks also spurred a number of senior reserve pilots to support the refusal movement. Accordingly, in his answer to the High Court of Justice, Halutz said that it is the policy of the Air Force to allow its pilots to exercise their own judgment and refrain from carrying out a mission if, when in the air, they consider that it might jeopardize civilians (HCJ 5757/04), thus weakening the potential for refusal among pilots.

Later, in May 2004, during a military operation in the town of Rafah, Justice Minister Yosef Lapid declared that the sight of an elderly Palestinian woman searching in the debris for her medication reminded him of his grandmother who had perished in the Holocaust. This criticism was one of the factors behind the cessation of the operation. Later on the army reaffirmed that its policy of house destruction was ineffective, at least partly because of international criticism.

Meanwhile, in another unprecedented move, while citing international law, in 2005 the High Court of Justice annulled the "neighbor procedure": an operational practice that allowed the army to use a Palestinian citizen as a human shield in order to inform his wanted neighbors of their arrest.

Similarly, in the light of the Intifada, international organizations started to exert pressure to put Israeli politicians and officers on trial for alleged war crimes, beginning with the attempt to indict Ariel Sharon himself for his part in the Sabra and Shatilah massacre in Lebanon in 1982. In September 2005, General Doron Almog, formerly head of the Southern Command, evaded an attempt to arrest him for questioning in Britain. IDF officers have thus been faced with a tangible threat. The influence of this threat on their behavior cannot be measured at the time of writing, but it is reasonable to assume that it will force the army to assess its activities in the light of international law, at least in order to defend its officers.

At the same time, the International Court of Justice began discussing the legality of the security fence, thus indirectly influencing decisions made by the Israeli High Court of Justice. The High Court, tending to provide legal approval for governmental actions, imposed a route for the wall that limited the damage caused to the Palestinian population while more than once rejecting considerations put forward by the security establishment. Considerations of security were increasingly subjected to norms in international law.

In these regards, the effects of globalization also impacted on internal power relations as Israeli organizations made use of both global rhetoric and international law to undermine the legitimacy of military actions. The changing international scene placed such organizations in a new political context and provided them with resources for collective action. Theoretically, globalization affords a political and cultural context for action in the local sphere that domestic actors can leverage to their advantage, including in issues pertaining to human rights, and impel the state to argumentatively respond to a globalized rhetoric. Domestic actors are also able to borrow models of action from other organizations and to establish cooperation based on transnational networks, not infrequently supported or inspired by international institutions (see Pieters, 2001; Risse and Sikkink, 1999; Tarrow, 2001). In other words, Israeli human rights and peace organizations regularly leveraged the local political discourse as a way of mobilizing international support while simultaneously conducting a dialogue with the state by invoking the global discourse.

Thus, for example, part of the legal rhetoric of conscientious objectors draws on the recognition for freedom of conscience in international charters.[6] Moreover, petitions by conscripts or candidates for conscription rely on the functioning of the Conscientious Objection Committee, which the IDF established in 1995, thus recognizing the need to exempt from service people whose pacifist worldview prevented them from joining the army. Even if the committee exempts very few people in practice, it created a normative and rhetorical framework for petitions, with the army recognizing the right to submit them.

The removal of obstacles also laid the infrastructure for civilian organizations among Palestinian citizens. For the first time they could enter a scene from which they had been historically excluded, namely, the military discourse. Historically speaking, the military discourse was based on clear rules that only allowed people who had contributed to the military effort to participate in it. The circle of fighters, in potentia or in actu, was the first to take part in the discourse, after its intimate boundaries had been broken following the 1973 War. In the 1990s, women expanded the circle, mostly calling on their contribution as mothers, thus penetrating this masculine field. From 2000 it was the turn of the Palestinian citizens, who were excluded from service, and thus also from the discourse, which was reserved for soldiers and their families. Unlike their predecessors, Palestinian citizens made systematic use of the legal system, which, regarding access to formal rights, was paying less and less attention to ethnic distinctions. Palestinian citizens were acting on the strength of their citizenship, and not according to the rules sketched out by the military discourse.

For instance, this is how Mohammed Bakri, director of the film *Jenin Jenin*, which represented the narrative of a slaughter in the refugee camp of

Jenin during *Operation Defensive Shield* (in 2002), overcame (at least partially) a coalition of reservists that endeavored to prevent him from screening the film. Meanwhile, the civil rights movement *Adalah*, led by Palestinian civilians, was party to the petition that led to the illegalization of the "neighbor procedure" as a military operational practice, and there are further examples. Against this background, it is not surprising to find that the sensitivity to globalization laid the ground for the return of Oslo, this time in the form of the Geneva Initiative, which had begun to gain support among businessmen, as a program that would return Israel to its global standing prior to the Intifada.

A further focal point of criticism was the army's activities at roadblocks in the West Bank. Putting up roadblocks throughout the West Bank was an inherent consequence of the reconquering of the area during the Al-Aqsa Intifada, and the humiliation of the civilian population was an inherent consequence of the roadblocks themselves, insofar as they dealt with a civilian population suspected of involvement in terrorist activity. In terms of public criticism of harm caused by the army to the civilian population, 2003 was a watershed: in that year the public voice of *Machsom Watch* became louder. In November 2004, *Haaretz* journalist Akiva Eldar published an article along with a photograph of a Palestinian man who had been stopped by IDF soldiers at a roadblock near Nablus and forced to play his violin (Eldar, 2004). The uproar caused by the article, because of its associations with images from the Holocaust, made the price that the army had to pay for its dealings with the Palestinian population even higher in terms of the IDF's legitimacy. This resulted in the security system reinforcing the roadblocks with trained personnel presenting a more humanitarian image, as well as the civilianization of some of the roadblocks (border crossings) and their removal from the army's hands.

As mentioned, in the summer of 2004, an organization of discharged soldiers, *Breaking the Silence*, was founded, exposing abusive acts against Palestinians. The years 2003–2004 also saw the strengthening of the refusal movement, not necessarily in terms of numbers (following the relative blossoming of *Courage to Refuse*, which weakened after *Operation Defensive Shield*; see chapter 4), but qualitatively, in the shape of the higher-ranking officers who signed up, the most senior of whom was a pilot in the Air Force with the rank of brigadier general. They were also joined by soldiers from elite units. For the first time, people who took no part in the fighting itself, but who wished to issue a protest against it in the name of the army and its ethics, had become activists. If the extent of refusal was limited, this was in no small part due to the IDF's strategy of keeping reserve units, where the potential for refusal is high, away from sensitive missions; of reaching informal agreements with those who insisted on refusing; of limiting public exposure of the phenomenon; and of taking recourse to public punishment only as a last resort. Increased rates of "grey refusal" was the result, as it was estimated that there were ten "grey" refuseniks for every soldier who officially pledged to refuse (Dloomy, 2005, 706–8).

In this spirit, journalist Molly Moore (2003) has rightly portrayed the situation in a comprehensive article for the *Washington Post*: "With the Israel Defense Forces in the fourth year of battle with the Palestinians, the most dominant institution in Israeli society is also embroiled in a struggle over its own character." This provides an indication of the extent to which the disobedience and other phenomena worried the army, who wanted to contain them tightly. Dov Weisglass, Prime Minister Sharon's bureau chief and the main architect of the Disengagement Plan, pointed to the growth of the refusal movement as one of the motivations behind the disengagement:

> And then [in the fall of 2003] we were hit with letters [of refusal to serve in the territories] from officers and letters from pilots and letters from commandos. These were not weird kids with green ponytails and nose-rings who give off a strong odor of grass. These were people like Spector's group [Yiftah Spector, a renowned Air Force pilot who signed the pilot's letter]. Really our finest young people. (quoted in Shavit, 2004)

These phenomena are related to the market ethos in two ways: first, their initiators relied on alternative sources of symbolic and social capital that had emerged from within the market and out of the decline of statism and traditional materialist militarism. After all, as the upper middle class voluntarily ceded its dominance over the army, it found itself with more autonomy to criticize the IDF, and was less willing to protect the army's legitimacy from the criticism of other groups. Groups that have acquired alternative sources of social and symbolic capital can act relatively freely toward the army, whereas in the past, if there was a conflict between one's feeling of responsibility and belonging on the one hand, and one's conscience on the other, the former would have overridden the latter. Second, attentiveness to these entrepreneurs' messages is related to increasing sensitivity to international norms under the auspices of globalization.

To summarize, these and other phenomena created a moderating public atmosphere that made it easier to expose information and pushed the military into dealing more meticulously with misconduct as a way of repelling external pressures. The relatively sterner instructions handed down by the Military Attorney General at the time, including a more marked tendency to punish wayward officers, were an indication of this moderate change.

This change of policy did not only mean intensifying internal supervision of the army, but also weakening its operational autonomy in policing the Occupied Territories. Normative restrictions were increasingly placed on the use of firearms. From the army's perspective, this increased the need to find alternative modes of fighting/policing. In particular, the novel characteristic of this collective action was in leveraging globalization so as to limit the army more than ever. While in the past civil rights organizations used to deal with irregular behavior on the part of the army on a case-by-case basis (see Ron, 2000 on the First Intifada), now the front expanded to include the IDF's very fighting methods themselves. Hence, the IDF's need to correspondingly alter its modes of fighting/policing, as Weisglass' words testified.

The erosion of the legitimacy of warfare was also reflected in the damage sustained to the IDF's internal control system as a result of ongoing friction with the civilian population. In general, the military organization aims to preserve organizational control by toughening the command hierarchy and sealing off the organization from external infiltrations that might upset that hierarchy. Its friction with a civilian population set the army a complex challenge to these principles of control. What diverse phenomena such as concern with the "neighbor procedure," house destructions, *Machsom Watch*, false reports from the field, debate over the practice of "confirming the kill," and *Breaking the Silence* all have in common, is the loss of control by the General Staff over its field forces. Tasks were carried out relatively autonomously at the field command level, characteristic of this kind of police fighting. Given the lack of direct and effective means of control, the General Staff's supervision of its troops was mediated by external bodies that reported on irregular behavior. Indeed, in the first years of the fighting, the General Staff relayed to the units that it was granting them freedom of action, thus practically blocking internal channels of information. Moreover, because they are carried out by small groups, and not within the framework of a large fighting team, policing missions empower the individual soldier.

Here there is a problem in controlling not only the soldiers, but also information. This explains why the military spokesperson was repeatedly criticized for unreliable reports, attributed to the "mediation gap" between the source of the information—the small and independent unit in the field—and the General Staff, which receives the information and processes some of it for public release. This, then, was another force for heightening the need to change the mode of fighting in way that would reduce the level of friction with the Palestinian population, namely, disengagement, thus enabling the deployment of concentrated forces under General Staff supervision. This is not to say that the General Staff was acting consciously, initiating the reacquisition of control out of a basic organizational need, but rather that the Disengagement Plan corresponded with this need.

MARKET POLITICS: THE "GOLD SACRIFICE" VERSUS THE "BODY SACRIFICE"

Following Porter (1994, 10), chapter 4 pointed to the differentiation between the "gold sacrifice," namely, the tax burden on the middle class in funding the military and bearing the brunt of economic slowdown as a result of war, and the "body sacrifice," that is, the fallen soldiers, who, from the mid-1990s, mostly came from religious and peripheral groups. Due to the new composition of the IDF, these two modes of sacrifice became differentiated and ceased to overlap. These divergent modes of sacrifice also embody distinct methods of political supervision of the military.

The "gold-sacrificers" are mostly concerned with the military's resources as taxpayers, as the above-mentioned criticism of the army's resources indicated. One political illustration of this trend was the dramatic rise of the Ashkenazi-based, middle-class *Shinui* Party in the elections of 2003, whose platform stressed policies that would improve the standard of living of its constituents, namely, upper-middle-class ex-soldiers. *Shinui* was politically energized by the double burden of its constituency, comprised of military service—especially in the reserves, where the upper middle class was still overrepresented—and the tax burden. At the same time, the party alleged that the Ultra-Orthodox did not share in either duty; on the contrary, Ultra-Orthodox families enjoy generous state subsidies channeled to nonworking yeshiva students (see Shalev and Levy, 2005). *Shinui* therefore restored the demand to link social rights with soldiering to the agenda by proposing to materially reward ex-soldiers and reservists, decrease the reserve burden, draft Ultra-Orthodox youngsters, and cut taxes. Nonetheless, this basically dovish party remained silent regarding the "body sacrifice" among other groups and refrained from speaking out against the losses caused by the fighting against the Palestinians.

In a similar fashion, an indicative glance at the press during the 1990s–2000s reveals that although it intensified its scrutiny over the military and consistently overcame traditional barriers such as the military censorship, relatively marginal issues were at the heart of its focus. Accidents and other military failures, intramilitary conflicts and struggles between military figures and politicians, failures in human resources policies, and ineffective economic management were among the issues. Criticism of the military gradually attracted the economic columns as well, where the focus was on issues of economically ineffective performance. However, substantive issues relating to the role of military thought in fashioning Israel's policies were neglected. It is hardly surprising, therefore, that the press overlooked the self-fulfilled prophecy implicit in the IDF's war preparations during the years 1997–2000 for what would become the Al-Aqsa Intifada, as well as the role played by the army in bringing about the fruitless collapse of Palestinian Authority during the 2000s, with the political vacuum that this created (see Dor, 2004).

"Issues of civilian control seem to escape the press," claimed historian Richard Kohn in regard to the erosion of the civilian control of the U.S. military. "Time after time, events or issues that in past years would have been framed or interpreted as touching upon civilian control now go unnoticed and unreported, at least in those terms" (2002). Israel is not an exception. It is part of the paradox that as political control over the military has been historically enhanced, Israeli politics have been militarized (Levy, 1997b).

On the other hand, the "body-sacrificers," with the national religious groups at their center, adhered to the traditional pattern of the republican citizen-soldier. According to this pattern, the military ought to be supervised by the soldiers staffing its ranks, if not directly (such as the reservists), then at least indirectly through their social networks, as signified by the religious camp's attempts to curb the withdrawal from the Gaza Strip (see chapter 6). Nevertheless, as the reshaped bereavement discourse shows, the new "body sacrificers" accepted their loss and focused their monitoring efforts on the political aspect of the IDF's missions. Therefore, only market-oriented pressures could drive the state to moderate its military policies, that is to narrow the IDF's freedom of action.

In the light of the expectation among civilian taxpayers that the providers of security should be held to account, the senior military staff entered into direct bargaining with its citizens-customers as a way of competing for resources and legitimacy in a competitive environment.

It is hardly surprising, then, that the Chiefs of the General Staff of the 2000s have nurtured a new perception of their role. They began to see themselves as beholden to the public, and not to the government, even stressing this in certain public comments. Accordingly, they were criticized for being "political Chiefs of the General Staff"; however, they were no different from their predecessors in the way they ran military affairs, but only in the medium through which they relayed their messages. Their dialogue with the public also brought heads of the army to lay out their unprocessed opinions firsthand, without relying on the mediation of politicians (for instance, Chief of the General Staff Moshe Yaalon's statements on the risks of a unilateral withdrawal from the Gaza Strip). The public's right to know clashed with the traditional foundations of supervision over the military, foundations that tend toward creating a partition and political mediating mechanisms between the army's commanders and the public, and negating soldiers' right to publicly disagree with their political superiors (for a comparative perspective see Johnson and Metz, 1995).

With this pattern of direct loyalty toward the public, the army moved away from its hesitant relationship with the media for the sake of much closer relations, to the point of actively marketing the military through the media. The consumerist motif of "direct marketing" spread to the military sector. "The perception of reality is more important than reality itself," said an IDF general during the Al-Aqsa Intifada, as part of a new outlook that primarily saw the military campaign as a battle over the public's conscience, in which the media play a substantial role. This outlook led the army to expose its various units, including elite units, to encourage junior officers to give interviews to the press, and to take the visibility of the fighting into account when making operational decisions. This factor became progressively more legitimate, and the army even began documenting operations, using its filming units for that purpose.

By marketing itself, the IDF worked to strengthen its legitimacy by giving an account of its activities to the taxpayers and parents of soldiers, and by persuading them that their resources are being aptly utilized. Thus, by revealing seemingly positive aspects of the organization's activities, the army can compete over resources and encourage enlistment from groups traditionally distant from the military. However, the media's invasiveness also weakened the IDF's internal organizational unity as the General Staff failed to prevent the unsupervised penetration of the media into various units.

Having partially abandoned the option of "voice," which entails the expression of collective interests through enhanced participation and the strengthening of the military's political accountability, citizen-consumers embarked on the "exit" option provided by the market model, that is, shifting between suppliers. In light of the monopolist nature of state-supplied security, "semi-exit" strategies were gradually employed, taking the form of alternative patterns of security consumption by relying on the market; in other words, the privatization of security. Among these patterns were private bomb shelters, local-municipal police forces to combat Palestinian infiltrators in upper-middle-class communities, gated communities, the private purchase of protective suits against chemical and biological threats, and even a local initiative to privately finance part of the security fence (see Ben-Porat and Mizrahi, 2005).

COPING WITH THE CHALLENGE—"PEOPLE'S ARMY" VERSUS "MARKET ARMY"

Criticism of the army's resources, the collapse in legitimacy of its recruitment model, and the implications of globalization on the political discourse such that militarily inflicted damage to a civilian population came under increasing censure, all gradually restricted the IDF's freedom of action. As an initial response, the army took considerable steps to subject itself to the rules of the market economy in order to strengthen its legitimacy and adapt its resources to the new market rules. This was not necessarily a conscious response, but rather the way in which an army sensitive to its legitimacy reacts to changes in its environment, within the boundaries of its cultural strategy.

The IDF dealt with the challenge of the market economy by playing with two tools, namely, belligerency versus adjustment to the market. First, when satisfactory rewards could be expected, it sharpened its combat profile. In other words, it portrayed itself as an entity providing an efficient and cost-effective response to external threats. Given that the army holds a monopoly on collective security provision against external threats, this is a mission that market forces are incapable of fulfilling.

This is the logic that led to the escalation of the Intifada in the 2000s, or at least its leverage, following the withdrawal of militarism during the Oslo period. It is also the logic that led to the leverage of the abduction of two reserve soldiers by Hezbollah in July 2006 to initiate the Second Lebanon War, after the IDF's status had reached a crisis point as a result of the withdrawal from the Gaza Strip. As chapter 1 suggests, this is the first step that the state will take when the republican equation is violated, a common enough occurrence when the symbolic rewards offered to the soldiers and their social networks are reduced.

On the other hand, when belligerence gradually demands an internal price beyond what leading social groups see as worthwhile, thus increasing their criticism of the army, the military is among the first to moderate the political echelon or cooperate with moves to moderation. This can be seen in the two withdrawals from Lebanon (in 1985 and 2000), the limitations on the use of military force in the First Intifada, and the withdrawal from the Gaza Strip in the Disengagement Plan. The reduction of military participation—the third of the state's strategic mechanisms—was then resorted to.

Beyond this basic maneuvering, the military has been expending great efforts to preserve the rhetoric of the "people's army," even though the historical model of the "people's army" has reached its end given the declining rate of enlistees (only 60 percent of Jewish men complete full military service) and reforms in recruitment that subject it to economic considerations. The "people's army" is primarily a mobilizing rhetoric. This is the meaning of the devotion to it on the part of the IDF's commanders and their political overlords, which made the recruitment model one of the most stable phenomena in the history of Israeli public administration—indeed, the model was unchanged from the early 1950s. This dedication to the "people's army," which positions the IDF above other institutions, thereby impacts on the military's resources as well. Competition over resources is thus alleviated, because military service is seen as having added value. In other words, the "people's army" is portrayed as a universal army, while other institutions, and especially market forces, are seemingly particularist, and therefore political or utilitarian. With this added value, symbolic rewards are produced by the soldiers. Furthermore, the rhetoric of a "people's army" also dampens political criticism when the army carries out controversial missions (Shelah, 2003).

Therefore, the shift to a model of professional recruitment, which would gradually yet unmistakably narrow the social base of military enlistment, is liable to damage the army's status, at least from the point of view of the military command. However, this mobilizing rhetoric can subsist in a (certain) level of tension between the symbolic and the real. Therefore, as far as one can judge from its activities, the preference of the General Staff is to implement a policy of selective recruitment that will gradually reconstruct the recruitment model of the "people's army," but without giving this explicit recognition, which might undermine its symbolic aspects. At the same time, and in order to maintain the army's representative profile, army chiefs, as mentioned, have been strengthening the IDF as a multicultural site while retreating from the pretensions of it being a "melting pot."

The military's alternative mode for dealing with market forces is adjustment, that is, to subject its conduct to the perquisites of the market economy, as can be seen in changes to its organizational culture and its recruitment model.

At the visible level, the IDF fitted its resources to the level of social willingness to allocate them, including efficiency drives and cutbacks. At a deeper level, however, the army used the change to try and deal with the degradation of its legitimacy in the eyes of the bearers of the market economy. In this regard, the new language and the organizational-cultural symbols that it adopted are no less significant than purely financial outcomes, as is typical of Western armies (see Kaldor, 2002). It may well be that the cultural need is more important than the bottom line, and thus not all of the army's market-oriented moves actually increased its efficiency. The IDF wishes to seem as if it is part of the market, and not opposed to it; it certainly does not want to appear as an economic "parasite." It is also possible that some of the efforts to attain legitimacy are influenced by the need of IDF officers to create anew social capital that would strengthen their professional convertibility in the civilian labor market, as well as their status in the army's internal power relations between combat officers and logistical staff.

In this framework, the army is carrying out a series of measures. First and foremost, it is conducting a gradual process of fragmentation into two armies.

The ground force is being reduced in favor of two new forces: a policing army, and a technological army. The policing army is designated to deal with the Palestinian militias and other ongoing security challenges along Israel's borders (including smuggling). This is the "old" army in its cultural and organizational sense: a "blue-collar" force, populated by lower-middle-class groups. An ethos of masculine and conservative militarism is cultivated, stemming from the character of the groups involved and their symbolic expectations from military service. At the same time, a management-technological army is emerging. This army is preparing itself for future and long-range threats (in terms of time and space), and for fighting against sophisticated terrorism. The militarism of this technological army is that of knowledge, and not the body, and as such is more suited to the market economy (Sasson-Levy, 2006, 218–22). The assimilation of technology constricts such military values as bravery and camaraderie in favor of knowledge. As a result, this array offers accessibility to women, as well as retaining a high level of attraction for educated groups from the middle class. The Second Lebanon War offered a refined expression of this distinction between the two armies: the "blue-collar" army failed as Hezbollah abducted two reservists in July 2006, which served as the trigger for the outbreak of war. In contrast, most of the weight of the war fell on the technological army, particularly the Air Force, while the ground forces wore themselves out in face-to-face fighting with Hezbollah.

In parallel, the army has been reshaping its organizational culture. To a large extent, it has been incorporating management principles similar to those of "New Public Management." In this sense, the IDF is perceived as a corporation with customers to whom it provides a service. In other words, the fighting is not seen to be serving the nation in an abstract sense. Each army unit has specific customers within the organization; training for war is the "input," while war itself is the "output." The image of the officer is no longer one of a leader, but rather that of a military expert (Gur-Ze'ev, 1997). Accordingly, control centers are places where the army "manages the war" while the commanders themselves have internalized managerial habits. Military language is focused on output ("the final outcome criterion"), and not on processes and inputs, and the new operative terminology has adopted market-oriented terms, such as "tender" among units competing over the execution of missions, or "leverage" as a mission aimed at impacting third parties. Against this background, the army is also striving to establish measurable standards for the security product it provides. In this framework, the army focuses on its combative core wherever that has a relative advantage, while changing its structure from a Fordist to post-Fordist one, whereby outsourcing is gradually replacing the internal provision of services (especially logistics and training).

In the long term, the increasing tendency to attach a price tag to security will accelerate the privatization of its provision.

In this spirit, and given that the recruitment model is still one of compulsory enlistment, the IDF has been internalizing the need to deal with the recruitment of youngsters as conscripts, and reservists even more so, in the face of competing demands from the civilian labor market. The means adopted to this end include greater material rewards, more sophisticated classification procedures, the use of mediators, such as parents, increased publicity for certain units as a marketing device, and the shaping or repositioning of military professions. The army did not even refrain from trying to reformulate its canonic military culture, as seen by the introduction of values that had previously been seen as contradictory to it. These values include the acknowledgment of the recruits' right for private consumption within the military, the institutionalized penetration of private cellular telephones, bargaining arrangements, flexible discipline, the recognition of parental involvement, and, of course, the cultural "diversity management" that has made the army an arena steeped with "identity politics." In parallel, the army has been gradually implementing differential salaries for its professional servicepersons in a way that takes competition for highly sought after professions in the civilian labor market into account. Differential salaries are also a kind of "language" that is deeply embedded in neoliberal discourse, in this case aimed at encouraging personal competitiveness while weakening the power of organized labor, naturally rooted in uniform wage agreements.

Finally, not only is the IDF narrowing its historical social roles, such as providing its soldiers with a basic education ("role contraction," in Cohen's [1995] terms), but it has been gradually introducing economic selectivity to its recruitment procedures. This is most notable in the reserve army: as mentioned, a reform was implemented in 1985 as part of cutbacks to the security budget, the most important aspect of which was the transfer of the burden of funding reserve duty from the National Insurance Institute to the IDF. From this point on, calling up reservists had a price tag, where previously their cost had been intangible, and hence disregarded. Moreover, this gave the army an incentive to cut back its reserve duty budget, and so it began to selectively call up reservists at the cost of an unequal distribution of the burden. The principle of selectivity, implemented de facto since the 1980s, was officially institutionalized in the reforms to the reserve army that were ratified by the government in 2005, and which are (at the time of writing) being written up as changes to the law. In a similar fashion, the army lent its weight to the public discourse calling for selectivity in compulsory enlistment too, and began implementing it as much as its manpower resources would let it. Most of those released from service were seen as making no economic contribution to the IDF.

Here too, a government decision to shorten the length of compulsory service and to adopt differential service routes in an attempt to attach a price tag to conscripts is institutionalizing de facto selectivity. In short, the army has relinquished the principle of universal conscription—one of the anchors of the concept of the "people's army"—in favor of selective recruitment, understood to be more efficient. Furthermore, this social policy recognizes the exchange between the scope of recruitment and the increased material rewards that can be provided to those who are recruited. Thus, in keeping with the market ethos, the IDF is coping with the "motivation crisis" by material means.

In summary, the processes discussed above are the main steps taken by the army to adapt its organizational culture to the prerequisites of the market and to narrow the gap between the two. This was not a thoroughgoing attempt to restore the army's legitimacy, but rather a move to narrow the gap. In consequence, these processes have actually created the infrastructure for intensifying the crisis the army has been dealing with from the 1990s.

THE OUTCOME: THE INTENSIFIED EROSION OF THE IDF'S LEGITIMACY

Because of the tension inherent between the constitutive rules of the market economy, and those constitutive of the military organization, the challenge of the market economy is the most significant of threats to the army's legitimacy. Hierarchy, discipline, solidarity, and sacrifice among the providers of this public product are held up against the contradictory values of business organizations, that provide mostly private products. From time to time the military endeavors to moderate this threat by amplifying once again the public product that it provides, namely, security, but only until the increasing costs of its provision once more clash with the ethos of the market.

As mentioned, the military's adaptation to the market does not necessarily rely on explicit organizational self-awareness, but rather on the organization's cultural strategy. In the case of Israel, the IDF's self-image as a "people's army" is not only a mobilizing rhetoric, but also a self-image that places limitations on its functioning. The most significant of these limitations is on the army's ability to position itself in politically controversial sites, and especially to clash with a social force that had once been the military's backbone, namely, the upper middle class, and that still forms a crucial source of the army's funding and legitimacy. The military's need for legitimacy, therefore, is material, as well as being a symbolic and cultural need anchored in its self-identity. Pressures such as those presented in this and previous chapters make the army back away from controversy.

The way that the IDF shapes its moves is not rational in the common sense of the term, but rather results from examining the alternatives via cultural filters (*adaptive rationality*, as termed by Johnston, 1995). Historical choices, analogies, metaphors, and precedents are invoked to guide choice. Cultural filters then simplify reality, restrict the range of possible decisions, determine what is taken for granted and what may be debated, and create a repertoire of scripts that the army is comfortable with shaping. The outcome is that the army adapts itself to the market rather than challenging it.

This limitation does not only impinge on the army as an organization, but also, and mainly, on the way it is politically operated. The political echelon acts in a cultural-political environment that curbs its ability to operate the military, while the army itself internalizes some of the limitations as reflected in its dialogue with the politicians.

Having to respond to the challenge of the market economy ensnared the army in an array of contradictions between its ranks and its relations with its social environment, which only served to erode its legitimacy even further. Within the army, there was tension between the various bearers of the market economy. These bearers, in this instance youngsters from the middle class, created expectations and pressures for increased material rewards for their service, while at the same time limiting the price the state could pay so as to meet them, on account of their intersecting expectation that the army's resources should be cut back. This is most clearly seen in the reserves: the IDF was obliged to become more efficient by calling up fewer reservists; but at the same time, and in contradiction to this, it was also required to distribute the burden equally. Accordingly, the army has to reward those carrying the burden, even as those rewards contradict pressures for budgetary cutbacks. As a result of the contradictory edicts of the market economy, the IDF has thus gradually begun to rely on alternative sources of manpower by creating new resources, in this case symbolic ones, which attract religious and peripheral groups that offer their services for low material rewards but high symbolic ones. A new social architecture was at work.

The tension between the army and the market is here reflected in the former's relations with its social surroundings: the IDF's new social architecture did indeed give the army more freedom of action in creating the conditions, if only temporarily, for autonomously escalating fighting while enjoying broad political support, which in turn contributed to the temporary expansion of its resources. However, the ongoing fighting with the Palestinians and its increasing cost brought the army back into both direct and indirect conflict with the market. More vocal criticism of the army's resources; the eroded legitimacy of the recruitment model with the shift from "obligatory" to "contractual" militarism and the reforms needed to deal with this shift; the influence of globalization on political discourse and its increased criticism of military activities that are perceived to contravene international norms; and damage to the army's very organizational solidarity—all these gradually narrowed the IDF's freedom of action once more, and, in particular, reduced its resources.

Theoretically, the crisis of legitimacy in Western states in the 1970s was the result of the contradiction between the direct intervention of the state on behalf of corporate elites and the official ideology of "free market capitalism," according to which social rewards should be distributed on the basis of individual achievement (Habermas, 1975). In the current instance, the very functioning of the army was creating contradictions between an economic ethics and a belligerent and nationalist ethics, while the economic ethics itself is creating internal contradictions between expectations from the army and its functioning.

Furthermore, the very over-legitimacy for the fighting in the first years of the Al-Aqsa Intifada created new spaces in which delegitimizing voices, leveraging globalization to challenge the military-political establishment, could appear later on. As a partial and intermediary response, the army went even further to adapt its activities to the rules of the market, thereby gradually becoming a "market army" in every aspect of the reshaping of its organizational culture. As an attempt to restore legitimacy, it was only partially successful.

Paradoxically, although the IDF regained broader freedom of action in administering belligerent policies, largely because of the new architecture of its social composition, it retained fewer resources with which to fund these policies, owing to amplified criticism with a market orientation. Freedom of action was not symmetrical to the army's shrinking resources.

To recall, there is an asymmetry between "body-sacrificers"—who expand the military's freedom of action—and "gold-sacrificers," who narrow it. At a deeper level, there is a gap between *the legitimacy to use force* and *the legitimacy to invest resources in the use of force*. While the path of belligerence retained its support among most groups in Israeli society, despite the challenges reviewed here, a gap opened up between ideological preference and the price that the leading groups were prepared to pay for it. For these groups, the potential corporeal price was already largely behind them, while the direct and indirect economic price was still seen as reducible.

Similar to previous instances of the use of force, here too the IDF implemented a policy of excessive force, which led to the imposition of certain restrictions. Indeed, the deployment of more moderate force, internal restraint similar to that exercised in the First Intifada, and the more frugal usage of reservists, may at least have delayed the appearance of direct and indirect challenges.

In such circumstances, the collapse of the Palestinian Authority following Israel's escalated attacks, to the extent that it ceased to be a dependable address for reining in its own forces, met with problems of legitimacy within Israel. In other words, even if there had been a military way of giving Israel the duties of the disintegrating Palestinian Authority (mostly by renewing the invasive pre-Oslo occupying regime), pressures from the market economy made this option impracticable. Therefore, and circularly, internal difficulties impeded the army's ability to find a way out of the dead end in the battlefield, while its limitations in the external sphere further increased internal pressures, which were burdensome for the fighting. Simply put, the state again exhausted the first mechanism targeted at balancing the republican equation, which is the manipulation of external threats. Accordingly, a cost-reducing change in the model of warfare was required.

At the same time, deescalation could have created another kind of problem for the military that would have trapped it within an intensifying clash of ethoses—the ethno-national ethos versus the ethos of the market economy—a clash that found expression in its ranks. In previous chapters, this clash of the ethoses was presented as fundamental to the political discourse in Israeli society, especially since the mid-1980s. What is new here is the clear extension of this collision into the army's system of legitimacy and its penetration into its ranks. This clash particularly intensified after the early years of the Al-Aqsa Intifada. Precisely as the army moderated the contradiction created by the market ethos between expectations for greater material rewards and the IDF's declining resources by increasingly relying on religious and peripheral groups, it thus committed itself to maintaining its combative profile as a way of making military service meaningful for those groups. While the ongoing belligerence during the Al-Aqsa Intifada contradicted the market economy, significantly reducing combativeness contradicted the expectations of the new groups to whom the army was committed, and even its own organizational interests.

The clash embodies the tension between the types of rewards reaped from military service. Groups from the upper reaches of the middle class—the bearers of the ethos of the market economy—have been distancing themselves in various ways from the army on account of the gap between symbolic rewards—including the progressive decline of their significance for those groups—and material rewards. Accordingly, such groups wish to reduce the costs of militarism by subjecting it to the market economy. The cultural manifestation of this approach is the contraction of militarism, that is, demilitarization, among certain groups in Jewish Israeli society. Parts of the secular Ashkenazi stratum insist on untying the Gordian knot linking soldiering with citizenship, while those who persist with military service make it conditional, or call for reductions in the army's resources. On the other hand, ethno-national groups are attracted to the army as a way of reaping symbolic rewards, and thus have an interest in raising the army above the market and giving meaning to their service. What these two ethos systems have in common, therefore, is the provision of conditional legitimacy to the army.

Ensnared in the ropes of the rhetoric and symbolism of a "people's army," the military strove to balance out the two ethoses so as to preserve the foundations of its legitimacy. From the IDF's perspective, the "clash of ethoses" is the expression of a contradiction between two bases of legitimacy. The clash is between the legitimizing base for allocating resources—legitimacy that rests on middle-class groups faithful to the ethos of the market economy—and the legitimizing base for supplying human resources, that is, legitimacy that rests on the groups that bear the ethno-national ethos. In other words, those sacrificing their "gold" and those sacrificing their "bodies" must be balanced out; otherwise, the army has difficulty functioning. To some extent, the required balance is between the varied state mechanisms involved in balancing the republican equation, that is, between manipulating the external threat versus regulating the internal burden when such manipulations fall short.

The IDF has indeed shed some of the burden of dealing with the middle class by means of its "new social architecture," but it must simultaneously cope with the financial burden that that group bears, as well as with the remainders of its corporeal burden. As mentioned, cultural-organizational change in the army only partially served this aim. Therefore, a change in the model of fighting with the Palestinians was required so as to reduce its costs, but without lessening the state of belligerence, which would threaten the army's organizational interests and undermine its commitment to the new groups staffing its ranks. Thus emerged the unilateral Disengagement Plan, the subject of the next chapter.

NOTES

1. Most of the criticism focused on the favorable retirement packages given to career servicepersons. These included the option of early retirement at around forty years of age, after which they would enjoy a generous army pension for the rest of their lives.

2. This section draws heavily from a coauthored article with Edna Lomsky-Feder and Noa Harel; see Levy et al., 2007.

3. Braverman Committee, *Reform in the Reserve System*. Israel Ministry of Defense, 2005 (Hebrew).

4. Ben-Bassat Committee, *Shortening Compulsory Service*. Israel Ministry of Defense, 2006 (Hebrew).

5. The *Geneva Initiative* was a joint Israeli-Palestinian effort that put forward a detailed model for a peace agreement to end the Israeli-Palestinian conflict on the basis of mutual compromises.

6. The Organization for Civil Rights, *Dror Boymal vs. the Defense Minister*, 20 February 2003.

Chapter Six

The "Embedded Military" and the Implementation of the Disengagement Plan

BACKGROUND AND PUZZLE

As outlined in chapter 5, despite the broad freedom of operation afforded to the IDF by its new social architecture, its scope began to narrow once more in the light of renewed tension between the army and the bearers of the market economy. This is the background to the Disengagement Plan, formulated in 2003 as a withdrawal from the Gaza Strip and the northern West Bank, and the evacuation of about 6,000 Jewish settlements from those areas. Prime Minister Ariel Sharon presented his plan to the public at the end of 2003. Following a political struggle and a series of protests by settler and right-wing organizations, the IDF carried out the entire evacuation over the course of a single week in August 2005.

The Prime Minister's announcement of the Disengagement Plan was made during a period of relative calm. The number of Israeli casualties in terror attacks was down 50 percent compared to 2002 (the IDF website). This was in some part attributable to the renewed military occupation of the West Bank during *Operation Defensive Shield*, carried out in March–April 2002. It was also partially the result of the renewal of American-sponsored indirect diplomatic talks between the Palestinian Authority and Israel. These discussions led to the Road Map, accepted by both sides in May 2003 as a framework for the gradual resolution of the conflict and the establishment of a Palestinian state. The Road Map forced an internal reorganization in the Palestinian Authority, including the appointment of a Prime Minister alongside President Arafat, which also led to the gradual political institutionalization—and hence increased military restraint—of the *Hamas* movement.

In Israel, the terrorist attacks themselves did not create internal pressure for diplomatic moderation, largely because, as mentioned, most of the military victims came from peripheral and religious groups. The same was true of the civilian victims: settlers, immigrants from the former Soviet Union, labor migrants, Ultra-Orthodox Jews, and those using public transport, who by their very nature do not come from the upper strata of society. The upper reaches of the middle class, where the power to effect political change lies, remained entirely unharmed. This stratum learned to fashion alterative modes for reducing risk, such as taking leisure in protected spaces, including going on vacation overseas, and consuming in secure environments such as malls and other gated areas (see Eckstein and Tsiddon, 2004). The peripheral groups lacked the ability to organize, though even had they possessed that ability, their ethno-national political ethos led them to support strong-arm tactics against the Palestinian population and to resist diplomatic concessions. In addition, the business community, the main loser from Israel's decelerated exposure to globalization as a result of terror attacks, exerted no serious pressure on the government to moderate its stance, as shown in chapter 3.

Against this background, the disengagement initiative grew directly and autonomously out of the state bureaucracy, specifically, a joint effort by the IDF's Planning and Policy Directorate and the Prime Minister's Office, headed by Bureau Chief Dov Weisglass. The process emerged from the understanding that Palestinian weakness in extending its authority over the armed militias in its territories was preventing the implementation of the Road Map. At the same time, Israeli fighting had reached a dead end, as it was unable to adequately fulfill the role of the Palestinian Authority in reining in terrorism, or even to bring itself to carry out that role as in the past. On the other hand, letting the situation stagnate carried the risk of Israel being drawn into a violent conflict that would call for the intervention of the international community and the external imposition of a comprehensive settlement. For the decision makers, the largest threat came from the Geneva Initiative, as mentioned in chapter 5. The ongoing violence was also detrimental to the Israeli economy and its internal solidarity, according to the architects of the plan, largely because of the growth of the refusal movement, as high ranking pilots and soldiers from elite combat units joined its ranks.

Therefore, from the perspective of Israeli policy makers, the government needed an initiative that would improve military deployment, preserve the Road Map as the sole diplomatic template, reduce international pressure on Israel, forge an internal consensus, and force the Palestinians into proving their ability to fully control any territory released from Israeli occupation. As hinted at by Dov Weisglass, the hidden agenda of the Disengagement Plan was to leave the bulk of the settlement project in the West Bank in place, at the cost of evacuating settlements in Gaza and small parts of the West Bank (Caspit, 2005; Shavit, 2004). And indeed, the political center, including pragmatic elements of the right wing, supported the Plan for exactly the reasons put forward by its architects.

At the margins of the process a hidden agenda was also attributed to the Prime Minister. By initiating the Plan, it was argued, Sharon was actually trying to bring about a new political agenda that would divert public attention away from the police investigations of bribery claims against his family, as well as consolidating a coalition of leftist parties around him—as the only person capable of leading Israel to make painful concessions—in return for a lenient approach to his breaking the law (Druker and Shelah, 2005, 365–67). This explanation was eagerly taken up by the right wing in an attempt to undermine the Disengagement Plan's legitimacy.

These explanations reflect only the tip of the iceberg of the structural processes detailed at length in the previous chapter. The erosion of the IDF's manpower and material resources increasingly restricted its freedom of operation, preventing it from forcing a military conclusion that would be accepted as legitimate, both internally and externally. To the extent that contractual militarism is a model that increases recruits' freedom of operation in relation to the General Staff, including the turn to selective refusal, it placed new restrictions on the freedom of operation of the army as a whole. At the same time, sensitivity to globalization laid down the infrastructure for the return to Oslo, this time in the shape of the Geneva Initiative, with its support from the capital elites, which Sharon's people hoped to rein in. Finally, the army's organizational solidarity was also damaged as a result of police-style fighting.

However, these explanations do not help us understand the effective implementation of the Disengagement Plan, especially in light of the opposition of the emergent *ethno-national political coalition*, which saw the Plan, and especially the evacuation of settlements, as endangering its interests. This coalition enjoyed the consistent support of around one-half of the public (including the more organized reserves of manpower), with a similar level of support in the Knesset. Furthermore, as seen in the IDF's new social architecture, the ethno-national coalition had even deepened its presence in the army. Yet despite all this, the IDF succeeded in evacuating the settlements quickly; in other words, *the army deployed the coalition's recruits against itself*. Moreover, not only did the evacuation take place quickly and without facing serious resistance, the IDF also managed to maintain unity in its ranks despite carrying out such a politically contentious mission. This, then, is the puzzle on which this chapter focuses.

Arguably, the Disengagement Plan took place because of its compatibility with the military's interests and power in the internal arena. The argument has two parts: (1) both the army and its political operators were interested in a plan that would halt the erosion of the IDF's legitimacy, which had been intensifying during the Al-Aqsa Intifada, a plan that would bring the fighting in line with the army's narrowing resources. Accordingly, the army supported a change in the model of warfare that would enable it to carry on the fighting as a way of maintaining its status, but that would also cost less to sustain, especially in the internal arena; (2) because of its initially low levels of legitimacy, the Plan's implementation was dependent on the successful deployment of the army in neutralizing the power of the ethno-national political-social coalition. The army's effective performance relied on its embeddedness in the social networks of the groups serving it, primarily the national religious groups. It implemented the Disengagement Plan by leveraging the groups' interest in preserving the IDF's ability to proffer mobility to their members and their status within the ranks, an interest that committed them to preserving the army's status as a "people's army" by holding themselves back from clashing violently with the evacuating forces.

THE DISENGAGEMENT AS A MILITARY PLAN

From the outset, the disengagement possessed only limited public legitimacy. Not only was the Plan inconsistent with the platform on which Sharon had been reelected as Prime Minister in 2003, but it was essentially portrayed as a kind of breach of a long-term contract between the state and the Jewish settlers of the Gaza Strip and the West Bank. Under this contract, the state encouraged the settlers to take up residence in the territories and granted them generous subsidies and military protection. The state portrayed this project as permanent, and did not make it conditional on future political arrangements. Now the evacuation of the settlers was required, and not as part of a bilateral agreement, but rather as a unilateral move whose political returns were not assured. Against this background, the settlers' leaders—from the more organized sectors of Israeli politics—focused on recruiting political support that tipped the scales inside the ruling *Likud* Party against disengagement, notwithstanding the fact that it had been initiated by the party's own leader and Prime Minister, Ariel Sharon. Unprecedentedly, the government acted in defiance of the ruling party. Many of the settler leaders even called for civil disobedience that would prevent the evacuation, as well as for conscientious objection within the army.

In these circumstances, the army's status as a legitimacy-building apparatus was strengthened, as the implementation of the Disengagement Plan was dependent on its support. In fact, the army was once more called upon to restrain opposition from the ethno-national coalition, similar to the pattern from the Oslo period (see chapter 3). The change in the IDF's composition, which had carried on apace following Oslo, made it much more representative of those social groups for which it had become a route for mobility. As such, it was the most effective tool for implementing the Disengagement Plan. For this reason the army's support—both rhetorical and practical—was crucial in furthering the Plan.

Beyond strategic considerations, the disengagement also dovetailed with the military's array of interests, which it served in two ways. First, the eroded legitimacy of the IDF meant that reduced friction with the Palestinian civilian population became a military interest, given that such friction was undermining the army's public image and undermining cohesion within the ranks, without conferring any operational benefits. The disengagement, by defining a border between Israel and the Palestinian Authority, could reduce the daily friction with a civilian population. Second, the lack of both human and material resources that resulted from public pressures to cut the defense budget and reform the existing recruitment system inclined the army to see a withdrawal as a way to cut back on its missions, thus reducing the burden on its resources. In particular, as the IDF was fighting the Palestinians, Iran's nuclear project added itself to the agenda, forcing the army to divert resources to a potential military response. On the other hand, having been born out of the need to change the model of fighting, the Disengagement Plan was fashioned as a military plan, thereby preserving the army's organizational interest in maintaining its status in shaping and maintaining a belligerent policy, an interest that fit its (not merely rhetorical) commitment to the new ethno-national groups manning it.

This is the backdrop for understanding the internalization of the acknowledgement that the military way had led to a dead end. As mentioned in the conclusion of the previous chapter, problems of internal legitimacy sharpened the feeling of deadlock, and vice versa, in a vicious circle. Accepting that it was at an impasse, from the summer of 2002 the army gradually toned down its activities. At the center of this process stood Prime Minister Sharon's recognition of the need to come to terms with the establishment of a Palestinian state, as against the majority position in his party's institutions. Having come to this conclusion—also constitutive of the Road Map—he stood for re-election, winning the elections of 2003 with an impressive majority. In parallel, the Disengagement Plan was clandestinely formulated, until it was made public in the winter of 2003. At this point, the army understood that it had to lend its support to a process that would break the stalemate.

The army might have rejected a unilateral move from the start. However, the upper echelons of the IDF, including the Chief of the General Staff himself,

Moshe Yaalon, were beginning to realize that their military options had run out, and that the army was having no impact on the Palestinians' conduct. Therefore, the fighting in its accepted format could not continue as the only means: either diplomatic channels should be exhausted, or new forms of military deployment should be considered (Asa and Yaary, 2005, 11–12). At a later date, Yaalon was to criticize the political echelon for failing to strengthen Abu Mazen during 2003. Following international pressure, Abu Mazen had been appointed the first Palestinian Prime Minister under the presidentship of Arafat; however, he resigned shortly afterward, having failed to enforce his authority over the military organizations (Harel and Yissacharoff, 2004, 317–20).

Not only did the military command internalize the need to change its approach, but this also happened at a time when, as mentioned, the army had made significant achievements in reining in terrorism, though without halting it entirely, meaning that the Israeli initiative was not portrayed as being driven by weakness. The army was particularly sensitive to this image, having speedily withdrawn under fire from Lebanon in the summer of 2000 in a way that made it look like it was fleeing. Moreover, even while fighting, the army had drawn criticism for what was perceived as its entirely unprecedented relinquishment of the ambition to settle the conflict through warfare. Instead, the IDF preferred the theme of *low intensity conflict*, that is, a conflict seen by the army as not constituting an existential threat, and that can thus be conducted over time without coming to a clear conclusion (Wegman, 2004).

In order to deal with the image of its weakness, the army was thus required to "stage a victory," to put forward its achievements as a triumph. As mentioned earlier, Chief of the General Staff Yaalon set the army a political aim— to "brand in the Palestinians' consciousness" the recognition that violence would not bring them positive results. In these circumstances, any moderation on the Palestinian side, such as took place with Abu Mazen's appointment as Prime Minister in 2004, was heralded as an achievement attributable to the Palestinians' "branded consciousness."

This was the background to making the Disengagement Plan a military plan in every way. The Plan was aimed at creating a new model of conflict management that would bring down the costs of fighting. In retrospect, we can see that Israel always sought ways of managing its occupation at low cost, from the model of the South Lebanon Army to Oslo, which turned the Palestinian security forces into "subcontractors" for the IDF and the *Shabak* (General Security Service). During the Al-Aqsa Intifada a new and improved model was tried out, namely, the renewal of the occupation following *Operation Defensive Shield* (2002), but without declaring military rule as long as the Palestinian Authority formally continued to exist. However, as mentioned, this model was also found to be expensive.

The apparent collapse of the Oslo model and the enduring difficulties of sustaining military rule that renewed the occupation de facto brought about the Disengagement Plan. The new post-disengagement model of warfare management had a number of features: (1) partial restoration of the Palestinian Authority's security forces to enable them to tackle terrorism in place of the IDF; (2) strengthening the infrastructure for empowering those forces by evacuating settlements, thus creating Palestinian territorial contiguity, at least in the Gaza Strip; (3) given the difficulty in exclusively relying on the Palestinian Authority's forces, a new actor was brought onto the scene, namely, the Egyptian army, sanctioned by Israel as a "subcontractor" to prevent arms smuggling along the Philadelphia axis in the area of Rafah; (4) maintaining indirect control over the Gaza Strip by overseeing its border crossings, supervising the construction of a seaport, and preventing the reopening of the Palestinian airport; (5) expanding the freedom of military action in response to hostilities from the Palestinian organizations as a result of the IDF's redeployment, effectively reverting the territory from its status as a "ghetto" under Israeli control to that of a "frontier" on the edges of the state and beyond it (to use once more the distinction suggested by Ron, 2003). In this way, Israel's responsibility for the civilian population was diminished; (6) expanding the use of precision weaponry that does not require risking soldiers' lives, methods that become available when a clear border is drawn. In this sense, the disengagement was seen as establishing a model of warfare that allowed Israel to control and influence the evacuated territories without its physical presence in them (Asa and Yaary, 2005). Indeed, the use of combat helicopters, artillery, and aerial observations increased following the withdrawal. The clearest manifestation of this mode of control was the "aerial curfew" imposed on the northern Gaza Strip in 2006 following the escalated firing of Kassam rockets by Palestinian militias. This model of warfare also restored to the General Staff control over its forces that, as mentioned, had been dented by the nature of police-like fighting; (7) the lack of linkage with further possible withdrawals from the West Bank, and an attempt to institutionalize the territorial detachment between the West Bank and the Gaza Strip.

Not by coincidence, the Disengagement Plan was brought into the world at the same time that the security fence between Israel and the West Bank was being constructed. The principles behind the fence were formulated during the Oslo period, and took on greater significance following the outbreak of the Al-Aqsa Intifada. Only in 2002 did Ariel Sharon's government approve the project following its previous reluctance, and began its construction under considerable public pressure. The fence's route has occasionally inspired protest by civil rights groups, with claims that it causes excessive harm to the Palestinian population, arguments that have sometimes been upheld by the Supreme Court. However, the barrier's route gradually sketched out parts of the border desired by Israel, that is, adjustments to the 1967 borders so as to include Jewish settlements blocs in the West Bank within Israel proper. To a large extent, the withdrawal from the Gaza Strip and the northern West Bank also established the principle of evacuating isolated settlements that cannot be included in Israel's side of the wall.

What the wall and the disengagement have in common is their preference for the unilateral manufacture of Israeli-Palestinian separation over a strategy for Palestinian state-building. State-building is generally based on a process whereby political institutions—in this case the institutions constitutive of the Palestinian Authority—strengthen their control over the territories they are responsible for and over the population living in them, and realize their monopolistic appropriation of the means of violence. This process takes shape through bargaining with the local population, by which the citizens accept the state's consolidating authority in return for rights, primarily personal and collective security, to be subsequently supplemented by political, economic, and social rights (Giddens, 1985; Tilly, 1992). Israel's decision to pull out might have created a space in which the Palestinian Authority could negotiate the disarmament of the armed militias in return for paving the way for Israel's withdrawal, which would in turn create further opportunities for the distribution of political rights (such as citizenship and political participation in the Palestinian state's institutions) and for economic development. Such steps would also have nurtured and strengthened the local middle class, which is, as ever, the linchpin of the state's rule. Political agreements, and especially those anchored in global regimes, can internally empower the state by affording it the legitimacy to impose its authority on insurgent factors, in this case the armed militias (see Phillips, 1998).

However, the unilateral moves in the Gaza Strip prevented Israeli-Palestinian negotiations that might have made the withdrawal conditional on the Palestinian Authority increasing its internal control. As a result, Israeli freedom of operation vis-à-vis the Palestinian Authority was also narrowed: all that Israel could offer in return for the Palestinian Authority tightening its grip on internal Palestinian affairs was assurances that Israel would refrain from renewing attacks against the Palestinian Authority or otherwise harming its sovereignty. This in turn made the Palestinian Authority less motivated to impose order on the armed groups in its territories, as well as reducing its legitimacy to do so. The political chaos that saw *Hamas* emerge victorious from the elections of 2006 was the consequence.

The security fence grew out of a similar logic. As an alternative to substantial demands that the Palestinian Authority control the arming of its territories, backed up with military cooperation between the sides (as in Benjamin

Netanyahu's tenure as Prime Minister), Israel in fact partially absolved the Palestinian Authority of this responsibility by erecting a barrier whose role was to prevent violent infiltrations into Israel's territory. At the same time, of course, the wall drove the Palestinians to develop high-trajectory weapons and other arms that can overcome the new barrier. If we add to this the other difficulties faced by the Palestinian Authority in functioning as a state-in-becoming, it is clear that Israel thus denied it a source of potential political power in the form of a monopoly over violence. The wall came to replace state-citizenry bargaining (for a theoretical approach see Krasner, 2005). It is hardly surprising, therefore, that thoughts of reinforcing Palestinian rule with a multinational force were advanced.

Moreover, as mentioned earlier, the discourse concerning the erection of the wall was largely economic—investment in the barrier in relation to its ability to reduce terrorist attacks, thereby contributing to economic growth (Eckstein and Tsiddon, 2004). The construction of the wall thus brought together two elements that the Oslo process had apparently shown to be mutually contradictory, namely, economic growth alongside ongoing fighting with the Palestinians. From the point of view of the Israeli business community, this concord makes the need for a political showdown less crucial. Globalization and militarism do not necessarily contradict one another, in contrast to emergent academic thought during the Oslo years (see mainly Shafir and Peled, 2002).

Israel has never devised a strategy for Palestinian state-building. Accordingly, the dead end that brought about the Disengagement Plan was not decreed by fate, but rather stemmed to a large extent from the collapse of the Palestinian Authority as a result of Israel's escalated attacks (see Bar-Siman-Tov et al., 2005), regardless of whether the explicit aim was to politically destroy the Palestinian entity (*politicide*, as termed by Kimmerling, 2003), or whether that was an unintended consequence. It is worth mentioning again that the recognition that the Palestinian Authority had ceased to be a reliable address for holding back the armed forces cultivated the perception of the Disengagement Plan as a unilateral move. In fact, only during Benjamin Netanyahu's tenure as Israeli Prime Minister did Israel adopt, if not explicitly, a partial strategy of Palestinian state-building, as his attitude of "if they give, they'll get" contributed to the strengthening of the Palestinian Authority's internal control and to security cooperation between the sides.

As a military plan, the Disengagement Plan thus sat well with the army's agenda for sustaining ongoing fighting, without which the IDF's institutional decline would have intensified even further. It also tallied with a model of lower-cost fighting, particularly in the internal arena, and restored control over the ranks to the senior command. It was the manifestation of the army's attempt to reconcile intersecting pressures from the ethos of the market economy on the one hand, and the ethno-national ethos—which had made its way in to the army through changes in its architecture—and its organizational needs on the other. Thus, the army actually became motivated to implement the plan, even in the face of opposition from the ethno-national coalition. Focusing on the IDF's motivation offers at least a partial explanation for its success in efficiently carrying out the evacuation, but its ability to overcome the challenge of legitimacy still requires explanation.

THE CHALLENGE TO THE ARMY'S LEGITIMACY

Originally, the task of evacuating the settlements was assigned to Israel's police force, but in light of the anticipated resistance to the evacuation by the settlers and their supporters, and following assessments that the police was incapable of contending with such a challenge on its own, the army was integrated into the mission by the government. Indeed, the IDF had long been the force responsible for the Military Administration of the territories being evacuated and their Jewish population. In other words, the army was charged with coping with civilian opposition to this controversial political decision. However, the army is not geared for policing missions, especially those that place it at the forefront of a clash with Jewish civilians. Such a mission, moreover, contradicts one of the fundamental principles of modern Western armies.

Preventing military involvement in domestic policing missions has historically been constructed as part of the relationship of trust between the modern state and its citizens. Within these relations, sectarian armed groups' acceptance of the state's monopolization of internal violence was based on their trust that the state would refrain from using the army to resolve internal political disputes. Violence was extruded from the immediate relations of production and civil society in general (see Giddens, 1985; Mann, 1993; Tilly, 1992).

Of course, there may be some exceptions to this principle (such as when Western armies are deployed to break up strikes), but nonetheless it is a firmly established one. Similarly, in Israeli-Jewish society, with the abolition of the Military Administration over the Palestinian-Israeli population in 1966, the army has almost completely been distanced from missions involving the imposition of internal order over civilians, apart from the Palestinian population in the Occupied Territories that had not been formally annexed to the state. The implementation of the Disengagement Plan violated this principle. Even though the evacuation of settlers from the town of Yamit (part of Israel's withdrawal from Sinai in 1981) was assigned to the army, the IDF was dragged into that mission without explicit awareness of its implications. This, though, was not the case with the disengagement.

However, following the social rearchitecturing of the IDF's field units, the challenge of ensuring legitimacy was extended to the army's own ranks. To recall, encouraging the enlistment of the ethno-national groups, with religious youngsters at their center, was not only based on considerations of human resources; rather, it was a type of contractual commitment based on the exchange of sacrifice for symbolic rewards. This contract replaced the old, and by now obsolete, republican contract between the military and the Ashkenazi middle-class groups. As for the IDF, its rearchitecturing attracted soldiers who displayed loyalty to the army and internalized the tenets of military culture, without mobilizing their civilian networks in protest against the army, as their secular Ashkenazi predecessors had done. As seen during the Al-Aqsa Intifada, this change had proven to be effective.

Despite the contract between the army and its recruits, the Disengagement Plan presented a potential threat to the achievements of ethno-national groups in the army, particularly the "knitted skullcap" group. The national religious grip on the army had mostly been felt in the field units, where, since the mid-1990s, they came to fill about 30 percent of the lower-command positions, more than their relative weight in the population, which stood at about 20 percent (Cohen, 2004).

For this group, the main symbolic return for its military participation was carrying out the mission of renewing Jewish control over what they perceived as the Holy Land. To a large extent, during the 1970s, the settlement project in the West Bank, imbued with religious meaning, brought Ashkenazi religious Zionism in from the margins of society, turning it into a central political and cultural stream. Increased recruitment to the army formed a complementary layer to the activity of *Gush Emunim* and with a younger sociological generation. For the national religious sector, serving in the IDF helped forge an alternative autonomous identity to the dominant secular Zionist ethos by taking part in promoting the newly defined "common good" of the Israeli community. However, the purported destruction of the settlement enterprise by the Disengagement Plan threatened to return religious Zionism to the status of just another sector in society, while also undermining the self-identity of a considerable number of conscripts as bearers of a national mission (Sheleg, 2006).

The evacuation, however, harmed not only religious, but other groups as well. A new combat model was heralded, based mainly on controlling the Occupied Territories without a physical presence, a model that entails eroding the significance of the military contribution of "blue-collar" soldiers, most of whom are recruited from the ethno-national groups. At the same time, the new model favors a transition to "hi-tech warfare," reliant on middle-class sectors of society.

In short, the army was faced with a complicated problem of legitimacy: not only was it ordered to carry out a domestic police mission, which contradicts the legitimacy of its operations and was perceived by some organized political groups in Israeli society as illegitimate; it also was faced with the prospect of a breakdown in its contract-like relationship with many of its conscripts. The army was essentially required to carry out an operation that conflicted with the interests of its own conscripts. This was the structural background for the concerns regarding mass disobedience that accompanied the disengagement process. Practically, a number of leading rabbis ruled that soldiers were forbidden by religious law to expel Jews from their homes, and urged them to refuse to take any part in uprooting settlements in the Land of Israel (Cohen, 2007). Their goal was to thwart Sharon's initiative. In light of the significant proportion of religious soldiers in the field units, the potential for conscientious objection posed a real threat to the IDF's cohesiveness as much as to its very capacity to carry out disengagement effectively, especially as hundreds of soldiers signified their intentions to obey the rabbis.

However, despite the resistance, over the course of a single week in the summer of 2005, the IDF unprecedentedly evacuated thousands of Jewish settlers from the Gaza Strip and the northern West Bank.

From the moment the task of evacuating the settlers was assigned to the army, it fully devoted itself to the mission. The army's evacuation tactics relied on the concentrated deployment of a large quantity of soldiers in the settlements being evacuated, thereby giving the army a significant numerical advantage over the settlers, who were expected to oppose their evacuation aggressively. Although this concentration of force and the manner in which the troops were organized may explain the success of the evacuation, it cannot account for the lack of large-scale or violent opposition on the part of the settlers.

After all, the opposition—the settler leaders—could quite easily have resisted forcefully. Despite their numerical inferiority, they could have made the event traumatic, thus largely defining the terms of any future evacuation of settlements on the West Bank. What has to be explained, therefore, is not only how the army managed to evacuate the settlers so swiftly, but also why the settlers (contrary to prior forecasts) reconciled themselves to their evacuation, resisting only passively, mainly via demonstrations. Also significant is the fact that the army maintained unity within its own ranks, even whilst executing a politically controversial mission. Early assessments that orders to evacuate the settlers would be disobeyed on a massive scale, particularly by national religious conscripts who identified with the settlement project, proved completely false.

At the broader level, at stake was the autonomous capacity of the state to implement the disengagement in defiance of the wishes of segments within Israeli society who wield significant clout. After all, the settler organizations in the territories and the ethno-national political coalition that backed them constituted a powerful political alignment, responsible for promulgating the view that the settlement project was irreversible. Ever since the Oslo Accords of 1993, successive Israeli governments have in fact internalized this restriction on their freedom of action, and have avoided committing themselves to evacuate settlements, let alone actually doing so. Instead, they have even encouraged the expansion of the settlement effort, albeit not necessarily through formal channels (Eldar and Zartal, 2004). From this perspective, the disengagement constituted a process that restored autonomy to the state, if only partially and temporarily, largely by means of assigning this police mission to the IDF.

THE IDF AS A PARTIALLY EMBEDDED ARMY

As argued earlier, the effective functioning of the IDF in this instance can be attributed to the degree to which it has become embedded within the social networks of the groups—primarily those affiliated with the national religious segment of the Jewish population who resisted the disengagement—that serve within it. The army implemented the Disengagement Plan by leveraging the interest of those groups in reinforcing the IDF's status as an apolitical and universal "people's army" by which they could preserve their mobility within its ranks. Thus, what prevented national religious groups from initiating massive clashes with the troops involved in the disengagement was their assessment that a confrontation of that nature could have undermined the army's status and, by extension, that of the resisting groups—both within the IDF and in civilian society too.

The Essence of Embeddedness

The classic Huntingtonian model of "objective" civilian control over the army posits that the social insularity of the military establishment and its senior officers from surrounding social forces has the effect of buttressing soldiers' goal-oriented professional values, which are thus insulated from political or social issues (Huntington, 1964; see also Cohen, 2002, 225–48). This theme is consistent with the *state-centered concept* of state autonomy—the ability of the state's bureaucracy to exercise power independently, in the face of resistance from internal social forces (see Domhoff, 1996; Evans et al.,

1985; Jessop, 2001; Migdal, 1988; Migdal, 2001; Seabrooke, 2002). Here too, state autonomy rests on the social isolation of state bureaucrats—the existence of unambiguous boundaries between the state apparatus and society. Accordingly, state-centered, as well as other statist approaches, regard the distancing of armies from missions concerned with domestic policing and the imposition of internal order to be one of the constitutive principles of the modern military in democratic systems.

An alternative approach is to substitute the binarism of state-society relations with a focus on what has been called the *state-society synergy*. This term refers to the mutual enhancement by the state bureaucracy and social groups of each other's operative efforts. This notion may be based on *embeddedness*, namely, the idea that public and private actors are informally enmeshed in the process of the production of public goods across the public-private divide. State bureaucrats may be closely embedded in the communities with which they work and do not remain at a distance from them, as statist approaches would expect, thus creating social capital that spans the public-private divide. Subcontracting public projects to local communities, and running projects that are comanaged by government and community representatives, are among the means through which the state can improve governability via the model of synergy. Improved governability might then take the form of mobilizing organized groups in support of state policies, building relations of trust rather than alienation, reinforcing the citizenry's commitment to the state, and the state's penetration into relatively autonomous societal segments (Evans, 1996; Evans, 1997; Ostrom, 1996).

The notion thus outlined can be extended to the military domain. Thus, militaries that are embedded within the social networks from which they draw their human resources may, under certain circumstances, become relatively autonomous in relation to the surrounding social forces. This kind of autonomous capacity may be fruitfully compared to militaries that base their autonomy on social isolation, as informed by the Huntingtonian model of *objective control*.

Militaries, unlike other state bureaucracies, do not work within and on behalf of distinguishable communities, but are mainly focused on external missions carried out for the benefit of the national community as a whole. Nevertheless, given that distinguishable communities serve in the military and are motivated by different opinions on national security goals, the borrowed concept of state embeddedness should not be rejected a priori. Embeddedness in this context means that the performance and conduct of specific military units are highly affected by the civilian networks from which the military draws its personnel.

To better understand the essence of embeddedness, it should be located within the hierarchy specifying the military autonomy vis-à-vis the ambient society. Moving up the hierarchy, *fusionism* is located one level above isolation (Fotion, 2003). Fusionism is the desired, normative openness of the military to the host society by incorporating the values of the latter within the framework of permeable boundaries between the social and military spheres in an attempt to gain legitimacy.[1]

Fusionism is elevated by *diversity management.* Diversity management refers to the organization's ability to integrate and administer the collective mixture of skills, values, and identities brought to the organization by various groups, and to manage itself in a way that appreciates and respects the differences between the groups. In the military context, such a policy might express the military's efforts, for various reasons, to integrate within its ranks previously alienated groups.[2] Diversity management may embrace the involvement of the military recruits' social networks in order to manage cultural aspects of military units, such as religion. Diversity management elevates the apparently normative openness of the military to the host society by incorporating the values of the latter within the framework of permeable boundaries between the social and military spheres in an attempt to gain legitimacy.

At the highest level of diversity management, embeddedness is formed, that is, units are comanaged by the military command and civilian networks, and hence enjoy greater autonomy vis-à-vis the senior command. Through this course of action, the values, beliefs and interests shared by the social groups involved could partly corrupt the military command's code of professionalism and distort the chain of command.

To move one level higher, extreme levels of embeddedness may lead to the civilianization of the army, a situation that Huntington terms *subjective control* (1964, 80), meaning that civilian groups define and monitor military activities in accordance with their specific interests. The demise of the military's professional identity is likely to result. Subjective control embodies the army's full embeddedness within the social networks from which it originated, and its lack of isolation in relation to them.

Unlike subjective control, embeddedness implies that the military is still "militarized," in the sense that only certain of its units are permeable to the civilian intervention that generates comanagement. Embeddedness is thus the balance point between isolation, fusionism, and diversity management on the one hand, and subjective control on the other.

To go one step further, embeddedness may enhance the military's autonomous status relative to the ambient social forces and make it more effective in this regard than socially isolated armies. The state's embeddedness can be seen as an exchange of institutional resources between the state and the surrounding social networks by which the state loses some institutional resources but in return enhances governability. Similarly, an embedded military shapes relations of exchange with part of its recruits in which the power groups accrue by means of the comanagement arrangements is traded for their loyalty to the army. Internal arrangements of this sort are valued against their social convertibility. Thus, whereas an isolated army typically holds tradable resources of this kind to a lesser extent than the more "open" armies, a "civilianized" army in the form of subjective control possesses resources that are poorly convertible because of its relatively low status. Embeddedness is again the balance point.

As demonstrated by the case of the IDF in the disengagement mission, embeddedness resulted from the rearchitecturing of its social composition, by which the IDF exchanged sacrifice on the part of the religious groups for symbolic rewards, which included special arrangements of diversity management generated by that exchange. It was the IDF's very embeddedness within the religious social networks that paradoxically heightened the army's capacity to evacuate the settlers without resorting to severe violence and without undermining its cohesiveness.

The IDF's Embeddedness

As argued earlier, the effective functioning of the army rested on its ability to exert its embeddedness within the social networks of the national religious groups that serve in it. Of particular relevance are two main forms of embeddedness that contradict the principle of an army isolated from society.

First, implicit in the symbolic rewards that the IDF offered to the national religious groups in return for their military contribution was a special arrangement through which the rabbis and their students could gain influence over the army's values and leverage the latter's military service to fulfill their ideological mission. Accordingly, as argued in chapter 2, the army fashioned a "dual hierarchy"—the simultaneous allegiance of some of the religious conscripts to their military commanders and to their rabbis, both of which represent "total institutions" (Cohen, 2004). This dual hierarchy generated (at least) seven forms of embeddedness: (1) the army's dialogue with the heads of the yeshivas over the character and terms of military service; (2) the bargaining over the religious soldiers' service conditions, such as allowances given to soldiers' wives and dependent children, became a matter of institutional rather than individual bargaining, unlike what had become customary for other recruits;[3] (3) the construction of an appropriate cultural and religious environment for religious soldiers, primarily arrangements and rules for positing men and women in integrated units; (4) many companies were established with a homogeneous religious composition, most notably the *hesder* companies; (5) rabbis were provided with free access to military camps in which their yeshiva students served and to whom the students frequently turned for guidance at the interface of religious and professional issues, such as the military's functioning during the *Sabbath*. In addition, rabbis served as de facto religious commissars, trying to educate secular soldiers as well, by means of their unprecedented access to military camps (Schiff, 2004); (6) in practice, the IDF tolerated the rabbis' inclination to issue religious decisions (*Piskei Halacha*) that related to professional issues, and subjected military discipline to theological considerations, such as rules banning religious conscripts from participating in the evacuation of settlements, or even military bases, in the West Bank, once the Oslo process began; (7) allowing religious conscripts to use their own formula during their enlistment ceremony, that is "I declare," while for other conscripts the text is "I swear" (see mainly Cohen, 2007).

In short, these and other arrangements gave the rabbis a foothold in the army in a manner that was not extended to other social groups. The army thus bent its professional principles in favor of its arrangements with this group. Embeddedness meant the provision of symbolic rewards.

The second aspect of this partial embeddedness could be found in the Occupied Territories themselves, in the synergistic relationship between the army and the settlers with a notable share of religious persons. From the early 1980s, the IDF began to arm the settlers and enable them to establish what to all intents and purposes were armed militias. Specifically, they were reserve units comprised of settlers who participated in the everyday protection of their communities. In this framework, the army allowed the settlers to keep their weapons with them, as befitting reserve soldiers. In practical terms, they became a kind of complementary wing of the army in maintaining the occupation, often committing abuses against the local Palestinians in exchange for generous state subsidies for the settlements and their residents. Over time, questions came to be frequently raised concerning the freedom of operation enjoyed by these forces vis-à-vis the military command, particularly since some of the senior commanders of the military, responsible for overseeing those settler units, live in the settlements themselves.[4]

In this instance, the model of diversity management implemented by the army with regard to the religious groups was relatively extreme (certainly in comparison to its implementation among other groups that the army integrated), to the point that it produced embeddedness. The IDF established arrangements that created its own dependence on sociopolitical groups, formed a model of joint military-civilian operations, and infringed upon the army's professional codes. In exchange, the army enjoyed access to a human resource that allowed it to function quite autonomously in executing politically controversial missions that kept the secular Ashkenazi center-left at bay, starting with the First Lebanon War, through the maintenance of control over the Occupied Territories (including during the Oslo process), and up to the fighting in the Al-Aqsa Intifada.

Paradoxically, rather than the IDF's embeddedness proving to be an obstacle, it actually enabled the smooth implementation of the Disengagement Plan, in ways that shall now be detailed.

THE STRATEGY OF THE EVACUATION

The effectiveness of the army's operation can be explained by the employment of a strategy that highlighted the IDF's character as a "people's army" embedded in the social networks from which a great number of its conscripts are drawn.

The Rhetoric of a "People's Army"

From the moment the decision was made to assign the evacuation of the settlements to the army, the IDF devoted all its energies to the mission by (both physically and psychologically) training its personnel, establishing special units, developing a media strategy, and more. As already noted, the army's tactics for the evacuation were based on the concentration of very large numbers of soldiers in the settlements being evacuated, thus creating a significant numerical advantage over the settlers, who were expected to object aggressively to their evacuation. Furthermore, the army worked to objectify and make the individual soldiers anonymous by issuing all of them with a standardized uniform (without the various symbols identifying the different corps), adopting a policy of thundering silence in the face of evacuees' provocations, and standing as a unified group in the face of such resistance as they encountered (Feige, 2005). However, this concentration of power and its organization can explain why the disengagement succeeded, but not why it did not encounter massive or violent opposition and significant disobedience.

The effectiveness of the IDF's operation relied largely on the manner in which the government used the army to carry out the Disengagement Plan: it not only deployed its human and organizational resources, but also drew heavily from its symbolic power as the "people's army"—meritocratic, depoliticized, socially engaged, and experienced by its members as overlapping with society.

At the conceptual level, it is worth emphasizing that whereas the political echelon explicitly and intentionally deployed the IDF's organizational and human resources, its political utilization was unintentional and well rooted in the *institutional heritage* that perceives the "people's army" as the preferred way of legitimizing politically contentious policies precisely because it is a "people's army" (see chapter 3 on Oslo),

The army's involvement contributed to the depoliticization of the Disengagement Plan. The army helped to legitimize the Plan by having its spokespersons present its positive aspects, or, alternatively, by refraining from criticizing it, thus playing down criticism from right-wing groups. The main source of the IDF's support for the disengagement, however, was in the symbolic sphere. From the moment it was decided that the evacuation would be undertaken by the army, the discourse surrounding the disengagement was largely diverted from debating the balance of advantages versus risks inherent in the process, to a discourse on state symbols. In the framework of the new discourse, the Plan's advocates stressed that hanging in the balance was nothing less than the very essence of Israeli democracy. They argued that it was crucial that the government should be capable of executing a decision legislated by its official institutions, thereby sidestepping discussion of the outcome of the withdrawal.

The army fell in line with this statist discourse, and senior IDF officers spoke of the need to implement democratic decisions made by the majority, with the army's subordination to the country's democratic institutions now coming under close scrutiny. These officers noted that the question of whether the army would be dragged into a political dispute or preserve its apolitical character was at stake. In other words, there was an expectation that despite the fact that the IDF was undertaking a politically controversial mission, its very involvement would neutralize any political opposition, which would prefer not to undermine the universality of the army, the main component of any "people's army" (see Shavit-Fradkin, 2006).

This symbolic discourse was most important in the context of the rearchitecturing of the IDF's social composition. As the new groups were granted a more equal status than in the past, or were at least offered equal access to mobility within the organization, they had something to lose should the army's status be challenged by being dragged into political dispute. In short, the new groups, and particularly the religious soldiers, were caught in a dilemma.

The Strategic Dilemma of the Religious Soldiers

The religious soldiers' dilemma may be outlined as follows: responding positively to the appeal from some of the leading rabbis to disobey orders to evacuate settlements would have salved the conscience of a significant number of religious soldiers. On the other hand, disobedience may erode the religious groups' status within the IDF, as was reflected in a three-layered discourse:

On the surface, weakening the IDF's symbolic status might have shattered a national symbol and affected its capacity to fulfill its military missions, which were nationally cherished by the Zionist-religious rabbinate. The symbols of the "people's army" were taken at face value, namely:

> Using the IDF to uproot the glorious settlement enterprise in Gush Katif [Gaza] is a distortion of the army's purpose and a blow at its cohesiveness. But this does not change its essential objective. We must show responsibility and partnership in building a strong IDF.[5]

Beneath the surface, dismantling that symbol, and hence undermining the IDF's status, implied belittling the significance of the current and potential status of the national religious groups within the army. "When you put on the uniform, you are wearing a kind of 'royal clothing' that becomes a source of strength and pride," as Rabbi Yuval Sherlo and Rabbi David Stav, joint heads of the Petach Tikvah *hesder* yeshiva, put their argument against disobedience,[6] implying that only a highly symbolized "people's army" can provide a reward of this kind to its recruits. Moreover, military service in a politicized army loses much of its ability to serve as a criterion for meaningful civilian privileges.

At an even deeper level, massive disobedience would have endangered the group's achievements since the 1980s, and would have raised questions regarding its ability to deepen its hold on the army and reach the very highest ranks, as envisaged by the group's leadership. Massive disobedience, both explicit and "grey," could cause the IDF's hierarchy to suspect the national religious groups' absolute loyalty to the army's values. First and foremost, this would impact on the promotion prospects of religious officers. It would also affect the willingness of IDF commanders to maintain the special arrangements with the religious leadership, upon which the army's embeddedness was constituted. Rabbi Yaakov Medan, a leading figure in the religious movement, summed up these worries when, shortly before the evacuation, he declared:

> But even if, God forbid, the decision is taken [for the IDF to carry out the evacuation]. . . , we must not support ideological disobedience, thus creating a stronger basis for ideological disobedience "to protect the settlers," currently on the margins of the left wing, and moving it into the center. We would also be distancing ourselves from the top ranks of the IDF, an idea that has been raised in various forums concerned about the religious right gaining control over the army. (Medan, 2004)

Incidentally, moreover, just prior to the implementation of the Disengagement Plan, the rabbis had been demanding the complete separation of religious male and female soldiers, to the point of establishing separate battalions, and not only companies, of religious soldiers. In other words, widespread disobedience might have caused the army to be hesitant about setting up "sub-armies" that would be decisively loyal to their rabbinic-political backers. Indeed, Danny Yatom, a major general in the reserves and a former head of the *Mossad*, warned on the eve of the pullout that a military coup is possible in the future if religious soldiers were allowed to become the majority within the top IDF brass.

In other words, not only was the group's status at stake, but also its ability to direct the IDF to protect the group's assets, such as the army's role in defending settlements in the West Bank, a mission that generated intensifying controversy. Furthermore, for the religious leadership, the very presence of its youth in the ranks is also part of a spiritual mission, by which the youngsters provide the IDF with the values the leadership sees as unique, namely, "bringing the fruits of Torah face to face with Israeli society," as put by Rabbis Sherlo and Stav.

At the same time, it became clear to the rabbis that a display of loyalty to the army by means of the test set by the Disengagement Plan could increase the future weight of their students, whose integration into the army would be that much smoother. An army with a high percentage of national religious soldiers could not easily be sent to implement the anticipated future strategy of evacuating most of the West Bank—the main focus of the religiously motivated settlement project. Rabbi Shlomo Aviner, the head of the *Ateret Cohanim* yeshiva in East Jerusalem, the rabbi of the Bet El Jewish community in the West Bank, and the most salient spokesperson against disobedience, expressed this concern when he said (Aviner, 2005):

> To leave the army is to leave the nation. It is disengagement from the people! . . .
> If you are not inside, you have no influence. You only harm yourself while others take your place—just as with the left-wing refuseniks.

What was hanging in the balance on the eve of the disengagement, therefore, was not only the abstract symbolic significance of the "people's army," but also the status of the organization as a mechanism that could potentially and practically grant mobility, especially to the religious groups, and realize their values. Representing the evacuation mission as a test of the IDF's universalism must thus be viewed in the context of what this meant to the groups whose status was linked in various ways to that of the army, and not just as an abstract political discourse. Accordingly, the notion, discursively inculcated by the IDF's command, that the very future of the "people's army" was at stake, and not just the fate of a few settlements, was echoed within the rabbis' rhetoric. The preservation of the military symbol of the "people's army" thus required that clashes between settlers and soldiers be avoided, and that the defection of religious soldiers during the evacuation of settlements be prevented.

Seen from a different perspective, the disengagement and its consequences were not the most prominent topic of interest to religious soldiers; they were far more troubled by a wide range of other issues, such as the relative merits of military service vis-à-vis torah study; *Sabbath* observance whilst on duty; interpersonal relations with secular troops; and gender relations in military units (Cohen, 2007). At the same time, the strong presence of religious officers worked to bind their loyalty to the military at the expanse of their ties to their rabbis. After all, military promotion, which determined the officers' prestige in their communities, was conditional on loyalty to the organization. Both conditions worked as a mechanism that may have reduced the potential political influence of extremist rabbis, as suggested by Rabbi Aviner (2005):

> Many soldiers are loyal to their commanders, and will follow them through thick and thin. It is religious arrogance to assume that that all of the religious officers and soldiers are in the rabbis' pockets.

In other words, the rabbis' intransigence could have distanced the conscripts from them. Therefore, embeddedness could also work to temporarily weaken the rabbis' bonds with their students, serving the interests of both.

The army deepened this dilemma in various ways. Thus, for example, while drawing on the abstract values of the "people's army" in order to criticize the development of the "dual hierarchy" of religious soldiers, the IDF concurrently continued to legitimize dialogue with the rabbis. By leveraging the advantages of embeddedness, this dialogue was intended to persuade the rabbis to advise their students to follow the army's orders. Alongside this dialogue, the heads of the army explicitly threatened either to cancel the *hesder* yeshiva program in its entirety and integrate the *hesder* soldiers with the rest of the army, or alternatively to halt the *hesder* arrangement with specific yeshivas whose rabbis were encouraging conscientious objection (Rapaport, 2005). The recognition of rabbinical authority was also manifested by the expansion of the role of the Chief Military Rabbinate, deployed as a religious authority to halt potential disobedience among religious soldiers.

Another mechanism for deepening the dilemma was the promotion of two religious major generals to the Head of the Personnel Directorate (Elazar Stern) and the Commander of the Central Command (Yair Nave), positions that entailed direct involvement in the evacuation mission. Through these appointments the army was acknowledging its limitations in enforcing discipline that ignored cultural differences. Both generals were expected to function as "middlemen," mediating on both a symbolic and institutional level between the soldiers and their rabbis, in order to reduce the potential for conscientious objection. It is even possible that their very appointment was an attempt to grant senior commanders added political-cultural value, beyond their purely military authority alone. Thus, the army presented the soldiers with a combined source of authority that could somewhat diminish the rabbinical authority imposed on a large share of the soldiers. At the same time, the IDF used these appointments to increase the representation of "knitted skullcaps" in its upper echelons. In exchange for this increased representation, the IDF expected the loyalty of the national religious sector, even if not necessarily explicitly (Levy, 2004b).

This being the case, the embeddedness of the IDF in national religious networks not only harmed the professional autonomy of the army in executing the withdrawal, but also deepened the strategic dilemma faced by the rabbis: endangering the achievements of the national religious group with respect to its upward mobility in the organization and its ideologically loaded missions, versus religious and ideological steadfastness.

The Social Construction of the Evacuating Forces

As well as deepening the strategic dilemma of the potential refuseniks, the IDF also acted to reduce the dilemma via the specific organization of the force that was to directly handle the evacuation (including forcefully removing settlers from their homes), in accordance with the hierarchy of the soldiers' professional (and hence political) loyalty. This was an advanced form of social architecture.

A considerable share of the direct evacuation work was assigned to the Border Police, a civilian policing force that receives manpower from the army and whose effectiveness stems from its combination of career service personnel with compulsory service soldiers. These soldiers join the Border Police with the economically motivated expectation that some of them will be able to stay on at the end of their compulsory service as regular salaried policepersons. Although a considerable percentage of the Border Police soldiers come from peripheral groups and often display aggressiveness toward the Palestinian population, not a single member of these units disobeyed orders to participate in disengagement operations. The professional ethos of serving in the police force, coupled with economic motivations, were strong enough to overcome a previously formed ideological orientation.

In addition to the Border Police, the IDF established and deployed improvised units of career officers of various ranks. These soldiers were gleaned from both rear units and command posts, and underwent brief training for their temporary positions. This had all the trappings of a professional army, concerned that the "people's army"—conscript soldiers, not to mention reservists—would not be able to withstand the pressure of the settlers' resistance. Along with the fact that this mode of organization fortified the army's ability to present a huge human mass, the career personnel naturally displayed a high level of loyalty to the army's orders, and there was almost no disobedience among them.

The career soldiers were joined by female soldiers, who accounted for about one-quarter of the inner circle of the evacuating forces. The latter were assigned to evacuating the women and children, and they successfully carried out their mission with no instances of conscientious objection whatsoever. On the one hand, it might appear that the gender-based division of labor in the military was reconfirmed. Looked at differently, however, the involvement of women soldiers represented a pattern of exchange—the women's loyalty to the army in exchange for their inclusion in a mission portrayed as a military operation (see Amram, 2006). Thus, the involvement of career personnel and women soldiers at least temporarily suspended the military division of labor between noncombat and combat soldiers, thereby assisting the military to overcome potential obstacles among the evacuating forces.

Even the outer circle, manned by military personnel, was organized to cope with the threat of disobedience. Reserve units—the most vulnerable to political influence, since they are composed of "civilianized soldiers" were completely excluded from the mission (Harel, 2005). Even more significant was the distancing from the inner circles of units with a high percentage of religious conscripts, including the Golani and Givati Infantry Brigades, and soldiers from some of the officers' schools.[7] The Golani Brigade had experienced various forms of internal protest prior to the disengagement, as about half of the officers from the level of company commander and higher were religious (Harel, 2006a). Similarly, the Ultra-Orthodox *Nahal* battalion was exempted from participating in the evacuation from the outset, on the assumption that it bore a high potential for disobedience (Rappoport, 2005).

At the same time, the IDF efficiently handled soldiers who announced their intentions to refuse, relieving such soldiers of their duties without penalizing them (Rotenberg, 2005). These were clearly instances of "grey refusal," which the IDF preferred to handle pragmatically, and away from the spotlight in order to minimize the challenge to the military's symbols as an allegedly apolitical organization.

The Responses of the Religious Groups

In the final analysis, the call to refuse split the leaders of the religious camp. In practice, most of the yeshiva heads opposed disobedience or refrained from expressing their views (Cohen, 2007), hence letting the soldiers decide by themselves. It is therefore safe to conclude that the religious and other rightist groups internalized the recognition that preserving the symbolic power of the "people's army" was in their interest, and particularly that of the religious conscripts. Embeddedness dominated over ideological proclivities to forcefully thwart the withdrawal. For some of the leaders and their military associates, this preference was based on the internalization of the IDF's symbolic power, while others were concerned about losing legitimacy due to damage to the symbol of the "people's army." Still others internalized the utilitarian motive to preserve the avenues for mobility in the IDF, which, owing to the symbol of the "people's army," were quite significant. Had the IDF remained an overt bastion of the secular Ashkenazi middle class, as it had been till the 1970s, its ability to discipline other social groups and even its own soldiers would have been lower; alternatively, had the IDF become professional, it would probably have encountered stronger civilian opposition, even if its ability to discipline its soldiers had been higher. Paradoxically, the change in the IDF's composition, upon which the republican equation was rebalanced, was therefore instrumental in developing its autonomous capacity both to fight, as expressed in combat against the Palestinians, and to moderate that aggressiveness (or give it a new form) via the Disengagement Plan.

Furthermore, instrumental to the military's success was the settlers' relative pragmatism. Unlike the West Bank settlers, for those in the Gaza Strip, many of whom were Mizrachim, the settlement project embodied social mobility, rather than fulfilling a national or religious mission. By moving to the settlements from their original development towns and moshavim in the Negev, with their negative image, they could build a community and give their life a new meaning that would replace their social and cultural peripheriality (Schnell and Mishal, 2005). Against this background, a mixture of economic and community incentives (such as moving as a community from Gaza to inside the Green Line), together with their deep-rooted respect for state symbols, with the IDF at the center, eased the settlers' dilemma in favor of pragmatism.

Not only were abstract values at work. During the evacuation, the spotlight fell on the emotionally charged personal encounters between the evacuators and the evacuees, who were connected by family, community, youth movement, and even military networks. Indeed, there was a broad social common denominator shared by the Gaza evacuees, many of whom were Mizrachim and had previously lived in development towns and moshavim in the Negev, and the evacuating soldiers, and even the police (Harel, 2006b). These personal meetings could have resulted in the collapse of the military effort, but they could also have had the opposite result, bringing about the collapse of the evacuees' resistance. After all, opposing the evacuating army meant harming a component of the evacuees' very identity, as they were socially associated with the army and the evacuators in various ways. Since the evacuees were the first to recoil from clashing with the IDF, not only did the personal encounters cause no harm to the military operation, but they even contributed to the IDF's legitimacy in that they represented the army as a humane body and not as an evil bureaucratic machine (Feige, 2005). Embeddedness, which also had social-emotional aspects, was translated into power.

Quite ironically, the settler leaders who called on soldiers not to refuse, or who abstained from calling for refusal, did so out of an internalization of the symbolic power of the "people's army" together with the rewards involved for the religious networks, thereby helping the IDF to evacuate them without any real opposition. Ultimately, this is what prevented substantial rates of refusal, which would have emerged if the evacuation had been particularly violent and drawn out, thus deepening the soldiers' dilemma.

In their soul-searching in the aftermath of the disengagement, therefore, the settler leaders and the rabbis had good cause to admit that they had erred, whether by "embracing" the army (both figuratively and physically, as in many instances the evacuating soldiers and the evacuees hugged and wept together), or by refraining to call for disobedience. The results of this soul-searching were evident in the "gloves off" policy in the violent opposition to the evacuation of a single, illegally built section of the West Bank settlement of Amona in February 2006.

In the final analysis, not only did the evacuation operation last only one week (while it had been planned to span a number of weeks), and not only was it unaccompanied by significant violence, but the scope of refusal was also low: only about 60 soldiers refused in a manner that drew public attention and required military legal action against them. Interestingly, most of them—fifty soldiers—had refused even before the evacuation had commenced (Bender, 2005), thus proving that the various preventative tactics had been effective, and that the layer of military personnel positioned at the front lines was one whose loyalty could be trusted. The IDF's status remained intact, at least in the short term.

CONCLUSIONS

The Disengagement Plan embodied the army's attempt to strike a balance between the ethos of the market economy, which urged the army to reduce the scope of its fighting, and the ethno-national ethos and its own organizational interests, both of which called for its continuation. The disengagement involved a change in the model of fighting that would satisfy these contradictory pressures. In this way, the political echelon successfully implemented a controversial move, as it deployed the "army of the peripheries" against its own social networks.

During the withdrawal, the IDF employed a strategy involving a dual rhetoric. On the one hand, it put forward its façade as an apolitical "people's army" whose status was under threat. Any harm caused to that status was portrayed as liable to affect the very social groups that resisted the disengagement, and which had been politically recruited in an attempt to prevent the army's involvement in the operation. While this approach required distancing the army from these groups and the portrayal of the IDF as above the sectoral divisions that characterize Israeli society, the army also employed a strategy of bargaining as an attempt to bridge the gap between the sides. This bargaining was facilitated by the IDF's embeddedness within the national religious networks, which had created dense interactions between the military command and the conscripts and their civilian communities. Bargaining and bridging served the need to make the groups aware of the price of harming the military, while at the same time making it easier for them not to follow their urge to oppose the army in a manner that could diminish its symbolic power, central to which was its being a distanced and apolitical "people's army." A duality of closeness and distance therefore characterized the dialogue between the IDF and the religious groups.

The IDF's moves were not necessarily typified by an explicit organizational self-awareness. Likewise, we have no indication that the political leadership directed the army's moves beyond the fundamental decision to assign the mission to the IDF and set the timetable for it. Rather, the organization's cultural strategy, informed by adaptive rationality, was at work again (see chapter 5). The IDF's self-image as a "people's army" constrained it to avoid or lessen conflicts with powerful Jewish groups, as part of its need for legitimacy. This explains the modes of bargaining with the religious leadership employed during the crisis, and the layers of forces involved in the evacuation as part of a deeply rooted social architecture of the ranks, and other moves.

Theoretically, under certain circumstances, an army that is embedded in the social networks from which it recruits its manpower is likely to increase its operational autonomy, as the case of the disengagement revealed, and not the opposite. The theoretical theme of state-society synergy can thus be expanded and adapted to the military's functioning as a state apparatus which enhances the state's autonomous status. Decisive are the convertible resources that the military accrues to its recruits, which it can trade for the groups' loyalty. Similar to the notion of synergy, an exchange of resources—institutional or symbolic—is at play.

An army insulated from society, as the IDF was in relation to some segments before the rearchitecturing of its social composition in the 1980s, or as a professional army is supposed to be, preserves the principle of the isolation of the state bureaucracy from social forces, as the Huntingtonian model of objective control clearly suggests. As seen by the professionalization of the U.S. military following Vietnam, for instance, a professional army provides the state with an autonomous capacity to maintain war readiness, and even to initiate war, as such an army faces less political resistance originating in military participation. In short, increased social isolation translates into extended autonomy (Moskos, 2001).

Nevertheless, when a professional army acts against the interests of groups serving within it (in performing policing missions, for example), this may exacerbate legitimacy difficulties that might hamper the military's performance. It is reasonable to assume that had the IDF been a professional army in 2005, it would have had to contend with much stronger opposition from the settlers that it evacuated. Even if the IDF had succeeded in maintaining unity within its ranks, it is doubtful whether it would have managed to carry out its mission, and certainly not without shock waves.

But the opposite type—an extreme level of embeddedness that leads to the civilianization of the army in the form of the Huntingtonian typology of subjective control—may produce a similar result. A high level of identification of the army with the interests of various groups will result in the disintegration of its image as a national-universal symbol. The army will thus function like any other organization in the labor market that practices a high level of diversity management, but not as a national symbol. Hence, it will encounter internal difficulties within its ranks in contending with domestic challenges, as the arrangements it shapes with the groups lack significant value. Such arrangements are poorly convertible as resources reaped in a "civilianized," nonprestigious army. Hence, the soldiers' motivation to display loyalty during an internal crisis when the army acts against their interests will be low. The army is therefore highly sensitive to changes in its relationship with the networks from which it recruits its soldiers and their attitudes to its missions, to the point that its ability to enforce total military discipline is hampered. An illustration of this is the massive desertion from units in the Confederate Army during the American Civil War with a homogeneous composition of soldiers from communities in which support for the war had eroded (Bearman, 1991).

Embeddedness is thus the balance point between isolation (and the more moderate forms that embody fusionism and diversity management) and subjective control, and exemplifies the combination of the two: an arrangement with certain groups is usually significant only if the army preserves its status as a universal-apolitical symbol. In other words, distancing grants significance to the closeness created by embeddedness. This balanced combination can be maintained as long as the army continues to isolate and distance other parts of the military from the social networks that provide it with manpower.

In the case of the IDF, even if the units with a high concentration of settlers and national religious soldiers had attained quite a high level of embeddedness, other units, and particularly the senior command, were still relatively socially isolated and distanced, in the sense that their relations with the IDF were placed at the level of fusionism/diversity management and not elevated to embeddedness. This combination ensured that the army was perceived by the religious groups as an entity that provided them with resources, especially symbolic ones, which, as stated, were contingent on the extent of its distancing, even if that distancing did not exist in the IDF's relations with the religious groups. This combination granted the state a resource that could be traded in exchange for a display of loyalty to the military way and the military organization.

Exchange relations were at work between the army and the new groups, particularly the national religious groups, by which the groups traded their internalization of the principle that the "people's army" is apolitical—as long as this principle is accepted by most of its units—for mobility both within the army and via the army to society. This exchange imbued their service with national meaning. This internalization now spread to the civic duty to refrain from clashing with the IDF as it undertook a politically controversial operation that digressed from the army's canonic mission, and even contradicted the interests of the serving groups. Paradoxically, the embeddedness of the army in the new groups' networks granted it the autonomy to act against the networks themselves. Owing to that level of performance, the IDF helped restore much of the state's autonomy by enabling it to act against the interests of the powerful settler organizations in an unprecedented way.

This means that the embeddedness/isolation balance is violated not only when the military is embedded too deeply and stripped of its universal symbolic resources, but even when it is not perceived as a wellspring for symbolic resources. It will especially take place when the very actions the army is taking are liable to denude the serving groups of their potential resources. Exchange of resources is thus rendered obsolete. It is therefore reasonable to assume that the continued deepening of the integration of national religious youth in the IDF will make it harder in the future for the army to assign a force to evacuate settlements in the West Bank, the primary Jewish settlement project. From the perspective of the soldiers and the networks from which they come, such a mission would completely divest them of their assets and their identity, thus easing the dilemma of opting for disobedience and opposition versus preserving the army's status, and will lead to broader disobedience.

But even in the shorter term, the state once again violated the republican equation in its post-Oslo version. In the past, the state had violated the equation by increasing the burden of service among the secular Ashkenazi groups just as their symbolic rewards were waning and material rewards were not growing at a proportionate rate. With this violation and the subsequent demilitarization, the ethno-national group became the anchor for the reconstitution of the equation by exchanging military sacrifice for symbolic rewards in the shape, among others, of the realization of its ideological values and the construction of embeddedness. The Disengagement Plan violated the symbolic aspect of the equation in relation to this group, and maybe even to other groups that are also motivated by the ethno-national ethos.

These circumstances mean that the IDF once more faces the need to adapt its architecture. The Disengagement Plan strengthened the foundations, which had been laid earlier on, for the gradual abolition of compulsory service, and the formation of a voluntary-professional army. From this perspective, the disengagement and changes in the recruitment model represent different aspects of the third mechanism in the state's strategy for balancing the violated equation, that is, redistributing the burden by transferring it from the middle class to other groups. Be that as it may, the army has not yet given up on the first mechanism, namely, the attempt to halt the erosion of its status and the emptying out of its symbolic arsenal by leveraging geopolitical opportunities to demonstrate its capailities, such as in the Second Lebanon War, as detailed in the following chapter.

NOTES

1. Openness of this sort was highlighted by Janowitz (1960), in contrast to Huntington (see also Burk, 2002; Schiff, 1995).

2. This policy could reflect power relations as much as an effort to (1) tap previously unexploited reservoirs of human resources, such as the policy toward minorities in the Dutch Army (see Richardson and Bosch, 1999); (2) serve the state's needs of control by recruiting specific groups, as in many ethnically divided societies (for different perspectives, see Enloe, 1980); (3) balance the power of other groups in the military, as Israel's case will indicate; (4) take affirmative action, for example toward women in the British Army (Woodward and Winter, 2006).

3. Edna Lomsky-Feder, private communication, 31 October 2006.

4. Keshev Report, *State Captured by Extremists*, October 2000.

5. See the manifesto published after the disengagement but reflecting the conventional view: *Our Way at this Time: A Document of Principles of Religious Zionist Rabbis*, 2006 (Hebrew). http://www.bneidavid.org/System/LessonInside.asp?LessonId=1489 (30 October 2006).

6. "A Letter to the Enlistee," *Hatzofe*, 29 July 2005 (Hebrew). But note that their institution, unlike many of the others, is not situated in the Occupied Territories.

7. Walla's website, 16 June 2005 (Hebrew).

Chapter Seven

The Second Lebanon War
The "Gap of Legitimacies" Syndrome

BACKGROUND AND PUZZLE

On July 12, 2006, a few hours after two IDF soldiers had been abducted by Hezbollah on the border between Israel and Lebanon, Israel launched the Second Lebanon War with a broad range of goals. The IDF opened up a heavy aerial assault that was focused on Hezbollah targets and its residential neighborhoods, while also striking at the Lebanese infrastructure, including the country's international airport. Hundreds of thousands of civilians became refugees, and hundreds were killed. In reply, Hezbollah gradually escalated its response, and fired missiles and Katyusha rockets at Israel's northern towns, including Haifa, killing tens of civilians, injuring hundreds more, and causing extensive damage to property, in what was the largest attack on Israel's civilian population since the 1948 War. In the second week of the war, Israel initiated ground raids aimed at pushing Hezbollah outposts away from the border. These raids were later expanded to take control of Katyusha launch sites almost as far north as the Litani River. After a month of fighting, the war was brought to an end by the cease-fire brokered by United Nations Security Council Resolution 1701, which also determined that the Lebanese army and a multinational force would be deployed in South Lebanon along the border with Israel. Although Hezbollah was not disarmed, it was weakened militarily, at least temporarily.

The war was spearheaded by the Prime Minister and the Minister of Defense, who together comprised the most civilian leadership any Israeli government had ever known. Unlike most previous incumbents, Ehud Olmert (who succeeded Ariel Sharon after the latter fell ill in the autumn of 2005) had not previously held any kind of position in the security system. Nor had

Defense Minister Amir Peretz, leader of the Labor Party, who had been chairperson of the *Histadrut* before arriving at Defense Ministry. Furthermore, the two were perceived as "civilians," not only because of their respective biographies, but mainly because of their political agendas, which favored a continuation of the disengagement. Olmert, who had been one of the architects of the Disengagement Plan, campaigned for election on a platform of support for the "convergence" plan, namely, the partial withdrawal of Israel from the West Bank. For his part, Peretz ran for prime minister on the platform of a dovish manifesto combined with a social agenda calling for cutbacks in the defense budget. Given the political agenda, puzzling questions surround the circumstances in which the Second Lebanon War erupted.

These questions are reinforced by the events leading up to the outbreak of the war. While in the summer of 2006 the IDF launched an aggressive assault on *Hamas* targets in Gaza in response to the abduction of a soldier whose unit had been positioned on the Israel-Gaza border, it nonetheless refrained from deploying a massive ground force in Gaza. Instead, the army delegated the bulk of the operation to the Air Force. At the same time, diplomatic efforts got underway to find a solution to the crisis based on an exchange of prisoners. More significantly, at that time a program was being drawn up in the Finance Ministry for an extensive cutback in the 2007 security budget. If we add to this policy the plans to reduce the scope of both reserve and compulsory military service, it would appear that the winds of war were certainly not blowing in the background. Yet despite all this, in response to Hezbollah's abduction of two reserve soldiers, the Israeli government instructed the army to launch the Second Lebanon War.

On the face of it, the military's response was the direct result of extensive contingency plans that had been created for use in the event of an abduction, as confirmed by the interim report of *The Winograd Commission*, that the government had appointed to investigate the war. However, while the IDF proposed implementing its plan, thereby inflicting a degree of damage on Hezbollah while recognizing that it could not actually be defeated without the IDF occupying large areas of Lebanon, the political echelon sought to expand the assault. Rather than launching a limited response, the government decided to bring about "a new order in Lebanon" by disarming Hezbollah, or at least removing it from the border with Israel, and deploying the Lebanese army in its place. Recovering the captured soldiers was not central to this goal.

In contrast to historical situations where the political echelon tries to restrain the army, or is dragged along behind it, in this case it was the politicians who broadened the goals that had been defined by the military. In other words, it is not the army's response that needs to be analyzed, but rather the freedom of operation afforded it by a political leadership committed to a civilian agenda. Moreover, the puzzle is even more complicated when we consider that despite the high levels of legitimacy and support that the war effort enjoyed at the beginning and Israel's military superiority over the Hezbollah militias, the war ultimately came to be regarded as a failure.

Accordingly, the central argument in this chapter is that the Second Lebanon War reflected the syndrome which I term the *gap of legitimacies*, that is, the widening of the gap that had emerged in the 1980s between high levels of political legitimacy for using force, and low levels of social legitimacy for making the attendant sacrifices. While during the 1980s these two values were largely congruent, as Israeli society became more market-oriented and the symbolic value of military sacrifice declined in the eyes of the upper-middle-class groups, and as the external threat was seen to be receding, the willingness to make sacrifices declined. This was mostly reflected in terms of increased sensitivity to casualties from the leading groups' social networks, the "motivation crisis" surrounding recruitment in its wider sense, pressures to divert resources from military expenditure to private consumption, and the internalization of the linkage between economic growth and security calm.

At the same time, military thought retained its supremacy over political thought, as illustrated by the Oslo process and the disengagement. The moves toward demilitarization in Israel in the 1990s were largely restricted to the upper reaches of the middle class, and did not stem from deep changes in the political culture. Instead, in keeping with materialist militarism, they emerged from the internalization of the limitations to the use of force, a decline in the preparedness to make sacrifices, and a reduction in the fruits of war. In the "peace camp," the Al-Aqsa Intifada even contributed to the deepening of mistrust toward Arabs, while the coalition of ethno-national groups supported a belligerent approach. Thus, the "gap of legitimacies" also reflects the "clash of the ethoses" and the tension between "gold" and "body" sacrificers and creates a tense coexistence between two values of legitimation.

Paradoxically, aside from the IDF's interest in rehabilitating its reputation by war, this syndrome gave rise to rapid decision-making as a means of avoiding the costly political debate that a prolonged decision-making process might cause. In addition, this syndrome also prompted the use of excessive military force to shorten the war and hold down its costs. In tandem, unrealistic war aims were leveraged in order to gain political support within an environment that was skeptical about the desirability of military sacrifice. However, this gap also imposed limits on the use of military force. Therefore, when measured against its unrealistic goals, the war was deemed a failure. As a result, the failure of the Second Lebanon War has laid the foundation for accelerating the conversion of the IDF from a drafted to a professional army.

MILITARY THOUGHT

Military thought in its post-1973 War form is no longer characterized by an agenda of territorial expansion or the defense of territorial assets for their own sake (unlike the years prior to 1973), but rather by minimizing the risks to what is perceived as the state's security. Military thought embodies an indistinctness between marketing (of the IDF's "services") and military command and strategic thinking. As mentioned in chapter 5, the army's sensitivity to its status, following criticism of its weaknesses issued in the framework of the primacy of the market economy, led it to struggle for increased legitimacy in a way that entailed a reduced willingness to take risks. Short-term solutions, flaunting its achievements, and reducing uncertainty by initiating combat and responding to complex problems as and when they arise, rather than dealing with them hypothetically, has characterized military thought since the 1970s, with occasional escalations following military failures. In such circumstances, a Shiite mini-state was not the kind of risk the army was prepared to take for an extended period of time.

Ironically, the systematic escalation of Israeli attacks on Palestinian militias in South Lebanon in the 1970s ("Fatah-land") empowered the Palestinian guerilla organizations and gradually turned them into a Palestinian mini-state controlled by the PLO, which ruled over significant areas in the south of what was then a divided Lebanon. A similar pattern was repeated in the 1980s with the entrenchment of a Shiite mini-state after the First Lebanon War. The difference between a guerilla organization and a state is vast. A mini-state has practical, if not formal, responsibility for a relatively defined area. It rules its territory with armed forces, which gradually take on the characteristics of a regular army. Like a state in every way—especially given the disintegration of the mother state—the political institutions that direct the armed forces are responsible for providing services to the civilian population under its control. As a result, the shift from guerilla organization to mini-state entails moderation and self-restraint—having territorial responsibilities means that the leadership has something to lose, not least because of the responsibility it has toward its "citizens."

Indeed, the transition from guerilla organization to state-like institution imposed moderation and self-restraint on Hezbollah, as manifested in the relative quiet that prevailed following the IDF's withdrawal. Hezbollah rarely initiated combat, and most of the incidents that occurred were the result of, or were at least justified by, disagreements between the sides that remained following Israel's withdrawal. These disagreements included prisoner exchanges, Israel's aerial incursions into Lebanese airspace, and the territorial dispute over the Shaba Farms at the foot of Mount Dov.

Following a combination of the hasty withdrawal from Lebanon and public charges that the army had promoted the seemingly failed "Oslo conception," thus purportedly bearing responsibility for arming the Palestinian militias, the risk threshold that the military was prepared to accept gradually dropped. Later on, criticism was added of the IDF's part in the Disengagement Plan, which was (mistakenly) said to have encouraged the firing of Kassam rockets at Sderot. In such circumstances, the IDF did not consider the presence of a Shiite mini-state to be a reasonable risk. Accordingly, instead of reconciling itself with it and establishing ground rules that would have ensured that the Lebanese border remained quiet, either until a Shiite state was officially formed or until the mini-state was assimilated in an orderly fashion within some kind of Lebanese federation, the army chose to react to violations with force. However, it is doubtful whether the army actually had an agenda for instigating the breakup of the Shiite entity. Evidently, the military entered the Second Lebanon War without a pre-planned strategy, without having trained its field units for combat with Hezbollah, without complete intelligence on its targets (or alternatively without relaying this information to the combat units), and without having prepared the emergency warehouse units or having prepared the rear.

All this suggests that an offensive was not on the IDF's agenda. The approach adopted by the political leadership under Prime Ministers Barak and Sharon, which was apparently not entirely opposed by the army, was to respect the balance of forces between Israel and the Shiite mini-state. Even if Hezbollah possessed long-range weapons that could reach deep into the Israeli heartland, it had control of South Lebanon and was conducting a rational policy vis-à-vis Israel (Benn, 2006). Therefore, the political echelon put the brakes on military plans and imposed restraint.

On the other hand, the political echelon ignored the diplomatic initiative that was repeatedly put to Prime Ministers Sharon and Olmert for a comprehensive agreement in Lebanon based on UN Resolution 1559, which had formalized Syria's withdrawal from Lebanon in 2005. In return for the deployment of the Lebanese army in the south, Israel was asked to resolve the above-mentioned disagreements (Oren, 2006). Such an approach might have made Hezbollah more willing to disarm, and in any case would have reduced any legitimacy it might claim about fighting to protect Lebanon. At the same time, Israel leveraged American hostility to Syria, the country with the most influence over Lebanon, to reject Syria's signals that it was interested in renewing peace talks. Israel knew that the outcome of these talks would require its full withdrawal from the Golan Heights.[1] The political cost of such a withdrawal was regarded as too high relative to the benefit of an agreement with a country whose decline in military capability meant that it was no longer considered a threat. Missed opportunities laid the groundwork for a renewal of violence.

THE VOLUNTARY PUTSCH

In Israeli historical memory, two incidents have been metaphorically defined as a military "putsch": the pressure applied by IDF generals on Prime Minister Levi Eshkol to embark on the Six Day War in 1967, and the "quiet putsch," as journalist Ofer Shelah termed the behavior of the army at the outbreak of the Al-Aqsa Intifada (2003, 63–82). Nevertheless, none of these resembles the moves that launched the Second Lebanon War.

On July 12, 2006, the Israeli government decided to bring about "a new order in Lebanon." Similar to the expanded goals of the First Lebanon War, an attempt was being made to use force in order to reshape Lebanon's fragile political order.

In the history of the relationship between the political and military leaderships of Israel, the government has never made such a significant decision so quickly, launching a war just a few hours after the crisis had broken. Under these circumstances, the military's contingency plan would have been the primary, if not the only, plan presented to the ministers. Absurd as it may sound, the government's decision to embark on the First Lebanon War was the result of a longer and more orderly decision-making process. The decision to launch the war embodies the renewed dominance of military thought over civilian thought, despite the erosion of the IDF's status and the civilian agenda that was brought to the fore by the elections of 2006.

A rushed discussion in the cabinet does not allow for the examination of nonmilitary options. Nor does it permit the full significance of a military operation to be discussed and realistic political goals to be defined. The accelerated process did not enable the ministers to discuss the practicality of the demand to deploy the Lebanese Army—part of which is Shiite—along the border, as a force capable of imposing its authority on the independent Shiite militias, which would have remained after the dismantling of Hezbollah, if in fact it were to be dismantled.

Indeed, it is doubtful whether the implications of the two possible outcomes of the Israeli military assault—a change in the fragile interethnic balance of power in Lebanon as a result of the disintegration of Hezbollah as an irreplaceable center of power, or, alternatively, its success in surviving the attack—could have been discussed in such a pressured time framework.

The lack of time also prevented the possibility of exploring the diplomatic option of a "package deal" for the implementation of UN Security Council Resolution 1559. It is also reasonable to assume that under such conditions the Foreign Ministry and the National Security Council would not have been able to present alternative viewpoints. And, of course, in all the excitement, the Sharon doctrine of restraint was in effect delegitimized, with no serious attempt made to examine whether it was worth preserving (see Maoz, 2006b).

Even if we assume that the price to be paid by the civilian population was clear to the cabinet, it nonetheless exposed the citizenry to real danger in exchange for what was presented as the removal of a future threat—but without enabling public discussion of the matter. Such a discussion may have been facilitated had the government opted for a "graduated escalation," which encourages debate over the balance of the gains versus costs of warfare.

Armies, by their very nature, are criticized because the excess of power that they accumulate enables them to dictate politically significant steps during times of crisis. In these situations, military contingency plans become the primary option available to politicians, which is why they tend to accept the army's viewpoint (Levy, 1986). The Second Lebanon War, however, was a particularly extreme case. Not only was the military plan the only plan, but the political leadership also voluntarily relinquished its responsibility to discuss it thoroughly. This action placed political thought, to which military thought is normatively subordinated, in a subservient position (see Michael, 2007).

Unlike in the past, when military moves had dictated policy, this time a political decision was made before embarking on any major operation. Unlike the metaphorical "putsches" of the past, this time the army did not put the government under any undue pressure. On the contrary, as shown by the reports cited above, the political echelon dictated the ambitious goals of this war, going far beyond the military's contingency plan of a forceful retaliation in response to Hezbollah's action. Moreover, unlike in the past, in the weeks immediately preceding the decision, not a single instance of the army's surprising the government had been recorded. In short, political control of the army, at least at the formal, institutional level, was not found to be lacking. On the contrary, it is possible that the generals were swept along by the politicians and refrained from using their legitimate professional authority to keep the political echelon within bounds. We are ultimately brought back to the supremacy of military thought.

The hasty and aggressive decision to go to war is explicable in terms of four mechanisms that incite belligerence, which are all anchored in the "gap of legitimacies."

THE MECHANISMS INCITING BELLIGERENCE

The first mechanism was the army's interests. The abduction presented the IDF with an opportunity to reintroduce a belligerent agenda in what was then a dormant Lebanese arena. This agenda fit with the army's organizational interest in continuing to carry out combat missions and demonstrate its abilities in a context where the logic of the market, together with an increasingly civilian agenda, were threatening the military's resources, not to mention its very character as a unique organization in terms of the identity and rewards that it offered its members. This argument is reinforced when we recall that, for the IDF, the withdrawal from Lebanon remained "unfinished business"—it had been imposed on the army by the political leadership, and the army saw it as a humiliating retreat. The army's interests must also be understood in the context of the consequences of the disengagement. Although the army was portrayed as having carried out its mission most effectively, the withdrawal came at the price of a schism between the IDF and the new backbone of its forces, namely, sections of the "knitted skullcaps." Warfare on a new front could help the army deal with this rift by producing new symbolic resources in place of those that the religious groups saw as having been diluted by the disengagement.

Given these circumstances, even if the army did not instigate the war, and even if its goals were expanded by the political echelon, the military was interested in leveraging the border incident into a sophisticated, lightning war that would bolster its status. This was not necessarily an explicit agenda, but rather part of the military's strategic culture (see chapter 5). The exploitation of this geo-political opportunity was at the very least fostered by the lack of an evaluation within the army that belligerence would, in this instance, harm its interests. Such evaluations in the past had led the army to support more moderate moves, but the current opportunity allowed it to act from a position of superiority over what it saw as an inferior adversary, and at a cost that was anticipated to be low. Thus, the eroded legitimacy for sacrifice served as the backdrop of the rationale for belligerency, while the strong legitimacy for using force was the catalyst for the war. The state's first strategic mechanism for balancing demands that challenge the burden of security came again into play, namely, manipulating the external threat.

The second mechanism that incited belligerence was the rapid decision to go to war. The government was trapped in the pillory of intersecting pressures deriving from the "the gap of legitimacies." On the one hand, a "civilian" government finds it difficult to display hesitancy in crisis situations within a political-cultural environment that legitimizes the use of force. In this type of context, the civilian leadership even finds itself calling on the army as a tool for political recruitment in legitimizing its civilian agenda. As mentioned, this was the situation with the Oslo agreements of the 1990s and the Disengagement Plan. Indeed, it is a state of affairs that will only intensify in the event of any future withdrawal from the West Bank or the Golan Heights, which, if it proves to be deeply controversial, will require the IDF's support. In this way, the civilian leadership comes to be dependent on military thought. In crisis situations, this dependency makes it harder to restrain the army, the institutional bearer of military thought, and the political leadership tends to broaden the army's freedom of operation and even to respond more aggressively than the army as a means of acquiring legitimacy. It should be emphasized that it is military thought itself on which the politicians are dependent rather than the army as an organization, which is subservient to civilian institutions. As its bearer, the army mediates between military thought and politicians.

A particularly striking example of the high level of legitimacy for deploying force was the media's unquestioning adherence to the military agenda during the war, with criticism being directed solely at the army's performance. This mode of criticism actually reinforced the superiority of military thought by strengthening the belief that this clash between nations had a military solution that would be attainable if only the army would function properly. Moreover, throughout the war, previous political and military leaders were blamed for having neglected the Lebanese arena and for tolerating the military buildup of Hezbollah. In other words, politicians and generals were condemned for not having initiated a preventive war. In circumstances such as these, discussion of diplomatic solutions was forced to the sidelines.

Comparatively speaking, militarily inexperienced leaders in the United States also extend the use of force to deal with interstate conflicts that do not represent a substantial threat to national security. However, unlike leaders who do have a military background, once they have deployed the military, these inexperienced leaders tend to place limitations on the use of force (Feaver and Gelpi, 2003).

The comparison with Israel is not fully applicable, but it would appear that the decision to deploy the military is treated more flexibly by a "civilian" leadership. Indeed, such an approach characterized the actions of Prime Minister Moshe Sharett (the 1950s' reprisal raids), Prime Minister Levi Eshkol (the escalation that led to the Six Day War), and Prime Minister Shimon Peres (*Operation Grapes of Wrath* against Lebanon in 1996). However, in similar circumstances a "military" political leadership, or a civilian leadership with a hawkish agenda, is better equipped to rein in the army. This was how Prime Minister Yitzhak Shamir (the First Gulf War, in which Israel refrained from retaliating against Iraq's scud missile attacks) and Prime Minister Benjamin Netanyahu (the "Western Wall Tunnel" incident) acted. Equally, governments headed by leaders with a military background have succeeded in advancing diplomatic solutions, sometimes against the advice of the army. Examples range from the governments led by Begin-Dayan-Weizmann (the peace agreement with Egypt), Prime Minister Yitzhak Rabin (the interim agreement of 1975 and the Oslo Accords of 1993), Prime Minister Ehud Barak (the withdrawal from Lebanon in 2000), and Prime Minister Ariel Sharon (the disengagement of 2005). Similarly, ex-generals serving in government have sometimes tried to moderate the exercise of military force. Examples of such individuals include Brigadier General Mordechai Tzipori in Begin's government (unsuccessful in curbing the attempt to broaden the goals of the First Lebanon War), and General Moshe Dayan during the Six Day War (failing to block the occupation of the Suez Canal). In the case of the Second Lebanon War, whereas the Sharon-Mofaz government, rich in military experience (General Mofaz was named Minister of Defense following his tenure as the Chief of the General Staff), had contained the military responses in Lebanon, Olmert and Peretz's "civilian" government gave the IDF unprecedented freedom of operation. Indeed, General Mofaz, serving as Transport Minister, unproductively tried to act as a moderating force in opposing the launch of a massive ground attack.

On the other side of the trap within which the government was caught, reduced legitimacy for military sacrifice gave rise to rapid decision-making processes that leveraged the crisis situation. A prolonged decision-making process, along with a graduated escalation of the combat, and a public discussion of the cost to the homefront as well as the price of the war itself—in both human and economic terms—might have provoked opposition. Such opposition could have come from the broad coalition of the proponents of the market economy wishing to restrict the military's power and resources and prevent the destabilization of the economy, itself dependent on regional stability.

Therefore, the limited legitimacy of a government trapped between intersecting pressures of the "gap of legitimacies," that reflected contradictory ethoses—military supremacy backed by an ethno-national orientation versus the market economy— contributed to the rapid decision-making process that led to the deployment of the army.

Analogically speaking, the Oslo process represents a similar case. Instead of dealing with the expected opposition to the Oslo process in the form of a political debate initiated by the ethno-national political coalition, Rabin's government led a "blitz" in the form of secret talks that led to an agreement only days after they had been revealed to the public. Here too, political weakness (among the Palestinian side as well) was translated into an apparent show of strength by means of a rapid process.

The third mechanism inciting belligerence is the tendency to shorten the length of war. The IDF is unable to wage lengthy wars. Since the 1948 War, there has been a clear trend in the military to formulate offensive doctrines as a way of shortening the length of combat. In contrast, a defensive strategy typically lengthens the duration of war. Given that long wars increase the profile of military participation, which is translatable into political participation, that is, demands for social and political rights in return for military sacrifice, long wars exact a high political cost in the internal arena. In the Israeli case, prolonged warfare also involves mobilizing the reserves, which is the main military force (Levy, 1997a, 75–76).

Given that the legitimacy for military sacrifice has declined since the First Lebanon War, the length of time that intensive combat can be waged has also been continually reduced, and military doctrine has had to be modified. As part of this process, there has been an increase in the use of technologies that reduce military participation and increase the remoteness of the combatant from his/her victims. Such technologies blur the awareness of the human meaning of war for victims and victimizers alike. *Operation Accountability* and *Operation Grapes of Wrath* illustrated the new model of "counter fire," that is, heavy reliance on aerial assaults with no use of ground troops. Such an approach resulted from the low level of legitimacy for deploying a ground force in Lebanon that would have suffered many casualties.

Thus, problems of legitimacy dictated the deployment of a massive military force, including the strategy of damaging civilian infrastructures in the area of Beirut, in order to ensure a swift conclusion to the fighting by creating pressure on Hezbollah to disarm, or at least retreat from the border with Israel. Graduated escalation was not an option. Simply put, the difficulty of fighting Hezbollah combatants face to face gave rise to the aerial bombardment of Beirut.

The fourth mechanism that incited belligerency was setting ambitious goals for the war. While the IDF wanted to weaken Hezbollah and deter it from carrying out attacks against Israel in the future, the government set out the grandiose, albeit unrealistic, goal of disarming Hezbollah by means of a military assault. Setting expansive goals serves the political leadership's need for legitimacy. Politicians use such goals to galvanize support among the leading social groups for making military sacrifices in an environment that has been less inclined to legitimize such sacrifices. In these circumstances, a more modest set of aims would have further decreased the legitimacy of military sacrifice. Under similar conditions, Western leaders have tended to rally their citizens for war by portraying it as a battle of "good versus evil" (Everts, 2002). Moreover, given the criticism directed at previous governments for having reconciled themselves to the empowerment of Hezbollah, the government's ability to realize any military-political outcome other than a fundamental change in the political order in Lebanon, primarily the disarming of Hezbollah, was limited.

In sum, the combination of a strong level of support for the use of military force, together with the eroded legitimacy for military sacrifice that came with a civilian agenda, brought about a massive military response. The army, which had not been sufficiently prepared, was now called upon to accomplish unrealistic goals. Paradoxically, the government's internal political weakness led to the use of massive force. However, the mechanisms that incited belligerence also determined the failure of the war.

CONDUCTING WARFARE WITH LIMITED LEGITIMACY

Not only did the emergent civilian agenda undermine the government's ability to restrain the military response, but it also eroded the legitimacy of sacrifice necessary for implementing that response. This erosion laid the foundations for shortening the war and ending it without accomplishing its declared goals.

One of the most symbolic aspects of the Second Lebanon War, reflected in the media's coverage of the event, was the manner in which the leading social groups divided their attention between the battlefield and the global stock exchanges where Israeli companies were trading. Concern that Israel's credit rating might be damaged by the war played a part in the agenda of the political leadership. Even when the war was just beginning, Prime Minister Olmert hastened to reassure the markets that it would not increase the state budget, but merely require an internal change in priorities. This plea for calm seems to have paid off, as the financial markets' trust in Israel remained stable.

The market's role in managing the war was also evident in the manner in which the homeland was defended. Northern settlements, from the border down to Haifa, were subjected to massive rocket and missile attacks that caused personal and property damage unknown since 1948. However, the state's approach was to practically privatize the defense of the homeland. The missile attack on Israeli cities during the First Gulf War (1991) can serve as a basis for comparison. One of the symbols of that war was the appeal issued by Shlomo Lahat, the Mayor of Tel Aviv (which was targeted by Iraqi missiles), to the city's residents to stay put, while he labeled those who decided to leave Tel Aviv as "deserters." This appeal and its implied notion of a community joined in solidarity facing up to an external threat under the leadership of state institutions had dissipated by the time of the Second Lebanon War. Neither the local nor the national leadership made similar pronouncements. Instead, they practically encouraged the residents of bombarded communities to abandon them in favor of cities further south. Even the decision and ability to leave were shaped by the marketplace. Many people had private resources that they could call upon while others relied on initiatives launched by nonprofit organizations and private donors who organized various types of refugee camps.

This shift can be explained primarily in terms of the changing cultural-political ethos, especially among the middle class. Recognition of the right to fear, the weakening of masculine-warrior machismo, and the privatization of bereavement, along with the placement of the victim, not his/her heroism, at the fore, were among the changes that made leaving the northern settlements more legitimate than in the past (see Rosental, 2001).

However, unlike the First Gulf War, the steadfastness of the civilian population was part of the equation of the war: the stronger the resoluteness of the people, the greater the IDF's ability to fight. Recognizing that certain sectors of society would potentially display weakness were they to suffer casualties, it was during the Al-Aqsa Intifada that the resilience of the civilian population became a factor in evaluating the IDF's capabilities. In such circumstances, it was in the state's interests that the residents of the north leave their houses, even if this reason was not explicitly acknowledged. It guaranteed that the less resilient but more organized population would be kept at a distance from the danger zone, instead of impeding the army's ability to fight by organizing protests, or at least publicly displaying weakness. Those left behind were from the weaker segments of the population, lacking the physical or economic means for moving south, and their ability to protest was also limited. Moreover, the government even avoided declaring a state of emergency as a means to avoid compensating residents and businesses for monetary damage caused by the war. Budgetary restraint, and the interests it serves, was never out of the government's sight, even during the war.

The limited legitimacy of military sacrifice was clearly reflected in the way that the war was managed. At the beginning of the war, having internalized the limited legitimacy for launching a costly ground offensive, the political echelon pledged that it had no intention of doing so, and the troops that were deployed were drawn mainly from the Air Force. Public sensitivity to fatalities was demonstrated after small-scale intrusions resulted in a relatively high number of casualties. Bad historical memories of being bogged down in the "Lebanese mud" for eighteen years bubbled to the surface, further eroding the legitimacy of sacrifice. At the same time, the government refrained from calling up more than a limited number of reservists. Sensitivity to mobilizing the reserves, particularly in light of the political and economic costs such an action incurs, also played its part in military decisions.

As a result, restrictions were placed on the manner in which the army was to conduct the war, and combat was generally restricted to an aerial and artillery campaign. The military, however, was faulted for failing to bring about two outcomes: accomplishing the goals of the war by creating a mechanism that would lead to the disarmament of Hezbollah, and stopping missiles and Katyusha rockets from being launched at northern towns. Nonetheless, the failure to realize these goals was in no way related to the initial decision to refrain from using ground forces. Hezbollah's armory included mobile and long-range missiles. Only by conquering large parts of Lebanon (beyond South Lebanon alone) could the IDF have paralyzed them, if at all. Forcing Hezbollah to disarm was an unreasonable expectation. At the same time, the aerial assault actually created the conditions for leveraging internal pressure in Lebanon, and consequently global pressure, to formulate an agreement that would distance Hezbollah from the border with Israel, even if the former retained its arms. From this perspective, a ground assault was unnecessary.

Herein lies the weakness of a government acting within a "gap of legitimacies," waging a surprise war with wide-ranging goals. The mechanism for initiating a surprise war was a double-edged sword. On the one hand, it enabled political mobilization by creating a rapid shift from routine to emergency under the cover of the abduction, itself represented as a security crisis. Characterizing the situation in these terms resulted in broad public support for the war's ambitious aims. On the other hand, the expectation that blind support for the government would be translated into effective performance was reinforced. Hence, as the gap between the objectives of the war and the IDF's performance began to emerge, and as the civilian population began to pay an increasingly heavy price, public criticism of the government intensified. This criticism did not question whether the war was a just one, nor did it challenge its goals; instead, the criticism was directed at the way in which the war was being fought. The media played a large role in systematically exposing operational failures and lapses, such as helicopter crashes, the lack of electronic defenses on a missile ship that led to its being hit by a rocket, complaints by reservists concerning the level of their training and equipment, and so on. The media's penetration of the army reached a level never before achieved during an emergency, and as such was publicly criticized for lack of patriotism (Weimann, 2007).

Given this state of affairs, the pressure for a ground operation emerged from the public as a means of ending the war swiftly. Achieving that goal was portrayed as dependent on reoccupying a strip along the Lebanese border in order to control the Katyusha launch sites. Such a reoccupation would require the launching of a ground operation. The "gap of legitimacies" thus trapped the government into a vicious circle. Given its lack of legitimacy, which had led it to expand the war's aims, the government found it difficult to end the fighting at its peak after only a few days. Thus, the government let slip the opportunity that was presented by the G8 Summit in St. Petersburg on the fourth day of the fighting, which called for an end to the fighting and a resolution of the conflict by implementing the existing UN resolutions. The government could not halt the fighting without having attained the original declared, yet unreasonable goals, even though it had by then succeeded in redefining the rules of the game with Lebanon and had weakened Hezbollah. The weakness of the "civilian" government thus led it to seek victory, even at a high cost that would further erode the legitimacy of the war.

The government's weakness spilled over onto the Chief of the General Staff, Dan Halutz, who was criticized for not incorporating the ground troops in the fighting. As the first pilot to have assumed the position of Chief of the General Staff, he was accused of a lack of familiarity with the deployment of ground forces. More than undermining the Chief of the General Staff's ability to make decisions, this lack of experience eroded the intra-organizational legitimacy of Halutz's decisions, erosion that spilled over into public debates.

All in all, it was the failure of the war—specifically the failure to prevent rocket attacks on the north—that strengthened the legitimacy for a casualty-heavy operation. The logic behind this development was latent in the state's functioning as a mechanism of "protection" (in the terms of Tilly, 1985). This logic demanded the exposure of the civilian population to danger in an attempt to thwart that danger, while the intensification of this danger merely strengthened the state's ability to mobilize support for its political decisions.

Legitimation difficulties also impinged on the way in which the ground operation was carried out when the government finally, halfheartedly, approved it. Not only was the operation delayed for some time out of sensitivity to the possibility that there would be casualties, and not only were the reserves called up late because of the political price of their mobilization, but the operation itself was also carried out hesitantly. Forces were inserted into Lebanon in order to take control of certain villages, and having completed their mission, were pulled back into Israeli territory in order to prevent further casualties. Meanwhile, Hezbollah returned to those villages, so that IDF forces were once more faced with the task of occupying them. Operational plans were changed at short notice, and officers claimed that they had been given contradictory orders. This kind of inconsistency increased the number of casualties, and thus intensified criticism of the army's performance and eroded the soldiers' trust in their commanders.

Moreover, caught in the trap of limited legitimacy, the government ordered the expansion of the ground operation after a cease-fire had already been agreed upon, taking advantage of the forty-eight hours before it came into effect. Not only did this assault fail to produce any significant achievements, but more than thirty soldiers also lost their lives. This debacle would later become one of the focal points for criticism of the government, including criticism leveled by the former Chief of the General Staff, Moshe Yaalon, who publicly claimed that this operation had been nothing more than "spin."

To a large extent, the war aims, as they were represented internally, served to increase political support, but the resources required to realize them did not accord with the low levels of legitimacy for sacrifice. At the same time, the goals also contradicted the limitations imposed by the international community on military activities. Central to these limitations was the United States' insistence that Israel refrain from harming Beirut's civilian infrastructure, damage that was aimed at shortening the war. Given the discrepancy between the aims of the war and the limited resources for waging it, together with the limitations imposed by the international community, the fighting was protracted and public criticism intensified.

Theoretically, states act in two arenas simultaneously—the domestic and the international. In both of these arenas, they strive to build coalitions in a manner that will reconcile domestic and international imperatives at one and the same time. Governments therefore endeavor to satisfy domestic pressures through international coalitions, but without making commitments that may have deleterious effects at home (Putnam, 1988). In this case, the domestic commitments that required a short war with ambitious goals did not correspond to international restraints, namely, Israel's commitment to its coalition with the U.S. government to avoid the deployment of excessive force that would demolish the Lebanese infrastructure and cause severe harm to civilians. These external restraints shattered domestic legitimacy.

Ultimately, despite the ground operation, rockets continued to be fired at Israel, and the IDF failed to establish a significant security zone. As a result, Israel was compelled to accept the Security Council's cease-fire agreement, which saw the distancing of Hezbollah from the border and the deployment of the Lebanese Army, with backing from a multinational force, along the border from which it had been driven away in the civil war of 1976.

The gap between the goals of the war and its actual achievements, combined with the difficulties faced by the ground operation in dealing with Hezbollah, gave the impression that the IDF, seemingly for the first time in its history, had not won the war. Many Israelis experienced a crisis of faith in the nation's political and military leadership, which diminished any strategic achievements the government claimed (see Makovsky and White, 2006).

In addition, the government had to handle criticism from reserve soldiers regarding the appalling level of their training and the lack of appropriate equipment provided to the units. The army's lack of preparedness was publicly exposed and criticized. This criticism also illustrated the "gap of legitimacies": the erosion of the preparedness of the reserve army was the direct result of cutbacks in the military's resources. On the eve of the war, arguments had been made repeatedly and publicly that, given the more moderate regional environment (especially following the defeat of Iraq), the army no longer needed all of its divisions. The scenario of a conventional war involving large numbers of troops seemed unrealistic, particularly in light of the policy of mutual deterrence related to Hezbollah's mini-state. Accordingly, the army acted rationally by diverting resources from the reserves to other missions. Its mistake was to support the initiation of a war for which it was unprepared. Public discourse demonstrated the gap between public demands for cutting military spending on the one hand, and the unwillingness to accommodate the use of force in line with these cutbacks on the other. The result was public protest.

MAPPING THE CASUALTIES AND PROTEST

More than in the Al-Aqsa Intifada, the bereavement discourse played a certain role in fuelling the protest movement following the war.

Mapping the casualties can provide a relevant comparison with the Al-Aqsa Intifada. Both events occurred in a period of time during which, on the face of it, neither the IDF's social composition nor the demographic weight of the various groups changed significantly. Table 7.1 illustrates this comparison.

The picture that emerges from Table 7.1 is that the four secular middle-class groups—the two secular Ashkenazi groups, the veteran kibbutzim and moshavim, and Mizrachim from the middle class and above—increased their presence in the casualties map from 45 percent to 54 percent, while the Druze and Israeli Palestinians reduced their share by 6 percent. As shall presently become clear, this increase stems from the significantly higher participation of soldiers from the veteran kibbutzim and moshavim. The participation of other groups did not change significantly, mainly that of the two religious Ashkenazi groups, Mizrachim from the middle class and below, together with Mizrachi settlers, and the cluster of immigrants.

Although the established secular middle class increased its presence in relation to the Al-Aqsa Intifada, it was still lower than its share of nearly 70 percent of the casualties in the first week of the First Lebanon War. Indeed, a comparison between the two Lebanon wars shows that this cluster of groups reduced its representation among the casualties by about 10 percent more than its reduction in its demographic weight. In other words, once again demographics cannot provide the explanation.

In order to trace this minor change in the composition of the casualties, differences in the forces that were deployed in the Second Lebanon War

Table 7.1. Comparison between IDF Casualties in the Al-Aqsa Intifada and the Second Lebanon War

The Group	Percentage of casualties—Al-Aqsa Intifada	Percentage of casualties—Second Lebanon War	The change	Group's proportion in the population	Percentage of Lebanon casualties in proportion to the population
Secular Ashkenazim—upper middle class	7.8	11.8	4.0	8.0	148
Veteran kibbutzim & moshavim	7.0	18.5	11.5	2.5	740
Secular Ashkenazim—middle class and below	13.1	11.8	-1.3	9.0	131
Mizrachim—middle class and higher	17.6	11.8	-5.8	14.0	84
Mizrachim—lower middle class	15.2	16.0	0.8	20.0	80
Mizrachi settlers	3.3	0.8	-2.5	1.5	53
Religious Ashkenazim (Green Line)	5.7	4.2	-1.5	7.0	60
Religious Ashkenazi settlers	3.7	5.9	2.2	1.5	393
Russian immigrants	12.3	11.8	-0.5	13.0	91
Ethiopian immigrants	2.5	2.5	0.0	2.0	125
Other secular immigrants	2.9	2.5	-0.4	2.0	125
Druze, Bedouins etc.	7.8	1.7	-6.1	19.0	9
Women	1.2	0.8	-0.4	1.0[1]	irrelevant
TOTAL	100	100			
N =	244	119			

[1] The Intifada's ratio (see Table 4.2).

Table 7.2. Casualties Differentiated by Corps, the Al-Aqsa Intifada and the Second Lebanon War (Percentage, Rounded)

War/corps	Proportion of each corps in total casualties	
	Intifada	Second Lebanon War
Infantry and elite units	44	50
Armor and engineering	6	30
Artillery, navy and Air Force	0	6
Special policing units	37	0
Border Police	7	0
Auxiliary units	6	14
TOTAL	100	100
Ratio of officers	18	21

compared to the Al-Aqsa Intifada must be taken into account. The Second Lebanon War differs from the first week of the First Lebanon War and the Al-Aqsa Intifada in that not all, or even most of the army, took part, including the regular army, as Table 7.2 illustrates.

Table 7.2 shows that the proportion of fatalities from infantry units was more or less similar, while casualties from the special policing units and the Border Police in the Intifada were replaced in Lebanon by soldiers from the armored corps. This shift in the composition of the combat force, from policing to aerial assaults and ground invasions, explains the reduction in the rate of Druze, Bedouins, and Israeli Palestinians, who, in the Intifada, were killed in Border Police units and the Desert Patrol Battalion. The change in the character of the combat also explains part of the increased contribution by the middle class, as the established groups are still relatively well represented in the Air Force and in elite infantry units. The dichotomy among those groups between *sayeret o'nayeret* ("elite unit or paperwork"; see chapter 5), which means that they stand out in positions that constitute only a minority of the combat forces, was reflected in the map of casualties in the Second Lebanon War.

Beyond the composition of the forces itself, the introduction of troops into Lebanon from "top to bottom" was crucial: at first only the Air Force and Navy were involved; later regular elite infantry units; following them, regular infantry and armored brigades; and finally reservists, though here too the elite units, mainly the reconnaissance companies, were introduced first. This hierarchy of introduction, which had not been a feature of previous wars, meant that the elite groups, within which the middle class was over-proportionally presented, were the first to suffer casualties, and at a relatively high rate. This leads us to conclude that the Second Lebanon War does not signify a halt to the erosion of the military participation of groups from the secular middle class, while the slight rise in relation to the Al-Aqsa Intifada is mostly explicable in terms of changes in the type of warfare and the order in which troops were drawn upon.

Breaking down the secular middle class groups in Table 7.1 reveals a decline in the presence of the Mizrachi middle class and above. This decline is to be explained by the fact that policing units from the Occupied Territories, in which they have a considerable presence, did not participate in the war, together with the increased presence of youngsters from the kibbutzim and moshavim in armored and infantry units in place of the upwardly mobile Mizrachi groups. At the same time, the slightly increased presence of the upper middle class is also notable. However, these were soldiers from families who joined this stratum at a later stage (such as residents of well-to-do community villages), while graduates of the leading high schools in Tel Aviv and Jerusalem—the solid core of this stratum—were almost entirely absent.

The most significant shift was among soldiers from the veteran moshavim and, especially, kibbutzim—both prominently Ashkenazi—who increased their share of the fallen by around 12 percent in comparison to the Intifada. Two figures will demonstrate the significance of this change. First, in the Second Lebanon War, the percentage of casualties who came from these communities was even higher than in the first week of the First Lebanon War— about 18 percent compared to about 12 percent—and was seven times greater than their proportion in the population. Given that the First Lebanon War represents the turning point in this group's relationship with the army, these figures take on added significance. The second datum is that while members of this group in the armored and engineering corps suffered no casualties whatsoever in the Al-Aqsa Intifada (as mentioned, around 18 percent of the total casualties in the war were from those corps, including armored forces carrying out policing duties), in the Second Lebanon War 17 percent of the fatalities in the armored and engineering corps were from the kibbutzim and moshavim, over a quarter of the casualties from that specific group. This indicates its increased hold on the armored and engineering corps, and not only on the Air Force and elite infantry units, where a rise has also been felt.

The mechanisms that had reduced the ratio of youngsters from the veteran agricultural sector in combat units—the erosion of historical symbolic rewards and the market economy (see chapters 2 and 4)—were still valid in the second half of the 2000s, but they had been balanced out by other mechanisms. While in the 1980s and 1990s, no public discourse accompanied the reduced presence of this sector in the army, from the late 1990s the national religious groups were represented as gradually taking the place of youngsters from the kibbutzim, not only in terms of quantity, but also in respect of their quality; in other words, they became the IDF's new "service elite." The kibbutz movement found itself on the back foot. With the disengagement project and the associated concern about religious disobedience, a counter-response in the kibbutz movement was triggered, which once more began to encourage its youngsters to make themselves prominent in the army. The growing strength of the "knitted skullcaps" was portrayed as a political-military danger, which the kibbutz movement had to rein in (Eyal and Frish, 2006). The flourishing of secular pre-military preparatory frameworks—a counterweight to religious frameworks—with the notable involvement of the kibbutz movement in some of them, also played its part. Given this background, one can understand why the heads of the kibbutz movement wasted no time in highlighting the high proportion of their constituency in the casualties map of the Second Lebanon War, thereby challenging the belittlement of their military contribution in the past. To a degree, the kibbutz movement, which has been undergoing cultural peripheralization since the 1990s as a result of processes of privatization that have blurred its uniqueness, needed to reemphasize its military contribution in order to leverage an improvement in its status.

The reaction of the kibbutz movement hastened the appearance of a discourse that highlighted the contribution of different social groups to the numbers of fallen soldiers. As mentioned in chapter 4, as a result of the adherence to the universalist ethos of the "people's army," the ethno-class segmentation of the casualties of war was never on the agenda in Israel. Against the background of the political-cultural struggle over control of the army that had been ignited by the disengagement, the Second Lebanon War contributed to breaking that particular taboo. From now on it became legitimate to discuss the ethno-class representation of the fallen. This discourse was accompanied by barbed comments made by certain groups—mainly those from the kibbutz movement and the leadership of the "knitted skullcaps" and the settlers—against the previous secular Ashkenazi-based service elite. This was the background for the criticism issued by the head of the IDF Personnel Directorate, General Elazar Stern, covered widely by the media, to the effect that children from veteran families in Tel Aviv, the core of the upper middle class, are not represented among IDF fatalities, thus spurring a public debate. In response, voices expressing the upper middle class opinion were heard saying that "Tel Aviv" symbolizes an alternative mode of civic contribution to society, or even that it makes a non-life-threatening military contribution to the army's technological sectors. In other words, the attempt to revive the republican discourse through the bereavement discourse was actually an effort to reattribute symbolic meaning to military sacrifice by groups who had been pushed aside by the market discourse. However, rather than being a republican discourse in its historical terms of contribution versus reward, the new discourse reflected the emerging experience of an intergroup struggle for control over the army, a struggle that will only intensify as the military becomes more selective and its missions become increasingly politically controversial.

Similar to the analysis of the Al-Aqsa Intifada, here too the casualties map has mainly political significance, this time stemming from the increased sacrifice made by groups from the secular middle class. When dealing with groups that are able to organize themselves politically, their recruitment and deployment in casualty-heavy missions comes at a political cost. Indeed, cracks in the wall-to-wall consensus over the war began to appear after the first wave of fatalities in the ground operation. Accordingly, the potential political cost played a part in the government's hesitancy in deciding to deploy ground forces and mobilize the reserves. The political price of calling up reserve soldiers was clearly understood by the government and the military command as part of a repertoire that had been learnt through experience accumulated since the First Lebanon War. This repertoire is made tangible both by the consolidation of a framework for organizations of reservists since the second half of the 1990s, as well as the fact that the reserve army is naturally reliant on the middle class—it reflects the compulsory army prior to the IDF's architectural change, and includes youngsters whose entrance into the labor market has made some of them upwardly mobile. The logic that led the reform of the reserve army is the same logic behind the hesitancy in deploying reservists in the Second Lebanon War.

The political cost was manifested more concretely after the war. Protests by bereaved families and organizations of reservists urged for the establishment of a state commission of inquiry to investigate events during the war, a demand that was partially met. Judging by comments made publicly, the reactions of the bereaved families expressed the mapping of the bereavement discourse as it had been reflected in the Al-Aqsa Intifada: religious families, primarily those of settlers, tended to criticize the government for preventing the army from succeeding, as well as for the IDF's ill-preparedness. This is a discourse well entrenched in military thought, which aims at deepening the meaning of losing a child in war. Secular families, and especially those from the higher strata, criticized the IDF's lack of preparedness as well, but also organized around the question of whether the war was a just one, pointing to the available diplomatic alternatives or to the missed opportunities for an earlier cease-fire. These voices, however, remained in the minority (Hasson, Grinberg and Rinat, 2006).

The changing composition of the army also left its mark on the reserves, whose spokespersons employed a more hawkish tone than in the past, certainly in relation to the First Lebanon War, when protest focused on whether the war was just, and not only on the way it was managed. Having said that, the relatively limited scope of the mobilization of the reserves, and the low proportion of middle-class reservists among those who were called up, reduced the critical mass needed to create mass protest over time. The main waves of protest largely dissipated a number of weeks after they began, though they continued at a level that kept the war on the agenda.

In addition to the reservists, retired generals also began to protest for the first time. As one would expect, this protest was primarily carried out through media appearances and meetings with senior military staff. The generals criticized the army's flawed performance, called for the resignation of the Chief of the General Staff, and some of them even offered their services in helping to rehabilitate the army.

The generals' protest was unprecedented in three ways. First, its very appearance as part of a disagreement between the military command and its former senior officers embodied a breach in the extremely tight-knit social network of current and former military persons, a network that advances their shared interests (see Barak and Sheffer, 2006). The generals' criticism of the senior command was liable to fracture even further the image of the very organization from which they received symbolic, and, indirectly, material rewards. It follows that their actions reflect their internalization of the acknowledgment that the army's image had reached such a low ebb that it justified an unprecedented protest by precisely those whose rewards are linked to that image.

Second, the generals who protested were mainly from the ground forces, and their protest was a kind of challenge to the unprecedented decision, which they portrayed as a failure, to appoint an officer from the Air Force to the position of Chief of the General Staff. Struggles over resources between air and ground forces, which had formerly been conducted deep within the military establishment, were brought out into the open, and gradually came to incorporate issues regarding the promotion of senior officers, the allocation of funds, military doctrine, and military symbols. Through their protests, the reserve generals were the voice of senior ground force officers still in the army.

Third, the relations of bargaining between the army and its social environment were taken to a new level. Until then, bargaining had been conducted over conditions of service at the individual and group level, or over the political nature of the missions handed down by the political echelon. Regarding the functioning of the army, however, contractual militarism restricted itself to issues external to the core of the army's functioning, such as accidents or sexual harassment. Now, though, the professional core of the military, namely, its performance in war, was being bargained over. At least for the reservists, this bargaining implied that their willingness to be called up in the future was conditional on improvements to the IDF's professional conduct. The barriers to what could be bargained over were lower than in the past.

Moreover, for the first time, broad sectors of the public were calling for the head of the army to be fired for his poor performance, a call that eventually led to Halutz's resignation in January 2007, the first Chief of Staff to step down in the wake of public pressure. In the past such voices had only been heard when the Chief of the General Staff had been perceived as carrying out politically controversial policies. Chapter 5 pointed to the direct dialogue between Chiefs of the General Staff and the public as part of the market economy discourse. The Second Lebanon War signified another step in the direction of the Chief of the General Staff becoming a public figure, with all the implications this has for how the army will deal with its public legitimacy in the future in a way that bypasses political mechanisms for monitoring the army.

SUMMARY AND AFTERMATH—THE ROAD TO A PROFESSIONAL ARMY

Since the 1970s, a combination of the "logic of the state" and the "logic of the market" has led Western countries to reduce the political costs of preparing for and waging war. As argued in chapter 1, this is a process that has gone hand in hand with a decline in the ability of the middle class—which has historically borne the burden of the military effort—to exchange its military sacrifice for civilian rewards at a high rate of convertibility. Reducing conflicts, phasing out the draft system, replacing symbolic rewards by material ones, downsizing armies, and increasing their reliance on technology have been some of the alternatives adopted by Western states in order to bring down the costs of war.

During the 1980s and 1990s, Israel gradually came to act according to this logic, with the Oslo Accords, the unilateral withdrawal from Lebanon of 2000, and the Disengagement Plan at the center of its policies. However, the Second Lebanon War was launched in contradiction to this logic. This time, the state went to war in such a way that it could not balance the contradiction between military thought—and the resulting military rhetoric—and the erosion of the legitimacy to make sacrifices in order to fulfill the goals of that rhetoric. The weaknesses in the rapid decision to launch a forceful and technological war, which was meant to bridge this gap, were revealed after only a short time. The political depiction of the war as a lightning operation to achieve unattainable goals that would once more demonstrate Israeli military superiority also laid the groundwork for undermining the legitimacy of the war, or at least the legitimacy for the way it was waged. At the same time, the difficulties in attaining unrealistic military aims temporarily heightened the legitimacy for military sacrifice, as evidenced by the support for a ground operation, but only in a limited fashion and not at a level that enabled the goals to be achieved.

Thus, the army was represented as having failed in the war, and certainly not as having won it. The attempt to leverage the war, albeit indirectly, to rehabilitate the army's standing ended in the accelerated erosion of its status, with the army seen as failing, and with most of its components subjected to critical external inquiry.

In addition to cutbacks in the military's resources, two structural factors also hindered the army's preparedness for the war. First, the policing missions in the Palestinian arena, which had occupied most of the ground forces since 2000, were destructive for the professional socialization of combatants for warfare in Lebanon. The employment of divided forces, the distance of the commanders from the battlefield, the lack of continuity in the mission, the IDF's absolute supremacy, and more, are among the factors that distinguish between the arenas. Moreover, the operational culture and its accompanying conceptual world blurred the missions for the forces on the ground when applied to the Lebanese arena. Second, a "market army" struggles to deal with well trained and highly motivated militia forces. In the IDF, the diversion of commanders' attention away from preparing their troops to issues such as the economic management of their unit, negotiations with parents and rabbis, media marketing, and so on, is one of the phenomena characteristic of the difficulties of warfare in a democracy. Had the state internalized these limitations on the use of force, particularly as they pertained to the internal arena, it might have avoided war entirely. At the very least, it would have ceased hostilities after only a short period of time and would not have involved ground forces. Furthermore, the state would have pursued goals that were in keeping with those internal limitations. Mass military participation—a combination of a high proportion of the civilian population engaged in the war, the mobilization of the reserves, and a heavy economic burden—contradicted the "logic of the state," which dovetailed with "the logic of the market." Both of these forces have shaped Western and Israeli attitudes in the past decades. Herein lies the explanation for Israel's perceived failure.

This failure served to sharpen political divisions in Israel: on the one hand, there were those who concluded that the army ought to be strengthened in order to provide a better military solution to Israel's regional problems, and to do away with political, or even international barriers to combat ("wiping out" villages instead of endangering the soldiers who are sent to fight in them). On the other, there were those who concluded that changes in the power of the Arab world place limitations on Israel's ability to use force, limitations that ought to lead to the pursuit of nonmilitary solutions.

Rather than balancing out the effects of the disengagement, the failure of the Second Lebanon War intensified them, and is gradually and inevitably leading to a change in the model of the IDF, from an army based on compulsory recruitment to a professional-volunteer army similar to most Western militaries. Despite the myth surrounding the conception of the "people's army," this mode of thought is no longer taboo in Israeli public discourse (see Levy, 2004a). And, as mentioned, since the 1990s the IDF has in any case been implementing a de facto policy of selective recruitment.

A series of vectors are acting to reestablish the army on professional foundations: (1) a reduced conventional threat (peace with Egypt and the weakening of the Syrian army), thus making the army less needy of large masses of assaulting forces; (2) cutbacks in the security budget, which also implies lower rates of recruitment; (3) the shift from labor-intensive to technology-intensive armaments; (4) the need to improve the professionalism of the army in response to the professionalization of adversary forces (as exemplified in the Second Lebanon War); (5) the strengthening of the liberal ethos that contradicts the principle of compulsory service, which denies the individual a degree of his/her freedom; (6) reforms taking place in other Western armies are also influential insofar as they provide the repertoire from which the IDF learns, as seen in the historical experience of transferring recruitment models from one country to another (for a theoretical approach, see Avant, 2000).

However, these vectors, which are changing the face of the army, also represent stronger forces. It can be argued that the army is marching toward its inevitable professionalization as the result of a spiral process that returns us to the balance between modes of reward, as depicted in Figure 7.1.

The military's arsenal of symbolic rewards gradually dried up following the 1973 War because of a combination of a decline in its prestige and the dominance of the market economy, and was further depleted following the disengagement and the Second Lebanon War.

Simply put, the IDF has gradually and systematically lost the confidence of various groups since the 1980s: the Ashkenazi upper middle class in the politically contentious First Lebanon War and the First Intifada, the national religious groups in the disengagement, and the middle-class reservists in the Second Lebanon War. When the war erupted and the reserve divisions were hesitantly mobilized and sent to fight for ambiguous goals, it became apparent that the IDF had simply violated its "psychological contract" with the reserve soldiers. According to the terms of this contract, the reservist is always ready to be called up, while the IDF guarantees that he/she will be trained, equipped, and effectively utilized. It is reasonable to assume, therefore, that in the wake of the war, the erosion of confidence

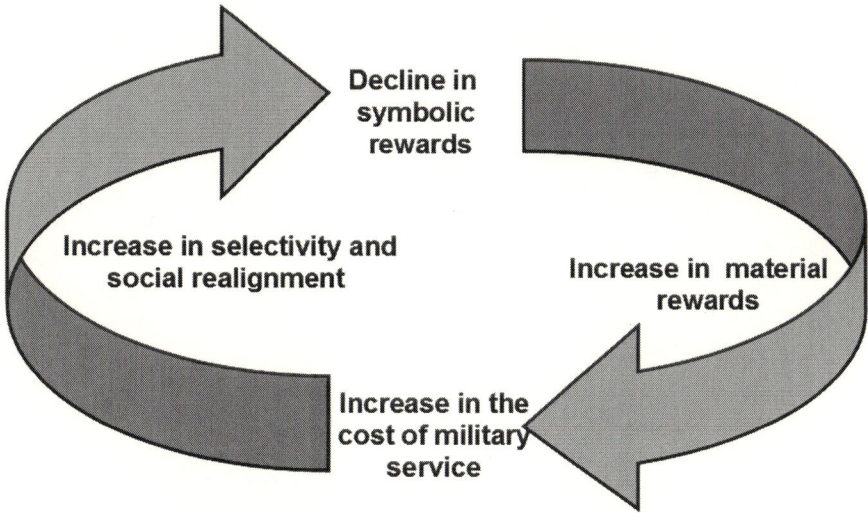

Figure 7.1. The Spiral of Rewards

will make it more difficult to draft and activate the reserves in the future. A similar effect, which enhanced the "motivation crisis," was experienced by the enlistees, as the war weakened their trust in the army's ability to protect their lives by deploying them effectively in essential missions. A decline in confidence also means a decline in the symbolic rewards reaped from military service, as it loses much of its significance. The outcome is the worsening of previous "symbolic deficits," thus making the professionalization of the army more feasible.

Since the 1990s, the erosion of symbolic rewards has heightened pressures for material rewards, a process that has been ongoing in the bargaining between the army and its recruits, primarily reservists (see chapter 2). However, the minor rewards offered by the army constituted a middle path: on the one hand, the improved rewards were not a sufficiently effective way of increasing motivation, while on the other hand, they raised the cost of military service, thus encouraging the pursuit of alternatives for reducing the number of "employees." This led the government in the years 2005–2006 (though before the Second Lebanon War) to ratify reforms in the recruitment system based on shortening the length of service, downsizing the army, increasing selectivity, and offering improved rewards, especially to those who would serve for extended periods of time. However, this did not mean a formal retreat from the principle of compulsory recruitment and the symbols of the "people's army."

Increased selectivity, heralded by the reforms, will accelerate the spiral process presented above. It will heighten material rewards, both directly and by eroding symbolic rewards, in a number of ways: (1) selectivity reduces the symbolic value of military service by weakening its totality, thereby bringing its recruits to see it as a kind of occupation requiring remuneration. Selective entrance into a highly prestigious organization enhances the actors' prestige, but not when the organization's prestige has already been eroded, as the case of the IDF suggests; (2) selectivity narrows the social basis of recruitment, the main consequence of which is the elevated presence of groups with low social status and religious groups, who are more highly motivated to serve. In turn, this process further alienates the upper middle class, which ceases to see the military as a social asset, instead treating it as just another professional arena, thereby raising their expectations for rewards, or reducing their motivation to serve; (3) selectivity increases the recruit's bargaining power, even if he/she was drafted. It provides more flexibility in decision making, both for the recruiter and the recruited. This bargaining power is directly proportional to the recruit's social status, seen as accessibility to senior position-holders, the media, and the legal system. Bargaining also reflects the availability of preferable alternatives in the civilian labor market (with academic studies providing an entry into the market), which heighten the enlistee's motivation to shorten his/her service or to avoid it altogether; (4) selectivity means that the burden is less equally distributed, thus leading to more intense pressure for higher rewards from the enlistees in order to compensate them for being overburdened.

However, whenever the army increases the material rewards for military service, this will once more increase selectivity so as to reduce the army's wage costs, by means of an exchange between increased rewards and reduced manpower, and so on and so forth.

The gradual depletion of the military's arsenal of symbolic rewards prevents it from stopping this spiral movement. As a means of creating "fresh supplies" of symbolic rewards, exaggerating the external threat—the first and most preferable state strategy for rebalancing the republican equation—has largely exhausted itself, as seen in the Second Lebanon War. Nonetheless, as in the past, it is reasonable to expect that the army will try to leverage geopolitical opportunities for belligerence that, in its opinion, will fill it once more with prestige. From this perspective, at the time of writing, the circumstances in which the Second Lebanon War ended may nurture a "second round" of fighting, whether with Lebanon or Syria (as long as the conflict over the Golan Heights is not resolved politically), which will be leveraged to make an improved display of the army's strength as a way of rehabilitating its internal status. Manipulation of the Iranian threat may have similar results.

With the worthlessness of rights allocated to the dominant groups—the second rebalancing strategy—and the above-mentioned breach of the "psychological contract," the stockpile of symbolic resources remains valid in two ways. First, remnants of ideological rewards remain, primarily for sections of the national religious group that are likely to struggle for supremacy in the army so as to prevent future withdrawals, and for some of the immigrants from the former Soviet Union, who perceive their service as their historical-demographic mission. Second, social mobility: for young Christian Russians as a way of acquiring citizenship along with a "friendly conversion process" that the IDF offers; and for women, as part of the feminist struggle, especially Mizrachi women, for whom military service is a means in their struggle against patriarchy. The army is also gradually becoming meaningful for the second generation of labor immigrants in Israel[2] as a test of their citizenship and assimilation into the new society, an option that is becoming increasingly accessible given the lenient approach shown to children of long-term labor immigrants who serve in the army.

Consequently, as the military's symbolic resources decline, they are unable to balance out the low level of material rewards. On the other hand, the ethos of the market economy restricts the military in two ways. Not only does it constrain the army to cut back the costs of warfare, which makes it harder to offer combat-based symbolic rewards to enlistees from the ethno-national groups, but it also places restrictions on its ability to offer material rewards to recruits from the middle class. This accelerates change in the architecture of the social composition of the military, turning it into a professional army based on rewarding low-status social groups by adopting a policy of economic selectivity. Having exhausted all the other mechanisms for balancing the republican equation—intensifying external threats, rewarding enlistees, and reducing military participation (by means of selectivity)—the shift to a professional army is the final means left in the state's arsenal. This is part of the mechanism of reducing military participation, in this instance by diverting the burden from the middle class, and "buying" it in exchange for money.

Cutting back on labor costs by hiring low-income employees is generally the strategy employers prefer when dealing with manpower scarcity or pressure for rising salaries from high-cost workers. In the military, the pay system appears to be oriented more to compensating personnel than rewarding them, and as such it is influenced by the recruits' cost of living (Carrell, 2004) and their own calculations regarding other options on offer in the labor market (Dunn, 2003). The cheaper recruits are those who are motivated by economic distress, ideological-militaristic drive, or an interest in social mobility, including women and immigrants. The alternatives offered by the civilian labor market to those recruits are less attractive, either financially or ideologically, thereby bringing them to make do with the rewards offered by the army.

However, as long as the model of compulsory, even if selective, recruitment remains in place, the spiral will not be broken. The army has no choice but to bargain over the price of the military service of the established middle-class groups who are subjected to the draft. Military service is thus a "hybrid," somewhere between market-regulated recruitment and nonnegotiable compulsory service. As a result, the soldiers' bargaining with the army will incorporate noneconomic values, such as a feeling of duty versus a sense of burden vis-à-vis those who are not serving, with the backing of lobbyists such as politicians, parents, and, in the future, possibly organizations of soldiers themselves. A possible outcome of this "hybrid" form may be that military service becomes more expensive, as was the case in several armies during the "twilight zone" between the declining draft and its formal phasing out. Stability will be partly attained when the recruitment model will finally become that of a volunteer and professional army, either fully or partially, with the army hiring its soldiers at the market price, neutralized from other considerations.

This outcome of the spiral of rewards may coincide with the army's own needs and increase its professional autonomy, which has been eroded since 1973 because of increased bargaining between the military and its recruits, either directly or via the mediation of their social networks, as discussed in chapter 5. The professionalization of the army is a strategic move that is liable to help reduce the army's permeability to political invasiveness. Transferring the military profession from the administrative field of jurisdiction of the state (in the form of compulsory service), which already incorporates semi-contractual relations between the state and the enlistees, to the field of the labor market (the soldier as a salaried employee), will reduce the army's dependency on such mechanisms of mediation with its recruits. As mentioned, these mechanisms include parents, rabbis, and other leaders of social networks from which the army tries to recruit. This dependency has expanded the bargaining space within which various groups can negotiate with the army, and has eroded the military's professional autonomy. Professionalization will reduce the power of those mediating mechanisms in favor of a pattern of "direct marketing," as is usually the case between an employer and a potential employee.

Not only is the military likely to increase its autonomy by adopting a professional model, but in the second half of the 2000s the army actually has the autonomy to instigate such a change. As the convertibility of military service and the military profession reduces, the army is increasingly able to reduce the rates of military participation without arousing significant political opposition. Experience teaches us that when the army has a significant impact in defining the social hierarchy, military service is attractive and the army becomes a contentious arena between groups that serve and those that are excluded and demand accessibility to the army in order to improve their status. Conversely, as the army loses its power to define the social hierarchy, and military service is no longer shrouded in myth, exclusion from the military becomes less significant (for theoretical approaches see Krebs, 2005; Leander, 2004a; Levy, 2007b).

Professionalization also strengthens the army's autonomy from another angle: it may help improve the quality of combat in the modern battlefield. This is particularly the case in situations where the gap is narrowing between the professional performance of IDF soldiers and Palestinian and Lebanese militiamen, with whom the army is (at the time of writing) having to deal in the "blue-collar" combat professions. The Second Lebanon War erupted as a result of Hezbollah's success in abducting two reservists. In other words, militias permanently stationed on a particular front prevailed over reserve soldiers who carry out their duties for only a short time each year. This failure of the "blue-collar" army ignited a war in which the bulk of the burden fell on the "technological army," mainly pilots, who embody the professional army. Meanwhile, acknowledging the inferiority of the IDF's "blue-collar" troops in relation to Hezbollah, or at best the even balance of power between them, large ground forces were not at first inserted into Lebanon, and they performed incompetently when they did eventually join the combat. In other words, the technological, professional army helped compensate for the inferiority of the militia-like "blue-collar" army, while the failure of the "blue-collar" army narrowed the state's freedom of operation and drove it to launch an assault on Lebanon after the soldiers had been abducted. Professionalization, therefore, may advance autonomy.

Finally, the shift to a professional model will also assist the military in its attempts to adapt itself to the ethos of the market economy by increasing its legitimacy in the eyes of the bearers of that ethos in a number of ways: (1) because of the exchange between higher salaries and the professionalization and the downsizing of the army's manpower, professional service is perceived, even if not necessarily correctly, as a cheaper model; (2) the "hidden tax" imposed on the families of servicepersons will be reduced in the spirit of the delegitimation of high rates of tax in public discourse; (3) the professional model implies downsizing the army, a move that accords with the ethos of "small government" with a trimmed-down public sector; (4) the professional model also limits the extent to which military service interferes with the labor market, in particular by reducing the cycles of manpower shifting back and forth between the military and civilian sectors; and finally, (5) the professional model releases in-demand civilian professionals from military duties.

As the army establishes its reliance on peripheral and religious groups, not to mention those driven by a militaristic ethos, it will adopt a more belligerent orientation. The weight of the middle class will decline in favor of society's more nationalistic and conservative groups, given the correlation between political outlook and ethno-class location. Those groups treat the use of force somewhat more lightly. They see their military service as a springboard for mobility, and hence have an interest in an aggressive army that will elevate its status, and by extension their own. Distributive conflicts are also likely to sharpen the militaristic orientation of peripheral groups as a way of attributing social meaning to their military contribution. The consequences of this process for the army's behavior were extensively illustrated in the discussion of soldiers' violence (see chapter 4), and are expected to be more acute in the future.

At the same time, because the very composition of its forces is politically unbalanced, the senior command's freedom of operation will be expanded. Contributive to this is the return of soldiering to the labor market. Commodification corrupts the republican principle of military participation, which is also meant to serve as a tool with which the political community can shape its own fate (see Sandel, 1998).

This corruption has two aspects: first, purchasing services, rather than recruiting soldiers, diverts the recruit's expectations from the sphere of symbolic rewards (such as realizing a political ideology) to that of material rewards. Military service will then be more depoliticized, as a professional soldier is naturally disinclined to disobedience. Professionalization will weaken the political expectations among both recruits and the civilian social groups from which they come, thereby reducing the motivation for the political monitoring of the army "from the inside." As mentioned, this may reduce the military burden at the moral level. The army's need to market itself as a universal, apolitical organization, open to all political groups, will also be reduced, and it will act as an employer in every way, endeavoring to persuade the labor pool that working for it is attractive (see Posner, 2003). Indeed, the experience of Western states shows that abolishing the draft is the preferred option for dealing with the eroded legitimacy of military service among the middle class (see Ajangiz, 2002; Burk, 2001).

Second, commodification will also be reflected in the shrinking social basis of recruitment. As shown by the analysis of the bereavement discourse in the light of the changes of the composition of the fallen in the Al-Aqsa Intifada, and as the distinction between "body sacrifice" and "gold sacrifice" suggests, when the army has a shrinking social base citizens have less bargaining power, at least at the level of motivation, if not legitimacy, to initiate collective action vis-à-vis the state with the aim of monitoring the army's behavior. This will intensify the elites' apathy to the army, with problematic consequences for democratic control over it.

The military's freedom of operation may also increase given the possibility that professionalization will lead the senior command to be somewhat oppositional in relation to the political echelon, as has happened in the U.S. Army and other militaries following the Cold War (see Avant, 1998; Desch, 2001; Feaver and Gelpi, 2003; Kohn, 2002). Thus, in the future, the senior command may make the use of military force in politically controversial missions conditional on the missions' legitimacy and on being able to use force with minimal restrictions, having drawn conclusions from the circumstances in which the army was brought into the disengagement and the Second Lebanon War.

CONCLUSIONS

The Second Lebanon War contributed to the depletion of the IDF's symbolic resources, and thus to its unavoidable professionalization. A reduction in the level of symbolic rewards increases the pressures for material rewards, which in turn narrow the army's recruitment base as part of the exchange between selectivity and rewards. The gradual outcome is the return of the military profession to the labor market. This process is combined with a reduction in the republican profile of the monitoring of the military. As with other Western countries, this is the only strategy left to Israel by which to balance the violated republican equation.

NOTES

1. Akiva Eldar, "Interview with Uri Sagie," *Haaretz*, 18 July 2006 (Hebrew).
2. In Israel there are approximately 200,000 labor immigrants.

Chapter Eight

Conclusions: Why Materialist Militarism Matters

The central aim of this book has been to inquire into the decade of fluctuations (from the mid-1990s to the mid-2000s) in Israel's military policies, and the army's role in directing and implementing them—from the Oslo Accords to the Second Lebanon War, via the Al-Aqsa Intifada and the disengagement. The dynamics of escalation and deescalation were largely explained in terms of the state's activities in maintaining and balancing the republican equation, which determines the level of social groups' military sacrifice as well as the legitimacy afforded to military policies. The concept of materialist militarism provided tools for understanding the dynamics by which the republican equation was constituted, violated and rebalanced.

THE REPUBLICAN EQUATION, ITS VIOLATION AND REBALANCING

A survey of the relations between the military and its social environment reveals the cyclical nature of the construction of the republican equation, its violation, rebalancing, repeated violation, and so forth. The balance between symbolic and material rewards, as well as that between their combination and the level of military sacrifice, are constitutive of the republican equation and the internal changes it undergoes. The outcome is reflected in the degree of the state's autonomy in maintaining and controlling the army.

Figure 8.1 summarizes the main trends (for simplicity's sake, the values are represented in a dichotomous fashion):

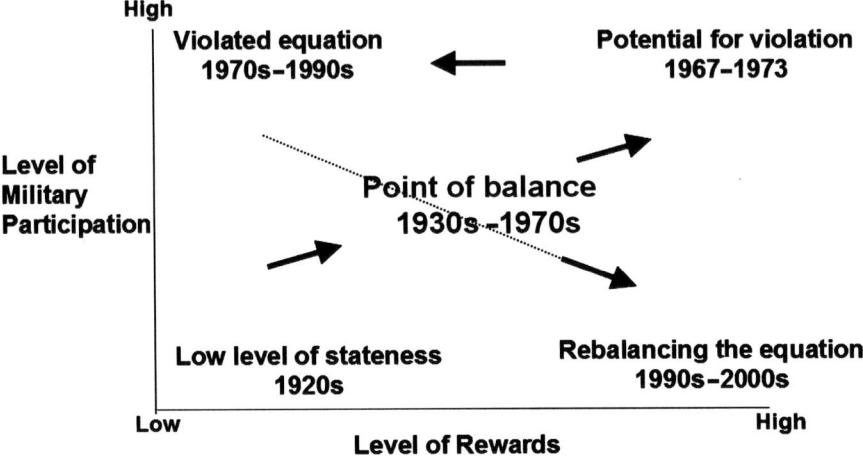

Figure 8.1. The Republican Equation: Reward versus Military Participation

Historically, low levels of both military participation and rewards characterized a low level of stateness. For a limited time, they were also characteristic of the early stages of the emerging Jewish community in Palestine. From the 1930s, and especially after the IDF had established itself as a central institution in the 1950s, the state succeeded in balancing military participation and rewards in a way that sustained the republican equation for a lengthy period of time. The army's role in defining the social hierarchy was central to the symbolic rewards it offered, which were also translated into material rewards in the social sphere mainly for the secular Ashkenazi stratum, then the backbone of the military effort. This balance ensured the state a high level of internal autonomy, which enabled it to realize its military policies. This was manifested in the state's inclination to belligerency, whenever permitted by the geopolitical circumstances.

Ironically, the "Golden Age" of militarism in Israel—between the years 1967–1973—was actually characterized by a fragile intermediary situation. Military participation rose considerably, partially with American funding, concomitant with the ability of the secular Ashkenazi middle class to reap the advantages embodied in military participation reaching its highest level. To a large extent, this was a situation on the verge of "overload," and as such it could only deteriorate: there were no new or alternative rewards to be gained, and the level of military participation could only have been reduced at the cost of the end of the Arab-Israeli conflict, a move that would have destabilized the dominance of the secular Ashkenazi groups. The equation tended to violation.

Against this background, following the 1973 War—which made the army's upkeep considerably more costly relative to the decline in the symbolic rewards for military participation—the potential for the violation of the republican equation was realized. Other circumstances, such as an ascendant market economy, reduced military prestige, while a less intense feeling of threat amplified this asymmetry. As a consequence, the secular Ashkenazi stratum curtailed its support for the military effort, signifying the emergence of what has been termed in this book a progressive motivation crisis, expressed in eroded legitimacy for the use of force, and lower levels of recruitment in the 1990s. As a result, the state's freedom of operation in initiating and sustaining bellicose policies diminished, and, with the army's backing, it reconciled itself to processes that were acting to deescalate the conflict. The Oslo process and the withdrawal from Lebanon in 2000 signify the peak of this development. Furthermore, it was at this time that the political monitoring of the army by those who bore its burden was at its highest level. This crisis, from the point of view of both the state and the army, was accompanied by demands for higher material rewards for military participation, some of which were met, but not in a way that the historical leading stratum in the army found satisfactory.

The second phase of the state's response to this violation of the equation, enacted mostly during the 1990s, was to attempt to rebalance it by changing the mode of military participation. This was primarily achieved through the rearchitecturing of the combat corps, characterized by an increased reliance on peripheral and religious groups as a replacement for the secular Ashkenazi stratum, alongside intensified use of technology. By rebalancing the equation, the state partly restored its capacity for autonomous action in the military arena, as manifested by the belligerent policies of the first years of the Al-Aqsa Intifada. Changes in the IDF's social makeup broadened the army's freedom of operation by weakening the political monitoring on the part of those social groups who had gradually distanced themselves from its ranks.

However, as the military's activities in the Occupied Territories reached a dead end, thus pushing up the cost of maintaining the army's fighting, the newly balanced republican equation was challenged once more. The ethos of the market economy undermined the military's legitimacy, while at the same time preventing the IDF from offering higher material rewards in compensation. Even though significant internal pressure to end the fighting against the Palestinians failed to emerge, the army's interest in restabilizing the warfare concurred with the political leadership's interest in blocking what it saw as painful diplomatic initiatives. Hence the Disengagement Plan.

To some extent, the forceful evacuation of Jewish settlements in the northern West Bank and the Gaza Strip was a breach of contract in the relations between the army and its national religious recruits, on whom the rebalanced equation of the post-Oslo period largely rested. This development, along with the continued distancing of the secular Ashkenazi middle class from the army, progressively reflected during the Intifada in the reduced resources and legitimacy afforded to the IDF, increasingly emptied the army of its symbolic resources. Against the background of the disengagement's impact on the army and the strengthening of a civilian, political agenda, the instigation of the Second Lebanon War further eroded the military's ability to provide symbolic rewards to its enlistees. This time, the stratum "lost" by the IDF was that of the middle-class reservists. At the same time, under the impact of its contracting resources, the IDF encountered difficulties in providing generous material rewards to its recruits in a way that would balance out the reduction in symbolic rewards. This predicament paved the way for a further downsizing of the IDF, parallel with its gradual conversion to a volunteer-professional army, suggesting that the equation could only be rebalanced if the army had a narrower social base and offered differential rewards. In other words, changes in the recruitment model would enable differential material rewards in return for heightened selectivity, rewards that would further attract peripheral groups to military service while simultaneously drawing professional manpower to positions requiring technological skills. At the same time, military service would continue to provide symbolic rewards to groups—also located at the social or cultural periphery—for whom it remains a social "entrance ticket."

THE POLITICS OF MATERIALIST MILITARISM

Materialist militarism not only illustrates the constitution and violation of the republican equation, but also the state's strategies for rebalancing it. The first strategy is the discursive intensification of external threats, which the state may leverage into geopolitical opportunities for military escalation in a way that the internal arena will not be expected to restrict. Quite simply, the price of the security product is raised. This strategy gives symbolic meaning to military sacrifice while reducing demands for other rights and products provided by the state besides security. As such, it suits periods during which the state, and especially the army, are in retreat in the internal arena. In Israel, this strategy was successful up until the 1973 War, and was temporarily adopted in the two Lebanon wars and the Al-Aqsa Intifada. The failure or exhaustion of this strategy brings the state to adopt an alternative strategy of trading sacrifice for various rights (after 1973 and the First Lebanon War), combining this bargaining with a reduction of the military burden when participation costs too much (mainly during the 1990s), and finally, rebalancing the equation by changing the basis of recruitment such that the army comes to rely on groups whose sacrifice comes more cheaply (largely in the years preceding the Al-Aqsa Intifada). As the ability to leverage escalation to produce new symbolic rewards exhausts itself, it becomes harder to recruit personnel without taking recourse to market-based mechanisms, in other words, without offering appropriate material rewards. Hence, this is a process that leads to the formation of a professional military. The theoretical analysis presented in chapter 1 demonstrated that the Israeli case is not so different from that of other Western countries; thus the book offers a template for analyzing the combined strategies of the Western state in general.

The concept of materialist militarism also enables a broader view of the army's status, and especially its freedom of operation, in light of how it responds to the intersecting pressures resulting from the clash between the ethno-national ethos and the ethos of the market. In general, the more the army is subjugated to one particular ethos, the greater its need to win legitimacy from the bearers of the other, "losing" ethos. Hence, with pressures from the ethno-national coalition prevailing over those of the market economy, the army had less need for political recruitment, as its aggressive policies themselves embodied the political recruitment of the ethno-national coalition. In these circumstances, the army enjoyed broader operational autonomy from the groups that make up the ethno-national coalition. Nonetheless, as the army becomes more belligerent, it finds itself in greater need of legitimacy from the middle class, the bearer of the market economy, which provides the material resources necessary for implementing the military's belligerent policies. This is the situation that characterized the Al-Aqsa Intifada, at least until 2003. Then, the need for legitimacy from the bearers of the market economy gradually led to the imposition of restrictions on the army's resources, which in turn necessitated military moderation and gave the upper hand to the ethos of the market economy. Both the disengagement and the failure of the Second Lebanon War, owing to internal problems of legitimacy, demonstrate this point.

On the other hand, the ascendancy of the market economy over the ethno-national coalition reduces the legitimacy afforded to the army and its resources; after all, the pressures exerted by the bearers of the market economy are intended to cut back military expenditure. At the same time, as pressure from the market-oriented coalition prevails over the expectations for belligerent policies on the side of the ethno-national coalition, the army's role in recruiting the social peripheries and highlighting military symbols becomes more important. This is a result of the need to strengthen the legitimacy of the market-oriented state, whose actions harm peripheral groups and contradict their conservative attitudes. The basic Western model of state-building, which combined the construction of a capitalist order with making the army a site for social mobility for traditionally nonelite groups as a way of recruiting their political support, embodies this structure (see Mann, 1987; Tilly, 1997a). This was also the situation during the Oslo period and, to a large extent, preceding the disengagement, when the military and the mode of thinking that it represents were central to the recruitment of the periphery.

The book also discusses intermediary situations, where a certain balance exists between the two vectors. Moderate military processes, that did not bring the army into confrontation with the ethno-national coalition, and that enjoyed broad legitimacy, such as the withdrawals from Lebanon (in 1985 and 2000), signify a kind of balance between the two poles of the market economy versus the ethno-national coalition. In other words, the advocates of the market economy overcame the ethno-national coalition, but not decisively. As a result, it was still necessary to recruit the periphery. At the same time, the army's resources were losing some of their legitimacy in a manner that spurred cutbacks in military expenditure following the withdrawals. Similarly, Netanyahu's premiership characterized a situation in which a balance was found between a most vehement anti-Oslo rhetoric on the one hand, and actual policy on the other, which in reality strengthened the arrangements that Oslo had constructed; that is, the vectors were balanced out. As a result, the government was able to weaken the legitimacy of the army's resources, in the form of budgetary cutbacks, while at the same time maintaining the military's role in recruiting the social periphery.

Much has been written about the lack of civilian control of the army. Analysts have strongly claimed that the level of control dropped even further with the outbreak of the Al-Aqsa Intifada (Michael, 2007; Peri, 2006; Shelah, 2003, 63–82). Nonetheless, the approach presented here places particular emphasis on the structural arrangements—themselves the result of social power relations—that gave military thinking its preeminence, and sees institutional supervisory arrangements at the political level as less important. After all, the army did not rebel in a determined fashion against the authority of the political echelon, but rather took advantage of the latter's weaknesses, or exploited the freedom of operation that politicians afforded it on the grounds of the primacy of military thinking in politics.

To a large extent, Israeli history reveals a transition from an "army without militarism" in the early 1950s, to "militarism without an army" in more recent years. The IDF of the early 1950s was a scrawny, old-fashioned army, dealing with alienated high school graduates and kibbutz youngsters. Its missions were drab and gray, and the army did not have a militaristic agenda:

hence, an "army without militarism" (see Maoz, 2006a, 581). Only in later years did the military emerge as a national symbol, particularly in the wake of the 1950s reprisal raids on the eve of the Sinai Campaign, and given its growing role in reproducing social inequalities. But the moment the political leadership opted to create a "mobilized," disciplined, and inequitable society by making the army a "nation builder" and routinizing war, politicians became dependent on the military. And even if the IDF's internal role has declined in the market society that Israel has become since the mid-1980s, it still plays a crucial role in the military and political mobilization of the peripheries' support for policies of deescalation, as demonstrated by the Oslo Accords and the disengagement. In other words, the political elites are dependent not only on the army as an organization, but also on military thinking itself. The dominant mode of military thought is not just limited to *the mode of thinking in the military itself*. Instead, it is a whole ideology that is deeply rooted in civilian-political thinking and is relatively autonomous from the army as an organization. Indeed, it also originates from sectors that are separate from, and might even challenge the army, such as the ethno-national apparatus, for example. "Militarism without an army," therefore, is flourishing.

The political monitoring of the military, then, is not the issue. In fact, formal monitoring of the army is steadily increasing, rather than weakening or remaining static, as is commonly claimed. The militarization of politics has contributed greatly to the monitoring of the army, and not the other way around. It has given the army an interest in being portrayed as a universal, apolitical organization that does the government's bidding, as well as creating the IDF's dependence on the political echelon as the supplier of the army's resources. Thus, fewer and fewer spheres of military action have remained autonomous, let alone hidden from the public eye. Since the Yom Kippur War, institutional monitoring (by civilian agencies) has become much more powerful, and has been backed up by public, noninstitutional supervisory mechanisms. Social movements have entered the arena, from *Peace Now* in the 1970s to *Adalah* in the 2000s. So pervasive have these efforts been that the army's professional autonomy is being eroded. Indeed, military analyst Stuart Cohen warned that the IDF has become "over-subordinated" by civilian institutions (2006). Consequently, calls to exercise greater control, by strengthening the National Security Council or giving the Knesset more supervisory powers, are misguided. Politically aimless military escalations will not be prevented by granting political institutions greater monitoring powers vis-à-vis the army, but rather by keeping military thinking subservient to political-civilian thinking.

The close monitoring of military operations did not strengthen substantive control over military policies and the IDF's role in fashioning them. Indeed, critical issues, such as broad strategic thinking, its linkage to Israel's political goals, and its implications for the IDF's preparedness for war, were overlooked by the public eye. This was not because of a lack of information, but rather due to a lack of interest among both the consumers and "brokers" (in the media and academia) of this information. One cannot find a better illustration than the Second Lebanon War, initiated by "civilian" politicians who themselves stringently monitored the IDF.

Paradoxically, as Bacevich (2005) has indicated, militarism prospered in the United States precisely during an era of increased political surveillance over the U.S. Army, with the flourishing of neoconservatism, a purely civilian culture, playing a central role in militarization. Militarism has origins external to the framework of the military organization, and military deployments in Iraq and Afghanistan have taken place just as the army's autonomy and capacity to leave its mark on foreign policy is diminishing. In the Israeli case, moreover, even with the IDF retreating from much of its social holdings, new forms of militarism have arisen, such as privatized security, which hinder the political community's ability to politically control the army (see, at the theoretical level, Avant, 2005). Accordingly, a reconceptualization of political control over the armed forces would seem to be called for (for such an attempt see Barak and Sheffer, 2006).

However, controlling the military institution is not as difficult, or as challenging, as controlling military thought. To this end, the sources of militarism should be exposed, including the military's hidden social roles. Materialist militarism, which helps us explore the functions of the multiple rewards that the army offers to its recruits, and especially to the social networks from which they come, furnishes us with a better analytical tool with which to recognize the flaws of political control. And as suggested by the theoretical framework and its accompanying empirical analyses, the modes of reward and the level of political control are mutually connected. Institutional mechanisms matter, but politics matters more.

THEORETICAL IMPLICATIONS

Materialist militarism is advantageous for understanding the sources and dynamics of modern militarism at several levels, as suggested by the Israeli case.

First, this concept fills the gaps left by other schools in tracing the mechanisms that routinized the cultural tenets of militarism, rather than accepting their existence as a point of departure. Materialist militarism relies on relations of exchange between the state and social agents, by which the agents exchange their military sacrifice for social rewards, thereby constituting the republican equation. The ideology of militarism, especially with the sacrifice that it may demand, cannot rest solely on the claims of the military establishment or on the revival and restoration of a dormant historical heritage; nor can it be seen as merely serving capital interests. Each of these theoretical notions leaves us with the key question of what accounts for the longevity of militarism, that is, what brings people to sacrifice either their bodies or their money for the sake of war. The concept of materialist militarism provides the missing link between corporate and organizational interests and ideologies on the one hand, and their realization on the other.

Second, by relying on the notion of convertibility, materialist militarism captures what has been missed by state formation theorists, namely, that fluctuating levels of militarism correspond to similarly fluctuating levels of convertibility. In other words, high rates of convertibility give militarism a higher profile, and vice versa. Furthermore, the transition from materialist militarism to post-materialist militarism demonstrates the former's contingency upon convertible rewards that may alter their form in accordance with their beneficiaries' motivation. Gender, ethnic, religious, community, and other sources of motivation are worthless when the rewards attained in the military are or appear to be, poorly translatable into civilian gains.

These dynamics stem from the very essence of materialist militarism as a kind of structural arrangement—the resource/sacrifice exchange. This structure is formed out of the very interactions of actors on the one hand, and the state and the army on the other, as an encounter of varied interests. Yet this is an arrangement with implicit contradictions. Agents can amass autonomous power, especially when there is a gap between the cost of maintaining militarism and the utility extracted from it, or when they find themselves in competition with one another because of unequal access to the fruits of militarism or the distribution of its costs. Therefore, unlike the perspective adopted by most studies on militarism, the concept of materialist militarism sees social agents not merely as subjects of state discipline via the army and militarism, but rather as having their own ability to resist the state. Relations of bargaining rather than discipline regulate the two sides. As an approach, materialist militarism can account for the changing level of militarism in society as reflected in the willingness of various groups to either support or resist it, thereby leaving their mark on the actual political and military consequences of their attitudes. For their part, states strive to balance and rebalance the republican equation by employing multiple strategies such as manipulating external threats, allocating rights, and reducing levels of military participation.

This is precisely how this book has explained the cycles of militarization in Israel up through the 1970s, the partial demilitarization up to the 1990s, and the renewed militarization of the first years of the new millennium, while zooming in on the puzzle of Israel's fluctuating military policies, and the army's role in fashioning them, during the decade from the mid-1990s to the mid-2000s.

Third, convertibility helps link militarism with inequality. The concept of convertibility enables us to differentiate the republican notion of the exchange of military duties for civil rights into different categories. In other words, convertibility works differently for different groups: for example, the attenuated convertibility of the secular Ashkenazi group's military resources from the 1980s led to higher convertibility for the Mizrachim (either by taking advantage of these new circumstances by rising through the ranks of the military hierarchy, or by capitalizing on the Ashkenazim's decline in prestige). It is argued that the military replicates civilian patterns of ethno-class and gender inequalities and helps to repattern and legitimize them in the social sphere. This is a relational view of inequality, according to which "inequality emerges from asymmetrical social interactions in which advantages accumulate on one side or the other, fortified by construction of social categories that justify and sustain unequal advantage" (Tilly, 2001, 362). The crystallization of an ethnic Mizrachi identity as institutionalized by *Shas*, for example, embodied the construction of a new social category that emerged from the nonmobile Mizrachim's inferior position, an inferiority that was also reflected in the IDF. In turn, this entrenched the group's disadvantageous position, largely due to its portrayal as a social parasite evading military service. Materialist militarism, moreover, is not only the framework in which inequality is legitimized (due to the sacrifice/rights equation), but is also ideologically nurtured by the motivation to sacrifice displayed by those groups that benefit from the hierarchy constructed by the military.

Fourth, using the rewards matrix (see Figure 1.1), the concept of materialist militarism provides tools for combining an analysis of both the modes of reward for military sacrifice as well as changes in the political monitoring of the army. The republican model, based on symbolic rewards, laid the foundations for the political community's broad partnership in controlling the army by converting the combination of "body sacrifice" and "gold sacrifice" into a political voice. This conversion was one of the original anchors of Western democratization and the formation of the welfare state. However, the erosion of symbolic rewards, gradually leading to the creation of a professional army with a narrow social base, laid the foundations for differentiating between the voices of the "body sacrificers" and the "gold sacrificers." Different social strata have different interests, and even ethoses, as seen in the changes in the Israeli bereavement ethos. Thus, the army's belligerency can only be limited by the "gold sacrificers" placing restrictions on its resources. The "gold sacrificers'" indifference to the "body sacrificers," as well as the latter's elevated motivation, expanded the army's freedom of operation, if only for short periods of time. The interaction between modes of reward is thus closely related to shifts between modes of supervision.

Fifth, materialist militarism can lay the foundations for a broader understanding of the military. The military operates more as a site than just an organization, quite unlike the way it has been analyzed by the mainstream of military sociology. It functions as a competitive arena in which soldiers, who are initially grouped into previously constructed categories, struggle over their military status and its convertibility, a struggle they often carry out with the involvement of the social networks within which they are nested. Competition and other forms of dialogue affect the construction and reconstruction of social identities, the motivation to serve, and loyalty toward the military command, and thus also affect the arrangements administered by the military for the sake of diversity management. Ultimately, these relations determine the military's status and thereby the extent to which recruited social groups can increase or decrease their access to convertible resources, which in turn determines their motivation to fight.

It follows that the army is not just a bureaucratic actor with unified organizational interests. Instead, the army is presented as a dual entity comprising an institution and an organization on the one hand, and a social site on the other. Its institutional interests are shaped by the encounter within its ranks between different groups, who are differentially rewarded for their recruitment and sacrifice. This impacts on the army's political freedom of operation in relation to the political supervision imposed on it, and its ability to serve or limit the interests of the political echelon. These different situations influence the army's modes of action and instigate changes in it, such as those seen throughout the Israeli "decade of fluctuations." Thus, by observing the attitudes of social groups to the army and militarism in general, and their expectations from the army in particular, the internal, social-political arena is brought to the center.

Sixth and finally, in tracing its dynamics, at least with regard to the army's status and performance, materialist militarism can be operationalized through the relations between the two modes of military reward: symbolic and material.

Symbolic/material rewards broaden the terms of institution/occupation offered by Moskos (1977). A national, socially respected calling is translated into material and symbolic rewards in the civilian sphere. In turn, a high level of convertibility increases the propensity to serve. The greater the social esteem for the calling, the stronger the institutionally oriented motivation to take it up. At least at the level of rhetoric, servicepersons will adhere to the source of their privileges, i.e., their calling. On the other hand, when this supposed calling is significantly less translatable into valuable social resources, demands are made for immediate, liquid rewards, and the notion of a calling is replaced by explicitly occupationally oriented motivations. This is Moskos' transition from institution to occupation, or from materialist militarism to its "post" form, in our terms. Convertibility is the key to tackling the changing dynamics in groups' abilities to accrue rewards from their military participation, thus shaping their motivation in a manner that impacts on the military's performance. These two modes of reward are mutually affected in the shape of the inverse relations identified between them. Symbolic and material rewards are thus no longer seen as lying on a binary scale, but rather as two variables generating relations of exchange. Furthermore, the analysis in this book shows how "institution," and not just "occupation," is translated into material gains.

Alongside the familiar symbolic resources—with social and political rights and social capital at their center—the Israeli case also demonstrates the army's ability to extract symbolic resources from its conduct as an arena with a multiplicity of cultures, where diversity management is also a way of regulating symbolic rewards. In an extreme version, diversity management embeds the army within some of the social groups that sustain it. Similarly, the international arena is also a field for the allocation of symbolic rewards, both within and via the military. Central to the state's strategy for political mobilization is interpreting the external environment as giving greater symbolic meaning to military contribution the more threatening it appears to be. On the other hand, difficulties experienced by the state in political mobilization both stem from and encourage a more critical interpretation of the external arena, one which is more open to moderate messages.

Furthermore, and most importantly, the interplay of rewards illustrates how the state possesses the power to regulate military participation in a manner that may fit its political agenda and to manipulate external threats as a mechanism for producing rewards. Accordingly, studies of the politics of recruitment may benefit from taking the impact of labor markets and the interplay between the modes of reward into account. After all, the politics of recruitment is affected by this interplay as reflected in the other side of the equation, namely, the changing motivations of the various groups to serve in the military.

This is not just a theoretical game. Indeed, the question of the appropriate model of recruitment for the modern military has been high on the global agenda since the end of the Cold War. Mapping the main values and variables is, therefore, essential. Their interplay will shape the military of the future and will have a bearing on its relations with the surrounding society, particularly with the social groups that staff the army, and those that fund and control it.

Bibliography

Ajangiz, Rafael. 2002. The European Farewell to Conscription? In *The Comparative Study of Conscription in the Armed Forces*, eds. Lars Mjoset and Stephen Van Holde, 307–35. Amsterdam: JAI Press.
Almog. Oz. 1997. *The Sabra: A Profile*. Tel-Aviv: Am Oved (Hebrew).
Amram, Sarit. 2006. *Disengagement, Masculinity and Feminine*. Paper Presented at the 37th Annual Meeting of the Israeli Sociological Association, Ramat-Gan, Israel, February (Hebrew).
Andreski, Stanislav. 1968. *Military Organization and Society*. London: Routledge and Kegan Paul.
Angrist Joshua D. 1990. Lifetime Earnings and the Vietnam Era Draft Lottery: Evidence from Social Security Administrative Records. *American Economic Review* 80 (3): 313–36.
Angrist, Joshua D. 1993. The Effect of Veterans Benefits on Veterans' Education and Earnings. *Industrial and Labor Relations Review* 46 (4): 637–52.
Appy, Christian G. 1993. *Working Class War: American Combat Soldiers and Vietnam*. Chapel Hill, N.C.: North Carolina University Press.
Aran, Gideon. 1985. *Eretz Israel: Between Politics and Religion*. Jerusalem: Institute for the Study of Israel (Hebrew).
Arian, Asher. 1995. *Security Threatened: Surveying Israeli Opinion on Peace and War*. New York: Cambridge University Press.
Arian, Asher, Shlomit Barnea, and Pazit Ben-Bun. 2006. *Auditing Israeli Democracy 2006: Changes in Israel's Political Party System: Dealignment or Realignment?* Jerusalem: The Israel Democracy Institute.
Arian, Asher, Shlomit Barnea, Pazit Ben-Nun, Raphael Ventura, and Michal Shamir. 2005. *The 2005 Israeli Democracy Index*. Jerusalem: The Israel Democracy Institute.
Aronoff, Myron J. 1993. The Origins of Israeli Political Culture. In *Israeli Democracy under Stress*, eds. Larry Diamond and Ehud Sprinzak, 47–64. Boulder, Colo.: Lynne Rienner Publishers.

——. 1999. Wars as Catalysts of Political and Cultural Change. In *The Military and Militarism in Israeli Society*, eds. Edna Lomsky-Feder and Eyal Ben-Ari, 37–53. Albany,: SUNY Press.

Aronson, Shlomo. 1992. *The Politics and Strategy of Nuclear Weapons in the Middle East: Opacity, Theory, and Reality, 1960–1991: An Israeli Perspective*. Albany, N.Y.: SUNY Press.

Asa, Haim, and Yedidya Yaary. 2005. *Diffused Warfare: War in the 21st Century*. Tel-Aviv: Yediot Achronot Books (Hebrew).

Avant, Deborah. 1998. Conflicting Indicators of 'Crisis' in American Civil-Military Relations. *Armed Forces and Society* 24 (3): 375–88.

——. 2000. From Mercenary to Citizen Armies: Explaining Change in the Practice of War. *International Organization* 54 (1): 41–72.

——. 2005. *The Market for Force: The Consequences of Privatizing Security*. New York: Cambridge University Press.

Aviner, Shlomo. 2005. Stop Dismantling the IDF. *Be'Ahavah Uve'Emunah* 500: 2–3 (Hebrew).

Avrahami, Yoash, and Miri Lerner. 2003. The Effect of Combat Service and Military Rank on Entrepreneurial Careers: The Case of Israeli MBA Graduates. *Journal of Political and Military Sociology* 31 (1): 97–118.

Azarya, Victor, and Baruch Kimmerling. 1998. New Immigrants as a Special Group in the Israeli Armed Forces. In *Studies of Israeli Society, Vol.8: Immigration to Israel—Sociological Perspectives*, eds. Elazar Leshem and Judith T. Shuval, 229–52. New Brunswick, N.J.: Transaction Books.

Bacevich, Andrew J. 2005. *The New American Militarism: How Americans Are Seduced by War*. New York: Oxford University Press.

Badger, T. A. 2005. Psychologist Says Abu Ghraib Conditions Ripe for Violence. *The Associated Press*, 3 February.

Bar Neta, and Eyal Ben-Ari. 2005. Israeli Snipers in the Al-Aqsa Intifada: Killing, Humanity and Lived Experience. *Third World Quarterly* 26 (1): 137–56.

Barak, Oren. 2005. The Failure of the Israeli–Palestinian Peace Process, 1993–2000. *Journal of Peace Research* 42 (6): 719–36.

Barak, Oren, and Gabriel Sheffer. 2006. Israel's 'Security Network' and its Impact on Policymaking: An Exploratory Essay. *International Journal of Middle East Studies* 38 (2) 235–61.

Barak-Erez, Daphne. 2005. *Women Pilots and Women Refusniks: One or Different Struggles?* http://www.tau.ac.il/law/workshops/seminars (Hebrew).

Baran, Paul, and Paul Sweezy. 1966. *Monopoly Capital: An Essay on the American Economic and Social Order*. New York: Monthly Review Press.

Bar-Joseph, Uri. 2001. *The Watchman Fell Asleep: The Surprise of Yom Kippur and Its Sources*. Tel-Aviv: Zmora-Bitan (Hebrew).

Barnea, Nahum, and Shimon Shiffer. 2006. What Would Halutz Say? *Yediot Achronot Supplement*, 25 August (Hebrew).

Barnett, Arnold, Timothy Stanley, and Michael Shore. 1992. America's Vietnam Casualties: Victims of a Class War? *Operations Research* 40: 856–66.

Barnett, Michael N. 1992. *Confronting the Costs of War: Military Power, State, and Society in Egypt and Israel*. Princeton, N.J.: Princeton University Press.

Bar-Siman-Tov, Yaacov. 1995. Security Regimes: Mediating between War and Peace in the Arab-Israeli Conflict. In *Regional Security Regimes*, ed. Inbar Efraim, 33–59. Albany, N.Y.: SUNY Press.

Bar-Siman-Tov, Yaacov, Ephraim Lavie, Kobi Michael, and Daniel Bar-Tal. 2005. *The Israeli Palestinian Violent Confrontation 2000–2004: From Conflict Resolution to Conflict Management*. Jerusalem: Jerusalem Institute for Israel Studies.

Barzilai, Gad. 1996. *Wars, Internal Politics, and Political Order: A Jewish Democracy in the Middle East*. Albany, N.Y.: SUNY Press.

———. 1999 War, Democracy, and Internal Conflict: Israel in a Comparative Perspective. *Comparative Politics* 31 (3): 317–36.

Bearman, Peter S. 1991. Desertion as Localism: Army Unit Solidarity and Group Norms in the U.S. Civil War. *Social Forces* 70 (2): 321–42.

Beilin, Yossi. 2001. *Manual for a Wounded Dove*. Tel-Aviv: Yediot Achronot Books (Hebrew).

Ben-Ami, Shlomo. 1998. *A Place for All*. Tel-Aviv: Hakibbutz Hameuchad Publishing House (Hebrew).

Ben-Ari, Eyal. 1999. Masks and Soldiering: The Israeli Army and the Palestinian Uprising. In *The Military and Militarism in Israeli Society*, eds. Edna Lomsky-Feder and Eyal Ben-Ari, 169–81. Albany, N.Y.: SUNY Press.

———. 2005. Epilogue: A 'Good' Military Death. *Armed Forces & Society* 31 (4): 651–64.

Ben-Ari, Eyal, and Edna Levy-Schreiber. 2000. Body-Building, Character-Building and Nation-Building: Gender and Military Service in Israel. *Studies in Contemporary Judaism* 16: 171–90.

Ben-Ari, Eyal, Edna Lomsky-Feder, and Nir Gazit. 2004. Notes on the Study of Military Reserves: Between the Military and Civilian Spheres. In *Building Sustainable and Effective Military Capabilities: A Systematic Comparison of Professional and Conscript Forces*, ed. Kristina Spohr-Readman, 64–78. Amsterdam: IOS Press.

Ben-Ari, Eyal, Daniel Maman, and Zeev Rosenhek. 2001. Military, State and Society in Israel: An Introductory Essay. In *Military, State and Society in Israel*, eds. Daniel Maman, Eyal Ben-Ari, and Zeev Rosenhek, 1–39. New Brunswick, N.J.: Transaction Books.

Benbenishty, Rami, and Ron Avi Astor. 2005. *School Violence in Context: Culture, Neighborhood, Family, School, and Gender*. New York: Oxford University Press.

Bender, Eric. 2005. 63 Refuseniks during the Disengagement. *Maariv-NRG*, 7 September (Hebrew).

Ben-Eliezer, Uri. 1997. Rethinking the Civil-Military Relations Paradigm: The Inverse Relation between Militarism and Praetorianism through the Example of Israel. *Comparative Political Studies* 30 (3): 356–74.

———. 1998. *The Making of Israeli Militarism*. Bloomington: Indiana University Press.

———. 2001. From a Nation-in-Arms to a Postmodern Army: Military Politics in 'New Times' Israel. *Democratic Culture* 4–5: 55–98 (Hebrew).

———. 2003. New Associations or New Politics? The Significance of Israeli-Style Post Materialism. *Hagar: International Social Science Review* 4 (1–2): 5–34.
———. 2005. The Civil Society and the Military Society in Israel. *Palestine-Israel Journal of Politics, Economics and Culture* 12 (1): 49–55.
Ben-Gurion, David. 1981. The Military and the State. *Ma'arachot* 279–280: 2-11 (Hebrew).
Ben-Porat, Guy, 2005. Business and Peace: The Rise and Fall of the New Middle East. *Encounters* 1 (1): 40–52.
Ben-Porat, Guy, and Shlomo Mizrahi. 2005. Political Culture, Alternative Politics and Foreign Policy: The Case of Israel. *Policy Sciences* 38 (2–3): 177–94.
Ben-Porath, Yoram. 1986. Diversity in Population and in the Labor Force. In *The Israeli Economy: Maturing through Crises*, ed. Yoram Ben-Porath, 153–70. Cambridge, Mass.: Harvard University Press.
Ben-Shalom, Uzi, Zeev Lehrer, and Eyal Ben-Ari. 2005. Cohesion during Military Operations: A Field Study on Combat Units in the Al-Aqsa Intifada. *Armed Forces & Society* 32 (1): 63–79.
Ben-Simon, Daniel. 1997. *A New Israel*. Tel-Aviv: Arie Nir (Hebrew).
Benn, Aluf. 2002. Israel's New Militarism. *Newsweek International*, 10 June.
———. 2006. We Need a Nasrallah. *Haaretz*, 6 July.
Benziman, Uzi. 1985. *Sharon—An Israeli Caesar*. New York: Adama Books.
Bergman, Ronen. 2002. *Authority Granted: Corruption and Terrorism in the Palestinian Authority*. Tel-Aviv: Yediot Achronot Books (Hebrew).
Berube, Allan. 1990. *Coming Out under Fire: The History of Gay Men and Women in World War Two*. New York: Free Press.
Bichler, Shimshon, and Jonathan Nitzan. 2001. *From War Profits to Peace Dividends: The Global Political Economy of Israel*. Jerusalem: Carmel (Hebrew).
Browning, Christopher R. 1992. *Ordinary Men: Reserve Police Battalion 101 and the Final Solution in Poland*. New York: Harper Collins.
Brubaker, Rogers. 1992. *Citizenship and Nationhood in France and Germany*. Cambridge, Mass.: Harvard University Press.
Burk, James. 1995. Citizenship Status and Military Service: The Quest for Inclusion by Minorities and Conscientious Objectors. *Armed Forces & Society* 21 (4): 503–29.
———. 2001. The Military Obligation of Citizens since Vietnam. *Parameters* 31 (2): 48–60.
———. 2002. Theories of Democratic Civil-Military Relations. *Armed Forces & Society* 29 (1): 7–29.
Calderon, Nissim. 2000. *Pluralists Despite Themselves: On Multiculturalism of the Israelis*. Haifa: Haifa University Press and Zmora Bitan Publishers (Hebrew).
Carmeli, Abraham, and Judith Fadlon. 1997. Motivation to Serve in the Israeli Army: The Gap between Cultural Involvement and Cultural Performance. In *Russian Jews on Three Continents: Migration and Resettlement*, eds. Noah Lewin-Epstein, Yaacov Ro'I, and Paul Ritterband, 389–405. London: Frank Cass.
Carmi, Shulamit, and Henry Rosenfeld. 1989. The Emergence of Militaristic Nationalism in Israel. *International Journal of Politics, Culture and Society* 3 (1): 5–49.

Carrell, Scott E. 2004. *Local Labor Market Effects on Air Force Reenlistment*. Department of Economics and Geography, U.S. Air Force Academy.

Caspit, Ben. 2001. How Hopes for Peace in Oslo in 1993 Became War and Despair in 2001. *Maariv Supplement*, 17 September (Hebrew).

———. 2002. Two Years of the Intifada. *Maariv Supplement*, 6 and 13 September (Hebrew)

———. 2005. How was the Disengagement Plan Prepared? *Maariv Supplement*, 16 July (Hebrew).

Cock, Jacklyn. 2005. 'Guards and Guns': Towards Privatised Militarism in Post-Apartheid South Africa. *Journal of Southern African Studies* 31 (4): 791–803.

Cockerham, C. William, and Lawrence E. Cohen. 1980. Obedience to Orders: Issues of Morality and Legality in Combat among U.S. Army Paratroopers. *Social Forces* 58 (4): 1272–89.

Cohen, Avner. 2000. *Israel and the Bomb*. Tel-Aviv: Schoken Publishing House (Hebrew).

Cohen, Eliot A. 2002. *Supreme Command: Soldiers, Statesmen, and Leadership in Wartime*. New York: Free Press.

Cohen, Stuart A. 1993. The Hesder Yeshivot in Israel: A Church-State Military Arrangement. *Journal of Church and State* 35: 113–30.

———. 1995. The Israeli Defense Forces (IDF): From a 'People Army' to a 'Professional Military'—Causes and Implications. *Armed Forces & Society* 21 (2): 237–54.

———. 2004. Dilemmas of Military Service in Israel: The Religious Dimension. *The Torah u-Madda Journal* 12: 1-23.

———. 2006. Changing Civil–Military Relations in Israel: Towards an Over-subordinate IDF? *Israel Affairs* 12 (4): 769–88.

———. 2007. Tensions between Military Service and Jewish Orthodoxy in Israel: Implications Imagined and Real. *Israel Studies* 12 (1): 103–26.

Cohen, Yinon. 1988. War and Social Integration: The Effects of the Israeli-Arab Conflict on Jewish Emigration from Israel. *American Sociological Review* 53 (6): 908–18.

Collins, Alan. 2004. State-Induced Security Dilemma: Maintaining the Tragedy. *Cooperation and Conflict* 39 (1): 27–44.

Dahan, Momi. 2002. The Rise of Earning Inequality. In *The Israeli Economy, 1985–1998: From Government Intervention to Market Economics*, ed. Avi Ben Bassat, 485–517. Cambridge, Mass.: MIT Press.

Dahan Kalev, Henriette. 2001. Tensions in Israeli Feminism: The Mizrahi Ashkenazi Rift. *Women's Studies International Forum* 24:1–16.

Dandeker, Christopher. 1990. *Surveillance, Power and Modernity: Bureaucracy and Discipline from 1700 to the Present Day*. New York: St. Martin Press.

Dar, Yechezkel, and Shaul Kimhi. 2004. Youth in the Military: Gendered Experiences in the Conscript Service in the Israeli Army. *Armed Forces & Society* 30 (3): 433–60.

Dayan, Moshe. 1976. *The Story of My Life*. Jerusalem: Edanim Publishers (Hebrew).

De Tray, Dennis. 1982. Veteran Status as a Screening Device. *American Economic Review* 72 (1): 133–42.
Desch, Michael C. 2001. *Civilian Control of the Military : The Changing Security Environment*. Baltimore, Md.: John Hopkins University Press.
Dloomy, Ariel. 2005. The Israeli Refuseniks: 1982–2003. *Israel Affairs* 11 (4): 695–16.
Domhoff, William G. 1996. *State Autonomy or Class Dominance? Case Studies on Policy Making in America*. New York: Aldine de Gruyter.
Dor, Daniel. 2004. *Intifada Hits the Headlines: How the Israeli Press Misreported the Outbreak of the Second Palestinian Uprising*. Bloomington: Indiana University Press.
Doron, Gideon, and Udi Lebel. 2004. Penetrating the Shields of Institutional Immunity: The Political Dynamic of Bereavement in Israel. *Mediterranean Politics* 9, (2): 201–20.
Drori, Zeev. 2005. *Between Faith and Military Service: The Haredi Nahal Battalion*. Jerusalem: The Floersheimer Institute for Policy Studies (Hebrew).
Druker, Raviv, and Ofer Shelah. 2005. *Boomerang*. Jerusalem: Keter (Hebrew).
Dunn, Lucia F. 2003. Is Combat Pay Effective? Evidence from Operation Desert Storm. *Social Science Quarterly* 84 (2): 344–57
Eckstein, Zvi, and Daniel Tsiddon. 2004. Macroeconomic Consequences of Terror: Theory and the Case of Israel. *Journal of Monetary Economics* 51(5): 971–1002.
Edgerton, David. 2005. *Warfare State: Britain, 1920–1970*. New York: Cambridge University Press.
Eldar, Akiva. 2004. Soldiers Force Palestinian to Play Violin at W. Bank Checkpoint. *Haaretz*, 25 November.
Eldar, Akiva, and Idit Zartal. 2004. *Lords of the Land*. Tel-Aviv: Dvir (Hebrew).
Emirbayer, Mustafa. 1997. Manifesto for a Relational Sociology. *American Journal of Sociology* 103 (2): 281–317.
Enloe, Cynthia. 1980. *Ethnic Soldiers: State Security in Divided Societies*. Athens: Georgia University Press.
———. 2003. *Maneuvers: The International Politics of Militarizing Women's Lives*. Berkeley: University of California Press.
Erez, Yossi, Yossi Shavit, and Dorit Zur. 1993. Is There Ethnic Inequality in Promotion Opportunities in the IDF? *Megamot* 35 (1): 23–37 (Hebrew).
Evans, Peter. 1996. Government Action, Social Capital and Development: Reviewing the Evidence on Synergy. *World Development* 24 (6): 1119–32.
———. 1997. Introduction: Development Strategies across the Public-Private Divide. In *State-Society Synergy: Government and Social Capital in Development*, ed. Peter Evans, 1–10. Berkeley: University of California Press.
Evans, Peter, Theda Skocpol, and Dietrich Rueschemeyer (eds). 1985. *Bringing the State Back In*. New York: Cambridge University Press.
Everts, Philip. 2002. *Democracy and Military Force*. New York: Palgrave.
Eyal, Nadav, and Felix Frish. 2006. Kibbutznik Officers Are Needed to Implement the Convergence Plan. *Maariv-NRG*, 18 June (Hebrew).

Ezrahi, Yaron. 1997. *Rubber Bullets: Power and Conscience in Modern Israel.* Berkeley, CA: University of California Press.
Fallows, James. 1993. Low-Class Conclusions. *The Atlantic Monthly* 271: 38–42.
Feaver, D. Peter, and Christopher Gelpi. 2003. *Choosing Your Battles.* Princeton, N.J.: Princeton University Press.
Feige, Michael. 2005. The Disengagement and Sociologists. *Sociologia* 33: 5–8 (Hebrew).
Feld, Maury D. 1977. *The Structure of Violence: Armed Forces as Social Systems.* Beverly Hills, Calif.: Sage Publications.
Ferguson, Niall. 2001. *The Cash Nexus: Money and Power in the Modern World, 1700–2000.* New York: Basic Books.
Ficarrotta, Carl J. 1997. Are Military Professionals Bound By a Higher Moral Standard. *Armed Forces & Society* 24 (1): 59–76.
Filc, Dani. 1996. Post-Populism in Israel: The Latin-American Model of Netanyau '96. *Theory and Criticism* 9: 217–32 (Hebrew).
Finer, Samuel. 1975. State and Nation-Building in Europe: The Role of the Military. In *The Formation of National States in Western Europe*, ed. Charles Tilly, 85–163. Princeton, N.J.: Princeton University Press.
Fishelson, Gideon, Yoram Weiss, and Nili Mark. 1980. Ethnic Origin and Income Differentials among Israeli Males, 1969–1976. In *Israel: A Developing Society*, ed. Asher Arian, 253–76. Tel-Aviv: Tel-Aviv University.
Fotion, Nicholas G. 2003. The Military and Its Relationship to the Society It Serves. In *Military Medical Ethics*, volume 1, eds. Thomas E. Beam and Linette R. Sparacino, 199–220. Falls Church, Va.: Office of the Surgeon General, U.S. Army.
Friedman, Thomas. 1995. I Dial Therefore I Am. *The New York Times*, 29 October, 15E.
Frisch, Hillel. 1993. The Druze Minority in the Israeli Military: Traditionalizing an Ethnic Police Role. *Armed Forces & Society* 20 (1): 51–67.
Fukuyama, Francis, and Abram N. Shulsky. 1997. *The 'Virtual Corporation' and Army Organization.* Washington, D.C.: Rand.
Gallo, Carmenza. 1997. The Autonomy of Weak States: States and Classes in Primary Export Economies. *Sociological Perspectives* 40 (4): 639–60.
Giddens, Anthony. 1985. *The Nation State and Violence.* Cambridge: Polity Press.
Giles, Wenona, and Jennifer Hyndman. 2004. Introduction: Gender and Conflict in a Global Context. In *Sites of Violence: Gender and Conflict Zones*, eds. Wenona Giles and Jennifer Hyndman, 3–23. Berkeley: University of California Press.
Gilroy, Curtis, Robert Phillips, and John Blair. 1990. The All-Volunteer Army: Fifteen Years Later. *Armed Forces & Society* 16 (3): 329–50.
Golani, Motti. 2002. *Wars Don't Just Happen.* Ben Shemen: Modan.
Goldstein, Joshua S. 2001. *War and Gender: How Gender Shapes the War System and Vice Versa.* New York: Cambridge University Press.
Gon-Gross, Tsippy. 2003. *The Family Joins the Army.* Tel-Aviv: Keter (Hebrew).
Gonen, Eyal. 2004. When Your Enemy Falls. *Yediot Achronot Supplement*, 19 November (Hebrew).

Gottlieb, Avi, and Ephraim Yuchtman-Yaar. 1985. Materialism, Postmaterialism, and Public Views on Socioeconomic Policy: The Case of Israel. In *Studies of Israeli Society, Vol. 3: Politics and Society in Israel*, ed. Ernest Krausz, 385–412. New Brunswick, N.J.: Transaction Books.

Grinberg, Lev. 2000. Why We Didn't Continue His Path? On Peace, Democracy, Political Assassination and the Post-Conflict Agenda. In *Contested Memory: Myth, Nationalism and Democracy*, ed. Lev Grinberg, 123–51. Beer Sheva: Humphrey Institute (Hebrew).

———. 2002. The Arrogance of Occupation. *Middle East Policy* 9 (1): 46–52.

Grinberg, Lev Luis, and Gershon Shafir. 2000. Economic Liberalization and the Breakup of the Histadrut Domain. In *The New Israel: Peacemaking and Liberalization*, eds. Gershon Shafir and Yoav Peled, 103–27. Boulder, Colo.: Westview Press.

Gross, Aeyal M. 2002. Sexuality, Masculinity, Military, and Citizenship: The Service of Gays and Lesbians in the Israeli Army in Comparative Perspective. In *Army, Society, and Law*, ed. Daphne Barak-Erez, 95–183. Tel-Aviv: Ramot (Hebrew).

Gur-Ze'ev, Ilan. 1997. Total Quality Management and Power/Knowledge Dialectics in the Israeli Army. *Journal of Thought* 32 (1): 9–36.

Gutwein, Daniel. 2004. Class Aspects of the Occupation: Some Remarks. *Theory and Criticism* 24: 203–11 (Hebrew).

Habermas, Jurgen. 1975. *Legitimation Crisis*. Boston: Beacon Press.

Hakak, Yohai. 2005. From the Army of God to the Israeli Armed Forces: An Interaction between Two Cultural Models. In *Gender, Religion and Change in the Middle East: Two Hundred Years of History*, eds. Inger Marie Okkenhaug and Ingvild Flaskerud, 29–45. Oxford: Berg Publishers.

Harel, Amos. 2003. 85% of Preparatory Course Graduates Are Combat Soldiers, 30% Are Officers. *Haaretz*, 11 December.

———. 2005. 8000 Reservists Will Be Called Up during the Disengagement. *Haaretz*, 17 June (Hebrew).

———. 2006a. The Skullcap Wearer. *Haaretz*, 20 May (Hebrew).

———. 2006b. The Class War. *Haaretz*, 3 February (Hebrew).

Harel, Amos, and Avi Yissacharoff. 2004. *The Seventh War*. Tel-Aviv: Yediot Achronot Books (Hebrew).

Hasson, Nir, Michal Grinberg, and Zafrir Rinat. 2006. 'What Was the Goal of the War?' the Bereaved Families Are Asking. *Haaretz*, 20 August (Hebrew).

Heiman, Ariel, Aryeh Neiger, Ofer Shelah, Boaz Munk, Daniel Tsiddon, Yagil Levy, Hadas Ben-Eliau, and Eyal Ben-Ari. 2004. Alternative Model for Reserve System. *Ma'arachot* 394: 95–107 (Hebrew).

Helman, Sara. 1997. Militarism and the Construction of Community. *Journal of Political and Military Sociology* 25 (2): 305–32.

———. 1999. From Soldiering and Motherhood to Citizenship: A Study of Four Israeli Peace Protest Movements. *Social Politics* 6 (3): 292–313.

Herman, Tamar. 2002. The Israeli Peace Movement: Situation and Prospects. *Shatil Library* 2002, http://www.shatil.org.il/data/tamar_herman_research.doc (10 June 2006).

Herzog, Hanna. 2004. Family-Military Relations in Israel as a Genderizing Social Mechanism. *Armed Forces & Society* 31 (1): 5–30;

Hirschel, Ran. 1997. The 'Constitutional Revolution' and the Emergence of a New Economic Order in Israel. *Israel Studies* 2 (1): 136–55.

Hirschman, Albert O. 1970. *Exit, Voice, and Loyalty: Responses to Decline in Firms, Organizations, and States*. Cambridge, Mass.: Harvard University Press.

Huntington, Samuel Phillips. 1964. *The Soldier and the State: The Theory and Politics of Civil-Military Relations*. New York: Vintage Books.

Inbar, Efraim. 2004. *Rabin and Israel's National Security*. Tel-Aviv: Ministry of Defense (Hebrew).

Inbar, Efraim, and Shmuel Sandler. 1995. The Changing Israeli Equation. *Review of International Studies* 21 (1): 41–59.

Inglehart, Ronald. 1977. *The Silent Revolution. Changing Values and Political Styles among Western Publics*. Princeton, N.J.: Princeton University Press.

Janowitz, Morris. 1960. *The Professional Soldier: A Social and Political Portrait*. New York: The Free Press.

———. 1976. Military Institutions and Citizenship in Western Societies. *Armed Forces & Society* 2 (2): 185–203.

Jessop, Bob. 2001. Bringing the State Back In (Yet Again): Reviews, Revisions, Rejections, and Redirections. *International Review of Sociology* 11 (2): 149–73.

Johnson, V. Douglas, and Steven Metz. 1995. *American Civil-Military Relations: New Issues, Enduring Problems*. Carlisle Barracks, Pa.: Army War College Strategic Studies Institute.

Johnston, Alastair Iain. 1995. Thinking about Strategic Culture. *International Security* 19 (4): 33–64.

Kaldor, Mary. 2002. Beyond Militarism, Arms Races, and Arms Control. In *Understanding September 11*, eds. Craig J. Calhoun, Paul Price, and Ashley S. Timmer, 159–76. New York: The Free Press.

Kanaaneh, Rhoda. 2003. Embattled Identities: Palestinian Soldiers in the Israeli Military. *Journal of Palestine Studies* 32 (3): 5–20.

Kaplan, Danny. 2002. *Brothers and Others in Arms: The Making of Love and War in Israeli Combat Units*. Binghamton, N.Y.: Haworth Press.

Kaplan, Rami. 2003. How to Make an Army from Unnecessary to Necessary. *The Left Bank* 27 June (Hebrew).

Karsten, Peter. 2001. The U.S. Citizen-Soldier's Past, Present, and Likely Future. *Parameters* 31 (2): 61–73.

Kashti, Or. 1997. The Ethnic Gap: The Melting Pot Is not Functioning. *Haaretz*, 14 May (Hebrew).

Kelman, Herbert, and Lee V. Hamilton. 1989. *Crimes of Obedience: Toward a Social Psychology of Authority and Responsibility*. New Haven, Conn.: Yale University Press.

Keren, Michael. 1989. *The Pen and the Sword: Israeli Intellectuals and the Making of the Nation State*. Boulder, Colo.: Westview Press.

Kimmerling, Baruch. 1985. The Reopening of the Frontiers, 1967–1982. In *Studies of Israeli Society, Vol. 3: Politics and Society in Israel*, ed. Ernest Krausz, 81–116. New Brunswick, N.J.: Transaction Books.

———. 1993. Patterns of Militarism in Israel. *Archives Europeenes de Sociologie* 34 (2): 196–223.

———. 2001. *The Invention and Decline of Israeliness: State, Society, and the Military.* Berkeley: University of California Press.

———. 2003. *Politicide: Ariel Sharon's War against the Palestinians.* London: Verso.

Kirby, Sheila Nataraj. 1996. *Enlisted Personnel Management: A Historical Perspective.* Washington, D.C.: Rand.

Klein, Naomi. 2004. Jobs Down, Thumbs Up. *Globe and Mail,* 13 May, A21

Kohn, Richard H. 2002. The Erosion of Civilian Control of the Military in the United States Today. *Naval War College Review* 55 (3): 9–59.

Krasner, Stephen D. 1984. Approaches to the State: Alternative Conceptions and Historical Dynamics. *Comparative Politics* 16 (2): 223–46.

———. 2005. The Case for Shared Sovereignty. *Journal of Democracy* 16 (1): 69–83.

Krebs, Ronald R. 2004. A School for the Nation? How Military Service Does Not Build Nations, and How It Might. *International Security* 28 (4): 85–124.

———. 2005. One Nation under Arms? Military Participation Policy and the Politics of Identity. *Security Studies* 14 (3): 529–64.

———. 2006. *Fighting for Rights: Military Service and the Politics of Citizenship.* Ithaca, N.Y.: Cornell University Press.

Lake, David. 1992. Powerful Pacifists: Democratic States and War. *American Political Science Review* 86 (1): 24–37.

Lavie, Aviv. 2002. In the Middle, Alone. *Haaretz,* 26 December.

Leander, Anna. 2004a. Drafting Community: Understanding the Fate of Conscription. *Armed Forces & Society* 30 (4): 571–99.

———. 2004b. Wars and the Un-Making of States: Taking Tilly Seriously in the Contemporary World. In *Contemporary Security Analysis and Copenhagen Peace Research*, eds. Stefano Guzzini, and Dietrich Jung, 69–80. London: Routledge.

Lebel, Udi. 2006. Postmortem Politics: Competitive Models of Bereavement for Fallen Soldiers in Israeli Society. *Journal of Modern Jewish Studies* 5 (2): 163–181.

Lebel, Udi, and Natti Ronel. 2005. Parental Discourse and Activism as a Response to Bereavement of Fallen Sons and Civilian Terrorist Victims. *Journal of Loss and Trauma* 10 (4): 385–405.

Lehman-Wilzig, Samuel N. 1991. Loyalty, Voice and Quasi-Exit: Israel as a Case Study of Proliferating Alternative Politics. *Comparative Politics* 24 (1): 97–108.

Lein, Yehezkel. 2002. *Land Grab: Israel's Settlement Policy in the West Bank.* Jeruslaem: B'Tselem.

Lev, Ozrad. 2005. *In the Rais' Pocket.* Tel-Aviv: Zmora Bitan (Hebrew).

Levi, Margaret. 1997. *Consent, Dissent, and Patriotism: Political Economy of Institutions and Decisions.* Cambridge: Cambridge University Press.

Levy, Jack S. 1986. Organizational Routines and the Causes of War. *International Studies Quarterly* 30 (2): 193–222.

Levy, Yagil. 1995. *Military Doctrine and Political Participation: Toward a Sociology of Strategy.* New York: Center for Studies of Social Change, New School for Social Research (research paper).

———. 1997a. *Trial and Error: Israel's Route from War to De-Escalation*. Albany, N.Y.: SUNY Press.

———. 1997b. How Militarization Drives Political Control of the Military: The Case of Israel. *Political Power and Social Theory* 11: 103–33.

———. 1998. Militarizing Inequality: A Conceptual Framework. *Theory and Society* 27 (6): 873–904

———. 2003a. Social Convertibility and Militarism: Evaluations of the Development of Military-Society Relations in Israel in the Early 2000s. *Journal of Political and Military Sociology* 31 (1): 71–96.

———. 2003b. *The Other Army of Israel: Materialist Militarism in Israel*. Tel-Aviv: Yedioth Achronot Books (Hebrew).

———. 2004a. Israel's Rough Draft. *Foreign Policy* 142: 84–86.

———. 2004b. The Politization of the Military Command. *Ynet News*, 22 December (Hebrew).

———. 2005. The War of the Peripheries. *Theory and Criticism* 27: 39–69 (Hebrew).

———. 2007a. Soldiers as Laborers: A Theoretical Model. *Theory and Society* 36 (2): 187–208.

———. 2007b. The Right to Fight: A Conceptual Framework for the Analysis of Recruitment Policy toward Gays and Lesbians. *Armed Forces & Society* 33 (2): 186–202.

———. Soldiers' Violence as a Competitive Test. *Sociologia Israelit* (forthcoming, Hebrew).

Levy, Yagil, Edna Lomsky-Feder, and Noa Harel. 2007. From 'Obligatory Militarism' to 'Contractual Militarism'—Competing Models of Citizenship. *Israel Studies* 12 (1): 127-148 .

Levy, Yagil, and Shlomo Mizrahi. Alternative Politics and the Transformation of Society-Military Relations: The Israeli Experience (n.d).

Levy, Yagil, and Yoav Peled. 1994. The Utopian Crisis of the Israeli State. In *Critical Essays on Israeli Social Issues and Scholarship* (Books on Israel, Vol. 3), eds. Russell A. Stone and Walter P. Zenner, 201–26. Albany, NY: SUNY Press.

Liebes, Tamar, and Shoshana Blum-Kulka. 1994. Managing a Moral Dilemma—Israeli Soldiers in the Intifada. *Armed Forces & Society* 21 (1): 45–68.

Liebman, Charles. 1989. Conceptions of 'State of Israel' in Israeli Society. *Medina, Mimshal Viyahsim Benleumiyim* 30: 51–60 (Hebrew).

Lifshitz, Yaacov. 2000. *Defense Economics: The General Theory and the Israeli Case*. Tel-Aviv: Ministry of Defense (Hebrew).

Linn, Ruth. 1996. When the Individual Soldier Says 'No' to War: A look at Selective Refusal during the Intifada. *Journal of Peace Research* 33 (4) 421–31.

Lissak, Moshe. 1984. A Response: Theses for Discussion or Preliminary Attitudes. *Medina, Mimshal Vihasim Benleumiyim* 22: 33–38 (Hebrew).

Lomsky-Feder, Edna, and Eyal Ben-Ari. 1999. From 'The People in Uniform' to 'Different Uniforms for the People': Professionalism, Diversity and the Israeli Defence Forces. In *Managing Diversity in the Armed Forces: Experiences from Nine Countries*, eds. Joseph Soeters and Jan van der Meulen, 157–86. Tilburg: Tilburg University Press.

Lomsky-Feder, Edna, and Tamar Rapoport. 2003. Juggling Models of Masculinity: Russian-Jewish Immigrants in the Israeli Army. *Sociological Inquiry* 73(1): 114–37.

Lubin, Daniel. 2001. The Legend of the Reserve Service (http://ipaper.co.il/cgi-bin/v.cgi) (Hebrew).

Lustick, Ian S. 1993. *Unsettled States, Disputed Lands: Britain and Ireland, France and Algeria, Israel and the West Bank-Gaza.* Ithaca, N.Y.: Cornell University Press.

———. 1996. To Build and to Be Built By: Israel and the Hidden Logic of the Iron Wall. *Israel Studies* 1: 196–223.

Lyons, E. William, and David Lowery. 1986. The Organization of Political Space and Citizen Responses to Dissatisfaction in Urban Communities: An Integrative Model. *The Journal of Politics* 48 (2): 321–46.

MacLean, Alair. 2005. Lessons from the Cold War: Military Service and College Education. *Sociology of Education* 78(3): 250–66.

Makover-Blikov, Sari. 2005. Why Should I Fight? *Maariv Supplement*, 11 February (Hebrew).

Makovsky, David, and Jeffrey White. 2006. *Lessons and Implications of the Israel-Hizballah War: A Preliminary Assessment.* Washington, DC: The Washington Institute for Near East Policy.

Maman, Daniel, and Moshe Lissak. 1990. The Impact of Social Networks on the Occupational Patterns of Retired Officers: The Case of Israel. *Forum International* 9: 279–308.

Mandel, Robert. 2001. The Privatization of Security. *Armed Forces & Society* 28 (1): 129–51.

Mann, Michael. 1987. The Roots and Contradictions of Modern Militarism. *New Left Review* 162: 35–50.

———. 1993. *The Sources of Social Power, Vol. II: The Rise of Classes and Nation-States, 1760–1914.* New York: Cambridge University Press.

Maoz, Ifat. 2001. The Violent Asymmetrical Encounter with the Other in an Army-Civilian Clash: The Case of the Intifada. *Peace & Conflict* 7(3): 243–63.

Maoz, Zeev. 2003. The Mixed Blessing of Israel's Nuclear Policy. *International Security* 28 (2): 44–77.

———. 2006a. *Defending the Holy Land: A Critical Analysis of Israel's Security and Foreign Policy.* Ann Arbor: University of Michigan Press.

———. 2006b. Questions for Inquiry Committee. *Ynet News*, 20 July (Hebrew).

Mateu-Gelabert, Pedro, and Howard Lune. 2003. School Violence: The Bidirectional Conflict Flow between Neighborhood and School. *City and Community* 2 (4): 353–69.

Mayseless, Ofra. 1993. Attitudes toward Military Service among Israeli Youth. In *The Military in the Service of Society and Democracy*, ed. Daniella Ashkenazy, 32–35. Westport, Conn.: Greenwood Press.

Medan, Yaakov. 2004. The Terror Balance Strengthens Sharon. *Nekuda* 273: 24–25 (Hebrew).

Meital, Yoram. 2004. *Broken Peace: Israel, the Palestinians and the Middle East.* Jerusalem: Carmel (Hebrew).

Michael, Kobi. 2007. Military Knowledge and Weak Civilian Control in the Reality of Low Intensity Conflict: The Israeli Case. *Israel Studies* 12 (1): 28–52.

Migdal, Joel S. 1988. *Strong Societies and Weak States: State-Society Relations and State Capabilities in the Third World*. Princeton, N.J.: Princeton University Press.

———. 2001. *State in Society: Studying How States and Societies Transform and Constitute One Another*. Cambridge: Cambridge University Press.

Mills, Wright C. 1956. *The Power Elite*. London: Oxford University Press.

Moore, Molly. 2003. Israeli Army Engaged in Fight over its Soul. *Washington Post*, 18 November, A01.

Morris, Benny. 1993. *Israel's Border Wars, 1949–1956: Arab Infiltration, Israeli Retaliation, and the Countdown to the Suez War*. Oxford: Clarendon Press.

———. 2001. *Righteous Victims: A History of the Zionist-Arab Conflict, 1881–2001*. New York: Vintage Books.

Moskos, Charles C. 1971. Armed Forces and American Society: Convergence or Divergence? In *Public Opinion and the Military Establishment*, ed. Charles Moskos, 271–94. Beverly Hills, Calif.: Sage Publishing.

———. 1977. From Institution to Occupation: Trends in Military Organization. *Armed Forces & Society* 4 (1): 41–50.

———. 2001. What Ails the All-Volunteer Force: An Institutional Perspective. *Parameters* 31 (1): 29–47.

Moskos, Charles C., and James Burk. 1994. The Postmodern Military. In *The Military in New Times*, ed. James Burk, 141–62. Boulder, Colo.: Westview Press.

Nahon, Yaacov. 1987. *Patterns of Educational Expansion and the Structure of Occupational Opportunities*. Jerusalem: Jerusalem Institute for Israel Studies (Hebrew).

Nevo, Baruch, and Yael Shor. 2002a. *The People's Army? The Reserves In Israel*. Jerusalem: The Israel Democracy Institute (Hebrew).

———. 2002b. *The Contract between the IDF and Israeli Society: Compulsory Service*. Jerusalem: The Israel Democracy Institute (Hebrew).

Ofir, Adi, ed. 2001. *Real-Time: The Al-Aqsa Intifada and the Israeli Left*. Tel-Aviv: Keter (Hebrew).

Oldfield, Adrian. 1990. *Citizenship and Community: Civic Republicanism and the Modern World*. London: Routledge.

Oren, Amir. 2006. Strategic Planning/Lebanon Was Waiting. *Haaretz*, 21 July.

Oren, Amiram. 2005. *The Spatial 'Price' of Security*. Haifa: University of Haifa, Chaikin Chair for Geostrategy (Hebrew).

Ostrom, Elinor. 1996. Crossing the Great Divide: Coproduction, Synergy and Development. *World Development* 24 (6): 1073–87.

Pappe, Ilan. 1992. *The Making of the Arab-Israeli Conflict, 1947–1951*. London: I.B. Tauris Publishers.

Peled, Yoav, ed. 2001. *Shas: The Challenge of Israeliness*. Tel-Aviv: Yediot Achronot Books (Hebrew).

———. 2004. Profits or Glory? The Twenty-eighth Elul of Arik Sharon. *New Left Review* 29 (2): 47–70.

Peri, Yoram. 1990. The Effects of the Intifada on the IDF. In *The Seventh War: The Effects of the Intifada on the Israeli Society*, ed. Reuven Gal, 122–28. Tel-Aviv: Hakibbutz Hameuchad Publishing House (Hebrew).
——. 2001. The Changing Security Discourse and the Change of the Concept of Citizenship in Israel. *Democratic Culture* 4–5: 233–66 (Hebrew).
——. 2002. *The Israeli Military and Israel's Palestinian Policy: From Oslo to the Al Aqsa Intifada*. Washington, D.C.: U.S. Institute of Peace.
——. 2006. *Generals in the Cabinet Room: How the Military Shapes Israeli Policy*. Washington D.C.: U.S. Institute of Peace Press.
Phillips, Nicola. 1998. *Globalisation and the 'Paradox of State Power': Perspective from Latin America*. Coventry: University of Warwick, Centre for the Study of Globalisation and Regionalisation, working paper 16/98.
Pieters, Jan Nederveen. 2001. Globalization and Collective Action. In *Globalization and Social Movements*, eds. Pierre Hamel, Henri Lustiger-Thaler, Jan Nederveen Pieterse, and Sasha Roseneil, 21–40. New York: Palgrave.
Porter, Bruce D. 1994. *War and the Rise of the State: The Military Foundations of Modern Politics*. New York: The Free Press.
Posner, Richard A. 2003. An Army of the Willing. *The New Republic Online*, 19 May http://www.tnr.com/doc.mhtml?i=20030519&s=posner051903 (20 June 2004).
Pundak, Ron. 2001. From Oslo to Taba: What Went Wrong? *Survival* 43 (3): 31–45.
Putnam, Robert D. 1988. Diplomacy and Domestic Politics: The Logic of Two-Level Games. *International Organization* 42 (3): 427–60.
Rabin, Yitzhak. 1979. *Service Book*. Tel-Aviv: Sifriat Ma'ariv (Hebrew).
Rabinovich, Itamar. 1991. *The Road Not Taken: Early Arab-Israeli Negotiations*. New York: Oxford University Press.
Ram, Uri . 2005. *The Globalization of Israel: Mcworld in Tel Aviv, Jihad in Jerusalem*. Tel-Aviv: Resling (Hebrew).
Rapaport, Amir. 2005. An Explosive Arrangement. *Maariv-NRG*, 7 July (Hebrew).
Rappoport, Meron. 2005. The Brigade of the Disengagement Opponents. *Haaretz Supplement,* 13 July (Hebrew).
Ratner, David. 2004. The IDF and the Consciousness Scene. In *The Low Intensity Conflict*, eds. Hagai Golan and Shaul Shai, 377–402. Tel-Aviv: Ma'arachot (Hebrew).
Raz-Krakotzkin, Amnon. 2000. Rabin's Legacy: On Secularism, Nationalism and Orientalism. In *Contested Memory: Myth, Nationalism and Democracy*, ed. Lev Grinberg, 65–88. Beer Sheva: Humphrey Institute (Hebrew).
Richardson, Rudi, and Jolanda Bosch. 1999. The Diversity Climate in the Dutch Armed Forces. In *Managing Diversity in the Armed Forces: Experiences from Nine Countries*, eds. Joseph Soeters and Jan van der Meulen, 127–57. Tilburg: Tilburg University Press.
Ricks, Thomas. 1997. The Widening Gap between the Military and Society. *Atlantic Monthly* 280: 66–78.
Risse, Thomas, and Kathryn Sikkink. 1999. The Socialization of International Human Rights Norms into Domestic Practices: Introduction. In *The Power of Human*

Rights: International Norms and Domestic Change, eds. Thomas Risse, Stephen C. Ropp, and Kathryn Sikkink, 1–38. Cambridge: Cambridge University Press, 1–38

Ron, James. 2000. Savage Restraint: Israel, Palestine, and the Dialectics of Legal Repression. *Social Problems* 47 (4): 445–72

———. 2003. *Frontiers and Ghettos: State Violence in Serbia and Israel.* Berkeley: University of California Press.

Rosenfeld, Maya. 2004. Sundays Morning at the Checkpoint: 'Pleasures of Duty' of the Occupiers, 'Duty of Sumud' of the Besieged. *Politica* 11–12: 41–56 (Hebrew).

Rosenhek, Zeev. Dynamics of Inclusion and Exclusion in the Israeli Welfare State: State Building and Political Economy. In *Generations, Spaces, Identities: Perspectives on the Construction of Society and Culture in Israel*, eds. Hanna Herzog, Tal Kochavi, and Shimshon Zelniker. Jerusalem: Van Leer (in print, Hebrew).

Rosental, Ruvik. 2001. *Is Bereavement Dead?* Jerusalem: Keter (Hebrew).

Rotenberg, Hagit. 2005. The Refusniks: The Real Story. *Arutz Sheva*, 6 October (Hebrew).

Roumani, Maurice M. 1979. *From Immigrant to Citizen: The Contribution of the Army to National Integration in Israel: The Case of Oriental Jews.* The Hague: Foundation for Studies of Plural Societies.

Sagie, Uri. 1998. *Lights within the Fog.* Tel-Aviv: Yediot Achronot Books (Hebrew).

Sandel, Michael J. 1998. *What Money Can't Buy: The Moral Limits of Markets.* The Tanner Lectures on Human Values Delivered at Brasenose College, Oxford, May 11–12.

Sasson-Levy, Orna. 2002. Constructing Identities at the Margins: Masculinities and Citizenship in the Israeli Army. *The Sociological Quarterly* 43 (3): 353–83.

———. 2003. Feminism and Military Gender Practices: Israeli Women Soldiers in 'Masculine' Roles. *Sociological Inquiry* 73 (3): 440–65.

———. 2006. *Identities in Uniform: Masculinities and Feminities in the Israeli Military.* Jerusalem: Magnes (Hebrew).

Savir, Uri. 1998. *The Process: Behind the Scene of an Historical Decision.* Tel-Aviv: Yediot Achronot Books (Hebrew).

Schiff, Rebecca L. 1995. Civil-Military Relations Reconsidered: A Theory of Concordance. *Armed Forces & Society* 22 (1): 7–24.

Schiff, Zeev. 2004. Religious Commissars in the IDF. *Haaretz*, 27 October.

———. 2006. Let's Get Real. *Haaretz*, 20 October.

Schnell, Itzhak, and Shaul Mishal. 2005. *Uprooting and Settlers' Discourse: The Case of Gush Katif.* Jerusalem: The Floersheimer Institute for Policy Studies (Hebrew).

Seabrooke, Leonard. 2002. *Bringing Legitimacy Back in to Neo-Weberian State Theory and International Relations.* Canberra: Australian National University.

Segal, R. David, and Janet S. Schwartz. 1981. Professional Autonomy of the Military in the United States and the Soviet Union. *Air University Review* 32: 21–30.

Selby, Jan. 2005. Post-Zionist Perspectives on Contemporary Israel. *New Political Economy* 10 (1): 109–22.

Shabtay, Malka. 1999. *Best Brother: The Identity Journey of Ethiopian Immigrant Soldiers.* Tel-Aviv: Tcherikover (Hebrew).

Shafir, Gershon, and Yoav Peled, eds. 2000. *The New Israel: Peacemaking and Liberalization.* Boulder, Colo.: Westview Press.

———. 2002. *Being Israeli: The Dynamics of Multiple Citizenship*. Cambridge: Cambridge University Press.
Shai, David. 2003. How to Ease the Burden on Reservists? *The Marker*, 3 January (Hebrew).
Shalev, Michael. 1992. *Labor and the Political Economy in Israel*. Oxford: Oxford University Press.
———. 2000. Liberalization and the Transformation of the Political Economy. In *The New Israel: Peacemaking and Liberalization*, eds. Gershon Shafir and Yoav Peled, 129–59. Boulder, Colo.: Westview Press.
Shalev, Michael, and Gal Levy. 2005. The Winners and Losers of 2003: Ideology, Social Structure, and Political Change. In *The Elections In Israel 2003*, eds. Asher Arian and Michal Shamir, 167–86. Brunswick, N.J.: Transaction Books.
Shavit, Ari. 2004. The Big Freeze. *Haaretz Magazine*, 8 October.
Shavit, Yossi, Yinon Cohen, Haya Stier, and Svetlana Bolotin. 1999. Ethnic Inequality in University Education in Israel. *Jewish Journal of Sociology* 41 (1–2): 5–23.
Shavit-Fradkin, Michal. 2006. *The Construction of Meaning of the IDF's Involvement in the Disengagement*. Paper Presented at the 37th Annual Meeting of the Israeli Sociological Association, Ramat-Gan, Israel, February (Hebrew).
Shaw, Martin. 1988. *Dialectics of War: An Essay in the Social Theory of Total War and Peace*. London: Pluto Press.
———. 2002. Risk-Transfer Militarism, Small Massacres and the Historic Legitimacy of War. *International Relations* 16 (3): 343–60.
Shelah, Ofer. 2003. *The Israeli Army: A Radical Proposal*. Or Yehuda: Kinneret Zmora-Bitan, Dvir (Hebrew).
Sheleg, Yair. 2000. *The New Religious Jews: Recent Developments among Observant Jews in Israel*. Jerusalem: Keter (Hebrew).
———. 2006. Religious Zionism as a Full Partner. *Haaretz*, 20 February.
Shenhav, Yehouda. 2006. *The Arab Jews: A Postcolonial Reading of Nationalism, Religion, and Ethnicity*. Stanford, Calif.: Stanford University Press.
Shlaim, Avi. 2001. *The Iron Wall: Israel and the Arab World*. New York: W. W. Norton & Company.
Shumsky, Dimitry. 2001. Ethnicity and Citizenship as Perceived by Russian Israelis. *Theory and Criticism* 19: 17–40 (Hebrew).
———. 2005. Orientalism and Islamophobia among the Russian-Speaking Intelligentsia in Israel. *Theory and Criticism* 26: 89–118 (Hebrew).
Silver, Beverly. 2004. Labor, War and World Politics: Contemporary Dynamics in World-Historical Perspective. In *Labour and New Social Movements in a Globalizing World System*, eds. Berthold Unfried, Marcel Van der Linden, and Christine Schindler, 19–38. Leipzig: Akademische Verlagsanstalt.
Sivan, Emmanuel. 1991. *The 1948 Generation: Myth, Profile and Memory*. Tel-Aviv: Ministry of Defense (Hebrew).
Skocpol, Theda. 1992. *Protecting Soldiers and Mothers: The Political Origins of Social Policy in the United States*. Cambridge, Mass.: The Belknap Press of Harvard University Press.

Smooha, Sammy. 1984. Ethnicity and the Military in Israel: Theses for Discussion and Research. *Medina, Mimshal Viyahsim Benleumiyim* 22: 5–32 (Hebrew).

———. 1993. Class, Ethnic, and National Cleavages and Democracy in Israel. In *Israeli Democracy under Stress*, eds. Ehud Sprinzak and Larry Diamond, 309–42. Boulder and London: Lynne Rienner Publishers.

Snider, Don M. 2003. Jointness, Defense Transformation, and the Need for a New Joint Warfare Profession. *Parameters* 33 (3): 17–30.

Snider, Don M., and Gayle L. Watkins. 2000. The Future of Army Professionalism: A Need for Renewal and Redefinition. *Parameters* 30 (3): 5–20.

Soysal, Yasemin. 1994. *The Limits of Citizenship: Migrants and Postnational Membership in Europe*. Chicago: University of Chicago Press.

Speaker, M. Kathryne, and George J. Petersen. 2000. School Violence and Adolescent Suicide: Strategies for Effective Intervention. *Educational Review* 52 (1): 65–73.

Strashnov, Amnon. 1994. *Justice under Fire*. Tel-Aviv: Yediot Achronot Books (Hebrew).

Sullivan, Andrew. 1995. *Virtually Normal: An Argument about Homosexuality*. New York: Alfred A. Knopf.

Sussman, Zvi. 1984. Why Is the Burden of Security So Heavy Upon Israel. In *The Price of Power*, eds. Zvi Offer and Avi Kober. Tel-Aviv: Ministry of Defense (Hebrew).

Swirski, Shlomo. 1981. *Orientals and Ashkenazim in Israel: The Ethnic Division of Labor*. Haifa: Machbarot Lemechkar Vlebikoret (Hebrew).

———. 1990. *Education in Israel: Schooling for Inequality*. Tel-Aviv: Breirot (Hebrew).

———. 1995. *Seeds of Inequality*. Tel-Aviv: Breirot (Hebrew).

———. 2005. *The Price of Occupation: The Cost of the Occupation to Israeli Society*. Tel-Aviv: Adva Center.

Swirski, Shlomo, Yaron Yehezkel, and Etti Konor. 1998. *Social Situation*. Tel-Aviv: Adva Center (Hebrew).

Szegedy-Maszak, Marianne. 2004. Sources of Sadism. *U.S. News & World Report*, 24 May.

Talmud, Ilan. 1985. *Between Politics and Economy: Public Consent versus Ideological Distinction in Israel*. M.A. Thesis, Department of Sociology, Tel-Aviv University (Hebrew).

Tamir, Moshe. 2005. *Undeclared War*. Tel-Aviv: Ma'arachot (Hebrew).

Tarrow, Sidney. 1994. *Power in Movement: Social Movements, Collective Action and Politics*. New York: Cambridge University Press.

———. 2001. Transnational Politics: Contention and Institutions in International Politics. *Annual Review of Political Science* 4 (1): 1–20.

Teachman, Jay. 2004. Military Service during the Vietnam Era: Were There Consequences for Subsequent Civilian Earnings? *Social Forces* 83 (2):709–30.

Thompson, Edward P., ed. 1982. *Exterminism and the Cold War*. London: New Left Books.

Thomson, Janice E. 1990. State Practices, International Norms and the Decline of Mercenarism. *International Studies Quarterly* 34 (1): 23–47.

Tilly, Charles. 1978. *From Mobilization to Revolution*. Reading, Mass.: Addison-Wesley.

———. 1985. War Making and State Making as Organized Crime. In *Bringing the State Back In*, eds. Peter Evans, Theda Skocpol, and Dietrich Rueschemeyer, 169–191. Cambridge: Cambridge University Press.

———. 1992. *Coercion, Capital, and European States, AD 990–1992*. Cambridge, Mass.: Basil Blackwell.

———. 1997a. Democracy Is a Lake. In *Roads from Past to Future*, by Charles Tilly, 193–215. Lanham, Md.: Rowman & Littlefield Publishers.

———. 1997b. Invisible Elbow. In *Roads from Past to Future*, by Charles Tilly, 35–48. Lanham, Md.: Rowman & Littlefield Publishers.

———. 1998. *Durable Inequality*. Berkeley, Calif.: University of California Press.

———. 2001. Relational Origins of Inequality. *Anthropological Theory* 1 (3): 355–72.

———. 2004. Trust and Rule. *Theory and Society* 33 (1): 1–30.

Tov, Imri. 1998. *The Price of Power*. Tel-Aviv: Ministry of Defense (Hebrew).

Turner, Bryan S. 2001. The Erosion of Citizenship. *British Journal of Sociology* 52 (2): 189–209.

Vasquez, Joseph Paul. 2005. Shouldering the Soldiering: Democracy, Conscription, and Military Casualties. *Journal of Conflict Resolution* 49 (6): 849–73.

Vigoda-Gadot, Eran, and Shlomo Mizrahi. 2005. *The Performance of the Israeli Public Sector: A Citizens Survey and National Assessment* (research paper #5). Haifa: University of Haifa, the Department of Administration and Public Policy (Hebrew).

Vos, Dan. 2006. Social Movements and Citizenship: Conscientious Objection in France, the United States and Israel. *Mobilization* 11(3): 277–95.

Wald, Emanuel. 1987. *The Curse of the Broken Vessels*. Tel-Aviv: Schocken Publishing House (Hebrew).

Weede, Erich. 1992. Some Simple Calculations on Democracy and War Involvement. *Journal of Peace Research* 29 (4): 377–83.

Wegman, Yehuda. 2004. The Trap of 'A Limited Conflict'. *Mideast Outpost* 166. http://www.afsi.org/OUTPOST/2004APR/apr3.htm (30 September 2006).

Weimann, Gabi. 2007. *The Media during the Second Lebanon War*. The Caesarea-Rothschild School of Communication, Tel-Aviv University (Hebrew).

Wendt, Alexander, 1992. Anarchy Is What States Make of It: The Social Construction of Power Politics. *International Organization* 46 (2): 391–425

Woodward, Rachel, and Patricia Winter. 2006. Gender and the Limits to Diversity in the Contemporary British Army. *Gender, Work and Organization* 13 (1): 45–67.

Yaish, Meir. 2001. Class Structure in a Deeply Divided Society: Class and Ethnic Inequality in Israel, 1974–1991. *British Journal of Sociology* 52 (3): 409–39

———. 2003. Israel's Class Structure. *Megamot* 43 (2): 267–86 (Hebrew).

Yiftachel, Oren. 1998. Nation-Building and the Division of Space: Ashkenazi Domination in Israeli 'Ethnocracy'. *National & Ethnic Politics* 41 (1): 33–58.

Yiftachel, Oren, and Alexander Kedar. 2000. On Power and Land: The Land Regime in. Israel. *Theory and Criticism* 16: 67–100 (Hebrew).

Yiftachel, Oren, and Erez Tzfadia. 2004. Between Periphery and 'Third Space': Identity of Mizrahim in Israel's Development Towns. In *Israelis in Conflict: Hege-*

monies, Identities and Challenges. eds. Adriana Kemp, David Newman, Uri Ram and Oren Yiftachel, 203–35. Portland, Ore.: Sussex Academic Press.

Yinon, Yoel, and Nili Freedman. 1977. Why Do Kibbutz-Born Soldiers Perform Better Than Do City-Born in the Army? *Megamot* 23 (1): 110–18 (Hebrew).

Yuval-Davis, Nira. 1985. Front and Rear: The Sexual Division of Labor in the Israeli Army. *Feminist Studies* 11 (3): 649–75.

Zagorski, Paul W. 1994. Civil-Military Relations and Argentine Democracy: The Armed Forces under the Menem Government. *Armed Forces & Society* 20 (3): 423–37.

Zureik, Elia. 2001. Constructing Palestine through Surveillance Practices. *British Journal of Middle Eastern Studies* 28 (2): 205–27.

WEBSITES

Breaking the Silence, http://www.shovrimshtika.org/testimony.asp (30 May 2006)

B'Tselem, http://www.btselem.org/Hebrew/Testimonies/index.asp (31 December 2006)

Courage to Refuse, http://www.seruv.org.il/english/default.asp (30 May 2006)

IDF, http://www1.idf.il/DOVER/site/homepage.asp?clr=1&sl=EN&id=-8888&force=1 (30 May 2006)

Machsom Watch, http://www.machsomwatch.org/eng/aboutUsEng&lang=eng (30 May 2006)

Soldier Testimony, http://www.soldiertestimony.org/Israel (30 May 2006).

Index

Adalah, 164, 253
adaptive rationality, 175, 207
alternative politics, 141
Ashkenazi secular, military service of, 24–25, 30–31, 34–40, 41–42, 46–47, 51, 53–55, 57–58, 60–62, 64, 65–70, 73, 75n4, 79–81, 82, 85, 86, 88, 89, 90, 102, 109, 111, 112, 118, 119, 120, 121, 122, 123, 124, 125, 127, 133, 135, 136, 137, 138–40, 142, 147, 155–59, 167, 178, 191, 197, 229, 230, 232, 238, 240–41, 248–50
Ashkenazi secular immigrants, military service of, 120, 122, 128, 230

Bedouins, military service of 84–85, 89, 90, 118, 119, 120, 121, 122, 123, 158, 229, 230, 231
bereavement, 24, 68, 69, 111, 115, 117, 128–31, 133, 142, 168, 225, 229, 233–34, 244, 256
body sacrifice, 129, 167–68, 176, 178, 215, 244–45, 256–57
Breaking the Silence, 131–33, 139, 140–42, 164, 166

citizenship, 10, 12, 16, 20–21, 31, 52, 60, 63, 66, 68, 82, 84, 113, 138, 148, 155, 157–58, 163, 178, 188, 241

citizen-soldier, 10, 14–16, 21, 30, 31, 36, 41, 63, 84, 142, 167, 168, 241; the severance of the link, 16, 20, 52, 62–63, 66, 82, 113, 138, 148, 157–58, 178
collective action, 4, 8, 13, 16, 17–18, 54, 56, 57, 112, 129, 133, 135, 143, 163, 166, 245. *See* also political protest, voice
conscientious objection. *See* disobedience
conscription policies, 6, 10, 12–13, 18, 19, 20, 29, 30–31, 35, 63, 66–68, 81, 85, 89, 100, 124, 128, 141, 144, 148, 154–55, 159, 163, 169, 170–71, 173–74, 176, 185, 210, 234, 238–45, 249–51, 258
convertibility, 12–18, 21, 22, 24, 26n3, 27, 31, 38, 41–42, 46, 48, 53–54, 63, 65, 69, 73, 81, 83, 121, 134, 135, 136, 138, 142, 149, 151, 157, 171, 196, 207, 208, 236, 242, 255, 256, 257
counter fire, 79, 223
Courage to Refuse, 132–133, 139, 140, 142, 164

disobedience, 2, 57, 68, 88, 99, 110, 132–33, 136, 139, 141, 156, 162,

163, 164, 165, 182–83, 184, 192, 198, 199–204, 206, 209–10, 233, 244
diversity management, 89, 173, 195–97, 208–9, 210n2, 257, 258. *See* also social identities
Druze, military service of, 75, 79, 84–85, 89, 90, 118, 119, 120, 121, 122, 123, 128, 158, 229, 230, 231

embeddedness of the military, 14, 25, 181, 184, 185, 193–98, 200, 202–3, 205, 206, 207, 208, 209, 210
Ethiopian immigrants, military service of, 41, 79, 84, 90, 118, 119, 120, 121, 122, 123, 127, 230
ethno-national ethos, 7, 53, 60–65, 80, 82–83, 84, 87, 92–96, 98, 100, 101, 102, 104, 107, 111, 112–13, 125, 127, 129, 137–38, 177, 178, 182, 190, 206, 210, 222, 251–53; ethno-national coalition, 74, 77, 90, 92–96, 112–13, 114, 158, 178, 183, 184, 185, 190, 191, 193, 210, 215, 222, 241, 251–52; and the clash with the market ethos. *See* market economy
exit, 17, 56, 139, 141, 169

Fatah, 104, 105, 107, 216
Fatah-Tanzim, 105, 107
feminism, 113–14, 158, 159, 241
Four Mothers, 1, 8, 58, 72, 88, 129–30,
frontier, 115n5, 187
fusionism, 195, 208–9

gap of legitimacies, 25–26, 176, 213, 215, 219, 220, 222, 226, 228
ghetto, 115n5, 187
globalization, 3, 7, 16, 23, 51–52, 72, 83, 92, 93, 95, 101, 114, 148–52, 160–66, 169–70, 176, 182, 183, 188, 189, 224
gold sacrifice, 129, 167–69, 176, 178, 244–45, 256–57

Gush Emunim, 61, 62, 63–65, 69, 85, 191

Hamas, 100, 107, 111, 161, 181, 188, 214
Hezbollah, 1, 71, 78, 79, 100, 103, 109, 170, 172, 213, 214, 215, 216–17, 218, 219, 221, 223, 226, 227, 228, 229, 243
Histadrut, 40, 95, 214

identity politics, 159, 173. *See* also social identities
institutional heritage, 100–1, 199
international strategy, 19, 72–73

kibbutzim, military service of 41, 52, 85, 118, 119, 120, 122, 124, 125, 126, 130, 131, 229, 230, 232–33, 252–53

labor market, 13, 16, 18, 21, 26, 32–33, 38–39, 53–54, 63, 70, 80, 81, 83, 90, 114, 144, 151, 171, 173, 208, 240, 241, 242, 243, 244, 245
Labor Party, 53, 62, 64, 73, 85, 105, 141, 214
liberalization, 46, 51–52, 82, 92–93, 151, 155, 158, 160, 238
Likud Party, 53, 57, 61–63, 71, 91, 93, 100, 104, 105, 184
low intensity conflict, 108, 186
loyalty, 17, 56

Machsom Watch, 140–41, 142, 164, 166
Mamlachtiyut (statism), 30–31, 36, 51–52, 60–61, 101, 149–51, 165
Mapai Party, 43
market army, 51–52, 147, 169–74, 176, 237
market economy, ethos of, 16, 23, 63, 81, 95, 102, 236; and the clash with ethno-nationalism, 52–53, 93–95, 177–78, 189–90, 215, 222, 251–52, 256; and the impact on the military,

24, 51–54, 66, 67, 69–70, 77, 109, 147–54, 160, 170–72, 174–78, 181, 206, 216, 222, 232, 238, 241, 243, 249, 251, 253
materialist ethos, 1, 48–52, 64, 150
material rewards, 12, 14–15, 17, 18, 19, 21–22, 23, 26, 40, 42, 50, 55, 56, 65, 68–69, 70, 73, 74, 77, 80, 87, 88, 89, 147, 151, 155, 157, 167, 173, 174, 175, 177, 210, 235, 238–45, 247, 248–51, 254, 257–58
melting pot, ethos of, 35, 36, 83, 101, 159, 171
mercenarism, 10, 14, 21, 78, 148
military hierarchy, 13, 34–36, 53, 80, 83, 84, 117, 166, 200, 203, 256; dual hierarchy, 87–88, 196–97, 202
militarism: contractual militarism, 69, 154–60, 176, 183, 235; general theory of, 8–11, 13–14, 19, 22–23, 26n2, 47–48, 254–58; materialist militarism, 11–15, 20– 23, 26, 31, 34, 47–48, 64, 69, 73, 74, 80, 85, 88, 89, 94, 138, 149, 150, 154, 165, 215, 247–58; obligatory militarism, 69, 154, 176; post-materialist militarism, 20–21, 22, 69, 80, 154, 255, 258
militarization, 3, 9, 10–11, 14, 20, 36–37, 41–42, 45, 46, 58–59, 144, 168, 253, 255; demilitarization, 9, 17, 20, 23, 30, 51–56, 59, 73–74, 92, 93, 115, 143, 144, 178, 210, 215, 255; gendered militarization, 113; remilitarization, 3, 20, 80, 93, 115, 138, 144, 256
military participation, 11, 15, 17, 19, 20, 25, 31, 40, 41–42, 50, 56, 63, 70, 79, 143, 144, 158, 170, 191, 208, 223, 231, 237, 241, 242–43, 244, 248–49, 255, 258
Mizrachim, military service of, 34–40, 41, 53, 61–63, 65, 69, 79–83, 86, 90, 102, 111, 118, 119, 120, 121, 122, 123, 124, 125–26, 205, 229, 230, 232, 241, 256

Moledet Party, 93
moshavim, military service of. *See* kibbutzim
motivation crisis, 56, 65–69, 70, 74, 80–81, 83, 84, 85, 86, 87, 109, 118, 125, 126, 154, 157, 174, 215, 239, 249

national religious, military service of, 23–24, 25, 30, 35, 41, 51, 52, 64–65, 69, 73, 77, 79–80, 85–90, 119, 120, 122, 123, 126–27, 135–36, 143, 147, 158, 159, 167, 168, 175, 177, 182, 184, 191, 192, 193, 196–98, 199–203, 204–10, 220, 229, 230, 232–33, 238, 240, 241, 244, 249, 250
National Religious Party, 93
neglect, 56
neoliberal ethos, 7, 51–52, 62, 63, 95, 101, 148–50, 153, 173
New Public Management, 172

Palestinian Authority, 4, 6, 7, 30, 84–85, 92, 98–100, 102, 103, 104–9, 110, 112, 153, 168, 177, 181–82, 185–89
Palestinian citizens, civil status of, 31, 33, 35, 38, 40, 52, 54, 75n2, 84–85, 93, 161, 163
Parents against Silence, 57
Peace Now, 57–58, 88, 91, 253
people's army, 25, 29, 31, 61, 67, 70, 85, 100, 117, 147, 159, 169–74, 178, 184, 193, 198–202, 204, 205, 206, 207, 209, 233, 238, 239
pioneer, 36, 38, 51
political control over the army, 3, 4, 10, 15, 18, 20, 21–22, 58–59, 114, 142–44, 166, 167–69, 193–96, 208, 210, 219, 233–34, 245, 247, 252–56, 258; objective control, 194, 208; subjective control, 195–96, 208–9; and the reward system, 21–22, 247–48, 256–57
political protest, 1– 2, 4, 6, 17, 23–24, 37, 38, 47, 56–60, 61–64, 65, 74,

75n3, 79, 91, 103, 109, 111, 117, 118, 124, 128, 129–31, 133, 138, 139, 140–41, 142, 153, 164, 181, 187, 191, 204, 225, 229, 234–36
privatization of security, 149, 169, 173, 254
professional army, 15, 19, 21, 26, 100, 143, 171, 173, 204, 205, 208, 210, 215, 238–45, 250, 251, 253, 256
professionalism: military's professional autonomy, 58–60, 79, 89, 112, 114–15, 128, 131, 133, 139–40, 142, 147, 152, 166, 175, 194–95, 196–98, 203, 205, 207, 242–43, 251, 253–54; military professionalism, 19, 21, 41, 100, 149, 156, 193–97, 203, 208, 238, 242, 243–45

quasi-exit, 141

reproduction of inequality, 12–13, 30–40, 45, 54, 94, 151, 253, 256
republican equation, 10, 11–15, 21–23, 30, 40, 47, 61–62, 73, 247–50, 255; rebalancing of, 18–21, 23–24, 30, 74–75, 77–79, 89, 114, 131, 143, 144, 177, 178, 205, 240, 241, 245, 247–50, 255; republican ethos, 10, 12, 13, 16, 18, 20, 30, 36, 51, 52, 53, 57, 60, 66, 82, 113, 125, 138, 143, 154, 158, 168, 233, 244, 256; violation of, 15–18, 21, 23, 26, 30, 48–60, 66–71, 74, 91, 114, 151, 154, 155–57, 170, 191, 210, 247–50
rights, 10, 11, 12, 14, 15, 18, 19, 20, 33, 40, 41, 51, 56, 59, 60, 61, 62, 65, 68, 69, 74, 80, 85, 93, 95, 113, 143, 151, 160, 161, 163, 167, 188, 223, 241, 250, 255, 256, 258
Russian immigrants, military service of, 41, 79, 83–84, 89, 118, 119, 120, 121, 122, 123, 127, 230, 241

settlements in the Occupied Territories, 24–25, 40, 46, 48, 64–65, 72, 78, 82, 90, 99–100, 101, 102, 104, 111, 133, 181, 182–83, 184, 187, 188, 190–93, 196, 197, 198–207, 208, 209, 250
settlers, military service of 78, 82, 86, 118, 119, 120, 126–27, 197, 209, 229, 230, 233–34
Shas Party, 62–63, 65, 67, 93, 95, 97, 113, 114, 256
Shinui Party, 7, 113, 114, 141, 153, 167
social architecture of the army, 23, 24, 30, 70, 73, 74, 77–90, 95, 96, 102, 111, 114, 115, 140, 143, 147, 152, 155, 175, 176, 178, 181, 183, 190, 191, 196, 199, 203, 207, 208, 210, 234, 241, 249
social capital, 13, 38, 54, 165, 171, 194, 258
social identities in the military, 13, 61, 62, 79, 80, 84, 85, 126–28, 158–59, 191, 195, 209, 220, 257
social inequality, 7, 23, 31–40, 45–46, 52, 54, 56, 61, 62, 63, 65, 67, 75n2, 83, 96, 113, 115n2, 135, 151, 253, 243, 256
social mobility (through military service), 10, 12, 16, 23, 25, 26n4, 54, 55, 80, 82, 83, 84, 95, 113, 125, 126, 128, 135, 136, 184, 185, 201, 205, 209, 241, 244, 252
Soldiers against Silence, 57, 88
state autonomy, 1, 2, 4, 15, 18–20, 23–24, 30, 40, 42–48, 69, 70, 73–74, 77, 96, 142–44, 182, 193–94, 207, 208–9, 247–49
state building, 14–15, 18, 188–89, 252
state-centered concept, 193–94
state formation, 9–11, 22, 255
state-society synergy, 194, 207
strategic culture, 49, 149, 220
symbolic capital, 13, 53, 68, 83, 165
symbolic rewards, 11–15, 17, 18, 20, 21–22, 23–24, 26, 30, 31, 34–40, 41, 42, 47, 48, 49, 50–56, 59, 60, 61, 62, 63, 65, 66, 67, 68, 69, 70,

73, 74, 77, 80, 82, 87, 88, 89, 96, 112, 113, 114, 130, 135, 142, 144, 147, 151, 155, 157, 170, 171, 175, 177, 178, 191, 196, 197, 200, 206, 210, 220, 232, 233, 235, 236, 238–45, 248, 249, 250, 251, 254, 255, 256, 257–58

threat (external), 3–6, 11, 12, 13, 15, 16, 17, 18, 20, 22, 29, 36, 42–43, 44, 48, 49, 50, 69, 71, 72, 74, 83, 93, 99, 101, 108, 132, 133, 143, 153, 160, 162, 169, 170, 172, 177, 178, 182, 186, 215, 217, 219, 220, 221, 224, 238, 240, 241, 250, 255, 258

Ultra-Orthodox, military service of, 35, 52, 62–63, 79, 86–87, 89, 113, 127, 138, 167, 204

voice, 17, 56, 129, 140, 141, 169, 256

warrior, 36–37, 42, 51, 54–55, 60, 64, 79, 81, 84, 135, 225

women, military service of, 9, 12, 19, 26, 30, 35, 41, 51, 52, 58, 61, 79, 80, 81–82, 88, 89, 90, 113–14, 115n1, 118, 119, 120, 121, 122, 123, 128, 140, 144, 159, 163, 172, 196, 204, 210n2, 230, 241

Yesh Gvul, 57–58, 88, 91, 132–33